Serving Physically Disabled People

Serving Physically Disabled People

An Information Handbook for All Libraries

Ruth A. Velleman

R. R. BOWKER COMPANY
New York & London, 1979

For Moritz

Published by R. R. Bowker Company
1180 Avenue of the Americas, New York, N.Y. 10036
Copyright © 1979 by Xerox Corporation
All rights reserved
Printed and bound in the United States of America

Library of Congress Cataloging in Publication Data

Velleman, Ruth A
   Serving physically disabled people.

   Bibliography: p.
   Includes index.
   1. Libraries and the physically handicapped.
2. Physically handicapped—Rehabilitation.
3. Physically handicapped children—Rehabilitation.
I. Title.
Z711.92.P5V44   027.6   79-17082
ISBN 0-8352-1167-3

Contents

Preface

In a sense this book has been in preparation for all of my professional life, which has been spent as the librarian in a school for physically disabled children and young adults and a rehabilitation center offering research and training in the area of employment of the disabled. When I first entered the field, there was not as much recognition of the needs and rights of disabled people as there is today. That this recognition has come about is a tribute to the many people, some of them mentioned in this text, who have devoted their lives to making it happen.

My own working knowledge, as it has developed over the years, has been shared in articles in *Library Journal, School Library Journal, School Media Quarterly*, and *Rehabilitation Literature*, as well as in many seminars and workshops on library service to disabled people. For the past few years I have been teaching a course in this field at the Palmer Graduate Library School of Long Island University, C. W. Post Campus, Greenvale, New York. I have found my students, some of whom are practicing librarians, eager to learn about service to this special population. I am indebted to them for telling me what they need to know. With this in mind, I decided to develop this work.

The book has many limitations. First of all, since events in the world of disabled people are moving so rapidly, one book cannot hope to convey a completely up-to-date or all-inclusive picture. The information it offers must be taken to represent the facts as they existed in 1979. Librarians should use it to help them as they open the door to the decade of the 1980s, in which exciting new changes will be taking place in the lives of disabled people and in the delivery of library service to them.

Second, since my work has been solely with physically disabled people, I have not attempted here to cover other disabilities. I hope that many books will follow, written by those more knowledgeable in related fields such as the mentally and emotionally disabled. I owe a very special debt of thanks to Professor Hanan Selvin and Alice Hagemeyer for sharing their own personal working and living experiences regarding the special needs of blind and deaf people.

The term *disabled* rather than *handicapped* has been used predominantly throughout the text as the author's preference; however, no attempt has been made to use it exclusively.

I am indebted to Judith Garodnick, editor-in-chief at R. R. Bowker, for her vision in recognizing the need for a book of this kind and for encouraging me to undertake the project; to my sponsoring editor, Corinne J. Naden, for her careful and temperate work on the manuscript; and to consulting editor, Nada Glick, for her cogent and wise suggestions.

I would like to thank my colleague and friend, Ronald S. Friedman, Ph.D., Director of Psychological Services at Human Resources School, for reading and offering constructive comments on the first chapter; Media Librarian Robert J. Hanley and Childrens' Librarian Donna Viscardi Shooltz for their support and cooperation; and Anthony J. Hendel, Director of the Interactive Television Project at Human Resources School, for the account of that program. For her able assistance in the preparation of the manuscript, I am indebted to Bernadette Lund. My friend and longtime colleague Joan A. Miller, Coordinator, Educational Programs and Studies Information Service (EPSIS), New York State Education Department, has been an invaluable source of information and sound advice throughout the years.

My dear niece Jill and her parents over the years have given me the firsthand knowledge and understanding that ultimately resulted in this work.

And, finally, to my husband, Moritz Velleman, who read each chapter, offered honest and incisive criticism, and gave me moral support and understanding throughout the project; and to my sons, Paul, David, and Daniel, for turning the tables and making me measure up to their expectations, my gratitude and love.

July 1979   Ruth A. Velleman

Introduction

Until recently, disabled people in the United States have been denied access—access to buildings, access to transportation and appropriate housing, access to education and employment, and access to information. Federal legislation has now made it clear that the United States will no longer tolerate second-class citizenship for its disabled population. Section 504 of PL 93-112, the Rehabilitation Act of 1973, has mandated equal rights for disabled people; PL 94-142, the Education of All Handicapped Children Act, guarantees an appropriate education for every disabled child in the country.

The effects of these laws have been far-reaching and all service professions are now involved in upgrading and improving services to the disabled population. The adaptation of all public buildings receiving federal funds, the provision of adapted transportation, recreational facilities, housing, and educational opportunity, and changing philosophies in the areas of job modification and attitudes on the part of potential employers have made it possible for people with disabilities to live more independent lives than ever before.

The library profession has very specific obligations to this large segment of the population—8 million children and almost 30 million adults—to supply them with special materials and services. Public libraries need to adapt physical facilities and programs and maintain basic information and referral collections for disabled people. School librarians need to acquire enough knowledge about physical disabilities to enable them to work with disabled children, to learn about sources for special curriculum materials for teachers and support staff, and to be prepared to assist parents with information pertaining to the daily living needs of their children.

The field of special librarianship is developing a new professional subspecialty in the health science area, called "Rehabilitation Librarianship." Rehabilitation, the process through which a disabled person is restored to his or her highest level of self-sufficiency, might better be defined as "habilitation" in the case of the congenitally disabled. It is achieved through a combination of medicine and therapy, education and vocational training, the ultimate goal being a life of dignity and independence. Many rehabilitation facilities do not yet have trained librarians on their staffs. Rehabilitation and librarianship need to be brought closer together to utilize the acquisition, organization, and retrieval skills of the professional librarian and to improve information delivery systems to disabled patrons and to the professionals who serve them.

Library schools in the United States have begun to respond to these needs by offering workshops and seminars in the field of library service to disabled people. A growing number have instituted course work in this area, but until very recently there has been little text material for the use of professors and students.

This book is offered as a guide to working librarians, to professors and students in library schools and schools of education, as well as schools offering course work in the area of rehabilitation counseling. Its objectives are to explore the informational needs of physically disabled people, to determine the role of the librarian in helping to meet these needs, and to offer pertinent sources of information.

Although librarians function in their communities as providers of a service, in a broader sense they are able to influence the thinking of their patrons. Because libraries are consulted for information by all segments of society—business, cultural, and educational, librarians have the opportunity to assume leadership roles in the community at large, in helping to shape attitudes and convey understanding about the special problems and needs of the disparate groups that form their public.

For this reason the first section of this book was written to offer librarians insight into some of the general problems faced by disabled people and help them acquire positive attitudes and a deeper understanding. All of the other objectives of this book should be placed within the context of this broader background.

Serving Physically Disabled People

PART I

Introducing Physically Disabled People

1
Attitudes and Understanding

This is a book mainly for librarians, to help them understand some of the needs of disabled people, people who may be their clients, their friends, their children, their colleagues—people who, although they may have special kinds of informational needs to help them function to the best of their abilities, are in the final analysis just people like anyone else.

It is estimated that 36,000,000 Americans are disabled in some way, either physically, mentally, or emotionally. About eight million of them are children in need of some adjustments in their educational opportunities. About one in six physically disabled Americans was born with his or her disability; the others become disabled through injury or accident or by contracting debilitating diseases such as multiple sclerosis or because of visual or hearing impairments.

In his book *Handicapping America*, Frank Bowe points out that we have designed the United States for the average able-bodied majority, without realizing the barriers we have placed in the way of the millions of our disabled citizens.[1] Many of these barriers are, of course, architectural. But, as one teenager once said, "You know, the real barriers are not architectural, they are attitudinal." Because of the standards that have become indigenous to American culture—youth and beauty and economic success—and our conformity to the image of perfection symbolized by the biggest, the tallest, and the prettiest as the most desirable measures for social acceptance, these barriers are in truth largely attitudinal.

Before we can deal with our roles as librarians in service to the segment of our population that we identify as physically disabled, it is necessary to examine our own attitudes in terms of how we perceive our fellow human beings. How has society looked at the less than physically perfect? What are the effects of labeling? How have the media contributed to a negative portrayal of the disabled? And, conversely, how do the disabled perceive themselves? What are their similarities to and differences from the able-bodied, and how are the disabled the same or different from each other? In terms of emotional problems, what are some of their very real difficulties and the difficulties of their families as they grow up in American society?

ATTITUDES TOWARD THE DISABLED

Beatrice Wright, in her book *Physical Disability: A Psychological Approach*, makes the distinction between the terms *disabled* and *handicapped:*

> A disability is a condition of impairment, physical or mental, having an objective aspect that can usually be described by a physician . . . a handicap is the cumulative result of the obstacles which disability interposes between the individual and his maximum functioning level.[2]

A *disability*, then, is a medical condition, whereas *handicapped* has a limiting connotation. Although many organizations (for instance, the Institute for Crippled and Disabled) dealing with the disabled (as well as many disabled individuals) still use such terms as *handicapped* or *handicapper* or even *crippled*, the use of the term *disabled* is increasing and is used throughout this book as the expression of the author's preference. Those who are not disabled are *able-bodied*. This term is infinitely preferable to the use of the word *normal*, which in speech is generally accompanied by quotation marks executed in the air, seeming to indicate that there is something "abnormal" about someone who has a disability.

In recent years, there has been a great deal written about attitudes toward the disabled. Frank Bowe's book has already been mentioned. Also, the Regional Rehabilitation Research Institute on Attitudinal, Legal and Leisure Barriers, in Washington, D.C., has published a fine set of pamphlets, including "The Invisible Battle: General Attitudes toward Disability"; "Free Wheeling: Attitudes toward People in Wheelchairs"; "Beyond the Sound Barrier: Attitudes toward the Deaf"; "Counterpoint: Attitudes of the Disabled toward the Non-Disabled"; and "Dignity," a booklet about the mentally retarded. Many of the popular attitudes that exist among the general public, as well as in social agencies, are handled with great competence and accuracy in these pamphlets. In addition, in the first chapter of their book *Notes from a Different Drummer: A Guide to Juvenile Fiction Portraying the Handicapped*, Barbara Baskin and Karen Harris pinpoint very effectively what have been traditional social responses to disability.[3] These books and pamphlets are worthwhile additions to all library collections.

There have also been many articles and some excellent films on this topic, and a short list is included at the end of this chapter.

Society has developed certain myths that surround our perceptions of disabled people. A true story about a young man known to the author speaks for itself:

> Andy was a high school student who had spina bifida (a disability involving the spinal column) and used a wheelchair. One night he was out with two able-bodied friends in an automobile when they were stopped for speeding. "All right," ordered the officer, "everybody out of the car." The two able-bodied youngsters scrambled out. Andy quickly put out his wheelchair and swung himself into it. "What's your name?" asked the officer, looking at one young man. "John Jones," replied the boy. Turning to the next one, he asked, "What's your name?" "Rick Smith" was the reply. And then, pointing to Andy but continuing to look at the other boys, the officer said, "And what's *his* name?"

In reality, Andy was a gifted drama student, well able to speak for himself. Similar stories are told by many disabled people, usually about being ignored in a restaurant as the waiter or waitress asks his (or her) companion, "What does *he* (or *she*) want to eat?" One friend who uses a wheelchair commented that often when he waits for an elevator, the operator will call out, "Let the wheelchair on first." He receives an instant image of his chair proceeding without him, as the comment effectively obliterates his image as a person.

There are two concepts involved here. One, which Beatrice Wright calls the concept of "spread," is the practice of assuming that if a person has one disability, he or she is totally incapacitated in all physical and mental areas.[4] For example, the blind person is considered to be also deaf. The person in a wheelchair may be considered "ill" or mentally handicapped; a deaf person is thought of as unable to communicate. (The old expression "deaf and dumb" hopefully has been laid to rest, although it is still heard at times.) Long after becoming adults, many people in wheelchairs are still treated as children, and "overprotecting" disabled people extends to organizations for the blind selecting reading materials for taping or brailling that do not represent a full range of what adults might choose to read.

The other and even more deeply significant concept is one of total depersonalization, as if having a disability makes a person less than a whole human being. This is perhaps the cruelest degradation of all, because it not only excludes disabled people from society but also totally obliterates them from the minds of others, thereby denying their existence.

Two more attitudes, seemingly opposites, are actually two sides of the same coin. One is that disabled people are to be pitied and the other is that the person, because of a disability, is somehow more courageous than other people. This latter attitude, one of overromanticizing, has led to the acceptance of disabled students into educational and vocational programs for which they are not legitimately qualified. Related to it is the phenomenon of "identification." Because people such as Franklin D. Roosevelt and Helen Keller or other less well-known, severely physically disabled, highly gifted, highly motivated people attain outstanding success in some way, others with similar disabilities should be able to do the same thing. "If she can do it, you can do it too" is the motivation offered, most of the time met, and justifiably so, with resentment. At the same time, the fact that these accomplishments are considered more laudable than accomplishments by similarly gifted, able-bodied people, and the extent to which they may be publicized by the media, put further undue emphasis on the disabilities and serve to set disabled people farther apart from their able-bodied peers.

The emotion of fear pervades our world—fear of the unknown, fear of the different, fear of the unusual. Able-bodied people are sometimes afraid in the presence of people with disabilities. Perhaps there is a fear of contagion, but more likely there is a fear of undue involvement, as if the disabled person is going to ask for help, requiring more time or emotional involvement than the able-bodied person is willing to give. Because our society places undue emphasis on the way people look, the aspect of a disabled person, less than physically perfect, often engenders a feeling of repulsion in the able-bodied.

When the Human Resources School for physically disabled children was first built, in Albertson, Long Island, the neighbors objected to the sight of children in wheelchairs when they looked out their windows. It was this sight that was the objection, far more than added traffic from school buses. One of the parents of the disabled children responded by saying, "My little girl is in a wheelchair, and I think she's beautiful." In the reaction of the neighbors in Long Island, repulsion extends to avoidance, as the able-bodied seek to put the disabled into a separate world, someplace else, where looking "at them" will not engender feelings of abhorrence or fear.

The use of image-loaded words connotes social attitudes toward the disabled. People are referred to as "afflicted" with a disability. Those who use wheelchairs are often said to be "condemned" or "confined" to their chairs. In the nineteenth century, people with developmental disabilities were called "mentally defective," and physically disabled people were described as "crippled" or "maimed." In 1859 the Massachusetts Residential School for Idiotic and Feeble Minded Youth was established by Samuel Gridley Howe, who also established the New England Asylum for the Blind, now the Perkins School.

All of these words are certainly loaded with many different emotions— the notion that a disability has been visited upon someone in payment for sinful behavior, the image of a less than perfect person, the image of the childlike person (as in Dostoevski's concept in *The Idiot*) somehow imbued with supernatural powers or with a purity beyond the ordinary.

One mainstreamed little girl in public school had only one arm. Her prosthetic arm was shunned by the other children because (they said) if they touched it, somehow it would put an evil spell on them, much like the evil eye of mythological literature. If we are to mainstream many more disabled children in response to the mandate of PL 94-142 (the Education of All Handicapped Children Act), such attitudes will need to be dealt with by parents and teachers. But placing severely disabled students into regular school settings without preparation in terms of attitudes may be courting failure. Often the disabled students are isolated socially, and this isolation is exacerbated by the fact that they are generally excluded from such special school programs and areas as physical education, science laboratories, cafeterias, field trips, and extracurricular activities. Thus differences rather than similarities are emphasized, making the disabled children feel devalued as human beings. In addition, after school, physically disabled children are often confined to their homes and have little contact with neighborhood youngsters and little opportunity to socialize and to develop friends in their neighborhoods. Most children will respond to healthy attitudes when they stem from sincere feelings on the part of the adults with whom they associate.

In order to deal positively with this problem, during the school year of 1974–1975, an interesting experiment with interaction between disabled and nondisabled children was conceived by Dr. Ronald Friedman, the psychologist at the Human Resources School.[5] Called the Peer-Peer program, its objectives and curriculum, as well as an attitude test and report of resultant attitudinal changes, have been described in a monograph entitled "The Peer-Peer Program: A Model Project for the Integration of Severely Physically Handicapped Youngsters with Nondisabled Peers (Ronald S. Friedman, Ph.D., Human Resources School, Albertson, New York 11507; copies of the monograph are available free of charge for as long as the supply lasts from the Human Resources School Library).

The objectives of the program were to:

1. Help reeducate the community to the abilities, as well as realistic limitations, of disabled people.
2. Help develop positive social attitudes toward the disabled.
3. Provide a rewarding experience for disabled youngsters, thus encouraging further contact with other nondisabled people.
4. Develop cooperative projects that would utilize the skills and talents of each child, disabled and nondisabled.
5. Provide a mechanism by which disabled children would feel a part of the larger community setting.

In this program, groups of students from a local elementary school for able-bodied children were matched with a group from the Human Resources School, and joint activities were planned under the overall supervision of Dr. Friedman, with the cooperation of teachers from both schools. A series of activity-oriented, small-group meetings was held, utilizing both school sites alternately. Activities emphasized the skills, abilities, and talents of each child, rather than his or her limitations. At the end of the planned program, an evening meeting featured presentations by each group to all parents.

Results of attitude tests conducted during this first year showed positive attitude changes among the children. However, in some ways the quantitative data do not reflect the degree of enthusiasm conveyed by the parents in evaluating the program. A parent of a nondisabled child commented that, at first, her child was afraid the children's disabilities might be contagious, then was in awe of the special school facility, and finally it became just a sharing situation in which the child was thoroughly comfortable with disabled people. A parent of a disabled child was pleased at the experience because the family was moving and planning to mainstream the youngster into a regular junior high school the following year. Another child was reported to have made friends with several of the nondisabled girls who came to her birthday party and continued to visit during the summer.

The program has been continued since that first year. Recently, a similar activity was begun with the Human Resources Junior High School group in cooperation with a local junior high school for able-bodied students. Children and parents who participate in this type of planned activity will respond to the healthy attitudes that stem from sincere, positive feelings on the part of the adults who are leading the program and with whom the children associate, as well as from the mutual respect stemming from rewarding experiences of the children with each other.

Since the late 1960s, programs that attempt to achieve integration in regular schools between disabled and nondisabled children have met with some success. In the article "Changes in Children's Attitudes toward the Physically Handicapped" by Jacqueline Rapier et al. in *Exceptional Children* (November 1972), the results of a well-planned integrated program and attitude study at the Loma Vista Elementary School in Palo Alto, California, are described.[6] After the integrated school experience with orthopedically handicapped children, these youngsters were seen as less weak and less in need of attention and help; that is, orthopedically handicapped children were perceived as more able to care for themselves than was originally thought. As a result of integration, the able-bodied children saw them more realistically as individuals on an individual basis, and attitudes became more positive.

Blindness

The disability of blindness has always engendered stereotyped attitudes among the sighted. Certain "mannerisms"—habits of rubbing or poking the eyes, holding the head rigidly, not looking toward the speaker, and maintaining a blank facial expression—are in reality the absence of sighted mannerisms, which can cause sighted people to be uncomfortable. The education of blind children and the rehabilitation of adventitiously blind (meaning people who were born with sight) adults or young adults include training in how to avoid these mannerisms.

Two sensitively written autobiographies graphically portray the experiences of growing up blind in a sighted world. *To Catch an Angel: Adventures in a World I Cannot See* by Robert Russell and *To Race the Wind* by Harold Krents are the life stories of men who became blind in early childhood.[7] Russell was educated in a school for blind children, while Krents was educated with sighted children in public schools. Their higher education, in Ivy League colleges and at Oxford University, and success in later life indicate that both are intellectually gifted and must not be considered typical of all disabled people. However, had they not been gifted, they could not have portrayed their childhood years so well. Both speak about loneliness, the lack of friends, the cruelty of other children and the sensitivity of a few, the rare understanding teacher, and the fact that they were looked upon as "blind boys" rather than as "boys who were blind."

The January 1972 issue of *Exceptional Children* magazine carried an article entitled "Changing Public Attitudes toward Blindness" by Velma March and Robert Friedman.[8] In the course of studying the attitudes of sighted students at Sierra High School in Whittier, California, it was found that they exhibited pity and sympathy for blind people, a belief that the blind are either incapacitated or retain extraordinary ability in their remaining senses, and an assumption that among the blind there is a similarity of interests and orientations. A small number of students either feared blind children or behaved maliciously toward them. To ameliorate this situation, a Vision Education program was initiated, taught in freshman health education classes at all ability levels. The article describes the program, which consisted of discussions of blindness, demonstration of visual aids, traveling with blindfolds on, and other activities. The program demonstrated positive results, showing that attitudes can be changed.

Deafness

The disability of deafness is a frequently misunderstood handicap. As with other groups of disabled people, much has happened in the 1970s in the education of deaf and hearing-impaired individuals. First, philosophies of teaching only lip reading to deaf children, espoused by the Alexander Graham Bell Society and used in most schools for deaf children until recently, have given way in many schools to the use of "total communication," the employment of all techniques of communication to enable the deaf to learn language and speech. American sign language, known as Ameslan, finger spelling, lip reading, writing, or any other method of communication can be used to allow deaf people to express themselves and to develop language skills.

A deaf person is a human being with a problem of communication through spoken language. Deafness has nothing to do with intelligence or ambition; deaf people do not want to be shut off from society, but often through fear of rejection, they isolate themselves from hearing people. Deaf persons have normal vocal organs and nearly all of them can speak, but because they are unable to modulate their voices, they may speak with what seems like a speech impediment. Sometimes listeners may find their speech unintelligible, and as a result, many deaf people choose not to use their voices in public. Many deaf people read lips, but even an adept deaf listener can only understand 30 to 40 percent of spoken sounds by watching the lips of the speaker.

There is no such thing as a "typical" deaf person. Hearing-impaired people are disabled in many different ways, ranging from persons who lost their hearing after they acquired language and speech, to prelingually deaf adults (deaf before the age of five) from deaf families who were able to help them acquire better than average language skills or from hearing families who may have had trouble communicating with them when they were young. Deaf people who are the products of oral programs often find themselves learning manual communication when they get older, but they are usually distinguishable because they habitually mouth when signing, or using manual sign language. Deaf children who attended public schools without the benefit of interpreting services are likely to have received little from their public school programs and usually have a habit of trying to look as if they are listening while absorbing very little from the conversation. Many have low verbal ability.

Because medical advances have succeeded in keeping more premature infants alive, there are now more prelingually deaf children than ever, many with multiple handicapping conditions. Similarly, more children with other types of physical handicaps such as spina bifida are surviving infancy.

An excellent book for developing a general awareness of the feelings of deaf people is Leo Jacobs's *A Deaf Adult Speaks Out*.[9] Jacobs explains that deaf people enjoy being together and have their own community. By reason of the fact that communication is such an important factor among human beings, until recently people who are deaf have been cut off from the hearing world. Deaf people experience feelings of isolation, and they are suspicious that people who wish to do something for them do so out of a sense of pity rather than wanting to develop activities that would be appropriate and worthwhile. It is important therefore that attitudes of the hearing population toward people with any degree or type of deafness be radically changed, that real attempts be made among the hearing population, who will be coming in contact with deaf people to a greater extent than ever before, to learn the language of the deaf or at least be ready to attempt communication in whatever way possible—body language, pantomime and gestures of all kinds, written communication, and lip reading.

A few sociometric studies of hearing-impaired children reveal that they are not as socially accepted as their hearing agemates in regular classroom settings. The presence of a hearing aid reduces social status because a visible disability is usually more disabling in terms of attitudes than a hidden disability. Children with hearing defects are chosen as playmates less often than other handicapped children, except for those with cerebral palsy—from a 1956 study by D. Force entitled "Social Status of Physically Handicapped Children," which appeared in *Exceptional Children*. These observations were made in an article entitled "Social Status of Hearing Impaired Children in Regular Classrooms" by Patricia Kennedy and Robert H. Bruininks, *Exceptional Children* (February 1974).[10]

The article states that until the time of the study, the focus of existing research was on children from 9 to 17 years, not on primary groups, and with those exhibiting mild rather than severe hearing loss. Previous studies were based on as few as six subjects, and these studies did not report whether the children had experienced preschool education (before the age of two years), including parental guidance, opportunities for social experience with hearing peers, and the benefits of early diagnosis and amplification. Also, little had been known about the concepts of self-worth of hearing-impaired young children and their perceptions of status within a group situation.

The present study centered on both moderately and severely hearing-impaired children who were enrolled in regular first- and second-grade elementary classrooms. Final results in choice of playmates indicated a higher acceptance of the profoundly deaf children by their peers than of either the mildly hearing-impaired or the able-bodied children. This study is of interest because the results differed markedly from those of earlier attitude studies. These young hearing-impaired children seem to have gained a degree of acceptance not before achieved, although there seemed to be differences based on the individual personalities of the children. Further studies should determine why this happened, what characteristics of these deaf children caused them to be so well accepted. Are young children more nurturant of the handicapped than older children? Did preschool programs play a role in enhancing social acceptance?

The whole question of "hidden handicaps" is one that needs further study. At the Human Resources School, one student who had hemophilia spoke about this. He felt that his peers who had visible physical disabilities might have had less difficulty accepting their own limitations and might have achieved greater acceptance by able-bodied peers than he, because his disability was not visible and his physical limitations not as readily understood. He himself felt ambivalent as he stood between the able-bodied and the disabled community. Beatrice Wright explains this seeming inconsistency by postulating that a person with a mild disability may, because he or she is "almost normal," have a greater push to hide and deny the disability, thereby thwarting adjustment.[11]

TREATMENT IN THE MEDIA

The media have contributed both negatively and positively to developing attitudes toward the disabled. Douglas Biklen and Robert Bogdan, writing in *Interracial Books for Children* (Bulletin VIII, Nos. 6 and 7, 1977), discuss media portrayal of disabled persons.[12] The authors surveyed a range of classic literature and popular contemporary media, and concluded that although a few books and films treat disability with sensitivity and accuracy, most do not. Stereotypes range from portraying disabled people as pitiable and pathetic to showing them as objects of violence or as sinister and/or evil. In *Handicapping America*, Frank Bowe cites as examples the evil Captain Hook in *Peter Pan*, Quasimodo in *The Hunchback of Notre Dame*, the monster in *Frankenstein*, and the classic good and evil example in *The Strange Case of Dr. Jekyll and Mr. Hyde*.[13] Pictorially, the disabled person is sometimes used for "atmosphere" in the background, further reducing the humanness of the person by relegating him or her to scenery, as in the frequently depicted blind newsstand dealer or musician.

In what Biklen and Bogdan call the "supercrip" concept, the character is often assigned supernatural abilities. Sometimes the disabled are portrayed as humorous, often as a burden to be taken care of by others, and almost always as nonsexual or totally incapable of sexual activity. In the latter case, a very successful departure from this was the paraplegic Vietnam War veteran portrayed by Jon Voight, for which he won an Academy Award, in the 1978 film *Coming Home*.

Some progress has been made in television and radio. On his television show for children, Mr. Rogers, on his Public Broadcasting Service program "Mr. Rogers' Neighborhood," made a positive attempt to include guests who have adapted to impairments. Some television stations are now signing news programs and commercials for the hearing-impaired, and on radio programs for the blind in many areas of the country newspapers and magazine selections are read. Under grants from the U.S. Office of Education, public television stations in Boston and Annandale, Virginia, are producing programs that portray disabled and nondisabled children interacting cooperatively. The television program "Zoom" has also occasionally featured disabled children.

But the image of disability has many facets. People find it easier to deal with the concept of "cuteness" in little children on crutches and in braces or wheelchairs than with disabled adults. The telethon phenomenon, where appeals for funds are made for research into the nature and causes of specific disabilities, bears out this attitude. Only good-looking children appear on these programs. In addition to appearance is the fact that disabled adults represent the "failures," the proof that the cure for the disability has not been found, whereas in children there remains the hope for improvement in their disabling condition.

The reality is that for disabilities such as cerebral palsy and muscular dystrophy, no cures have yet been found, although a great deal of research is going on. But money is also sought for services to furnish appropriate educational opportunities, provide needed therapy and equipment, develop job possibilities and independent living situations, and generally to improve the quality of life for people with these disabilities. These reasons, no less legitimate in the quest for funding where the government cannot or, in any case, has not provided the funds, are nevertheless far less appealing and effective in the minds of the public.

More extensive examples of both good and bad portrayals of the disabled in literature are offered in the already mentioned *Notes from a Different Drummer*.[14] The various forms of media are somewhat limited in the extent to which they can influence attitudes toward the disabled. It is the position of the President's Committee on the Employment of the Handicapped (Library Committee), however, that constant efforts should be made to work toward the objective of portraying the disabled positively in all forms of the media. Book publishers have been contacted toward this end, the objective being to persuade writers and publishers and particularly illustrators to portray the physically disabled in positive ways. Where he or she may not be a main character, a disabled person in an illustration should be a positive portrayal. An excellent example is in the picture book *Moon Man* by Tomi Ungerer, in which an elderly gentleman in a wheelchair is pictured at a board meeting, obviously a very important member of a scientific group.[15]

Almost any type of portrayal of disabled people in the media will be successful if handled with a solid positive attitude and with accuracy. One outstanding example was Lily Tomlin's characterization on the stage of the indomitable quadriplegic young lady named Crystal, who traveled across the United States in her puff-n-sip wheelchair. A risky experiment at best, this attempt at humor about the subject of quadriplegia could have been a disaster in the hands of a less skilled performer than Tomlin. However, disabled people who saw her performance were not only vastly entertained and amused but also astounded at the knowledge she displayed of her subject, making it clear that Tomlin had done a tremendous amount of research before tackling it. Her monologue, one of the first real attempts to utilize humor in a positive way about physical disability, was published in *Disabled USA*.[16]

ATTITUDES OF DISABLED PEOPLE

In May 1977, a White House Conference on Handicapped Individuals was held in Washington, D.C. It was a large gathering, attended by disabled people as well as members of the helping professions, and it reflected all of the major concerns that disabled people share as they work toward economic and social independence. Cross-cutting all other concerns, however, was the great need for campaigns that emphasize the abilities rather than the disabilities of disabled people, as well as their diversity.

Underscoring this point was the variety of special-interest groups that met during the conference to consider specific issues. A nonwhite caucus asserted that racism contributes greatly to the condition of the 40 percent of disabled people who belong to nonwhite groups.[17] There was also a Hispanic caucus, a disabled women's caucus, and a mental health caucus. Most interesting, from the point of view of attitudes among disabled people, was the caucus for an alternative conference report. This caucus was formed by disabled persons who felt that some of the issues presented at the larger conference did not express their concerns. This group published an alternative conference report, which was included in its entirety in Volume II, Part A, of the final report of the main conference. (Single copies of the report are also available from the Clearinghouse on the Handicapped, Department of Health, Education, and Welfare, Room 339D, HHH Building, Washington, D.C. 20201.[18])

This report recognized the concept of flexibility and self-determination in noting the different generic labels in current use in different parts of the country: *handicapped; individuals who are handicapped; individuals with a handicap; disabled; individuals who are disabled; individuals with a disability; handicappers; individuals who are handicappers;* and *able-disabled.*

In the area of attitudes, one concern was that blanket legislation, recommendations, and approaches toward issues affecting all handicapped groups lack specificity. Sometimes different categories of handicapped people have different or even opposite problems, and the able-bodied do not always know what is best for specific categories of disabled people. It was resolved, and the recommendation made, that the issues and concerns of the conference be analyzed and grouped according to each special handicap, in order to meet more properly the needs of each group, and that consideration be given to position papers and recommendations from special groups of the handicapped, particularly from those consumer organizations now representing the disabled that are under the leadership of handicapped individuals.

More and more disabled people are heading these groups, serving on the boards of projects for independent living and in many other ways taking charge of their own affairs. Significantly, in the light of this development, Section VII of the report, entitled "Removal of Attitudinal Barriers," opens with a recommendation that there should be a strong emphasis on assertiveness-training groups for the handicapped, to be conducted if possible by qualified handicapped people. The disabled need to have this training to help them overcome the results of overprotectiveness or the "institutional mentality" syndrome. Constant association with professional groups that profess to help the disabled in reality sometimes causes them to assume an attitude of inferiority, which must be overcome.

The White House Conference, as well as the meeting of disabled people in the alternative group, was noteworthy because many disabled people are ambivalent about joining in activism with other disabled people, believing that such action will tend to cut them off from associating with the able-bodied. There are among disabled people some strong feelings of hierarchy, so that some disabled individuals are considered inferior by people with other disabilities. The development of diverse independent living projects that include disabled people in their management but allow the disabled to live among the nondisabled may be a partial solution to this problem.

EMOTIONAL AND SOCIAL PROBLEMS OF DISABLED PEOPLE

Certain principles of human behavior apply to all individuals with or without disabilities. Usually, however, the strengths and weaknesses in the individual are intensified in persons with physical disabilities. Young adults, for example, go through a painful growing-up period. A large nose or a pimple to a teenager may seem as disabling as a serious facial disfigurement for a disabled person. Conformity to the norm among young adults is terribly important. How difficult, then, is it for a young adult who is physically disabled, undersized, or in some other way nonconforming to the norm for his or her age?

The normal growing pains of adolescence are magnified in the presence of a disability. Sexual development for the disabled teenager holds all of the struggles that confront the able-bodied teenager, but they are magnified. Sometimes the disabled female fears adulthood less than does the disabled male, since the image of a woman in a wheelchair does not connote a loss of femininity. Usually the disabled female has her menstrual period, and often she can bear children. But the American macho image of maleness can cause disaster for a male in a wheelchair, who must look up to women. Spinal cord injury and spina bifida often result in some degree of sexual dysfunction. The problem exists for the professional to help the disabled male achieve a strong self-image in the face of these disadvantages. The topic of sexuality and the disabled is an important one, and sources of information in this area are found in Chapter 4.

Disability is a state of mind and a matter of degree. Individual concepts of self-worth—how we perceive ourselves—depend on how we were handled by our parents, our teachers, and the society around us. And so it is with disabled individuals. Many disabled people, each one different from the other, have differing concepts of self-worth and different degrees of disability. Some feel very handicapped indeed, while others do not perceive themselves as particularly disabled, but rarely does the physical condition cause this difference. Mildly disabled individuals may feel very disabled; severely disabled individuals surmount tremendous physical barriers to accomplish anything they wish.

It is possible, however, to generalize somewhat about the social and emotional strengths and weaknesses of disabled people, and about some of the problems they encounter as they grow up. The question often asked is whether the congenitally disabled are better adjusted than those who are disabled later in life. This can be reasoned either way, and there is evidence to support both positions. The child who is born disabled has a much longer time to be influenced by overprotective parents, or, conversely, to learn to cope with his or her disability, helped by wise and supportive parents. The newly disabled adult, however, brings to the experience all the emotional strengths and weaknesses that were a part of his or her nondisabled personality. Wright maintains that no tests have conclusively shown a difference, and we find much individual variation here.[19]

One student entered the Human Resources School after experiencing a stroke, and he exhibited socially objectionable and hostile personality traits. Upon conferring with the psychologist at the school he attended before the stroke, it was determined that testing done when he was eight years old showed the same characteristics. The parents were in therapy and had been alternately together and apart. His teachers found him difficult to cope with. It would have been easy to blame brain damage for the behavioral pattern, but this youngster was the same person before and after his disability.[20]

The person who has had an accident experiences many personality changes, and generally goes through a series of stages—first denial (it has not happened, or, if it has, it is not going to result in permanent disability), then hostility (why did this have to happen to me?), then depression (which Wright calls the "period of mourning" for the lost healthy body). In the face of this kind of experience, most people after a period of time become the same person they were before. That time period may be months or it may be years, and some people who have had accidents show intensification of strength and very great courage.

> Gerry came to the Human Resources School after an automobile accident and time spent in a rehabilitation institute. He was a paraplegic, having suffered a spinal cord injury. For two years he exhibited extreme hostility, followed by depression. Communication with him was extremely difficult. He stayed on an extra year to make up schoolwork, and during that third year he began to thaw out. In time, Gerry became the charming, warm individual he was before his accident. He went on to college and is now working productively.

Can the psychological limitations of a disabled person be traced back to the way he or she was handled as a child? Yes, of course, in the same way that any parent has influence on a child's development, with perhaps a little bit extra. Because children are seen as extensions of the parent, bearing a child who is less than physically perfect can be taken by the parent as a personal failure. The parent must then deal with feelings of grief at the loss of the anticipated healthy child and go through what Beatrice Wright says is a period of mourning for that child.[21] This period is similar to that experienced by the young adult or adult who has an accident. Time for adjustment cannot be estimated but depends on individual cases. Parents' reactions to handicapping conditions in an older child are similar to the response at the birth of a disabled child, with one major difference. When the child becomes handicapped later in life, the parents have already formed a strong attachment. With the newborn, the attachment is not yet formed and is more easily interfered with.[22] Lack of contact at birth, because of prolonged medical treatment in the hospital, for example, further disrupts the formation of this attachment.

Some parents respond to the birth of a disabled child by rejection. This withdrawal may be temporary or it may result in the disabled baby's being placed in an institution. A visible disability is harder to deny than an invisible one and consequently will engender the greater reaction from both parents and the rest of society. One stage in a parent's adjustment to what may be a life-long disability is denial that it will be permanent. Parents comment that they tried to place a child in a regular school program, whether or not it was the most advantageous placement for the child, simply to be able to say to themselves and to their friends that the child was in a regular school and thus not really disabled. Denial over a long period of time can, of course, interfere with proper medical management, as well as appropriate school placement and education or vocational plans for the future.

All parents face the occasional wish that their children—able-bodied or disabled—did not exist. But parents of disabled children feel this way more often because these children make so many more demands on their time. The feelings of anger and resentment at the extra burden can produce guilt feelings, all of which the disabled child may perceive and use to pressure the parent and make more demands. The result is very often overprotection, a common reaction of parents, many of whose children need a certain amount of physical protection and care. Overprotection is caused by the parents' need to feel less guilty about their negative feelings. It also allows the parents to atone to the child for the disability, a need that comes in part from the parents' sense of guilt at having "given" the child a defective endowment.

Overprotection is also emphasized in the isolation that parents of chronically ill children sometimes experience as they retreat from relationships with their neighbors, hesitate to take their handicapped children on vacations, and often discourage socializing by the disabled son or daughter. There are, however, some very beautiful exceptions to this situation. The parents of one young man, severely disabled with osteogenesis imperfecta and on a home instructional school program, encouraged him to acquire a license as a ham radio operator. This put him in verbal touch with the entire world. He also held classes for neighborhood children, who were thus encouraged to visit him, and this made him seem less homebound. When this young man finally entered the Human Resources School at the age of 15, his social adjustment was outstanding. He finished high school, college, and law school, and he is now practicing law for the disabled.

Other parents have encouraged their severely disabled children to attend sleep-away summer camp, thus forcibly breaking the protective ties and enabling the children to develop into socially and emotionally independent individuals, even though they might always need a certain amount of physical care.

One serious problem affecting families of disabled children is a lack of communication between husbands and wives. There is a high rate of disrupted marriages in families with handicapped children, usually, but not always, with the father leaving a situation he cannot tolerate and the mother remaining isolated with the children. However, in some situations the mother has left the child with the father because he was better able to accept the situation.

One way in which parents can deal positively with the fact of having a disabled child is to inform themselves fully about the disability and work within the parent organizations that have been formed to encourage educational opportunities and research about the condition. (Some of the literature these groups have issued is listed in Chapter 2.) Sometimes, with a need to approach the problem intellectually, a parent or other concerned adult will consult a librarian at a public library in search of information. While the librarian must make every effort to help find material, often this is a sign of "shopping around." The information given by medical or other professional persons has not been accepted as adequate or final, and the person's quest for more acceptable answers goes on. Librarians must develop a sensitivity to this while making every effort to help supply the asked-for information.

Problems of adolescence can be heightened by parental attitudes. Most of the time the parent's overprotective attitude serves to help keep the adolescent asexual. Most handicapped adolescents in their own group discussions move far more quickly into issues of sexuality than do their parents.

Parents for the most part are now encouraged to care for disabled children at home rather than to place them in institutions. There are now more educational and other services to help ease the very real burdens that fall upon the parents of severely disabled children.

The effects of a disability within a family, however, also extend to the siblings of the disabled child. Often parents must direct most of their energy and attention to the care of the disabled child, at the expense of the rest of the family. Observations seem to indicate that siblings of disabled children often experience more emotional problems than do other children. According to some studies, some siblings have benefited from having a handicapped sister or brother and as young adults are more tolerant, compassionate, and aware of prejudice than others of their age. But bitterness, resentment at the family situation, anger, and feelings of deprivation do seem to be more the general reaction. In general, the family that includes a disabled child experiences a great deal of stress and many more problems than do the families of able-bodied children.[23]

Families in which one member becomes disabled later in life experience problems involving disbelief and anger as well as a certain amount of "shopping around" for help. Ultimate readjustment will depend on which family member has become disabled. When it is the husband or wife, there may be role reversals in terms of employment and/or household duties. Added duties and responsibilities for able-bodied family members, decreased income, early maturity for children, and changes in recreation and travel patterns require flexibility of each family member. Since people typically resist changes that require personal sacrifices or concessions, the impact of disability upon the family may be extremely traumatic.

These and other views are expressed in an article by Carroll Ault entitled "The Impact of a Blind Member on Others in the Family" in the journal *Blindness* 1977–1978 (an annual published by the American Association of Workers for the Blind, Inc., 1511 K Street N.W., Washington, D.C. 20005).[24] Ault's position, stated in the article, that the impact of blindness on the family is more traumatic than that of other disabilities is one to which this author cannot subscribe. Rather, the problems stated, it would seem, do apply to families in which one member develops any kind of severely disabling condition.

WHAT THE LIBRARIAN CAN DO

Some librarians, with the very best of intentions, will feel awkward when actually faced with helping a disabled patron for the first time. A few simple dos and don'ts may help to put them at ease.

1. Offer assistance as you would to anyone else, for example, to push a wheelchair or to guide a blind person. The person will indicate whether or not the help is needed, and a "no, thank you" must be respected. Most disabled people will not hesitate to ask for needed help and will be specific as to how it should be given; for example, the blind person usually prefers to take your arm rather than to have you grab his or hers.

2. Noticing an obvious disability is not rude; however, asking personal questions about it is inappropriate.

3. Always talk directly to a disabled person rather than to the person

who may be accompanying him or her. Never talk about a disabled person to the person he or she is with as if the person did not exist. This would include an interpreter for a deaf person.

4. Do not be concerned if you use the words *walking* or *running* when talking to a person in a wheelchair or "Do you see?" when talking to a blind person. Disabled people use these words themselves and think nothing of it.

5. Do not avoid using words like *blind* or *deaf* when associating with people with these disabilities. Disabled people know that they have them and do not need to be shielded from the facts.

6. When talking with a person in a wheelchair for any length of time, it is better to sit down in order to be at the same eye level. It is very tiring for a person to look up for a long time.

7. Be sensitive to architectural barriers in your libraries. By law they should be removed. Everyone must be concerned and alert to this very real problem.

8. Remember that if a person does not turn around in response to a call, it may be that he or she is deaf. A light tap on the shoulder to get a person's attention makes sense.

9. Never gesture about a blind person to someone else who may be present. This will inevitably be picked up and make the person who is blind feel that you are "talking behind his or her back."

10. Lip reading by deaf persons can be aided by being sure that the light is on your face and not behind you, and by taking all obstructions such as pipes, cigarettes, or gum out of the mouth, keeping the lips flexible, and speaking slowly. Additional communication could include body language, pantomime and gestures of all kinds, and written communication if necessary.

SUMMARY

The elimination of barriers so that disabled people may live among the able-bodied in dignity and equality will count for nothing unless the first and most important barrier of all—prejudice—is eliminated. Stereotyping people because they look "different" from the norms, which society has established, must cease. We, as librarians, in order to give service to all segments of society, must look within ourselves to deal with our attitudes toward all patrons so that we may give service with the necessary care and sensitivity.

BIBLIOGRAPHY

Anderson, Consuelo Escoe, and Presberry, Rosa L. *Pick A Title: A Collection of Children's Books and Other Media about the Handicapped.* Maryland State Department of Education, 1978. Books, films, professional references, publishers, and producers.

Anthony, W. A. "Societal Rehabilitation: Changing Society's Attitudes toward the Physically and Mentally Disabled." *Rehabilitation Psychology*, 19 (1972): 117–126.

Baskin, Barbara H., and Harris, Karen H. *Notes from a Different Drummer: A Guide to Juvenile Fiction Portraying the Handicapped.* New York: R. R. Bowker, 1977. Chapters on society and the handicapped, literary treatment of disability, an annotated guide to juvenile fiction portraying the handicapped, 1940–1975.

Bowe, Frank, *Handicapping America.* New York: Harper & Row, 1978. How society handicaps its disabled people.

Brooks, B. L., and Bransford, L. A. "Modification of Teachers' Attitudes toward Exceptional Children." *Exceptional Children*, 38 (1971): 259–260.

Lazer, Alfred L., Stodden, Robert L., and Sullivan, Neil V. "A Comparison of Attitudes Held by Male and Female Future School Administrators toward Instructional Goals, Personal Adjustment, and the Handicapped." *Rehabilitation Literature*, 37, no. 7 (1976): 198–201.

Newman, J. "Faculty Attitudes toward Handicapped Students." *Rehabilitation Literature*, 37 (1976): 194–197.

Payne, R., and Murrey, C. "Principals' Attitudes toward Integration of the Handicapped." *Exceptional Children*, 41 (1974): 123–125.

Poznanski, Elva O. "Emotional Issues in Raising Handicapped Children." *Rehabilitation Literature*, 34, no. 11 (Nov. 1973): 322–326.

Rapier, J. et al. "Changes in Children's Attitudes toward the Physically Handicapped." *Exceptional Children*, 39 (1972): 219–223.

Re: Search. A publication of the Regional Rehabilitation Research Institute on Attitudinal, Legal, and Leisure Barriers, George Washington University, Washington, D.C. 20036. Vol. II No. 6 (February 1979) issue is on *Labeling* and contains some provocative ideas and good references. Barrier Awareness Series includes: *The Invisible Battle: Attitudes and Disability; Beyond the Sound Barrier . . . Attitudes toward People with Hearing-impairment and Deafness; Free Wheeling . . . Attitudes toward People Who Use Wheelchairs; Counterpoint . . . Attitudes of Disabled People toward Nondisabled People* (companion to *The Invisible Battle*); *Dignity . . . Attitudes toward People with Mental Retardation; Overdue Process: Providing Legal Services to Disabled Clients . . . Attitudes of Legal Professionals toward Disabled People;* and *Partners . . . Attitudes of Rehabilitation Counselors and VR Clients toward Each Other.*

———— Panieczko, S. *Attitudes and Disability: A Selected Annotated Bibliography,* 1975–1977.

Shotel, J. R., Iano, R. P., and McGettigan, J. F. "Teacher Attitudes Associated with the Integration of Handicapped Children." *Exceptional Children*, 38 (1972): 677–683.

Smith-Kanen, Sandra. "Socialization of the Physically Handicapped." *The Journal of Applied Rehabilitation Counseling*, 7 (Fall 1976): 131–141.

Weinstein, G. W. "New World for Deaf Children." *Parents Magazine*, 47 (November 1972): 58–59.

Wright, Beatrice A. "Changes in Attitudes toward People with Handicaps." *Rehabilitation Literature*, 34 (1973): 354–357, 368.

───────. *Disabling Myths about Disability*, rev., 1977. Pamphlet. Paper originally presented at the 1961 annual Easter Seal Convention. Distributed by the National Easter Seal Society, Chicago, Ill.

───────. *Physical Disability: A Psychological Approach*. New York: Harper & Row, 1960.

Audiovisual Materials

The following references have been reproduced with permission from the annotated bibliography "The Special Student: Selected Media for Special Education," by Robert J. Hanley, *Previews* 7, no. 5 (January 1979).

Changes. 16mm, color, 28 min., Crystal Productions, Aspen, Colo., 1976. Life-styles of people with spinal cord injuries.

Get It Together. 16mm, color, 20 min., Pyramid Films, Santa Monica, Calif., 1977. A 1977 blue-ribbon winner at the American Film Festival in New York City and an Academy Award nomination. Insightful visit with a recreational therapist who is a paraplegic.

Gravity Is My Enemy. 15mm, color, 26 min., Churchill Films, Los Angeles, Calif., 1977. Academy Award winner for best short documentary dealing with the artistic abilities of a quadriplegic, his philosophy of life, the support of his family. Mark Hicks died at the age of 28, leaving a body of artistic works that are exceptional in their conception and execution.

Handicapped Adults and Their Life Styles: Making It (series). Cassette, automatic, color, 4 strips with 2 cassettes with teacher's guide. Eye Gate Media, Jamaica, N.Y., 1979. Includes "Lee Bean: Advocate for Justice"; "Alice Hagemeyer: A Member of Two Committees"; "Susan Bowmaster: A Different Point of View"; "Zeddie Hart: Overcoming the Odds." Excellent for career education. Shows four well-adjusted adults living with handicapping conditions.

I'll Find a Way. 16mm, color, 26 min., National Film Board of Canada (prod.), Media Guild, Solana Beach, Calif. (dist.), 1977. Academy Award winner about a nine-year-old girl with spina bifida. Many of her problems are common to all children. Excellent for familiarizing children with those who have handicaps.

I'm Just Like You: Mainstreaming the Handicapped (set). Cassette, automatic and manual, color, 2 strips with 2 cassettes with teacher's guide. Sunburst Communications, Pleasantville, N.Y., 1977. Includes "Taking It in Stride," and "Dealing with the Problem." Case histories of handicapped children mainstreamed into regular public schools. Designed to give parents, educators, and students an awareness of the needs and abilities of handicapped people.

Kevin Is Four: The Early Development of a Child Amputee. 16mm, color, 27 min., Ohio State University, Columbus, Ohio, 1965. Demonstrates how naturally a child can develop despite his handicap. Attitudes of parents and needs of the child.

Stress—Parents with a Handicapped Child. 16mm, color, 30 min., Films, Inc., Wilmette, Ill., 1966. Five British families in an unscripted film. An insightful documentary that looks at problems of raising a handicapped child.

Swan Lake: Conversations with Deaf Teenagers. 16mm, color, 15 min., Total Communication Laboratories, Western Maryland College, Westminster, Md. Interviews with deaf teenagers who express their views on various aspects of life. In sign language with a spoken narrative interpretation. (Other films on deafness and hearing loss available from Total Communication Laboratories.)

To Climb a Mountain. 16mm, color, 15 min., BFA Educational Media, Santa Monica, Calif., 1975. Blind and partially sighted mountain climbers seek to expand their own horizons. Sharing their experience will affect attitudes toward visual impairments.

Understanding the Deaf. 16mm, color, 21 min., Perennial Education, Northfield, Ill., n.d. Develops an awareness of how deaf people communicate.

Walter. 16mm, color, 15 min., Churchill Films, Los Angeles, Calif., n.d. A well-adjusted, productive, physically disabled college student shares his world with viewers.

Additional Films

Crip-Trips. 16mm, three short films, black and white, President's Committee on Employment of the Handicapped, Washington, D.C., n.d. Three disabled people tell about themselves.

Everyday Champions. 16mm, color, 30 min., Michigan Bell System, Detroit, Mich., n.d. Employment of the disabled by the Bell System.

The Good People. 16mm, color, 30 min., Hughes Aircraft, Gemini Productions, Hollywood, Calif., n.d. Employment of the disabled at the Hughes Company.

Mimi. 16mm, black and white, 17 min., Billy Budd Films, New York, N.Y., n.d. Young physically disabled girl talks about her adolescence, growing up, and marriage.

When You Meet a Blind Person. 16mm, color, 13½ min., American Foundation for the Blind, New York, N.Y., 1971. Winner of several film awards, an excellent introduction to how to meet and behave in social situations with a blind person. Sighted person meets and fumbles situations such as guiding a blind person along the street and dining together. The fumbled scenes are repeated, showing the correct manner in which to participate in such situations with a blind person.

NOTES

1. Frank Bowe, *Handicapping America: Barriers to Disabled People* (New York: Harper & Row, 1978), p. viii.

2. Beatrice Wright, *Physical Disability: A Psychological Approach* (New York: Harper & Row, 1960), p. 17.

3. Barbara H. Baskin and Karen H. Harris, *Notes from a Different Drummer: A Guide to Juvenile Fiction Portraying the Handicapped* (New York: R. R. Bowker, 1977).

4. Wright, *Physical Disability*, p. 118.

5. Ronald Friedman, Ph.D., *The Peer-Peer Program: A Model Project for the Integration of Severely Physically Handicapped Youngsters with Nondisabled Peers* (Albertson, N.Y.: Human Resources School, 1975).

6. Jacqueline Rapier et al., "Changes in Children's Attitudes toward the Physically Handicapped," *Exceptional Children* 39, no. 3 (1972): 219–223.

7. Harold Krents, *To Race the Wind* (New York: Putnam, 1972), and Robert Russell, *To Catch an Angel* (New York: Vanguard Press, 1962).

8. Velma March and Robert Friedman, "Changing Public Attitudes toward Blindness," *Exceptional Children* 38 (1972): 426–428.

9. Leo M. Jacobs, *A Deaf Adult Speaks Out* (Washington, D.C.: Gallaudet College Press, 1974).

10. Patricia Kennedy and Robert H. Bruininks, "Social Status of Hearing Impaired Children in Regular Classrooms," *Exceptional Children* 40, no. 5 (1974): 336–341.

11. Wright, *Physical Disability*, p. 53.

12. Douglas Biklen and Robert Bogdan, *Interracial Books for Children*, Bulletin VIII, nos. 6 and 7 (1977).

13. Bowe, *Handicapping America*, p. 109.

14. Baskin and Harris, *Notes*, p. 15.

15. Tomi Ungerer, *Moon Man* (New York: Harper & Row, 1967).

16. Lily Tomlin, "Crystal the Terrible Tumbleweed," *Disabled USA* 1, no. 5 (1978).

17. White House Conference on Handicapped Individuals, summary, final report, Office of Handicapped Individuals, Washington, D.C., DHEW pub. No. (OHD) 78-22003, p. 119.

18. Alternative Conference Report, representatives of the handicapped at the White House Conference on Handicapped Individuals for an Alternative Conference Report, vol. 2, part A, final report of the White House Conference on Handicapped Individuals, Washington, D.C., 1978.

19. Wright, *Physical Disability*, p. 154.

20. M. Marie Meier, "The Psychology of Disability" (speech, Greenvale, N.Y., Palmer Graduate Library School, C. W. Post Center of Long Island University, August 1–6, 1976).

21. Wright, *Physical Disability*, p. 110.

22. Elva O. Poznanski, "Emotional Issues in Raising Handicapped Children," *Rehabilitation Literature* 34, no. 11 (November 1973): 322–326.

23. Ibid.

24. Carroll Ault, "The Impact of a Blind Member on Others in the Family," *Blindness* (1977–1978), p. 180.

2
Defining Disabilities

We live in a society in which everyone is expected to conform to certain physical standards. How one looks often influences how one is treated. It takes some time before an individual's personality emerges, takes over, and creates an impression on the observer that is closer to the truth. What *is* the truth? Every person has certain abilities that can, with appropriate education and training, be developed to their maximum function. The truth about each individual lies somewhere among his or her innate capacities, how well these capacities have been developed, with the assistance of family and professionals, and the degree of emotional strength the person brings to his or her life experiences.

One tends to think of physically disabled people as a cohesive group, with certain similar characteristics. To some extent this is true, and some of these similarities have been explored in Chapter 1. There are, however, many differences, and in particular many physical differences, among the disabled. All persons in wheelchairs or using crutches or braces do not have the same kinds of physical problems.

Physical disabilities fall into three basic anatomical categories: those involving the skeletal structure, the muscular system, and the neuromuscular system. Special health problems are also included among the physical disability groupings.

The major skeletal disabilities include various forms of dwarfism, osteogenesis imperfecta, amputees (congenital and traumatic), arthrogryposis, and rheumatoid arthritis. The major muscular disability is muscular dystrophy; other major muscular disorders are related and included under this heading. Neuromuscular disabilities include cerebral palsy, postpolio, and multiple sclerosis. Special health problems include hemophilia, epilepsy, cardiac diseases, diabetes, sickle cell anemia, and many other of the so-called hidden disabilities.

Some disabilities may involve more than one basic anatomical category; spina bifida, for instance, affects both the skeletal structure and the neuro-muscular system. The disabilities discussed in the following pages are listed in alphabetical order, with the anatomical category or categories noted in the text.

Some of these disabilities are well known and a great deal has been written about them. Others are fairly rare and it has not been easy in the past to acquire information. This chapter discusses some of the well-known disabilities as well as some of the rarer types, probably being encountered for the first time by the general public. Sources for more extensive information will be offered to aid librarians in assisting parents, educators, rehabilitation counselors, and disabled patrons themselves. (Types of disabilities involving visual and hearing impairments are discussed in Chapters 6 and 7.)

Many of the parent organizations have published pamphlets dealing with disabilities in lay terms. These are often free of charge and are so indicated here. Fortunately, there is now an excellent source for both public and school libraries that offers definitions of many of these disabilities, using simplified medical terminology—*Physically Handicapped Children: A Medical Atlas for Teachers* by Eugene E. Bleck, M.D., and Donald A. Nagel, M.D.[1] This book would make a fine addition to reference and teacher information collections.

AMPUTATION

A missing limb is the result of acquired or congenital amputation. In acquired amputation, the person was born normally, but through accident or surgery (most often for a malignant tumor), a limb was removed. Congenital amputation means that the child was born without the limb, in part or in total. The Greek word for limb is *melus*. *Hemimelia* means half a limb; *amelia* means total absence of a limb. *Phocomelia* (*phoco* means seal) is a small appendage of what might have been a full limb.

The cause of total or partial congenital limb absence is a failure of fetal limb bud development in the first three months of pregnancy. Artificial limbs (prostheses) and training in their use are the treatment for this condition. The absence of both upper or lower limbs presents obvious problems, which must be solved on an individual basis and, in some cases, with special electric prostheses and devices.

Generally, the intellectual capabilities of children with amputations do not differ from those of the general population. But education of the child must take physical limitations into consideration. The use of a prosthesis with the upper limbs will depend on the height of the amputation. Sometimes children discard the prostheses, particularly when engaging in sports. Children will know what is best for them.

With the total loss of upper limbs, children sometimes become adept at using feet or toes. In our cosmetically oriented society, this can prove disturbing, and in some cases children are restricted from doing so. However, this is an example of optimum functional use of residual assets.

Bilateral (both legs) above-the-knee amputees are usually very handicapped and need wheelchairs for at least part-time use and conservation of energy. Swimming is an excellent exercise for such people. Below-the-knee amputees walk well with artificial limbs. Such handicapped children can be mainstreamed without any trouble, with adequate attention paid to the attitudes of their classmates.[2]

ARTHRITIS

The word *arthritis* means inflammation of a joint. However, it is widely used to cover almost 100 different conditions that cause aching and pain in the joints and connective tissues throughout the body. More than 12 million people in the United States are limited in their activities by arthritis. There are five kinds of arthritis:

Rheumatoid arthritis is the most serious and painful. It is inflammatory and chronic and can affect the whole body. It primarily attacks the joints and can flare up unpredictably, causing progressive damage to the tissues. Crippling can result. Women are affected three times more often than men. When occurring in children, it is known as juvenile rheumatoid arthritis (see below).

Osteoarthritis is principally a wear-and-tear disease of the joints, which occurs with age. It is usually mild and not inflammatory.

Ankylosing spondylitis is a chronic, inflammatory arthritis of the spine, which affects men ten times more often than women, usually beginning in the teens or early twenties.

Rheumatic fever is a disease that follows a streptococcus infection, and frequently damages the heart. It also causes arthritis in the joints, which subsides quickly and does not cause crippling.

Gout, also called gouty arthritis, is an inherited disease that usually attacks small joints, especially the big toe. It mostly attacks men and is very painful.

The purposes of treatment programs are to relieve pain, reduce inflammation, prevent deformities or damage to joints, and retain mobility. Treatment involves medication, exercise, splints, heat, walking aids, surgery, and rehabilitation therapy. Since there is no cure (except for remissions), treatment must continue. Most of the time arthritis does not prevent people from functioning in employment and other daily activities.

Juvenile Rheumatoid Arthritis

Juvenile rheumatoid arthritis may occur in children as early as six weeks of age. Estimates of the number of children with this disease in the United States vary. Most children with rheumatoid arthritis have a type called polyarticular arthritis, with severely affected joints. These children are usually in pain and will tend to sit very still so as not to feel it, with a subsequent loss of range of motion and contractures. Frequently, the children are small for their age, since the disease interferes with growth and sexual maturation. Complications may include an eye disease and some degree of joint damage. These can be controlled if the disease is treated early and properly.

Treatment consists of medication (aspirin, as in adult rheumatoid arthritis, is most frequently used), rest, appropriate exercise, and in some cases surgery. Rest is of utmost importance.

In the classroom, children with rheumatoid arthritis are often uncomfortable, and consequently tend to become depressed, inhibited and shy, or, conversely, angry. Pain may vary, depending on what kind of night the child had or what time of day it is. Attendance may be poor, as these children tend to get a late start in the morning. Teachers, therapists, occupational therapists, and school nurses must be aware of the child's problem and be able to show sympathy without being overprotective. Time must be allowed for the child to move from one class to the other. A high aspirin dose may cause temporary loss' of high tones in hearing. Vision problems may be first detected by a teacher and should be reported.[3]

A pamphlet entitled "Arthritis: The Basic Facts" has been published by The Arthritis Foundation (New York Chapter, 221 Park Avenue South, New York, New York 10003). Additional information may be obtained from the national headquarters of The Arthritis Foundation (1212 Avenue of the Americas, New York, New York 10036).

ARTHROGRYPOSIS MULTIPLEX CONGENITA

From the Greek words *arthro* (joints) and *gryposis* (curved), this congenital disease begins *in utero*. It involves the muscles, or more accurately the spinal cord cells that control muscle contraction, resulting in failure of muscle function. This causes lack of movement in the joints and consequent stiffness and deformity. Arthrogryposis is not hereditary.

Children born with this disability are stiff-jointed, usually with their arms fixed in a permanently twisted position. Surgery may sometimes allow the arms to bend so that the hands can be used. However, once in a bent position, the arms often cannot be straightened. Some of these children walk with a stiff-legged gait; others are in wheelchairs. There is often hip dislocation. Surgery may be needed to correct knee and/or foot deformities. Scoliosis (spinal curvature) is corrected by surgery and spinal fusion.

Children with arthrogryposis have normal intelligence and speech, but physical rehabilitation is limited. Educationally, children with this condition should be given the opportunity for academic achievement. Accommodations will need to be made in the areas of mobility and handwriting. Sometimes the use of a typewriter can help.

The parents of children with this disability have formed a national association. Two contacts for the association are Mrs. V. Hamby, 3204 K Street, Vancouver, Washington 98663; and Mrs. Nancy DiNunzio, 106 Herkimer Street, North Bellmore, New York 11712. Since this parent organization is very young, it has not yet published any pamphlet materials. Persons wishing information should contact the association, which will certainly be producing some literature in the near future.[4]

CEREBRAL PALSY

Cerebral palsy results from damage to the brain, usually at birth. *Cerebral* refers to the brain and *palsy* to lack of control over the muscles. It is a nonprogressive condition that remains throughout life. In addition to lack of motor control, there may be seizures, spasms, mental retardation, abnormal sensation and perception, or impairment of sight, hearing, or speech —all in varying degrees. Teeth often require special attention. When the tongue muscle is involved, eating and talking are affected. Sometimes involvement of the facial muscles can cause grimaces, which can hide the normal personality of someone with cerebral palsy. Medicines usually play a minor part in treatment, although experimental surgery on the brain is being attempted. Neurosurgeons hope to find successful surgery to end spasticity or uncontrolled movement.

Cerebral palsy is caused by defective development, injury, or disease. Chief among its causes is an insufficient amount of oxygen reaching the fetal or newborn brain. Other causes may be premature birth, Rh or A-B-O blood type incompatibility between parents, German measles in the mother, or other viruses or bacteria.

There are three main types of cerebral palsy: *spastic*, the largest group, having tense, contracted muscles; *athetoid*, constant uncontrolled motion; and *ataxic*, a poor sense of balance that may cause falling. Some cerebral palsied people have a combination of spasticity and athetosis.

It is estimated that 750,000 children and adults in the United States have one or more symptoms of cerebral palsy. Approximately 15,000 babies are born with this condition each year. Preventive programs include better testing during pregnancy to try to prevent the causes.

Management of children with cerebral palsy consists of trying to help them achieve maximum potential growth and development. Programs utilize physicians, therapists, educators, nurses, and social workers. In some cases surgery and braces are used. Children range in mental ability from mentally retarded to extremely bright, with no correlation between the severity of physical impairment and mental condition.

School programs must be highly individualized, requiring a great deal of attendant care for the most severely disabled children. When a child with cerebral palsy is bright, it is imperative that adequate schooling is offered. New college programs, geared to acceptance of the severely physically disabled, now make it possible for bright cerebral palsied individuals to go on to higher education. Support services for the cerebral palsied young adult must include psychological counseling, special living accommodations, and a realistic understanding of possible life goals.

To date, people with cerebral palsy have found little success in the employment field and have been the objects of much prejudice on the part of the able-bodied community, as well as the community of people with other disabilities. New ways of thinking about how people with cerebral palsy can make a contribution to society are sorely needed.

The United Cerebral Palsy Association, Inc., the national organization to help parents and children with cerebral palsy, was formed in 1949, and six years later the United Cerebral Palsy Research and Educational Foundation, Inc., was established to stimulate and fund research and training of professionals. At the local level, direct services are provided by affiliates, including medical diagnosis, evaluation and treatment, special education, career development, social and recreation programs, parent counseling, adapted housing, advocacy, and community education. There are 300 state and local voluntary agencies in the United Cerebral Palsy network.[5] The National Easter Seal Society also has information about available services. Persons with cerebral palsy who cannot turn book pages may borrow talking books under the program of the National Library Services for the Blind and Physically Handicapped of the Library of Congress.

Free pamphlets on cerebral palsy include "Cerebral Palsy: Hope through Research" (U.S. Department of Health, Education, and Welfare, PHS, NIH Publication No. [NIH] 75-159, Superintendent of Documents, Washington, D.C.) and "Cerebral Palsy—Facts and Figures, Fact Sheet," May 1977 (United Cerebral Palsy Association, Inc., 66 East 34 Street, New York, New York 10016). Also see Nancie R. Finnie, *Handling the Young Cerebral Palsied Child at Home* (New York: E. P. Dutton, 1975).

CYSTIC FIBROSIS

First described in 1936, this is the most common chronic lung disease in Caucasian children, usually resulting in early death. When first reported, almost all deaths occurred before the age of one year. With improvement in treatment, the average life expectancy is now fourteen years, with an upward trend so that a large percentage of children reach adulthood and function well. Adult males with cystic fibrosis almost always are sterile.

It is estimated that one in 1,500 children is born with this hereditary disorder. Approximately one in every 25 whites carries the gene. The disease occurs much less frequently in black youngsters and is very rarely reported in Oriental children.

Originally thought to be a disease involving only the pancreas and the lungs, cystic fibrosis is now known to be caused by an abnormal mucus secreted in these and other organs as well. The basic reason for the abnormality has not been found. In 1952 it was discovered that children with cystic fibrosis have an abnormal concentration of salt in their sweat, providing evidence that nonmucus-secreting glands were also involved. Cystic fibrosis is a simple recessive genetic disorder. When two parents carrying the gene produce a child, there is a one in four chance that the baby will have cystic fibrosis, two in four that he or she will be a carrier, and one in four that he or she will not carry the gene. Recent research may soon become the basis for a method to identify carriers.

The prime emphasis in treatment of cystic fibrosis involves the lungs. Lungs must be kept clear of mucus and free of infection as much as possible. The use of antibiotics has slowed the course of cystic fibrosis somewhat.

The teacher of a cystic fibrosis child should be aware of the fact that he or she may cough frequently, which is important to clear the lungs. The child will have a large appetite and will need to go to the bathroom often because he or she has an excessive number of stools. The child may need to take medication during class hours. Cystic fibrosis children should not engage in strenuous play in hot weather, as excessive perspiration causes loss of salt from their bodies.

Cystic fibrosis children are no more or less bright than their peers, although they may appear brighter because their interests tend to be intellectual rather than physical. They should be treated as much as possible like other children in the class. School and public librarians wishing literature on cystic fibrosis should send for "Guide to the Diagnosis and Management of Cystic Fibrosis," "Living with Cystic Fibrosis: A Guide for the Young Adult," and "Your Child and Cystic Fibrosis"—all from the National Cystic Fibrosis Research Foundation (6000 Executive Building, Suite 309, Rockville, Maryland 20852).[6]

DWARFISM

An individual who is smaller than others to a marked degree is considered to be a dwarf. Either his or her rate of growth, the length of time for which growth continues, or both have been inadequate. Early diagnosis is critical because once a certain stage of growth has been reached, nothing can be done to accelerate it. There are many different types of dwarfism, and only simple definitions are given here, as well as sources of information that will enable a better understanding of differences in diagnosis and treatment.

Hypopituitarism, a condition of unknown cause, begins early in life. Height, weight, and bone age are symmetrically depressed. Pituitary hormones are affected, and thyroid and adrenal functions are mildly or severely impaired.

Primordial dwarfism refers to the individual who is unusually small at birth, although born at full term. Growth is slow from earliest infancy. Bone age generally keeps pace with chronological age. Sexual maturation is normal and at the usual time. The child develops into a miniature adult, comparatively normal in every way save size.

Nutritional dwarfism means short stature that may result from inadequate intake of calories, proteins, or certain vitamins.

Chondrodystrophy is a group of conditions, of which achondroplasia is a major disorder. The slightly enlarged skull and disproportionately shorter extremities typical of this disease generally can be seen at birth and are due to a major defect in chondrogenesis (the function of cartilage).

There is a group of miscellaneous disorders associated with short stature in which the mechanisms of defective growth are not established. One of these is Turner's syndrome, in which short stature is associated with many abnormalities in glandular functions, chromosomal abnormalities, and other congenital defects.

Fortunately, it is now possible to diagnose dwarfism, using such information as height of parents and siblings, birth height and weight, current height and weight, roentgenograms of the hands and the lateral skull to exclude the possibility of certain types of tumors, and X rays of the knees to detect chondroplasia.

Until the twentieth century, no remedy could be found for any type of dwarfism. In 1908 it was discovered that hypopituitary dwarfism was related to a dysfunction of the pituitary gland. In 1945 a hormone extracted from animal pituitaries was shown to produce growth in animals. However, at that time it was not successful with humans. In the early 1950s, growth hormone was obtained from over 20,000 monkeys as a result of the work producing the Salk vaccine, and it was shown to be effective with humans.[7] In 1956 it was discovered that hormones extracted from the pituitaries of deceased humans was effective, demonstrating that hypopituitary dwarfs can grow for years and that other types of dwarfs may respond as well. The therapy has no ill effects.

Hypopituitary dwarfs need the hormone from one pituitary gland daily, and these glands must be obtained by donation after death. While the exact number is unknown, there are estimated to be between 3,000 and 7,000 people with this type of dwarfism. The number of Turner's syndrome children is probably larger, and they need two to five times as much hormone per day. It is estimated that the number of glands required is equal to three-quarters of the annual deaths in the United States.

In 1963 the National Pituitary Agency (210 West Fayette Street, Suite 503-7, Baltimore, Maryland 21201) was formed, with the sponsorship of the College of American Pathologists and the National Institutes of Health. Its objective is to collect pituitaries from every death in the United States. The cooperation of all physicians is needed, and the agency can be contacted for shipping instructions, shipping containers, reimbursement procedures, and complete information concerning techniques of collection.

Pituitary hormones also have uses in the treatment of other diseases. This information, of utmost importance to one segment of our population, should be on file in all libraries.

When treatment is started early, a child suffering from dwarfism may have a chance to reach average adult height and thus avoid the psychological problems associated with extreme short stature (see Chapter 13). All dwarfs are capable of having a regular sex life, the biggest problem being to find an appropriate partner. Many dwarfs are able to have children, who may or may not be dwarfs. Schooling for this group of young people should be commensurate with intellectual ability. Some architectural problems will exist and must be overcome. Vocational training, if suitable, can lead to successful employment and a satisfactory life adjustment.[8]

Research in the 1960s and 1970s has been increased, sponsored by the National Institute of Arthritis and Metabolic Diseases, and foundations began to form to deal with dwarfism. The Human Growth Foundation (Maryland Academy of Science Building, 601 Light Street, Baltimore, Maryland 21230) was formed by parents of children with growth problems, particularly dwarfism. They support medical research and assist in the spread of knowledge. Little People of America, Inc. (P.O. Box 126, Owatonna, Minnesota 55060) is a society in which a condition of membership is dwarfed stature, with a maximum allowable height of five feet.

Pamphlets in this area are "This Child Is a Dwarf" (National Pituitary Agency, Baltimore, Maryland); and "Human Growth Hormone" (U.S. Department of Health, Education, and Welfare, PHS, NIH, National Institute of Arthritis and Metabolic Diseases, Bethesda, Maryland).

EPILEPSY

The term *epilepsy* comes from the Greek word for "seizure." It describes a disorder of the central nervous system, which causes seizures or convulsions resulting from uncontrolled electric discharges in the brain. Seizures vary in type and severity. Until quite recently, epilepsy has been surrounded by myth and distorted ideas. Research has indicated that there is still great prejudice against persons with epilepsy.[9] Two percent of the population, or about four million Americans, have some form of epilepsy, although accurate statistics are not easy to obtain, since many people still hide the fact that they have the disorder.

Grand mal seizures (general convulsions) take the form of blackouts and violent shaking of the entire body, accompanied by irregular breathing and drooling. Sometimes there is a pale blue color in the face, fingernails, or lips. A warning called "aura" before a seizure is sometimes experienced in the form of spots before the eyes or skin tingling. After the seizure, the patient may seem confused or feel tired and may fall asleep.

Petit mal seizures usually start to occur between the ages of 6 and 14. Sometimes they seem to be just daydreaming spells and may cause behavior or learning problems in children. They may also include rapid eye blinking or twitching movements. These seizures may occur as often as 100 times a day, usually lasting less than a minute.

Infantile myoclonic and akinetic convulsions affect muscle control and movement and can seldom be controlled by medication. They have been nicknamed lightning seizures because they may occur from 5 to 300 times a day. This disorder should be suspected in infants who seem apathetic or in 6- to 18-month-old children with colic, poor eating habits, or slow motor development. The baby may have muscle jerks or twitching, may draw his or her body into a ball, and the facial color may change to pale or red or blue. The older child or adult may suddenly fall to the ground, sustaining frequent bumps and bruises.

Psychomotor seizures arise from a specific area in the brain and may occur at any age. They take many forms, including lip smacking, staring, headache and stomachaches, buzzing or ringing in the ears, dizziness, or strong emotions such as fear or rage.

Focal motor seizures originate in the area of the brain that controls muscle movement. The individual is conscious throughout a motor seizure and is left only with some muscle weakness in the area affected.

Autonomic seizures consist of repeatedly occurring symptoms of headache, stomachache, nausea, vomiting, or fever, which may contribute to periodic behavioral, learning, and emotional problems. The patient does not lose consciousness.

It is possible for an epilepsy patient to have more than one type of seizure, and careful diagnosis and individual treatment are very important. Seizures that can be traced to a specific brain injury are called *symptomatic* and are sometimes caused by faulty development of brain tissue before birth, injury during birth, tumors, abscesses, or blood clots in the brain, severe head injury, or brain infections such as meningitis or encephalitis.

Seizures with no determinable cause are called *idiopathic*. Heredity seems to play a small role in this type of epilepsy, which usually does not appear until after the age of five. As persons grow older, the incidence of the onset of convulsions diminishes. There are now many drugs for the control of most epilepsies, enabling most people with this disorder to enjoy normal lives.

Parents of children with epilepsy are encouraged to allow them to be active. With understanding and support, children can meet with academic success. People with epilepsy exhibit the same wide range of intellect as the population in general, and most children with epilepsy are able to attend regular classes. It is imperative that all teachers and support staff be provided with general information about epilepsy so as to forestall hostility or teasing on the part of other children. The School Alert program of the Epilepsy Foundation of America (EFA) provides materials to enhance understanding of the disease, as well as on emergency aid techniques.

Adolescent epileptics experience the same problems as other adolescents, sometimes magnified by the medical and social problems connected with the disease. EFA chapters often provide special services for them. For example, in Denver, Colorado, teenagers with epilepsy have formed a group called Epi-teens.

Those children whose seizures are part of severe brain damage may be referred to an institution. One that EFA suggests is the National Children's Rehabilitation Center in Leesburg, Virginia, which is specially equipped to educate and care for children with severe epilepsy.

Epileptic students often go on to college. In any case, all epileptics should consider training for future employment. Prejudice, which used to exist against employment of epileptics, has been combated successfully through educational campaigns by EFA. Some employers, however, are still reluctant to hire the epileptic person. Sheltered workshops offer employment to people whose seizures are not well controlled. State laws that used to restrict marriage among people with epilepsy have been removed. A decision to marry must be made on the basis of emotional maturity, ability to support and raise a family, and proper genetic counseling.

Should librarians encounter persons with epilepsy who are having problems of any kind, they should be referred to the Office of Vocational Rehabilitation or to a local EFA chapter for assistance. For further information, send for "Medical and Social Management of the Epilepsies" and "The Person with Epilepsy: Life Style, Needs, Expectations" (Chicago: National Epilepsy League, 1977). A research study entitled *Plan for Nationwide Action on Epilepsy: Vol. I* was published by the Commission for the Control of Epilepsy and Its Consequences (U.S. Department of HEW, PHS, NIH, Pub. No. [NIH] 78-0276, Washington, D.C., August 1977).

FAMILIAL DYSAUTONOMIA

Also known as Riley-Day syndrome and originally described in 1949, familial dysautonomia is a recessive genetic birth defect, with both parents carrying the gene, although they are normal. There is at present no genetic test. However, most cases reported to date have been in Jewish families of Eastern European extraction (Ashkenazim) and have included equal numbers of males and females.

Familial dysautonomia is a disorder of that part of the nervous system controlling sensation and autonomic functions. The severity of symptoms varies among individuals and at different ages in any one individual; however, early symptoms generally include difficulty in sucking (in the infant) and swallowing and drooling. Vomiting is common, and blood pressure and temperature fluctuate widely. Blood does not circulate oxygen to the brain sufficently, and as a result dizziness or an actual cessation of breathing sometimes occurs in the slightly older child. Skin blotches come and go with excitement and sweating is profuse, but both decrease with age. Lack of overflow tears with crying is one of the most distinctive signs of familial dysautonomia, and eye dryness, combined with decreased sensation in the cornea, makes these children particularly prone to corneal abrasion or ulcers. To supplement eye moisture, methyl cellulose eyedrops or similar eye lubricant must be used about four times a day.

Loss of sensation causes lack of taste, lack of sensitivity to hot and cold, and loss of feeling; thus care must be taken to avoid any injuries or burns. The pitch of the voice is also affected, and speech will appear immature. Coordination problems occur in areas of gross motor movement, and gait will often be awkward.

There is an overall slower growth rate and weight gain, and the average height is usually less than that of the shorter parent. Spinal curvatures occur in almost all dysautonomic children and can be aided by bracing. For all of these reasons, these children may appear somewhat younger than their actual age and may also show emotional immaturity. Sexual maturation is delayed in both males and females, commonly occurring in the late teens. The oldest known dysautonomic to date is in the mid-thirties, and several are now in their twenties.

While there have been a few marriages reported, there have been no known pregnancies, and it is not yet determined whether pregnancy would be hazardous to a dysautonomic woman. Dysautonomic individuals will be carriers of the disease, so genetic counseling is advisable. Older dysautonomics would like to be able to work and should, depending on stamina and educational level, be able to do so. Travel, however, can be a problem. Driving a car may not be feasible, since perception and coordination are poor for most dysautonomics.

The school-age child is somewhat delayed in verbal intelligence, but should not be classified as mentally retarded. Motor ability is often poor and perceptual handicaps fairly common, but with careful educational planning, many can do average or above-average work. Many of the dysautonomic children who have been followed have been able to complete high school, and several have gone on to college.

Parents of these children are usually very knowledgeable and should be consulted by school districts and medical and nursing personnel. Because of the serious nature of the physical problems, early special education is often advisable. However, often this education does not offer appropriate intellectual stimulation.

Excellent literature about this disease is available from the Dysautonomia

Foundation, Inc. (370 Lexington Avenue, New York, New York 10017), which publishes "Caring for the Child with Familial Dysautonomia," a complete description of dysautonomia in lay terms, written especially for parents and professionals. It contains detailed sections on home care, including dietary management, respiratory techniques, eye care, dental hygiene, accidents, and so on. A special section tells about plane and car travel (some airlines have been known to cooperate even in such things as adjusting flying altitudes). The foundation also publishes "Familial Dysautonomia: Diagnosis, Pathogenesis and Management" by Felicia Axelrod, M.D., Richard Nachtigal, M.D., and Joseph Dancis, M.D., reprinted from *Advances in Pediatrics* (Volume 21, 1974). This is a clinical article for the use of physicians and other medical personnel, and includes extensive bibliographic references to medical articles published within the past 20 years. *Familial Dysautonomia: A Nursing Care Plan* is a complete nursing plan written for hospital nurses who may encounter these patients. It is also extremely valuable for school nurses who may see children with this disability for the first time.

HEMOPHILIA

The term *hemophilia* is used to describe a hereditary condition in which the blood has difficulty in clotting. Descriptions of this disease date back almost 2,000 years, and the royal families of Russia and England figure in its history. There are many bleeding disorders. Blood clots are formed by chemical reactions aided by clotting proteins, which are molecules that circulate in the blood. There are 12 different clotting substances represented by I through XIII. (For some reason, the number VI has never been assigned.) A deficiency of any one of these substances can cause a serious bleeding disorder. Factor VIII (classic hemophilia) and Factor IX (parahemophilia) are the causes of the most common and most severe forms of hemophilia, accounting for over 90 percent of serious bleeding disorders.

Both Factor VIII and Factor IX are transmitted as sex-linked recessive, meaning that the abnormality is carried by the female, who has a 50 percent chance of passing it on to her son. A female carrier also has a 50 percent chance of passing on the disorder to her daughter, who will then become a carrier. A male hemophiliac will pass the disorder on to all his female offspring, who will become carriers. Males do not inherit hemophilia from their fathers. Children born to female carriers of hemophilia, therefore, have a 50 percent chance of being completely free of the disease.[10]

One of the major physical problems in children with hemophilia is recurrent joint bleeding, which causes thickening of the joint lining and finally extensive destruction of the whole cartilage lining of the joint. Degenerative arthritis then sets in and can cause crippling joint disease in early adult life. Braces may be necessary for children who have this problem.

Children with hemophilia can bleed from minor cuts or lacerations, and trauma to the head and neck can cause life-threatening bleeding into vital areas. Neurological symptoms such as headache, sleepiness, nausea, and vomiting should be recognized as serious. Even more serious are unequal pupil size of the eyes, slurred speech, disorientation or muscle weakness, or dark brown urine, of which school nurses, teachers, and others working with hemophiliacs should be aware.

Children with hemophilia usually have average to above-average intelligence and may be educated in either public or special school situations, depending on the severity of their condition and the willingness of the school to take the responsibility for maintaining the child on a modified physical recreation program. They should not be involved in any contact sports, but exercise is important for maintaining strong muscles and well-functioning joints.

Adults who handle children with hemophilia should be cautioned against overprotection. A hemophiliac will not bleed to death from a cut finger, and often spontaneous internal bleeding occurs, which is nobody's fault. Hemophiliac children should be provided with home or hospital instruction whenever necessary.

In the 1970s, medical progress was made to enable hemophiliacs to maintain themselves in good condition. Factor concentrates to replace the deficient VIII and IX are now available, although costly, and patients can infuse themselves at home with these concentrates whenever clotting is needed. This is a tremendous step forward for parents and children who had to spend so much of their time in emergency visits to the hospital.[11] However, ideally, hemophiliacs should always live fairly near a large hospital that has facilities for treating hemophilia and is familiar with all of the problems.

Marriage for the adult hemophiliac should involve genetic counseling. Wives must be willing to provide supportive assistance during bleeding episodes, and the couple must understand that if they have female children, who will become carriers, any male grandchildren may have hemophilia. The question of having children naturally or adopting should, of course, be settled before marriage. A large number—30 percent of hemophiliacs—never marry. Of the 70 percent who are married, approximately one-half have children.

Solutions to everyday problems of hemophilia are well handled in a paperback book entitled *How to Live with Hemophilia* by James M. Vogel, M.D. Vogel discusses the types of homes in which hemophiliacs should live and how to handle shaving, dental care, types of anesthesia during dental extractions or operations, travel, recreation, and much more.[12] He maintains that employment for the hemophiliac is a major problem and that unemployment is four times the national average.

The appendix of Vogel's book offers addresses of special hemophilia centers at the time of printing. The author submits that the list is incomplete and that more detailed information can be obtained from the National Hemophilia Foundation (25 West 39 Street, New York, New York 10018).

For travelers, the World Foundation of Hemophilia (Suite 806, 1420 Rue Street, Mathieu, Montreal 108, Quebec, Canada) supplies addresses of centers in many countries.

LEGG-PERTHES

This is a temporary orthopedic disability, also called Legg-Calvé-Perthes disease. Early in the 1900s, the development of X-ray examinations of the hip enabled doctors to see changes in children between the ages of four and five years who complain of pain in the knee, thigh, or occasionally in the hip joint and who start to walk with a limp. Boys are more frequently affected than girls. The disease consists of the destruction of the growth center (epiphysis) at the hip end of the thigh bone (femur). Over a period of two to three years, there is a repair of the growth, consisting of resorption of the dead bone and laying down of new bone. Treatment during this period of healing involves absolute rest, usually by immobilizing the leg with a special brace, or both legs with a brace if both hips are affected. In some cases, surgical repair is indicated.

In most cases, the child must receive special attention for two to three years during the time of elementary education, necessitating special architectural accommodations for braces or wheelchair use in schools and classrooms.[13]

MULTIPLE SCLEROSIS

Multiple sclerosis is a disability that affects the central nervous system. An estimated 500,000 Americans have this disease. It usually attacks adults in the 20- to 40-year age bracket. Onset before the age of 18 or after 45 is uncommon. It is caused by the destruction of patches of the myelin with which many nerve fibers are coated. This destruction causes nerve impulses to have trouble traveling past the damaged areas. Why this happens has not yet been discovered. Symptoms of multiple sclerosis include:

numbness in parts of the body

prickling sensation in parts of the body

double or otherwise defective vision, such as involuntary movements of eyeballs

extreme weakness or fatigue

loss of coordination

tremors of hands

noticeable dragging of one or both feet

speech difficulties, such as slurring

severe bladder or bowel trouble (loss of control)

partial or complete paralysis of parts of the body[14]

Three or more of these symptoms are danger signals and should not be ignored. Sometimes symptoms disappear for periods of several years, and occasionally never return. Multiple sclerosis is usually progressive, proceeding in a series of attacks, each one causing further disability. However, many patients remain at a constant level or plateau of capability with no noticeable increase in disability.

There is no cure for multiple sclerosis and no definitive diagnostic test. No treatment will halt or alter its progress. Many drugs have been tried without long-term success. Treatment can and should be given for prevention of upper respiratory and other infections. Physical therapy and braces can be prescribed for stabilizing limbs and keeping the patient as active as possible. A variety of nursing needs of long duration, as well as architectural modification of living facilities, must be anticipated.

The National Multiple Sclerosis Society has 178 chapters and branches in the 50 states and the District of Columbia, all staffed by volunteers. The society offers patients equipment, aids to daily living, nursing services, counseling, and physical and occupational therapy. Its research programs operate in cooperation with the National Institute of Neurological and Communicative Disorders and Stroke, a branch of the federal government. The aim is to find the cause, prevention, and cure of multiple sclerosis, and much progress has been made toward this goal. Literature on this disease is available from the National Multiple Sclerosis Society (55 W. 44th Street, New York, New York 10036) or through local branches or chapters. Titles include "Facts: Multiple Sclerosis"; Molly Harrower, Ph.D., "Mental Health and Multiple Sclerosis"; and "You and Multiple Sclerosis: A Pamphlet for Patients."

MUSCULAR DYSTROPHY

Muscular dystrophy is a general designation for a group of chronic diseases whose most prominent characteristic is the progressive degeneration of the skeletal or voluntary musculature.

The age of onset and the muscles affected, as well as the rate of progression, vary according to the type of dystrophy. These diseases are, for the most part, hereditary, although spontaneous occurrences as the result of genetic mutation are not uncommon. The cause is some as yet undetermined error in the hereditary materials that brings about a metabolic defect. It is not yet known whether the primary lesion is in the muscles themselves or in some other part of the body.

There are seven types of muscular dystrophy as well as two muscle diseases classified as myotomas. In addition, polymyositis and dermatomyositis, five myopathies, and six disorders classified as neurogenic atrophies, the neuro-muscular disease myasthenia gravis and Friedrich's ataxia are listed in this grouping. A chart available from the Muscular Dystrophy Association lists all of these disorders and their types of inheritance, clinical onset, progression, and treatment.

There is no cure for any of the dystrophies. Medical management is limited to relieving symptoms of the disease. Orthopedic devices may be prescribed at appropriate stages in the progression. Because muscular dystrophy is not a reportable disease, there is no way to determine accurately the number of people who are afflicted. It is estimated that approximately 200,000 men, women, and children in the United States have dystrophy, with two-thirds of these children between the ages of 3 and 13.[15]

The principal type of muscular dystrophy that occurs in childhood, and that educators are most likely to encounter, is muscular dystrophy—Duchenne type. It was first identified by Guillaume Duchenne in 1868. This disease predominantly affects boys, and it is an inherited form due to a gene carried by the mother and transmitted to her sons. Early symptoms include an awkward gait around the age of three, tiptoeing, and swayback posture. By the time children enter kindergarten, they are sometimes diagnosed as learning disabled or having minimal brain damage.

Batteries of tests are in order at this time to identify the disease. In time, with the progression of the disease, children will fall a great deal and need to stand up by "walking up their lower limbs" with their hands. Eventually a wheelchair will be indicated, usually by the time the child is in the fourth to seventh grade. If a regular school is architecturally accessible, the child may be mainstreamed. Otherwise a special school equipped to handle orthopedically disabled children will be necessary. With the progression of the disease, a good deal of nursing care is needed. Children may be obese because of flabby musculature, or else become excessively thin. This causes posture problems (scoliosis), sometimes necessitating braces. Pain can occur when the child is seated in one position for too long, and positioning may be needed during the day and also at night when parents generally take turns turning the child many times.

Upper extremity weakness is progressive, rendering the child very disabled by early teens. Cause of death, usually in the late teens, is from heart failure, as the heart muscle weakens, or lung infection due to weakened breathing muscles. Nursing information can be found in *Physically Handicapped Children: A Medical Atlas for Teachers* by Eugene Bleck and Donald Nagel.

Relatives of people with these disabilities have an extremely active organization working to provide services and information, and to fund and encourage the research that will bring the hoped-for breakthrough to a cure. Headquarters of the Muscular Dystrophy Association, Inc., is at 810

Seventh Avenue, New York, New York 10019. Its national chairman, Jerry Lewis, has been instrumental in raising large sums of money for the organization, which encourages a wide range of research, sponsors, university fellowships, and scientific meetings. Today there are 227 chapters of the Muscular Dystrophy Association in the 50 states, the District of Columbia, Puerto Rico, and Guam, providing a full range of medical services, orthopedic aids, transportation, and 92 summer camps in 36 states. Many services are provided to patients and their families free of charge.

Association chapters have established a national network of hospital-affiliated outpatient clinics providing medical and counseling services. Services are described and locations of chapters and clinics are listed in the booklet "Muscular Dystrophy Association Services to the Patient, the Family and the Community," available from the Muscular Dystrophy Association. Additional literature, also available from the association, includes Elizabeth Ogg, "Milestones in Muscular Dystrophy Research"; "MDA Fact Sheet," revised May 1977; and "Muscular Dystrophy Fact Sheet." Pamphlets are also available on individual dystrophies.

SPINAL MUSCULAR ATROPHIES

The spinal muscular atrophies are a less common form of muscular dystrophy. Until recently they were divided into Werdnig-Hoffmann disease (early death, usually before school age) and Kugelberg-Welander disease (later onset and longer life), but Koehler points out that this subdivision is artificial and can be misleading.[16] In reality, it is a disease that takes a variable course, and many of the children will die before school age. Less severely affected children will be seen in regular schools, while the more severely affected will be in special schools.

Sometimes clinical arrest and stabilization occur, with prolonged survival. Children must be educated in the least restrictive environment with the physical aids needed to compensate for hand weakness. Bracing and therapy to avoid joint and bone complications involve daily moderate exercises.

These students should be given realistic vocational goals so that they can lead productive lives that will be commensurate with their physical capacities.

AMYOTROPHIC LATERAL SCLEROSIS

Amyotrophic lateral sclerosis is caused by damage to the motor nerve cells of the spinal cord and the brain, resulting in gradual loss of strength and muscle control. The myelin sheath surrounding each nerve fiber is the tissue primarily injured in multiple sclerosis. In amyotrophic lateral sclerosis, however, myelin damage is secondary to damage to the motor nerve cells and the nerve fibers of cells in the outer layer of the brain.

Amyotrophic lateral sclerosis was brought to public attention as the illness of Lou Gehrig. Symptoms generally appear in later life, between ages 35 to 40 and 70. It is more common in men than in women. Length of life after diagnosis varies greatly, from 3 to 21 years. There is no known treatment or cure, although research has tended to center, as with multiple sclerosis, around changes in the myelin sheath.

A number of voluntary health agencies have formed who concern themselves with this illness:

Amyotrophic Lateral Sclerosis Foundation, Inc., 2840 Adams Avenue, San Diego, California 92116

Amyotrophic Lateral Sclerosis Society of America, 12011 San Vicente Boulevard (P.O. Box 49001), Los Angeles, California 90049

National ALS Foundation, Inc., 185 Madison Avenue, New York, New York 10016

In addition, both the National Multiple Sclerosis Society and the Muscular Dystrophy Association provide services for those people with amyotrophic lateral sclerosis. The following pamphlets are available: "Amyotrophic Lateral Sclerosis: A Disease of the Central Nervous System" (Multiple Sclerosis Society, 205 East 42 Street, New York, New York 10017); and "A.L.S." (distributed by Muscular Dystrophy Association, Inc., 810 Seventh Avenue, New York, New York 10019).

FRIEDRICH'S ATAXIA

Friedrich's ataxia is a genetic disorder resulting in progressive deterioration of the nervous system, causing an inability to coordinate voluntary muscle movements. Intelligence and the special senses are unimpaired. Damage occurs to nerve cells in parts of the brain, spinal cord, and peripheral nerves. Exact causes of Friedrich's ataxia are unknown and no cure has been discovered.[17]

The onset of the disease is between the ages of 10 and 15. It usually starts with an unsteadiness in the legs. Within approximately eight to ten years, ambulation becomes difficult. There is an absence of tendon reflexes, and weakness and loss of coordination of arm and hand movement, which causes difficulty in writing. Death usually occurs on an average at 36 years, not because of the primary disease but because of complications such as degeneration of the heart muscle. Nearly three-fourths of the fatal cases are attributed to heart failure, although the reason is unknown. It is possible, however, for someone with Friedrich's ataxia to live with a minimally progressive or atypical form of the disease for a long time.

Children with Friedrich's ataxia should be kept in regular classrooms as long as possible until loss of motor function is severe enough to require special schooling. Special devices, such as dowels to enable the child to write or use an electric typewriter, may be needed. Therapy and some vocational training with the avoidance of fine motor skills are indicated for those with milder forms of the disease, since these people will be able to function in society within certain limits.[18]

The Friedrich's Ataxia Group in America, Inc. (P.O. Box 11116, Oakland, California 94611) is a nonprofit organization. It was started by patients as a clearinghouse for information about the disease, and is now fund raising for research. A quarterly newsletter is published for patients and friends. Friedrich's ataxia is one of the disabilities included for care under the Muscular Dystrophy Association's authorized program of patient and community services, and information may be obtained by contacting the nearest Muscular Dystrophy Association office. Available pamphlets are "What Is Friedrich's Ataxia?" (Friedrich's Ataxia Group); "Friedrich's Ataxia Fact Sheet" (Muscular Dystrophy Association, Inc., 810 Seventh Avenue, New York, New York 10019), and "Friedrich's Ataxia: Fact Sheet" (U.S. Department of HEW, PHS, NIH, Pub. E [NIH] 78-87, 1977).

OSTEOGENESIS IMPERFECTA

Osteogenesis imperfecta is a skeletal disease that affects between 10,000 and 30,000 people in the United States, or one out of 50,000 babies born. In translation from the Greek, *osteo* (bone) *genesis* (beginning) *imperfecta* (imperfect) means imperfect bones at birth. A deficiency in the manner in which the protein fibers in the bone are arranged causes a reduction in bone salts (calcium and phosphorus) and a consequent weakening of structure. The resultant breaking of bones has given this condition the name of "brittle bone disease," although this popular term is an oversimplification.[19]

Osteogenesis imperfecta is classified in two major categories: congenita and tarda. The tarda group is further divided into tarda I and tarda II.

Osteogenesis imperfecta congenita children are born with numerous fractures, some appearing *in utero*, and suffer repeated fractures in childhood, which result in skeletal deformities such as malfunctioning joints, stunted growth, barrel chest, and often scoliosis (curvature of the spine). Eventual deafness is a possibility. A characteristic facial appearance includes bulging forehead and temples and a triangular shape, blue discoloration of the whites of the eyes, and poorly formed teeth. The disease is not inherited; rather it is the result of a spontaneous change in the genes (mutation).

The tarda I child has many of the same symptoms as the congenita child; however, the symptoms do not appear at birth but within the first year of life. The symptoms are not as severe and affect the legs only. The second group is sometimes so mildly affected that the bones never fracture and there is no deformity and no shortness of stature or dwarfism, which are so apparent in the other two groups.

In both tarda groups, there has been a family history of osteogenesis imperfecta. Proper genetic counseling is advisable to patients and families in all three groups, but especially to those in the tarda II group, as the mildness of its symptoms results in a higher incidence of marriage and parenthood.

Since the nature of the disease is unknown, treatment is directed toward the symptoms. To prevent deformities and reduce the number of fractures, metal rods, called Harrington Rods, are threaded through the bones of the legs in a surgical procedure. This allows some ambulation, although children with the congenita type use wheelchairs most of the time. Often a person with osteogenesis imperfecta in a wheelchair is able to walk limited distances. New research has developed telescoping rods designed to "grow" with the bone and there are new improved techniques for insertion. However, research into drug therapy has proven nonproductive.

Physical therapy is an important form of treatment to prevent the wasting away of muscles and ultimately of bones, and swimming is an ideal exercise. Each child must have a physical therapy program specially tailored to his or her needs and capabilities.

Proper schooling is important, as there is a prevalence of average and above-average intelligence among osteogenesis imperfecta children. Early stimulation at home and proper school placement will enable them to benefit from normal education.

In April 1970, parents of osteogenesis imperfecta children formed the Osteogenesis Imperfecta Foundation, Inc., a voluntary national organization, which has area representatives in most states and active chapters in ten. The national address is Osteogenesis Imperfecta, 1231 May Court, Berlington, North Carolina 27215. Pamphlets published by the foundation can be obtained free of charge by writing to Osteogenesis Imperfecta, Clinic of the Hospital for Special Surgery, New York, New York 10021. They were written in collaboration with the New York chapter of Osteogenesis Imperfecta Foundation, Inc. (P.O. Box 245, East Port, New York 11941).

PARAPLEGIA AND QUADRIPLEGIA

Paraplegia means paralysis of the legs, affecting both motion and sensation. Quadriplegia means a degree of paralysis of all four limbs. Weakness of the upper limbs may range from limited use to total paralysis, depending upon the level of injury to the spinal cord. Paraplegia and quadriplegia are caused by injury, either at birth or in accidents such as automobile, motorcycle, diving, and other types of sport injuries or bullet wounds. Often it is the most active young people who sustain injuries, making adjustment to disability difficult.

Paralysis is caused by damage to the spinal cord or, in some cases, a fracture of the spine. Interruption of the nerve connection between the brain and the limbs will cause the disability. Since these connections are in the spinal cord, pressure on the cord from bone fragments or other damage will cause the injury. Some repair techniques now exist and much research is being done to improve them so as to repair more of these injuries.

Emergency measures are very important to the spinal cord injured. The way in which the patient is moved after an accident, emergency hospital treatment, and the fact that rehabilitation must begin as soon as possible after injury should be widely known. Morale is, of course, of primary importance (see Chapter 1).

Problems involved with paraplegics and quadriplegics include loss of bowel and bladder control and skin breakdowns, called decubitus. Physical limitations will range from use of crutches and braces to wheelchair use. When the patient returns home, steps must be taken for return to school, employment if possible, and, in general, an active life. Many people who become adventitiously disabled have been active in sports. For these, there are wheelchair sports of all kinds in which they can participate. Upon returning home, the patient should make contact with his or her office of vocational rehabilitation for the assignment of a rehabilitation counselor who will help guide the person's future.

All libraries should have information available about paraplegia and quadriplegia. There are many pamphlet materials, such as "What You Should Know about Paraplegia" (Department of HEW, Publication SRS-RSA-119-70, Washington, D.C.: U.S. Government Printing Office, 1970).

The National Spinal Cord Injury Foundation (369 Elliot Street, Newton Upper Falls, Massachusetts 02164) publishes pamphlet materials, as well as the magazine *Paraplegia Life*. Paralyzed Veterans of America, Inc. (4330 East West Highway, Suite 300, Washington, D.C. 20014) also publishes a great deal of material, as well as the magazine *Paraplegia News*. *Accent on Living* magazine (Cheever Publishing, Inc., P.O. Box 700, Gillum Road and High Drive, Bloomington, Indiana 61701) also carries many advertisements for commercial products useful to paraplegics and quadriplegics. Spinal cord injury research is being carried on in nine hospitals in the country, which are a part of the Rehabilitation Research Network (see Appendix IV).

SICKLE CELL ANEMIA

Sickle cell anemia is an inherited disease found in black people or individuals of black heritage. It occurs when an altered type of hemoglobin is present in the red blood cells. These take on a sickle-shaped form, which gives the disease its name. General symptoms include weakness, jaundice, leg ulcers, malfunction of certain organs, and a lowered resistance to infectious disease. Most patients die before their thirtieth year. No treatment has yet been discovered for sickle cell anemia.

Sickle cell anemia is inherited from parents, and between 8 and 13 percent of American blacks are carriers of the disease. If both parents are carriers, one in four of the children may be born with the disease, while two may be carriers. The disease seems to have developed as a protective mechanism against malaria in Africa and the Mediterranean area. In the United States, this is no longer useful but constitutes a serious health problem. To date, the only prevention is genetic counseling, although research is in progress to determine the basic nature of the disease.

Children with sickle cell anemia may be able to attend school if they are careful in bad weather and stay away from people with contagious diseases. Limiting sweets and carbohydrates in diet is indicated. Adults with sickle cell anemia should refrain from physical labor.

Information on the disease is available from the National Institutes of Health (Public Health Service Information Office, National Institute of Arthritis and Metabolic Diseases, Bethesda, Maryland 20014), which publishes pamphlet No. 1745-0058, available from the U.S. Government Printing Office.[20]

SPINA BIFIDA WITH MYELOMENINGOCELE

This is one of the most serious handicapping conditions that affect children at birth. Until the 1940s, very few of these babies survived beyond infancy. However, treatments developed in recent years have improved conditions so that these children are able to survive and live into adulthood. Many of them are able to pursue active, productive lives.

In spina bifida, some of the vertebrae that normally cover the spinal cord fail to develop fully. In one type, called spina bifida occulta, the spinal cord and the skin covering it are normal, and this condition occurs in more than 30 percent of all births. Most adults who have this condition are unaware of it unless a low back problem with subsequent X rays uncovers this mild structural abnormality. Spina bifida with myelomeningocele describes a condition in which the spinal cord protrudes from the surface of the body in some area of the back and is covered only with the membranes that normally cover it when it lies within the vertebrae. This condition is called spina bifida manifesta.

The term *myelomeningocele* describes the spinal cord when it takes the shape of a flat plate, as it does in this condition rather than its normal tubular shape. In spina bifida myelomeningocele, one part of the nervous system has not developed as it should, and the baby may not be able to move the muscles in his or her legs. The lower extremities may also be insensitive to pressure, friction, pin pricks, heat, and cold. Paralysis and insensitivity only occur below the point where the protrusion exists. The arms, shoulders, and chest can become very strong with training.

A less severe condition is called spina bifida with meningocele, where the spinal cord does not bulge out and paralysis is not usual, although other aspects of the disability may be present.

A major problem for children with spina bifida is the lack of voluntary muscle action for bowel and bladder control, causing them to be incontinent in childhood. In older children, special surgical procedures allow them to handle their own bladder and bowel problems. Since the bladder is never completely empty, however, odor is often a problem unless very careful hygienic measures are used. Care must always be taken to avoid urinary tract infections, and a urologist is very often a member of the team of specialists caring for the spina bifida child. Constant medication is often used to prevent infection.

Persons with spinal cord injury often have similar problems of incontinence. Also similar is the problem of decubitus ulcers, raw skin openings resulting from constant wetness and poor skin care and circulation. Buttocks and feet must be checked constantly for this condition. These skin sores may, on occasion, become so deep as to require plastic surgery.

Sometimes fluid, which originates normally inside the brain and is absorbed at a regular rate, leaks into the myelomeningocele sac, allowing for possible infection. Also, in about 75 percent of spina bifida cases, there is interference with the circulation and absorption of the fluid and pressure can increase beyond normal levels, causing hydrocephalus, an abnormally rapid and excessive enlargement of the head, with resultant brain damage. Neurosurgeons have developed a procedure called shunting to prevent this occurrence. Shunts must be constantly watched and changed as the child grows.

Physical therapy is an important aspect in the early care of spina bifida children. Gentle exercise of the legs, performed by the parent even with young babies, will help prevent joint deformities. Most spina bifida children need wheelchairs, but some are able to ambulate with braces and crutches. Often trunk muscle weakness will cause scoliosis, dislocation of hips, club feet, or other deformities. Orthopedic surgical procedures are used to prevent these problems. A team of specialists is needed to cope with the considerable physical problems of the spina bifida child.[21]

Except where mild hydrocephalus has caused minimal brain damage, many spina bifida children have normal intelligence and may do acceptable schoolwork. Until recently, incontinence in childhood, plus a high level of school absence, has not made it possible for these children to be mainstreamed, and special education programs or home instruction were indicated. More sophisticated bladder management has enabled some children as young as the first grade to be able to function independently in this area and consequently to attend regular school. This is successful only where the nursing, physical therapy, and other professional staff have been prepared to handle the considerable medical problems. Many adults with spina bifida now in their thirties are holding responsible positions in the working world, many living independent lives.

In September 1959, the first spina bifida parent group was organized. More than 50 spina bifida parent groups have grown up across the United States, and in 1972 the Spina Bifida Association of America was formed. This national organization now includes nearly 5,000 families and may be contacted for information at Spina Bifida Association of America, 104 Feston Avenue, New Castle, Delaware 19720. The pamphlet "The Child with Spina Bifida" by Chester A. Swinyard is available from the Spina Bifida Association of Greater New York (P.O. Box 805, Radio City Station, New York, New York 10019).

The above disabilities have been described in some detail because until very recently it was difficult to find information about many of them that was not entirely medical in nature. The emergence of individuals with these physical disabilities into the mainstream of life, schools, and work makes it imperative that graduate library school courses and courses in schools of education incorporate some knowledge of these disabilities into their curricula.

NOTES

1. Eugene E. Bleck, M.D., and Donald A. Nagel, M.D., eds., *Physically Handicapped Children: A Medical Atlas for Teachers* (New York: Grune & Stratton, 1975).

2. Bleck and Nagel, "Amputations in Children," p. 15.

3. John J. Miller III, Ph.D., "Juvenile Rheumatoid Arthritis," in Bleck and Nagel, p. 233.

4. Bleck and Nagel, "Arthrogryposis," p. 21.

5. United Cerebral Palsy Association, "Cerebral Palsy—Facts and Figures, Fact Sheet" (May 1977).

6. Birt Harvey, M.D., "Cystic Fibrosis," in Bleck and Nagel, p. 109.

7. "Human Growth Hormone," Department of Health, Education, and Welfare, Public Health Service, National Institute of Arthritis and Metabolic Diseases, Bethesda, Md. (1965).

8. John Money, Ph.D., "Dwarfism: Questions and Answers in Counseling," *Rehabilitation Literature* 28 (May 1967): 134–138.

9. Bruce O. Berg, M.D., "Convulsive Disorders," in Bleck and Nagel, pp. 101–108.

10. Thomas J. Leavitt, M.D., "Hemophilia," in Bleck and Nagel, p. 155.

11. Robert Massie and Suzanne Massie, *Journey* (New York: Knopf, 1975). A graphic account by his parents of Robert Massie's struggles with hemophilia.

12. James M. Vogel, M.D., *How to Live with Hemophilia* (New York: Interbook, n.d.).

13. Donald Nagel, M.D., "Temporary Orthopaedic Disabilities in Children," in Bleck and Nagel, p. 196.

14. National Multiple Sclerosis Society, "Facts: MS," 205 (1977).

15. Muscular Dystrophy Association, "1977 Fact Sheet," Muscular Dystrophy National Office, New York.

16. Judith Koehler, M.D., "Spinal Muscular Atrophy of Childhood," in Bleck and Nagel, p. 255.

17. Friedrich's Ataxia Group in America, *What Is Friedrich's Ataxia?* (Oakland, Calif., 1977).

18. Koehler, "Friedrich's Ataxia," in Bleck and Nagel, p. 139.

19. Bleck and Nagel, "Osteogenesis Imperfecta," p. 205.

20. Leavitt, "Sickle Cell Disease," in Bleck and Nagel, p. 241.

21. Bleck and Nagel, "Myelomeningocele, Meningocele, Spina Bifida," p. 181.

PART II

THE PUBLIC

LIBRARY

3

Benefits Under the Law

Public libraries are the backbone of library and information services in the United States, and they have always led the way in providing special patrons, such as the blind, the homebound, and the institutionalized, with basic reader services. In the decade of the 1970s, however, disabled people have been emerging in far greater numbers than ever before from homes and institutions and making great strides toward becoming active participants in society. "Access" has become the word that characterizes this phenomenon —access to education, employment, housing, and recreation, access to the right to live in dignity with some measure of independence, whether or not employment is feasible. For all people the quality of life is the most important goal, not its length or its economic productivity.

Information services to this growing special population need to reflect their changing life requirements. Most public libraries do not have the basic reference materials for the disabled that will answer questions about such needs as housing, transportation and travel, educational opportunities and much more. Library service to the deaf and hearing-impaired population is still very much in its infancy. The 1980s must become a decade of information delivery to the disabled by all libraries.

Recent Library Services Construction Act (LSCA) grants in the area of library service to special groups reflect some attempts to provide more effective service to the disabled.

How did the 1970s become the decade of the emerging disabled? Early in this century, concern for individuals with disabilities was first reflected with rehabilitation legislation for the injured veterans of World War I, which established the Veterans Administration, and ultimately with the passage of the Vocational Rehabilitation Act Amendments of 1943, which marked recognition of the fact that people with handicaps could be educated and trained for employment. In 1947, the President's Committee on Employment of the Handicapped was established. Created by executive order rather than legislation, this committee, made up of subcommittees in various professional areas, has no enforcement rights. Its only power is one of public education and persuasion. The Library Committee of the President's Committee is committed to encouraging library service to the disabled in all libraries, to stimulating the development of courses in library service to the disabled in library schools, and to the portrayal of the handicapped in the media in a positive way. Also in 1947, the first National Employ the Handicapped Week was observed.

Subsequent rehabilitation amendments increased expenditures for rehabilitation services, created the Rehabilitation Services Administration within the Department of Health, Education, and Welfare, and strengthened the network of state and local offices concerned with the rehabilitation of disabled people. By 1973, awareness of the needs of the disabled culminated in the far-reaching Vocational Rehabilitation Act of 1973.[1] In Title 5 of this act, Section 501 provides for the employment of the disabled in the federal government; Section 502 created the Architectural and Transportation Barriers Compliance Board; and Section 503, the Affirmative Action clause, states that private businesses receiving $2,500 or more in federal funds must take "affirmative action" to search out and employ the disabled. The historic Section 504 provides that the disabled shall have equal access to all programs that receive federal funds.

A parallel development was PL 94-142, the Education for All Handicapped Children Act, which states that all disabled children in the United States are entitled to a free education in the most appropriate and least restrictive environment.[2] Somewhat inaccurately called the Mainstreaming Act, PL 94-142, together with Section 504, encourages large numbers of disabled people to enter the mainstream of American life.

In 1978, the Rehabilitation Act of 1973 was amended with PL 95-602, The Rehabilitation, Comprehensive Services and Developmental Disabilities Amendments of 1978.[3] A new definition of developmental disabilities is an important feature of the law, major provisions of which include the establishment of a National Institute of Handicapped Research, a program to increase the fostering of employment opportunities for the handicapped, a comprehensive service plan to foster independent living for the severely handicapped, and a significant strengthening of Section 504 of the Rehabilitation Act of 1973.

Included in the 1978 amendment is a reiteration of the need, expressed in the Rehabilitation Act of 1973, for a Central Clearinghouse of Information for the Handicapped. Thus Congress recognized that the provision of information is an important component in the education and rehabilitation of the disabled.

This chapter and the two following present information for librarians that will enable them to make programs and premises accessible to the disabled. Outlined are the civil rights provided by law to the disabled, as well as the special information needs that must be represented in information and referral services and the architectural modifications needed to make libraries accessible. It is important that librarians understand the basic civil rights of the disabled and know which agencies concern themselves with these rights so that proper referrals can be made in response to inquiries for information. Local addresses cannot be supplied in a book of this kind; however, state and local agency addresses can be obtained and kept on file in the reference rooms of all public libraries.

CIVIL RIGHTS

Disabled people have certain rights guaranteed by law: rights to education, employment, health care, and any other public or private services that receive federal assistance. It is the responsibility of the Office of Civil Rights in the Department of Health, Education, and Welfare to enforce federal laws prohibiting discrimination because of physical handicaps and to investigate discrimination complaints brought by individuals under these laws.

Legal rights of the disabled are now the primary concern of many lawyers throughout the country who are specializing in this field. Coordination of information is being handled by the National Center for Law and the Handicapped (211 West Washington Street, Suite 1900, South Bend, Indiana 46601). The National Center publishes the bimonthly magazine *Amicus*, which offers up-to-date reports on the fine points of law and the disabled community. Case studies reported in the magazine will be of professional interest to those concerned with this topic.

At the May 1977 White House Conference on Handicapped Individuals, a lawyer's caucus, composed of nearly 50 lawyers and others working in the area of law and the handicapped, met and launched the Legal Advocacy Network for the Disabled (LAND), with goals of dissemination of names and addresses of interested persons, a directory of persons active in the field, and clearinghouse services.[4]

The National Center for Law and the Deaf at Gallaudet College (Seventh Street and Florida Avenue, Washington, D.C. 20002) is a project of Gallaudet College and the National Law Center of George Washington University. They publish information in the field of the law and the deaf and hearing-impaired community.

In California, Senior Adults Legal Assistance (SALA) established, in October 1978, a Disability Law Center. The organization publishes *Dis-*

ability Law News (newsletter, available from Johanna Wallace, editor, 624 University Avenue, Palo Alto, California 94301, for a small donation). Undoubtedly, other areas will be establishing such centers, and it is hoped that these will be noted in a LAND directory or through *Amicus*.

Certainly, a basic right of all Americans is the right to vote, and this right should be exercised by disabled people, who need to make themselves knowledgeable about the laws that affect them and begin to make their legislators aware of how they feel. Many states have laws requiring that polling places be made accessible, and advocates are working toward passage of a federal law. Meanwhile, all disabled people who cannot enter a voting place are entitled to absentee ballots, which can be obtained from the local board of elections.

THE BIG TEN—CIVIL RIGHTS OF THE DISABLED

I. The Right to Live in a Barrier-Free Environment

Federal and state laws providing for the accessibility of public buildings to the disabled have existed since the late 1960s. Public Law 90-480, the Architectural Barriers Act of 1968, states that "any building constructed or leased whole or in part with federal funds must be made accessible to and usable by the physically handicapped" (US Code, Title 42, Section 4151.56). Public Law 93-87, the Federal Highway Act of 1973, states that the secretary of transportation may not approve any state highway program that does not provide for curb cuts on all curbs constructed or replaced at pedestrian crossways on or after July 1, 1976 (US Code, Title 23, Section 402). Many state laws make similar provisions where state and local public funds are used.

For several years, PL 90-480 was not enforced with determination. Then the Architectural and Transportation Barriers Compliance Board was established to ensure compliance with the standards (US Code, Title 29, Section 792, PL 92–112, Section 502, and PL 93-516, Section 111, Rehabilitation Act Amendments of 1974). This legislation does not affect buildings erected without government money. However, disabled and able-bodied people alike are trying to make communities aware of their responsibility to make churches, museums, parks, theaters, and certainly libraries architecturally accessible.

In May 1977, the Compliance Board launched a public awareness campaign with the trademark "Access America" to draw attention to the barriers that still exist and to promote barrier-free design in the United States. For further information or to file a complaint, write to the Architectural and Transportation Barriers Compliance Board, Washington, D.C. 20201, or phone (202) 245-1801. References for agencies, publications, and bibliographies in the area of architectural barriers are listed in Chapters 8 and 11.

"Access" to deaf individuals means communication. The provision of interpreter services at public functions and in educational institutions is now the law under Section 504. It is also possible for deaf people to communicate with other people if both sender and receiver have teletypewriter systems (TTYs). A TTY is an electronic device that permits communication over regular telephone lines. A visual signal will tell the deaf person when the phone rings. The telephone is then placed in a coupler and the message typed out. Many government agencies now have TTYs and special numbers so that deaf people can communicate with them. As a matter of law, all federal agencies and institutions receiving federal funding will be required to have TTY hookups.

At present, most deaf people do not have TTYs in their homes. They are expensive, and TTY calls, because they are slower, are much more costly than telephone calls. In the future it should be made possible for deaf people to operate TTYs at a reduced charge, and any business or service agency wishing to communicate with deaf people should consider installing TTY equipment. What a tremendous service it would be if public libraries could install such equipment! Then deaf patrons could go to the library, if they did not have home TTYs, and call, over toll-free lines, to government agencies from which they might need information.

Deaf people are usually not able to comprehend much of what they see on television. Turning down the sound on your television set will give you some idea of what deaf people experience. Attempts have been made to caption television programs in the same way that foreign films are captioned. However, open captions (which would appear on all screens) were found to be disruptive to persons with normal hearing, and the networks opposed this move. Since 1972, the Public Broadcasting System has been testing the use of closed captions on television programs. Closed captions can only be seen on the screen by the use of a decoder.

In the spring of 1979, two of the major networks, NBC and ABC, announced that they would begin using closed captions on their stations. A national Captioning Institute, to be located near Washington, D.C., will be responsible for coordination of the project. A home decoder, purchased by the deaf individual, will enable the captions to be seen. It was announced that the commercial rights to sell these decoders were obtained by Sears, Roebuck, which will market them at approximately $250 each.

Since TTYs and caption decoders cost in the hundreds of dollars and since, until now, many deaf people do not have high-paying jobs, the purchase of these items still poses a hardship for the average consumer. Hopefully, these items will be made available at a nominal fee or without charge by public funding.

II. The Right to Appropriate Housing

Everyone has a right to live in comfort and dignity. However, the lack of suitable housing for the disabled is a fact only now beginning to be remedied. Private construction cannot be counted on until builders become sensitive to the architectural requirements of the disabled and are willing to be of help. However, federally funded housing construction must make provisions for the disabled in response to Section 504 and because the Department of Housing and Urban Development (HUD), which funds most housing and urban development projects, is now committed to accessible housing.[5]

Historical Background

Since 1937, the federal government has been attempting to provide suitable housing for its citizens. Attempts at assisting the private housing industry to meet these requirements proved inadequate, whereupon the government assumed greater responsibility for meeting the housing needs of the low-income population, especially the elderly. In the late 1950s and early 1960s, recognition was also given to the special needs of the physically handicapped. Legislation from 1964 through the next ten years attempted to make suitable housing available to them. It was not until 1974 that the Housing and Community Development Act included the developmentally disabled among the special user groups eligible for federally assisted housing.[6]

The Housing and Community Development Act of 1974 (PL 93-383) is a very comprehensive piece of legislation that encourages the building of housing suitable for the handicapped and elderly by providing federal dollars for this purpose to private builders.[7] Under Section 8 of this act, HUD's Housing Assistance program attempts to provide decent housing for families that had not been able to afford such housing in the past by assisting in the renovation for accessibility of existing housing and the building of new, accessible housing units.

Section 202 of PL 93-383, the Direct Loan programs, stimulates private builders to build accessible housing by making loans for this purpose. The developmentally disabled are specifically mentioned under eligibility for these loans. The section interprets "accessibility" as meaning the provision, in addition to architectural modifications, of a whole range of support services, including health, continuing education, and homemaking counseling, as well as transportation to these services. This provision reflects the independent living philosophy, as opposed to institutional living, which primarily young adult disabled people are now espousing in great numbers. (See Chapter 4 for an account of this movement.)

Under the act's Rent Subsidy programs for the families of low-income handicapped and elderly, a family is now defined as one or more single elderly or handicapped individuals living together; one or more such individuals living with an attendant; or a family of two people or more.

The Housing Authority Act of 1976 prohibits rent subsidies provided under PL 93-383 from being considered income to persons receiving Supplementary Security Income support. In June 1977, HUD established an Office of Independent Living and announced that 5 percent of all new family units constructed under the Section 8 and public housing programs must be designed for use by the handicapped.

To help disabled people to find out about housing eligibility, rent subsidies, or other benefits under the law, librarians should have them contact HUD's office for Independent Living for the Disabled (Seventh and D Streets S.W., Washington, D.C. 20410).

A handicapped individual who wishes to adapt a private home to meet certain needs may be eligible for a Federal Housing Authority insured loan, which may be used to remove architectural barriers or other unacceptable features. These loans are available through banks or other financial lending institutions.[8] To repair a home on a farm in a rural area, low-income disabled people may be eligible for loans from the Farmers Home Administration. Information may be obtained from Farmers Home Administration, Department of Agriculture, Washington, D.C. 20250.

Helpful publications that librarians may wish to obtain for housing files are Marie Maguire Thompson, *Housing and Handicapped People* (President's Committee on Employment of the Handicapped, Washington, D.C. 20210); and "Housing for the Handicapped and Disabled: A Guide for Local Action" (National Association of Housing and Redevelopment Officials, 2600 Virginia Avenue N.W., Washington, D.C. 20037, March 1977). For information about adaptations of home interiors, as well as alternate types of living situations for the disabled, see Chapter 4.

III. The Right to Transportation

Mobility is of primary importance to everyone. Mobility means freedom. The ability to get around—to go to a job, to school, to shop, and to travel— is basic to a way of life that ensures maximum independence. People with physical disabilities often are unable to use conventional transportation and consequently remain homebound. During the 1970s, the federal government recognized the very formidable barriers that existed in the field of transportation and acknowledged its obligation to remove them. Federal concern was marked by a 1969 research study called *Travel Barriers: Transportation for the Handicapped* (PB No. 187-327, available from the Clearinghouse for Federal Scientific and Technical Information, Springfield, Virginia 22151). The study was supported by a contract with ABT Associates, Inc., of Cambridge, Massachusetts, and sponsored by the Office of the Secretary, Department of Transportation (DOT). A summary of the findings of this report is contained in *Travel Barriers* (No. 0-386-217, U.S. Government Printing Office, 1970).

Local communities that are interested in adapting their transportation facilities will find the report helpful. It covers very precisely the physical adjustments to be made in all systems of transportation, including turnstile collection, ramps, modification of escalators, design of elevators, stair lifts, bus redesign, subway design, and air and train travel.

Federal laws now in operation include PL 91-453, the Urban Mass Transportation Act of 1970; PL 93-87, the Highway Act of 1973; and PL 93-503, the Mass Transit Act of 1974—all of which encourage special efforts in the planning and design of mass transportation for accessibility, especially where federally funded projects are involved.[9] Public law 93-503 also states that rates charged to the elderly and handicapped will, during nonpeak hours, be one-half the rate for other persons traveling during peak hours. Information about these policies may be obtained from the Department of Transportation Programs and Policies, Office of Environmental Affairs, 400 Seventh Street S.W., Washington, D.C. 20590.

Amtrak Corporation is taking steps to eliminate architectural barriers on its trains. For further information, contact Amtrak Consumer Affairs, 955 L'Enfant Plaza, Washington, D.C. 20024; or Department of Transportation, Federal Railroad Administration, Office of Financial Assistance, 700 D Street S.W., Washington, D.C. 20590. For additional information about rail, air, and interstate bus travel, as well as information for handicapped drivers and accessible highway stops, refer to Chapter 4.

The Story of Transbus

Problems for the general handicapped public, which often includes many people with limited financial means, concern the very difficult area of mass transit within cities and other localities. The problems were laid out in a September 1975 study entitled *The Disabled and the Elderly: Equal Access to Public Transportation* by James J. Raggio et al. (Public Interest Law Center of Philadelphia, 1315 Walnut Street, 16 Floor, Philadelphia, Pennsylvania), published by the President's Committee on Employment of the Handicapped.

In the report, all of the transportation legislation up to 1975 is summarized and its implications analyzed. As it states, until the mid-1970s, the Urban Mass Transportation Association (UMTA), which administers the federal Mass Transit Assistance programs, had not made a real commitment to designing fully accessible equipment. Efforts centered around providing special parallel services (called paratransit services), such as specially equipped vans and taxis to meet transportation requirements for the disabled. Public Law 93-112, which created the Architectural and Transportation Barriers Compliance Board (Section 502), spurred renewed efforts in this field of mass transportation for the disabled. Section 504 of the same act requires that transit systems receiving federal funds make provisions for accessibility by the disabled.

A number of lawsuits filed in the mid-1970s began to challenge the purchase of buses that were not fully accessible to the elderly and disabled, in particular, people using wheelchairs. Controversy over whether or not it is possible to develop a fully acceptable urban bus has continued.

In 1971, UMTA initiated a research project to develop an accessible bus. American Motors, General Motors, and Grumman Flexible Corporation worked on prototypes for such a bus, to be called Transbus. In 1973, GM opted to stop the research and continue work on its own model, called Rapid Transit Series (RTS). In 1976, the federal government dropped the Transbus project. Grumman continued to work on its own design, and American Motors also stopped work on the project.

On May 19, 1977, Secretary of Transportation Brock Adams announced that all new public buses financed by DOT grants should be designed for access by handicapped and elderly persons.[10] This announcement, coming after the government had abandoned the project, was a victory for the "Transbus 12" group, led by the American Coalition of Citizens with Disabilities and 11 other advocacy organizations for the disabled that had lobbied and sued for Transbus without further delay.

Yet, we are still very far from having a prototype Transbus on the streets. The August 4, 1978, issue of the newsletter *Handicapped Americans Reports* carried a special article on this situation. For many reasons, including disputes on varying design features, Transbus as yet exists only on paper.[11] For up-to-date information, contact the Transbus Group (1315 Walnut Street, 16 Floor, Philadelphia, Pennsylvania 19107).

Paratransit

The viable alternative in use for public transportation of the disabled is vans and taxis. UMTA has been experimenting with a prototype of a small vehicle, but no working models are yet produced. For information, write for "Paratransit: An All New Vehicle for Public Transportation" (UMTA, Office of Public Affairs, U.S. Department of Transportation, Washington, D.C. 20590).[12]

As yet only three fairly new subway systems in the country—BART in San Francisco, MARTA in Atlanta, and METRO in Washington, D.C.— are accessible to the disabled. METRO is the only one designed to warn deaf passengers of incoming trains, with a row of lights at the edge of the platform. Elevator buttons have raised printing and are brailled for the blind, and half fares apply at all times for the disabled. A TTY service provides routing and scheduling information for the deaf.[13] Renovating older subway systems, such as that in New York City, to make them accessible would be prohibitive in cost, and thus such a solution seems unfeasible.[14]

Those wishing to pursue this topic in depth can send for "Transportation for the Handicapped: Selected References (April 1975, Bibliographic List No. 8, U.S. Department of Transportation, Office of Administrative Operations, Library Services Division, Washington, D.C. 20590).

IV. The Right to Financial Assistance

There are two basic federal programs that provide financial assistance to disabled persons. The acronyms for these programs sometimes cause confusion. They are Social Security Disability Benefits (SSDB) and Supplemental Security Income (SSI).

Social Security Disability Benefits

The purpose of SSDB is to provide continuing income for families or persons whose incomes have been reduced because of disability. Disability is defined as a physical or mental impairment that prevents a person from working, is expected to last or has lasted for at least 12 months, or is expected to result in death (US Code, Title 42, Section 423). This protection against loss of earnings because of disability became part of Social Security benefits in 1954.

Benefits are available to persons disabled since childhood if parents or guardians have paid into Social Security during their working years, and to persons disabled as adults, available through their own Social Security contributions paid when they were in the work force. A person disabled before the age of 31 may need 18 months of Social Security credit to receive assistance. Blindness is included under the law, the definition for legal blindness being 20/200 even with glasses or a limited visual field of 20 degrees or less. Monthly benefits will be paid to

1. Disabled workers under 65 and their families.
2. Disabled spouses, disabled dependent spouses, and (under some conditions) disabled surviving divorced spouses of workers who were insured at death. Benefits may be payable at age 50 in these instances.
3. Persons disabled before age 22 who continue to be disabled. If the disability is permanent, benefits will last a lifetime and will continue after the death of parents.

It is important to apply for Social Security benefits soon after the disability is incurred, since payments generally do not begin until the sixth full month of the disability. A person disabled for more than six months before applying may receive some benefits for the months before the application. Back payments are limited to the 12 months preceding the date of application. A person disabled in childhood may be eligible for benefits as soon as one parent begins receiving retirement or disability benefits, or dies. A disabled worker or a person disabled in childhood who returns to work in spite of the disability may continue to receive disability benefits for up to 12 months. This trial work period is to give the disabled person a chance to test his or her ability to work and to allow for an adjustment period.[15]

When applying for Social Security benefits, it is helpful to bring along

Social Security number or card

Date of last working period

Date of injury or illness

Date of recovery or return to work, if no longer disabled

Dates of treatments for disability

Proof of age

Name of illness or sickness

Names and addresses of doctors, hospitals, or clinics

Names of jobs held before becoming disabled

Supplemental Security Income

An individual who is blind or disabled and whose income and resources are very limited may be eligible for SSI benefits. SSI came into effect in January 1974 as an amendment to the Social Security Act, which provided that the federal government take over state programs of assistance to the disabled and people aged 65 and over. SSI is designed to provide a minimum monthly income for those whose disability prevents them from gainful employment and who, because of disability, may not have been able to contribute to the regular Social Security system. Excluded from benefits are persons in public institutions, drug addicts, and alcoholics, unless they are undergoing appropriate treatment.

This law is very complex. A person may have some income and still be eligible for SSI. However, financial holdings such as stocks and bonds or jewelry, pensions, Social Security checks, workmens' or veterans' compensation, or even gifts would reduce monthly payments.

SSI is available to disabled children, defined as unmarried persons under 18 years of age. Responding to a congressional mandate, on December 3, 1976, the Social Security Administration issued proposed criteria for making SSI disability determinations among children under the age of 18. Under previous regulations, a single list of impairments was applied to both children and adults. This section was retained, but a new subdivision was added to deal with the evaluation of disabling conditions peculiar to childhood.

The most noteworthy features of the proposed criteria are (1) Children with IQs of 59 or below would be considered disabled, whether or not another handicapping condition existed, rather than the adult standard of 49 IQ or below. (Actually, the Social Security Administration had been using the standard of IQ 59 for some time.) (2) Children with IQs of 60 to 69 must have a physical or other mental impairment that restricts their functional or developmental progress or must have chromosomally proven Down's syndrome in order to be found disabled. Additional regulations govern epileptic and cerebral palsied children.[16]

Full-time students are eligible for SSI until the age of 22. In some states, additional payments are available from separate state programs. Income maintenance programs are sometimes (as in California) offered to pay for such special living requirements as attendant care (see also Social Services, below).

A person may have to wait two to four months after applying for SSI before receiving the first check. If financial resources are very limited and the person meets the requirements of the local department of social services, he or she may be eligible for emergency assistance while waiting for the checks. In such cases SSI will provide a letter of referral and the department of social services will loan the money under the "home relief" category until the SSI checks begin arriving.[17]

In both the SSDB and SSI programs, vocational counseling, rehabilitation and training, and possible job referral are mandatory for all applicants.

To avoid having SSDB and SSI checks stolen from mailboxes, or for persons who have difficulty getting around, disabled people should arrange to have their checks deposited directly into their bank accounts. Direct deposit form SF-1199 is available at all banks and should be filled out to arrange for this transaction. Librarians should be aware of this information to pass along to disabled patrons. Notices from Social Security are available in braille upon request, accompanied by a written letter (also available in Spanish) should the blind person wish someone to read the notice.[18] Requests should be sent to the Department of Health, Education, and Welfare, Social Security Administration, Baltimore, Maryland 21235.

The publications listed can be obtained from the local Social Security office or from the U.S. Government Printing Office, Washington, D.C. 20402. They should be made available in all public library reference rooms or at the front desk where pamphlets are displayed—"Disabled? Find Out about Social Security Benefits"; "If You Become Disabled"; "Your Disability Claims"; "Your Social Security Rights and Responsibilities—Retirement and Survivor Benefits" (revised January 1977); "Pocket History of Social Security" (March 1977); "Social Security, Rulings on Federal Old-Age, Survivors, Disability, Health Insurance, Supplemental Security Income and Minors Benefits" (Social Security Administration, Baltimore, Maryland 21235); "Supplemental Security Income for the Aged, Blind and Disabled"; "Pocket Guide to Supplemental Security Income"; and "Helping the Aged, Blind and Disabled" (also available in Spanish).

V. Health Care

The primary sources of federal medical assistance for disabled persons are Medicare and Medicaid, Crippled Children's Services, and the Early Periodic Screening Diagnosis and Treatment Program (EPSDT).

Medicare and Medicaid are two different programs administered in different ways. Medicare is run by the Bureau of Health Insurance of the Social Security Administration, Department of HEW. It is made up of two parts: (1) Hospital insurance and related health services after the patient leaves the hospital, such as nursing care or other home health visits, at no cost.

(2) Medical insurance to help pay doctor bills and other approved medical services, for which there is a small monthly charge. This part is voluntary.

Eligible for Medicare are people 65 years or older, as well as disabled people who have had Social Security or Railroad Retirement disability annuities for two years or more, and people who are insured by Social Security or Railroad Retirement and are in need of dialysis treatment or kidney transplant because of permanent kidney failure. Wives, husbands, and children of insured people may also be eligible if they need maintenance dialysis or a transplant.[19] This program is not based on income and is available regardless of financial need.

Insurance benefits cover a wide range of services, including outpatient clinic or emergency room, home health visits under specified conditions, outpatient physical therapy and speech pathology services, X rays, casts, braces, artificial limbs or eyes, wheelchairs or medical equipment, ambulance services, and anything else prescribed by a physician.[20]

Medicare must be applied for at local Social Security offices or information may be obtained from the Health Care Financing Administration (Medicare Bureau, Health Education Inquiries Branch, Lowrise, Room GB3, Baltimore, Maryland 21235). For vertical files, librarians should send for two booklets entitled "Your Medicare Handbook" and "A Brief Explanation of Medicare."

Medicaid is a joint federal and state medical assistance program. It is financed by the federal government on a sliding scale, from 50 percent to the richest states to 78 percent to the state with the lowest per capita income. Forty-nine states participate in the program (Arizona does not have a Medicaid program), as well as the District of Columbia, Guam, Puerto Rico, and the Virgin Islands. The program is run by state governments with federal guidelines. The Medical Services Administration of the Social and Rehabilitation Service (SRS), Department of HEW, is responsible for the federal aspects of Medicaid.

Medicaid provides physical and related health care services to persons with low incomes. The payments do not go directly to the individual, but to the service provider. Since Medicaid is administered by the states, eligibility is determined by state social services programs on the basis of broad federal guidelines. Persons eligible for Medicaid are those on welfare, those receiving SSI benefits, the medically needy, the blind, and the disabled. Individuals with higher incomes may be eligible for Medicaid or their children may be eligible if medical expenses exceed a given percentage of annual income. There are some geographic differences between eligibility requirements and types of services covered because each state establishes its own eligibility requirements for Medicaid.

Medicaid services include necessary medical, dental, and other medically related care, nursing services in all institutions, outpatient or clinic services, home health care services, drugs, sickroom supplies, eyeglasses, and prostheses. When applying, the individual should have such information as name, address, age, Social Security number, annual income and income of persons in the family, amount of savings, cash value of insurance, and market value of any stocks, bonds, or other investments.

Further information on Medicaid and how to apply is available from local or state departments of social services or the Health Financing Administration, Medicaid, Switzer Building, 300 Independence Avenue S.W., Washington, D.C. 20201. Librarians should have on file "Medicaid—How Your State Helps When Illness Strikes" (available from Medical Services Administration, SRS, Department of HEW, Washington, D.C. 20201).

Medic Alert Foundation International is a voluntary nonprofit organization that provides an emblem (to be worn on a bracelet or necklace) and a wallet card to persons who need special consideration when being given emergency medical service. The emblem lists a phone number to be called for complete medical information on the tag wearer. There are over 40 million people in the United States who have hidden medical problems, such as diabetes, heart conditions, severe allergies, and epilepsy, to mention only a few. Other medical services supply a wallet card with a complete medical history. People with special medical problems should be made aware that such services are available. A physician should be able to recommend such a service.[21]

VI. The Right to Certain Social Services

There are many additional services available to disabled people who are unable to work or care for themselves because of physical or mental problems, including meal planning, nutrition, shopping service, and homemaker service. Contact should be made with the local social service department by telephone, letter, or in person. Libraries should have on hand for disabled patrons the booklet "Social Services for the Aged, Blind and Disabled," obtainable from the local department of social services.

Crippled Children's Services

Crippled Children's Services (CCS) is a joint federal/state program to provide medical and related services to handicapped children from birth through age 21. All states must provide medical diagnosis and evaluation free for all children, without the requirement of a state residency period. All programs accept Medicaid, Blue Cross and Blue Shield, and other medical insurance payments. For further information, contact local, county, or state health deparments.[22]

Early Periodic Screening, Diagnosis, and Treatment Program

The EPSDT program screens children from poor families to find out if health care or related services may be necessary. Children receiving state Aid to Families of Dependent Children and children whose parents or guardians receive Medicaid and/or local or state public assistance benefits are eligible. Programs vary from state to state and are administered by state public assistance (welfare) or health departments.[23]

VII. Insurance and Tax Benefits

Benefits under various types of insurance can provide coverage for disabled people.

Workmen's Compensation

This insurance provides payments in lieu of salary to those who become disabled as a result of injury or disease related to employment as well as payments for necessary medical services. Types of benefits and amounts paid vary from state to state. The second injury clause limits the liability of the employer who hires a disabled worker. Contrary to the belief of many prospective employers, workmen's compensation insurance rates are not higher for a disabled employee than for a nondisabled one. If a disabled worker has an accident on the job, under the second injury clause the employer is only liable for the percentage of disability that results from the second injury, not for any part of the disability that existed before the injury.

Salary Continuance

This form of insurance can be purchased by an individual or by a company for its employees. Such a policy provides the worker with an income while wages are discontinued due to an accident or illness that occurs during the policy period. Amounts of payments vary with the type of policy.

Life Insurance

If someone has life insurance and becomes disabled, he or she may not, in many cases, have to pay the premiums. Many possibilities exist under certain circumstances. Information can be obtained from the Institute of Life Insurance (277 Park Avenue, New York, New York 10017), which publishes the guide "Life Insurance for Your Family Security."[24] Various types of health insurance are explained in the booklet "Consumer and Community Services" (Health Insurance Institute, 277 Park Avenue, New York, New York 10017).

Tax Benefits

Under PL 92-178, US Code, Title 26, Section 214, disabled people may deduct certain medical and dental expenses from earned income. In the case of a disabled child, the deduction would be allowed to the parents. The Internal Revenue Service (IRS) allows deductions for orthotic items such as motorized wheelchairs, specially equipped automobiles and telephones, prostheses such as artificial teeth and limbs, eyeglasses, hearing aids and their component parts, and crutches. Also included for deductions are guide dogs for the blind and the deaf.

The Tax Reform Act of 1976, explained in "Your Federal Income Tax" (1977 edition), allows a tax credit for the cost of a disabled child or disabled spouse's care (a greater tax benefit than a tax deduction). A tax credit is taken off the final amount of tax to be paid after it has been computed. A tax credit of 20 percent of the payments for attendant care of a disabled family member is allowed if this enables the taxpayer to be involved in gainful employment. Payments to relatives who provide this care can be included in some circumstances.[25] Form No. 1040 must be filed to claim this credit. For further information, contact the local IRS office or the Commission of Internal Revenue (1111 Constitution Avenue N.W., Washington, D.C. 20224).

VIII. The Right to Work

People with disabilities would like to be able to work as productive members of society if at all possible. In our society much status is attached to receiving a paycheck and being self-supporting. Perhaps even more important is the need to feel that one is doing something worthwhile and making a contribution to society. Two events have gone a long way toward helping disabled people achieve this goal of economic independence. The first was the establishment of the vocational rehabilitation network in the United States, which serves all disabled people through counseling, testing, training, and placement in appropriate fields of work. The second, and no less significant, was the affirmative action section in the Rehabilitation Act of 1973, designed to ensure that disabled people would be hired for jobs in the mainstream of society. Slowly but surely the old attitudinal barriers are falling, and this, combined with architectural and job accommodations and the willingness to make such accommodations on the part of many forward-looking businesses, is making it possible for disabled people to achieve gainful employment in larger numbers than ever before.

Vocational Rehabilitation

All people who have a disability that interferes with their ability to work outside the home, to be a homemaker, or to function in any segment of society are eligible by law to vocational rehabilitation services, supported by the federal government but administered through the states. These services must be sought at the local level through vocational rehabilitation offices. These agencies are called by slightly different names in different parts of the country. To apply, check the telephone directory under state listings for department of vocational rehabilitation, department of rehabilitation, or office of vocational rehabilitation. Services will be provided if there is a possibility that some form of employment will result, whether it is competitive, self-employment, sheltered employment, or homemaking.

A wide range of services, financial assistance, and training includes evaluation of rehabilitation potential through counseling, medical rehabilitation, training and/or higher education, financial assistance, interpreter services for the deaf, and reader services, as well as mobility training for the visually impaired, transportation, and sensory and other technological aids and devices. On-the-job help may be provided if needed. Expenses borne by the program will vary widely from case to case and state to state. Each state's financial resources and administration of programs are different. In many states the vocational rehabilitation services for the blind are handled separately.

Vocational rehabilitation services are provided under the Rehabilitation Act of 1973 (PL 93-112) and the 1974 Rehabilitation Act Amendments (PL 93-516). Final regulations were issued on November 25, 1975. Final standards for evaluating vocational rehabilitation programs and projects were published by the Rehabilitation Services Administration (RSA) on December 19, 1975. Regulations implementing the Randolph-Sheppard amendments of 1974 (PL 94-516) were issued by RSA on December 23, 1975. Under these regulations, the state vocational rehabilitation agency for blind individuals is designated as the licensing agency to administer vending facilities programs for the blind. Priority of licensing to blind vendors, as well as blind operators of cafeterias, are set forth in these regulations, and a set of rules governing the maintenance and operation of these facilities on federal properties is also listed.

The Commission for the Visually Handicapped also provides services such as eye examinations, general examinations, training in mobility and homemaking, and information about recording devices, college and training fees, specific small business equipment, transportation costs, and small business enterprise aid programs. Some of these services are dependent upon the economic needs of the family. Services for older visually handicapped people supplied by the commission include instruction in braille typing, handcrafts, training in mobility, and orientation to the environment and safe travel.

Under the Wagner-O'Day Act (PL 92-28, PL 93-358), sheltered workshops serving blind and severely handicapped persons receive special preference in bidding on government contracts for products and services. At least 75 percent of the direct labor involved in making the commodity or providing the service must be performed by blind or other severely handicapped persons.

The Rehabilitation Services Administration, Department of HEW, Washington, D.C. 20201, will supply further information about these services. Information also can be obtained from the Association of Rehabilitation Facilities, 5530 Wisconsin Avenue, Suite 955, Washington, D.C. 20015.

Affirmative Action

Section 503 of the Rehabilitation Act of 1973 forbids discrimination on the basis of disability by requiring that business firms and organizations receiving $2,500 or more in government contracts actively seek out disabled people for employment. It is also mandated that job accommodations be made to a reasonable degree. Handicapped workers must also be given equal opportunity for advancement.

Section 501 of the act requires that federal agencies not discriminate against the disabled in hiring practices. In addition, a small number of federal jobs, called special "A" appointment positions, are set aside for handicapped individuals on a noncompetitive basis, should there be a need for special consideration. Special services are also offered: for the blind— readers or oral tests; for the deaf—sign language interpreters and written rather than oral tests; and for the orthopedically handicapped—extra time or help because of the disability in marking answer sheets.

Federal job information centers are maintained by the Civil Service Commission throughout the country to provide local job information. These offices are listed in telephone books under U.S. Government, but if none is listed in a particular area, one can dial (800) 555-1212 for the toll-free number of the federal job information service in a particular state.[26]

Section 504, which applies to all recipients of federal funds, including government agencies, schools, hospitals, colleges and universities, and social agencies, requires equal access to premises, programs, and jobs. Violations in any of these areas should be reported to the Office of Civil Rights (Department of HEW, 300 Independence Avenue S.W., Washington, D.C. 20201).

State employment offices are also required to help disabled people find jobs. Two pamphlets that might be useful for library vertical files are "Seven Services—How the Employment Service Helps the Handicapped" (Superintendent of Documents, Washington, D.C. 20402), and "Employment Assistance for the Handicapped" (President's Committee on Employment of the Handicapped, Washington, D.C. 20210).

CETA, the Comprehensive Employment and Training Program, was created to provide employment and training for the unemployed, underemployed, and economically disadvantaged. Many disabled people fit its eligibility criteria. Local CETA offices can be found through the telephone book, the local department of labor, or mayor's office.

Veterans' Benefits

Veterans should apply to regional Veterans Administration offices to ascertain benefits available to them. For all veterans disabled by injury, accident, or disease or permanently and totally disabled for reasons not traceable to service, there are many benefits, including partial payment on automobiles and automobile adaptations, mechanical aids and guide dogs for the blind, monthly disability payments, clothing and prosthetic and orthotic appliance payments, educational assistance, money for home remodeling, hospitalization, life insurance, and attendant care.

Veterans of World War II are eligible for vocational rehabilitation under certain conditions. Vietnam veterans may be assisted in getting jobs through the Vietnam Veterans Readjustment Act of 1974. For information, write to Affirmative Action to Employ Disabled Veterans and Veterans of the Vietnam Era, President's Committee on Employment of the Handicapped, Washington, D.C. 20210. For further information, send for "Federal Benefits for Veterans and Dependents" (Superintendent of Documents, Washington, D.C. 20420); and "Benefits for Veterans and Their Families" and "Educational Benefits for Veterans and Their Families," both available from the State Division of Veterans' Affairs. Find the address in the telephone directory under Veterans' Affairs, Division of.[27]

Small Business Loans

The Small Business Administration (SBA) makes business loans on reasonable terms to any handicapped individual who wishes to establish, acquire, or operate a small business. It also assists certain businesses that employ disabled individuals. SBA loans may not exceed $350,000 at an interest rate of 3 percent per year for a term not to exceed 15 years (PL 92-595, US Code, Title 15, Section 636). For further information, contact the Small Business Administration, Washington District Office, 1030 15 Street N.W., Washington, D.C. 20417. Librarians should send for the "Fact Sheet on Handicapped Assistance Loans" from SBA.[28] Also available is "Government Business Opportunities" (Government Services Administration Business Service Center, Washington, D.C. 20405), which tells how to do business with the federal government.[29]

IX. Education

The right to educational opportunity has been legislated under the Education for All Handicapped Children Act of 1975, which required that all states initiate a Project Child Find to locate and provide appropriate education in the least restrictive environment for all disabled children ages 6 to 17, by September 1, 1978. Disabled young adults ages 18 to 21 must be located and appropriate schooling offered to them by September 1, 1980 in those states where such public education is required. Disabled children ages 3 to 5 must be found and educated in those states with laws mandating public education at these age levels.

All disabled children must have individualized educational plans made for them, and parents have the right and the obligation to participate in the final decision for educational placement of their children. Placement outside the public schools, in special or private school facilities, must be at no cost to the parents. Auxiliary services such as therapists, transportation, and special technical aids must also be provided at public expense.

Final responsibility for implementing PL 94-142 rests with the state education departments. See also Part IV for a fuller explanation of the education of exceptional children and for school library services to them.

Higher education is now being made available to a greater extent than ever before to those disabled young adults eligible for college programs. These may be funded by vocational rehabilitation services if higher education is considered realistic. By 1977, over 500 college campuses in the United States had been made architecturally accessible to the disabled and were offering special services to physically disabled students. By June 1980, it is required that all colleges and universities receiving federal funds be made accessible to the disabled. Complaints about noncompliance with the law may be filed with the Office of Civil Rights, Department of HEW, Washington, D.C. 20201.

Refer to Elinor Gollay and Alwina Bennett, *The College Guide for Students with Disabilities* (Cambridge, Mass.: Abt Associates); and *Getting through College with a Disability: A Summary of Services Available on 500 Campuses for Students with Handicapping Conditions* (President's Committee on Employment of the Handicapped, Washington, D.C. 20210).

X. Consumerism—The Rights of Disabled Consumers

One of the most important books in the area of consumerism is Lilly Bruck's *Access: The Guide to a Better Life for Disabled Americans* (New York: David Obst Books, Random House, 1978). For many years Bruck has been involved in consumerism, and this training in the rights of citizens as buyers of goods aided her as she wrote this extremely useful book for the disabled consumer. It should be found in the reference rooms of all libraries, and circulating copies should be made available to disabled people and the professionals who serve them. It will help librarians who wish to aid disabled patrons in their attempts to become participating members of society. The book includes legal rights information, as well as information in all areas of activities of daily living for the disabled.

Unique to Bruck's book is her thesis that the disabled person is a consumer of goods who spends money in the marketplace. But it is the disabled consumer who is often severely restricted by environmental and transportation barriers. Moreover, attitudinal obstacles prevent many disabled consumers from obtaining quality service, and often products needed to overcome the effects of disability are expensive and unreliable.[30]

Bruck asserts that the disabled people of the United States have never received a fair deal in the marketplace. Perhaps in future generations, when able-bodied and disabled children, educated together and growing up together, will be more accustomed to each other, rejection and fear of people with disabilities will no longer exist. Today, however, salespeople generally continue to reflect the suspicions that society exhibits toward disabled people. They must be taught, perhaps in management training seminars, how to deal with a diversified public that includes people with various disabilities.[31]

Discussing catalogue shopping by mail by the homebound, Bruck directs that complaints about mail orders, including fraudulent advertising, be addressed to (1) Direct Mail Marketing Association, 6 East 43 Street, New York, New York 10017; (2) Local consumer affairs offices; and/or (3) Federal Trade Commission, Washington, D.C. 20580. "Mail Fraud Laws" and "Shopping by Mail, You're Protected" are available free from Consumer Information Center, Pueblo, Colorado 81009. To learn more about how to avoid pitfalls that come with the door-to-door sales pitch, send for "Three Days to Cancel: Door-to-Door Sales," Buyers Guide No. 15 (Federal Trade Commission, Room 130, Washington, D.C. 20580).

Bruck's information section about credit cards, establishing a credit rating, and shopping on credit is as valuable to the able-bodied as to the disabled, as is the section on food shopping. She states that persons receiving Social Security and SSI benefits may be eligible to participate in food stamp programs and may use food stamps, if disabled and elderly, to purchase meals from home delivery services, commonly called Meals on Wheels. Local senior citizens centers or food stamp offices can provide information about this. Also, special diets are deductible as a medical expense.

Highlights of the section on the purchase of goods and services include purchase of medicines and their deductibility for tax purposes, how to find out about the products for the disabled that have been developed through space age technology, and how to comparison shop for the items most suited to personal needs. There is a useful section on hearing aids and an account of some of the work being done by the Telephone Pioneers, a volunteer service organization of the Bell Telephone Company, who use their inventive skills to make things for disabled children and adults. Local chapters of this voluntary organization are in many areas of the country and can be reached through the telephone company.

The section on eyeglasses would certainly affect countless numbers of people, as would the information on banking services, how to choose the most advantageous and most convenient method of banking, and suggestions on repairs of household appliances and home improvements.

Such ideas as electric and heating bills written in braille, a service recently instituted by Con Edison in New York City at the request of a blind user, and the suggestion of installing TTY phones so that deaf subscribers might have access to information about their bills (not yet done) are ideas whose time has come. All companies that service the public in the future will have to accommodate disabled users in such ways.[32]

SUMMARY

Disabled people have certain basic rights legislated by the federal government. Many people are unaware of their rights and do not take advantage of the benefits to which they are entitled by law. People who turn to the public libraries for information should find them equipped to help locate appropriate social agencies and consumer services.

NOTES

1. PL 93-112, 93rd Congress, Washington, D.C., September 26, 1973.

2. PL 94-142, 94th Congress, Washington, D.C., November 29, 1975, Education for All Handicapped Children Act of 1975.

3. PL 95-602, 95th Congress, Washington, D.C., November 6, 1978, Rehabilitation Amendments of 1978.

4. White House Conference on Handicapped Individuals, summary, final report, Department of Health, Education, and Welfare, Office for Handicapped Individuals, Washington, D.C., DHEW Pub. No. (OHD)78-22003 (1978), p. 122.

5. Lilly Bruck, *Access: The Guide to a Better Life for Disabled Americans* (New York: Random House, 1978), p. 51.

6. Marie McGuire Thompson, *Housing and Handicapped People*, The President's Committee on Employment of the Handicapped, Washington, D.C. (1976), p. 5.

7. Ibid., p. 10.

8. "For the Disabled Person . . . A Pocket Guide to Federal Help," Department of Health, Education, and Welfare, Office for Handicapped Individuals, Washington, D.C. (September 1978).

9. James J. Raggio et al., *The Disabled and the Elderly: Equal Access to Public Transportation*, Public Interest Law Center of Philadelphia, Philadelphia, Penn. (September 1975), published by the President's Committee on Employment of the Handicapped, Washington, D.C., p. 11.

10. Bruck, *Access*, p. 59.

11. *Handicapped Americans Reports*, Plus Publications, Washington, D.C., August 4, 1978.

12. Bruck, *Access*, p. 61.

13. Ibid., p. 62.

14. Access Chicago: The Rehabilitation Institute of Chicago, Northwestern University Medical Rehabilitation Research and Training Center No. 20, Proceedings of Access Region V, May 13 and 14, 1976, p. 107.

15. "Financial Assistance for the Disabled," INA Mend Institute, Booklet No. 3, Human Resources Center, Albertson, N.Y. (1975), p. 17.

16. Key Federal Regulations Affecting the Handicapped, 1975–1976, Department of Health, Education, and Welfare, Washington, D.C. (September 1977), pp. 48–49.

17. INA Booklet No. 3, p. 19.

18. Bruck, *Access*, p. 66.

19. Ibid., p. 68.

20. INA Booklet No. 3, p. 21.

21. Bruck, *Access*, p. 72.

22. "For the Disabled Person," p. 11.

23. Ibid., p. 12.

24. INA Booklet No. 3, p. 8.

25. Bruck, *Access*, p. 50.

26. Ibid., p. 45.

27. INA Booklet No. 3, pp. 28, 29.

28. Ibid., p. 30.

29. Bruck, *Access*, p. 86.

30. Ibid., p. 7.

31. Ibid., p. 107.

32. Ibid., p. 191.

4

Information for Living

Human beings have certain basic needs, which, when fulfilled, enable them to function as active members of society. Good health, as well as appropriate clothing, housing, education, employment, and transportation, and recreation and a satisfactory adjustment as sexual human beings are taken for granted by most of us. But for a large segment of the population, fulfillment of these basic needs sometimes presents seemingly insurmountable problems. These are physically disabled people, who are between 10 and 20 percent of the national population.

Until recently, physically disabled people made up a large percentage of the population of institutions, unless their families kept them at home, and then they were usually homebound. Often they lived alone as shut-ins. Today, dramatic changes are occurring in the lives of the disabled. They are emerging from their previously protected environments, and they are demanding to be heard. Legislation such as PL 93-112, the Rehabilitation Act of 1973, and PL 94-142, the Education of All Handicapped Children Act, and the May 1977 White House Conference on the Handicapped have responded to these changes. As a result, disabled people are searching for information in all areas of their activities of daily living.

In response to this need, many new advocacy organizations have come into existence in the 1970s, while older organizations have updated their goals by modernizing and broadening their services and informational activities. New developments ranging from research in innovative areas such as rehabilitation engineering to changing attitudes in many of the general service fields have combined to effect significant improvements in the lives of the physically disabled.

Librarians, who are the first-line information officers for the general public, will see more and more of this new client population. The ones they do not see are out there, nevertheless, and must be reached in innovative ways. Events have moved so quickly that many disabled people are still unaware of the facilities, the new technology, and the opportunities being made available to them. Often the public librarian is the first one to whom they turn for information. And all too often the reference shelves and vertical files do not hold the answers.

In Chapter 2 mention was made of literature that librarians can obtain for their vertical files at little or no cost concerning the physical nature of various disabilities. This chapter will outline some of the basic information needs of the disabled and will offer sources, again at very little cost, which public librarians and school librarians dealing with the parents of disabled children or with disabled young adults can add to their collections. The institution and hospital librarian will also wish to collect this information for patients who, taking advantage of new methods in education, rehabilitation, and training, are now aspiring to more active lives in their communities. Reentry into the community can be facilitated by the astute librarian who can supply the practical information needed for independent living.

One important guide that deserves a spot on all library reference shelves is *National Resource Directory: A Guide to Services and Opportunities for Persons with Spinal Cord Injury or Disease and Others with Severe Physical Disabilities* (Newton Upper Falls, Mass.: National Spinal Cord Injury Foundation, 1979). The first section covers sources of medical and rehabilitation services, as well as instructions for personal care at home. Addresses of comprehensive care facilities for the spinal cord injured are listed by state. A section on emotional adjustment explains the feelings that people have when they first become disabled, as well as the problems encountered by families, and details the kinds of professional psychological services available to help deal with them.

There is a good bibliography of books, films, and addresses of ongoing seminars on the topic of sexuality for the spinal cord injured. A section on independent living offers addresses of independent living centers. (However, this list will be outdated quickly. The Office of Handicapped Individuals in Washington, D.C., which is keeping an ongoing listing of such centers and updating it every few months, is a more accurate source of information here.)

The rest of the directory offers valuable and concrete information about such important aspects of living as financial assistance, addresses of state welfare offices, VA offices, equipment suppliers, and rehabilitation engineering centers.

Listings for the state offices of vocational rehabilitation, local chapter addresses of the National Spinal Cord Injury Foundation, organizations offering recreation and travel for the handicapped, as well as listings of guidebooks to cities in the United States and titles of journals, newsletters, and pamphlets on spinal cord injury, paraplegia, and quadriplegia complete this valuable guide. On the last page there is one small paragraph about library services for the physically handicapped, which deserves mention simply because of its brevity. It states that persons with physical disabilities are eligible for talking books, large print books, and reading aids, as well as art prints "to brighten up a room" and home delivery of books. That's it! Let us hope, however, that very soon library service for the physically handicapped will include information and referral services in *all* areas of daily living, employment, and education.

LIVING WITH A DISABILITY

The physically disabled person must make certain accommodations to live comfortably within his or her environment. This requires, first of all, proper prostheses (devices attached to the body, such as an artificial arm or leg) and orthotics (devices used by the disabled person, such as a wheelchair, cane, or crutch). These items should be prescribed by a medical rehabilitation team at a rehabilitation hospital, in the case of a person who has been newly disabled by accident or injury, or by the family physician, in the case of a person disabled from birth. However, very often a disabled person seeks further information for the purchase of specific items and will turn to the librarian for assistance. The following sources will give the reference librarian the basic information needed to answer such requests, which may come from a disabled patron, a parent of a disabled child, or a professional support person such as a social worker or visiting nurse.

For the person who must live in a wheelchair, the chair becomes an extension of his or her own body, somewhat as a prosthesis does for someone with an amputation. A wheelchair should be prescribed by a medical team, based on the individual's life-style. Wheelchairs vary in many respects—chair size, wheel size, reclining or straight-backed, with or without armrests, collapsible or not, electric- and battery-powered as opposed to hand-operated.

A helpful pamphlet for a disabled person seeking information on a purchasing choice or a decision to change chair style is *Wheelchair Selection: More than Choosing a Chair with Wheels* (Rehabilitation Publication No. 713).[1] Published by the Sister Kenny Institute, it describes different types of chairs for adults and children, types of chair cushions, and chairs for agencies (useful data should a local agency call the library for information). Major wheelchair manufacturers are listed at the back. Librarians who provide access to commercial catalogues may wish to acquire some of the ones on this list.

The Training and Education Department of Everest Jennings Company (1803 Portius Avenue, Los Angeles, California 90025), a major producer of wheelchairs, has issued several excellent booklets in its Wheelchair Prescription series, available free of charge. The titles are *Things to Consider When Buying or Renting a Wheelchair; Measuring the Patient; Safety and Handling;* and *Care and Service.* The overall emphasis of the first two booklets is the need for some professional help in choosing a chair. Booklets three and four, however, are excellent references for an attendant or anyone else who is called upon to help a person in a wheelchair.

Some physically disabled people do not need wheelchairs, but use canes, crutches, braces, or walkers. As in the case of wheelchairs, obtaining some of the commercial catalogues of major companies handling these items will enable the library patron to discover if there is a piece of equipment to meet a specific need.

The library patron who has lost full or partial use of an arm may present a special kind of challenge when seeking information. To help in all aspects of daily living, *The One Hander's Book*, written by Veronica Washam and based on personal experience, contains a wide range of information to meet these needs.[2] Throughout the book, hints are offered for ways in which to give gentle use to the nonfunctioning or prosthetic arm. Suggestions are offered for everyday needs such as carrying keys and change and managing doors and newspapers. Dressing, grooming, and housekeeping suggestions, child care, and situations such as school, recreation, or work are covered. The book is interesting because it suggests no gadgets and only provides the kind of helpful ideas that the author, herself a one-hander since the age of two, has personally discovered. She even suggests a variation to enable a one-handed person to use an electric typewriter.

Clothing

Looking attractive is important to everyone, and today it is possible to look attractive without spending a great deal of money. Some people, both disabled and nondisabled, can sew and make their own clothing. Many disabled people, however, will be looking for information sources on inexpensive clothing adapted to their physical needs. These sources do exist, and for very little money the librarian can have this information on reference shelves or in the vertical file.

The disabled generally need garments that are easily put on and removed, soil and crease resistant, with concealed zippers where necessary to suit orthopedic needs, and with elasticized waistbands. Underarm reinforcements are necessary for crutch users, and extra knee width in pants accommodates the wheelchair user. Women in wheelchairs need to avoid narrow skirts and look best in full, longer skirts or pants. Well-placed pockets are helpful for carrying small necessities.[3] If a person has a problem of incontinence and uses a collecting device under clothing, the right kind of clothes will make it possible for him or her to be in public without embarrassment.

The mail-order house Fashion-Able, Rocky Hill, New Jersey 08553, offers all types of clothing for the disabled. Its catalogue wil be sent upon request. The Vocational Guidance and Rehabilitation Service of Cleveland, Ohio, has an ongoing program in which it develops and tests new clothing designs for disabled people. Its catalogue, available for a small charge, gives styles and designs. Menswear fashions are available in adaptations for wheelchair use (shorter, less bulky jackets, short legs), special trouser closings for bathroom needs, and wider legs to accommodate braces or a prosthesis. Leinenweber, Inc. (69 West Washington Street, Chicago, Illinois 60602), has researched these clothing needs and a catalogue is available on request.

The book *Independent Living for the Handicapped and the Elderly* by Elizabeth May, Neva Waggoner and Eleanor Hotte contains an informative section on what to look for in clothing for the handicapped. Although the 1974 edition, an update of the original book, retains some outdated bibliography, it is still a good buy for library shelves because of the very practical information in this and other areas that is still useful. The authors state that dressing is made easier for the disabled when clothes are amply cut through armholes and waist, with fasteners that are easy to manipulate. Clothes that are well and cleverly cut can help to minimize a structural deformity and, in general, allow for ease and comfort in wearing. A special section deals extensively with special needs in children's clothing, and an appendix offers directions for making simple clothing alterations.[4]

"Clothing for the Handicapped: Fashion Adaptations for Adults and Children" (Rehabilitation Publication No. 739) is a monograph by Miriam T. Bowar, R.N., O.T.R. (Minneapolis, Minn.: Sister Kenny Institute, 1977). It would be a useful addition to vertical files. Disabled people at the institute contributed many suggestions concerning their special needs. These problem areas are listed with possible solutions, followed by sketches and patterns for easy sewing. Alterations for clothing manufactured for the ablebodied are also suggested. A directory lists many of the sources mentioned here and adds two companies that offer patterns for adaptive clothing: Kwik Sew Pattern Company, 300 Sixth Avenue North, Minneapolis, Minnesota 55401; and Natural Creations by Kay Cadell, Textile Research Center, Texas Tech University, P.O. Box 4150, Lubbock, Texas 79409.

Housing

No need is more basic than the need for shelter. Historically, in the United States during the nineteenth and early twentieth centuries, persons who were different, either mentally or physically, were placed in institutions. Through the first half of the twentieth century, these institutions grew larger and correspondingly more impersonal, less efficient in terms of service, and a financial burden to the community. The 1970s was the decade for change as the disabled became more visible in society. Rehabilitation studies are proving that various living arrangements, as alternatives to large institutions, are more economically efficient and certainly less dehumanizing.

Considerations in the choice of a living situation for a physically disabled person must include the degree of physical disability as well as emotional independence. Sometimes a severely physically disabled person will be able to manage a more independent living situation than a less physically disabled person, who may not be able to work out an independent situation without a great deal of support care.

Many variations in living arrangements are becoming available to the physically disabled person. Librarians who want to be information officers for disabled library patrons will need the most up-to-date information in their files. A few basic sources on reference shelves and some vertical file material represent very little outlay in terms of money and will provide a wealth of pertinent information.

Physical Adaptations

What makes living easier today for the disabled is, first of all, the physical adaptations now available. Taking advantage of new technological developments and architectural design possibilities, the knowledgeable physically disabled person can have a comfortable physical environment to suit individual needs. A fairly recent book in this area, and the most complete, is *Housing and Home Services for the Disabled: Guidelines and Experiences in Independent Living*, by Gini Laurie.[5] Laurie deals with the entire spectrum of physical adaptations and alternate living arrangements.

In the chapters dealing with architectural adaptations, Laurie states that "adapting to disability is a two-way street; the individual must adapt to the environment and the environment must adapt to the individual."[6] The chapter "Adaptations to Housing" is a mixture of ideas from various sources —the experiences of disabled persons, books by therapists, pamphlets, and information that, over the years, has been published in *Rehabilitation Gazette* (formerly the *Toomy j. Gazette*) published by Laurie and her husband Joseph. This book could form the basis for a collection of information in this area. Laurie recommends other pertinent sources, and the book is valuable not only for such source material but also for its mention of equipment and sources for purchase. The book also provides general specifications for ramps, door widths, telephone alarm systems, kitchen and bathroom adaptations, and environmental control systems.

There are also several monographs offering specific information in these important areas. *Home in a Wheelchair: House Designs for Easier Wheelchair Living* (1977), by Joseph Chasin and edited by Jules Saltman, is one of a series of three monographs published by the Paralyzed Veterans of America, Inc. (PVA), an advocacy organization. The others are *Wheelchair in the Kitchen* (1973) and *Wheelchair Bathrooms* (n.d.). All three are available from PVA (7315 Wisconsin Avenue, Washington, D.C. 20014) or free of charge from the Eastern Paralyzed Veterans of America in New York City.

Home in a Wheelchair offers general advice of the type given to anyone buying or building a house: the need to take into consideration how much one can spend, the location of the property, the grade of land, whether to design and build or buy from a model (as many disabled persons do) and then make adaptations in the floor plan, and so on. Specifications are offered for the grade of ramps, for car ports or garages, width of doors (single), specifics for folding doors (double), sliding (if possible), or automatic (ideal if possible). Details such as types of door handles are important to a disabled person with hand weakness.

Chasin discusses methods of communication, including telephones, alarm systems, CB radios, and intercoms. Much of this information is covered in the Laurie book, but is obtainable here in abbreviated form. Descriptions of electrical systems, placing of wall outlets, optimum window designs, home elevators, and chairlifts are followed by several ideas for kitchen design, laundry and storage areas, an exercise area, floor coverings, and bathroom and bedroom designs. Three floor plans for demonstration houses are shown with wheelchair specifications, followed by a bibliography. The monograph ends with a list of the commercial sources for the items mentioned in the text—32 compact pages of extremely useful information for very little or no cost.

Wheelchair in the Kitchen, also by Chasin and edited by Saltman, is in a format as compact as its companion volume. It includes measurements of wheelchairs, how much space is needed to turn corners, and how to negotiate hallways and doors. Optimum kitchen layouts are shown, including counter heights and cabinet widths, sink space, and dishwasher design. For refrigerator and storage space, ingenious ideas are offered for revolving shelves and pullout racks. Ideal laundry room designs to be used by persons in wheelchairs, as well as ideas for tools to use in kitchens to grasp items beyond reach, are included. Suggestions are also offered for alternate ways of doing things when remodeling is not feasible, and what to look for when apartment hunting. Safety tips and a bibliography are included.

Wheelchair Bathrooms, by Harry A. Schweikert, Jr., was written in the early 1970s and is an up-to-date revision of literature published by PVA in the late 1950s. This 20-page monograph uses very simple terminology and clear illustrative drawings with measurements of the bathroom itself, types of toilets, with grab bars or overhead trapezes, raised seats, commode chairs and bedside commode chairs, and sinks—wall hung, counter, and corner types. Legs must be avoided for wheelchairs.

Tubs are pictured, with or without shower doors, and plans are also given for stall showers. These are best installed at the end of the room, with a floor slanted toward the drain and without a lip so that a person in a shower wheelchair can be wheeled right in. Bidets, or perineal baths, are a suggested improvement. A bibliography and a list of commercial sources are included.

Independent Living for the Handicapped and Elderly, described earlier, also includes work simplification principles by the late Lillian M. Gilbreth, industrial engineer, applied to all areas of household tasks, from doing laundry to child care. The focus of the book is primarily on people with orthopedic disabilities. It offers special devices to simplify food preparation and methods for making house cleaning easier for those in wheelchairs. The chapters on kitchen and bathroom planning give many useful ideas. Particularly valuable are the appendices, which show designs for special equipment for child care, special devices (for example, for lifting a wheelchair into an automobile), commercial sources, and agencies and publishers.

An extremely useful pamphlet is *Adaptations and Techniques for the Disabled Homemaker,* by Miriam Bowar Strebel, (Minneapolis, Minn.: Sister Kenny Institute).[7] It presents information about devices and adaptations to make life simpler for the disabled homemaker, and in some cases, construction information is supplied so that items can be made in a workshop. Many of the items mentioned are available in hardware stores. Commercial sources are indicated throughout the text. The author cautions against suggesting this pamphlet unless a disabled person is knowledgeable about his or her capabilities. Often a medical or rehabilitation counselor is needed to make appropriate suggestions.

Helpful work-saving hints are given, such as eliminating unnecessary tasks and selecting foods that minimize preparation, such as packaged mixes and frozen and canned goods. In preparing main dishes for more than one meal at a time, work at comfortable heights in a seated position, and so on. Food preparation hints include how to crack an egg with one hand and peeling and slicing techniques. For work and storage areas, gadgets such as reachers and lap boards are pictured. For refrigerator and storage areas, various adaptations, such as overhead mirrors, are suggested for those with weak arms and hands. This booklet concentrates exclusively on meal preparation and kitchen use and would be a worthwhile addition to vertical files, providing a wealth of practical information for very little cost.

Many handicapped or elderly homemakers have no contact with rehabilitation personnel or institutions. Often visiting nurses or social workers are in need of practical information for these clients, especially in the area of food preparation. *The Mealtime Manual for People with Disabilities and the Aging* offers solutions for practical kitchen management problems for handicapped homemakers.[8] Compiled by Judith L. Klinger, O.T.R., M.A., editor, Institute of Rehabilitation Medicine, New York University Medical Center, the manual is helpful for the elderly, one-handed, arthritic, wheelchair users, and/or people with upper-extremity weakness. It includes useful hints for the upper-extremity amputee, people with limited vision, loss of sensation, or lack of muscular coordination.

Important chapters include small electrical appliances, gadgets for opening boxes and cans, modified kitchen design, and kitchen storage. It also includes information on food preparation, serving food, entertaining, shopping, and managing alone. Some of the gadgets are listed as available from the American Foundation for the Blind. Others are available from commercial sources, which are listed along with names of organizations and agencies. This useful book can be obtained from Box 38, Ronks, Pennsylvania 17572.

The largest single source of information for devices of all kinds is *Aids to Independent Living: Self Help for the Handicapped*, by Edward Lowman, M.D., and Judith L. Klinger (New York: McGraw-Hill, 1969). Although it has not been revised, the scope of its contents has not been duplicated in any one place, and most of it is still valid. The authors are on the staff of the Institute of Rehabilitation Medicine, New York University Medical Center. The information is useful for groups who work with the disabled without benefit of medical centers, such as general practitioners, public health nurses, occupational and physical therapists, and vocational counselors, and the disabled themselves.

The tasks of daily living are organized into 65 categories for easy reference. Chapter headings include basic dress and grooming, ambulation, housing, transportation and travel, communication, and recreation. The book also offers lists of sources of commercial publishers and their addresses. Although this is an expensive book, libraries that can afford the purchase will find it a good investment.

INDEPENDENT LIVING

There have always been disabled people willing to take risks in order to live independent lives. But the average disabled person, unable to be gainfully employed, has found it almost impossible to surmount the formidable financial obstacles standing in the way of independent living. Able-bodied adolescents develop a need to leave their families, and usually do so in their late teens upon entering college or their early or middle twenties with marriage and/or employment. In the past, too often disabled people whose families were no longer able to care for them were placed in institutions. In many cases young people were housed with the elderly and the intellectually able with the developmentally disabled. The regimentation and depersonalization of institution living are familiar to anyone who has had occasion to check conditions in such places.

To avoid institutional living and alleviate the isolation of being a shut-in, there has long been a need for new kinds of living arrangements for the severely physically disabled. These arrangements must include architectural adaptations plus some support services and, when needed, the availability of attendant care. For the severely disabled who cannot be gainfully employed, appropriate government subsidies are needed to make all of these services economically feasible.

The most exciting and fastest moving of the developments in the growing awareness of the needs of the physically disabled has been the independent living movement. The idea that disabled people have the right to live with a measure of dignity and independence, as part of the able-bodied community whenever possible, was initiated in the United States and moved forward by enterprising disabled young adults, with the later cooperation of the federal government. Librarians in public, high school, or institution libraries who come in contact with disabled adults or adolescents could do no better than to inform themselves of the growing diversification in life-styles and housing arrangements that give physically disabled people the possibility of choice such as never before.

The concept of independent living is based on the premise that disabled people have the civic right to support services that will enable them to live as part of the general community, whether or not they can be gainfully employed. Support environments must include elimination of architectural barriers, attendant and household chore services, counseling, equipment repair, legal and medical services, adapted transportation, and vocational and educational services. For these services to be protected from exploitation and control by individuals who do not depend on them, these programs must include the severely handicapped in their planning and management.[9]

For many years the National Rehabilitation Association has supported the idea of an independent living program separate from the traditional government emphasis on vocational rehabilitation. Originally, the federal administration did not support this "independent living" concept; however, the idea gradually began to gain favor. The Rehabilitation Act of 1973, Sections 501, 502, 503, and 504, called for barrier-free work areas and educational facilities, affirmative action in employment programs, and the creation of an Architectural and Transportation Barriers Compliance Board. It also included authorization of a major study for the comprehensive needs of the severely disabled.

In 1974 the Vocational Rehabilitation Act was amended (with PL 93-516), and it authorized a White House Conference in May 1977. The Social Service Amendments of 1974 (PL 93-647), adding Title 20 to the Social Security Act, aided the severely disabled to achieve financial self-sufficiency. (Send for *Social Service '75*, No. 75-23038, free, from SRS, Department of HEW, Washington, D.C.) This was followed by several Supplemental Security Income Amendments and the National Housing Act Amendments of 1975, Title 1 of which included provisions for the removal of barriers in housing for the handicapped. In June 1977, an Office of Independent Living was established in HUD, with the objective of creating independent living centers across the country and making more and better housing available to the handicapped.[10] (For more detailed explanation of these laws, see Chapter 3.)

The concept of housing for the disabled has changed therefore from large institution-type projects to encompass a range of housing alternatives providing a selection of support services based on individual needs. Many concepts have been developed, including group homes and cooperative residences such as the Cheshire Homes project in England and now under consideration for duplication in New Jersey. Another type of arrangement is the total living community such as Het Dorp, the town in Holland. Drawbacks to these communities rest in the fact that they are made up totally of disabled people, with no opportunity for integration into the able-bodied world.[11]

In the move toward achieving independence, mental barriers are sometimes more difficult to surmount than physical ones, making it advantageous to have some sort of transitional environment. In the area of public housing, there have been HUD-assisted housing projects, established during the 1960s and 1970s. In addition, some experimental living projects have been started as adjuncts to rehabilitation hospital centers. In the United States, some college campus living projects have been expanded into group home or independent living programs. Legal problems sometimes exist in the case of group homes in order to change town ordinances that bar group living in residential areas.

Three types of disabled people benefit from some sort of group residence. Severely physically disabled persons who need attendant or skilled nursing care and housekeeping may require this type of arrangement on a permanent basis. Some disabled people use the group home as a transitional facility where they can receive peer counseling while taking a step toward independence. Some people simply prefer to live in a somewhat sheltered environment. On the other hand, integrated housing helps to make the disabled individual feel more a part of the community and promotes independence. Most young disabled people prefer to live among the able-bodied. However, there have been some successful segregated housing developments.

Resogin House was set up by Eastern Paralyzed Veterans of America, and consists of several apartments for the spinal cord injured where residents can share costs and services. Glass Mountain Inn, Inc., in Anaheim, California, is a group home for ten disabled men and women and five attendants who form a family.[12]

The Boston Center for Independent Living (BCIL) was started in 1974 as a residential college program and remains an outstanding example of an independent living project that recognizes the need for a transitional living period of training for disabled young adults and adults who have never lived on their own, managed money, marketing, and household chores, or directed attendants to care for their physical needs. The project includes campus living, cluster housing with attendant care, and independent apartment living. Literature from BCIL is available by writing for "BCIL Report," Peter Reich, editor, Boston Regional Medical Rehabilitation Research and Training Center No. 7, Tufts (July 1977).[13]

Additional projects are now being established in other areas of New England. And projects also exist in Texas (New Options), Colorado (Atlantis), and several other places in the country, each with some form of transitional living program combined with housing clusters offering support services.[14]

California became the first state to pass homemaker/chore legislation to supplement federal benefits, thus enabling the severely disabled and elderly to have sufficient funds to hire attendants to help care for survival needs.[15] The Center for Independent Living (CIL) at Berkeley (2539 Telegraph Avenue, Berkeley, California 94704) is the first and the best known of the independent living centers in the United States. The Berkeley center was an outgrowth of the Physically Disabled Student Project at the University of California Berkeley campus. Run from its inception by disabled students and former students, the program provides services and counseling to enable all physically disabled people, including quadriplegics, to live independently, most of them for the first time. Members of the center live in apartments in the Berkeley community, with the help of support services, which include an attendant pool, legal and medical services, wheelchair repair, transportation, peer counseling, and much more.

The objectives of the project are to show that a consumer-based organization can deliver services and facilitate independent living within the able-bodied community. The center at Berkeley has encouraged the establishment of 15 additional centers in California, all stimulated by California's favorable state financial benefits. In 1974 the Berkeley project became a center for the training of rehabilitation counselors, in collaboration with the Department of Rehabilitation of the state of California, and in 1975 the federal government contracted with CIL to demonstrate the effectiveness of its peer counseling approach to the rehabilitation of the severely disabled.

The Berkeley center has demonstrated the necessity for having the physically disabled represented in the majority on the boards of directors of independent living projects so that they can direct project development. The 15 centers in California have now formed themselves into a coalition, and it is the objective of the directors to form a national coalition. Whether the passage of Proposition 13 will affect monies to the disabled in California remains to be seen. For a listing of independent living projects, see Appendix.

Housing and Home Services for the Disabled by Gini Laurie is the first book that details the physical adaptations available to the disabled and, in addition, gives a detailed account of the state of the art in the area of independent living for the handicapped. Living projects of all kinds now in existence, as well as some that have been attempted and have failed for one reason or another, are discussed in this comprehensive work.

Although no one text can be complete or remain up-to-date in this fast-moving field, purchase of only Laurie's book will give librarians a tremendous source of information for disabled patrons hoping to achieve a measure of independent living. Laurie's chapters on adapted environments and devices are followed by personal independent living experiences, how to handle problems of attendant care, and an account of various types of home care services. Different types of living arrangements are detailed, including transitional projects, apartment living arrangements, cluster housing, long-term residential facilities, mobile homes, HUD-assisted housing projects, and much more. Information is also presented on living experiments worldwide. Projects for the developmentally disabled are included too.

An interesting alternative in housing for the handicapped was developed at St. Andrews Presbyterian College in Laurinburg, North Carolina. St. Andrews has had a program for handicapped students since 1961. In 1976, with a grant from HUD, research was carried on for the design of mobile homes for the handicapped.[16] The rationale for this project was the fact that mobile homes, being so much less expensive than other types of housing, could be afforded by many disabled people. Standard mobile homes were purchased by the college, and adaptations made in their design to accommodate handicapped students.

The project produced a monograph, "Mobile Homes: Alternative Housing for the Handicapped" (Superintendent of Documents, Washington, D.C.). Several different plans are given for such mobile home construction. It was hoped that the federal government could influence mobile home manufacturers to produce these models for general use, and at some time in the future this may happen. Meanwhile, the monograph is a good item for vertical files, as it would be useful to disabled people and to architects or builders who have been asked to deal with this situation.

COMMUNICATION

During 1977 the author was involved in trying to obtain information for a disabled young girl who had lost most of her ability to speak. Lisa K. is severely physically disabled with dystonia, which involves a loss of muscle tone. At one time she was able to communicate, but she gradually found it more and more difficult to produce sound. Her schoolwork (always good, as Lisa is very bright) was suffering, and she was unable to make herself understood to her friends and her family. Lisa's mother, a rehabilitation professional, joined with the library staff and speech therapist at Lisa's school in an attempt to find information on the latest technological advances in this area. This book was prompted by the difficulties encountered in this and many searches like it, and the knowledge that numerous other disabled people find such information almost impossible to locate.

Many disabled people cannot speak because of neuromuscular problems, damage to the larynx, or other disability. For them, communicating —the lifeline in our society, the way in which we make contact with the rest of the world—sometimes consists of anything from eye blinking in Morse code to crude alphabet boards for pointing (where there is an available hand). Intelligence and emotions remain largely locked within.

In the spring of 1978, a newsletter, *Communication Outlook*, was created for the purpose of focusing on communication aids and techniques for the severely disabled.[17] Published jointly by the Artificial Language Laboratory and the TRACE Center for the Severely Communicatively Handicapped, University of Wisconsin at Madison, the newsletter's purpose is to report on all of the new developments in this area. The newsletter states, and rightly, that while exciting advances have been made in this field, the impact is yet to be felt on the lives of the majority of human beings whom this new technology can potentially serve. And this is largely true because it is so difficult for the average disabled person, rehabilitation counselor, teacher, speech therapist, or physical therapist to obtain information in the fast-growing field of technological aids for the disabled.

Librarians can now subscribe to this newsletter, which, it is hoped, will continue to give information on new and existing products such as artificial voice units, calculator-type devices, special typing devices, and other electronic communication boards.

Experience has shown that only the person who is to use it can really make the final decision as to which piece of equipment is best. Lisa indicated her preference for a machine called Handi-voice, small enough for her to hold, which "speaks" with an artificial voice and can be programmed with a microcomputer to encompass a large vocabulary. Lisa's only objection was the fact that the "voice" sounded male. She, naturally, preferred to have her artificial voice sound female. This comment has been passed along to the developers.

A great deal of activity is going on in this area at research engineering centers such as the Biomedical Engineering Center at Tufts-New England Medical Center. The Cybernetics Research Institute has, for some time, been developing man-machine communication and control systems. For further information, contact Haig Kafafian, Llewellyn Park, West Orange, New Jersey 07052.

Communication can also be a problem for disabled people with limited or no hand use. The telephone company offers instrument adaptation for persons with various physical disabilities. A two-year study at the Institute of Rehabilitation Medicine, New York University Medical Center, under the sponsorship of AT&T, investigated how standard telephone equipment could be adapted for use by the physically disabled. Types of disabilities were identified and equipment matched to the disability. A rehabilitation monograph, *Telephone Services for the Handicapped*, Rehabilitation Monograph XXXVII (available from the Institute for Rehabilitation Medicine, New York University Medical Center), resulted from this study and provides information for medical personnel in helping meet the needs of clients. The study concluded that it is technically possible to meet the needs of virtually all persons disabled by neuromuscular or skeletal disorders who are able to communicate orally with one or another variation in equipment. The advent of touch-tone dialing has simplified these adaptations even further.

Each Bell Telephone Company has a marketing coordinator of services for the handicapped. Other phone companies have departments of marketing and engineering. Library information and referral files should contain the information that a client need only contact the telephone company and list his or her needs in order to obtain a telephone adjustment.

Typewriting rehabilitation is a particularly interesting possibility because it provides a skill that is useful on a personal living level, as well as in a school or work situation. The real difficulty is in locating teaching materials. *Type with One Hand* by Nina K. Richardson was originally copywrited in 1959 and marketed by South-Western Publishing Company. Although the material is not new, nothing better seems to have been developed. Luckily, *Type with One Hand* is still available and is listed in the 1978 edition of the South-Western Publishing Company, T09 textbook catalog.

SEXUALITY AND THE HANDICAPPED

The obvious fact that disabled people have sexual feelings like everyone else has been ignored for too long. All people are sexual beings, and human sexuality can be expressed in many ways. Body image—how we perceive ourselves—is important to all people, and no less so to the disabled. Disabled males, whether congenitally handicapped or paraplegic or quadriplegic because of injury or illness, find it particularly difficult to express themselves as males because it is believed, often mistakenly, that they are impotent. Disabled women may feel that their bodies do not conform to the stereotyped female standards for beauty. Research in the very important area of sex and the handicapped has just begun to develop.

A few years ago disabled people complained that they were unable to find any information in this area. However, many articles are now available in professional journals on this topic. Bibliographies are listed in Chapter 8. In addition, there are several paperback books available at very little cost. These should be a part of all library collections, particularly public and institution libraries and certainly in libraries serving rehabilitation counselors.

Sexual Adjustment: A Guide for the Spinal Cord Injured by Martha Ferguson Gregory is available from Accent on Living Publications (P.O. Box 700, Bloomington, Illinois 61701). It was written by a rehabilitation counselor whose husband is a quadriplegic as a result of an automobile accident. Gregory's book offers an overview of paraplegia and quadriplegia that would be very informative to anyone seeking information in dealing with the physically disabled. The author explains that, contrary to popular belief, most types of spinal cord injuries do not preclude some form of sexual activity. It becomes extremely important for the psychological well-being of the paraplegic male that he not consider himself to be sexually impotent and that he find some accommodation in this area.

Gregory also details typical psychological stages that most accident victims who become paraplegic or quadriplegic pass through on their way to emotional recovery (see Chapter 1 for details on this concept).

Valuable and detailed information is offered about the sexual capabilities of paraplegic males. The sexual adjustment of the disabled female is somewhat easier in that the female can play a more passive role. In any case, it is necessary that rehabilitation counselors begin to understand the implications of sexual problems for the disabled as they affect the nondisabled marriage partner and the family.

A very beautiful pamphlet was developed by Planned Parenthood of Snohomish County, Inc. *Toward Intimacy*, and a companion pamphlet, *Within Reach*, which is a guide for health care personnel who would like a greater understanding of their disabled clients, can be obtained from Human Sciences Press (Order Department, 72 Fifth Avenue, New York, New York 10011). *Toward Intimacy* was written for disabled women and the professionals who counsel them. It is based on interviews with disabled women who shared their experiences. Unlike the Gregory book, this one tells about women with a wide range of disabilities, both congenital and acquired, including cerebral palsy, rheumatoid arthritis, spinal cord injury, burns, strokes, and others. Several basic premises are stated: (1) sexuality is a right of all people; (2) disabled persons are sexual; (3) to talk and learn about sex is good; and (4) sexual expression is natural.

The goal is intimacy. The number or type of orgasms and erections is not necessarily what makes people feel close to each other. *Toward Intimacy* includes such topics as body image, how people feel about their bodies, alternate sexual methods, and ways of expressing affection. It also includes information on family planning. A chart indicates some sexual problems for each of several physical disabilities. However, the range of degree of disability and physical capability is so varied that this attempt is not as successful as the rest of the booklet. Illustrations are sketches by Katie Venables.

A book that seeks to dispel some of the myths generally surrounding the sexual ability of disabled people is *Sexual Options for Paraplegics and*

Quadriplegics by T. O. Mooney et al. (Boston: Little, Brown, 1975). It contains very explicit photographs, and high school librarians may be wary of placing it on open shelves. It should certainly be made available to counselors working with disabled adolescents and to librarians in institution and public libraries who wish to provide materials for disabled patrons.

Sexual Options makes the point that for the person with spinal cord injury and disabilities such as spina bifida, which are believed to cause impotence in some cases, there are alternate ways of giving and receiving sexual pleasure. It offers specific methods that have been used by disabled people and their partners and found to be satisfying. The important points are made that (1) whatever is satisfying and pleasurable to a couple is acceptable as long as they mutually agree; (2) it is important for people to experiment and discover what is satisfying; and (3) it is important for couples to communicate with each other what they find pleasing and satisfying.

All of these books stress the importance of communication and of thinking as sexual beings, and above all, of keeping a sense of humor about possible outlandish physical situations. Making these sources available to patrons would be an invaluable service on the part of the library staff.

Another book, more clinical and not as necessary in the public library, might be an important purchase for librarians dealing with professional rehabilitation counselors and/or institutional medical personnel. *Not Made of Stone: The Sexual Problems of Handicapped People* was written originally in Dutch by Dr. K. Heslinga, in association with A. M. C. M. Schellen, M.D., and A. Verkuyl, M.D., specialist in rehabilitation. Published originally in The Netherlands, it was translated from the original and published by Charles C. Thomas in 1974.

Not Made of Stone contains a chapter on the male and female reproductive systems and one on general genetics. It details the influence of specific disabilities on sexual ability. Sex education for disabled children is offered in the context of sex education for able-bodied children, and the book also deals with the sexual adjustment of disabled adults. Marriage, use of attendants and nurses, and whether or not to have children are handled sensitively.

For additional references in this area, see Chapter 8.

RECREATIONAL ACTIVITIES

The recognition that physically disabled people have a need to participate in recreational activities should be obvious. However, the truth is that this concept began to receive national attention only within the last few years. Until then, although many disabled people had managed to travel, dine out, or attend the theater, there was not the concerted effort that now exists in this area. Now that many more disabled people are entering the general population, librarians will most certainly begin to receive requests for information in the many areas of recreational activity, including sports and cultural activities, and the closely related topics of transportation and travel. The following sections offer a general survey of these related fields to enable librarians to answer requests for information.

Sports

In 1977 the Paralyzed Veterans of America published a pamphlet entitled "Recreation and Competitive Wheelchair Sports." In it the point is made that some form of recreational activity increases upper-extremity strength for persons with paraplegia. Increased blood circulation helps to prevent pressure sores, and increased fluid intake helps to prevent kidney and bladder infection.

Wheelchair sports actually began toward the end of World War II. Before then, there had not been a very significant paraplegic population because people with spinal cord injuries seldom survived. In her book *Wheelchair Champions: A History of Wheelchair Sports* (New York: Thomas Y. Crowell, 1978), Harriet May Savitz recounts the history of the development of wheelchair sports. As a member of the National Wheelchair Athletic Association, she travels with the teams to all competitions, and her book has an authentic ring, offering many human interest stories about wheelchair athletes. Her story begins in the 1940s with Harry C. Jennings, an engineer, and his friend Herbert A. Everest, also an engineer, who was paralyzed with a broken back and rendered virtually immobile in a wooden, noncollapsible wheelchair. Jennings, wishing to help his friend, designed the first lightweight collapsible metal chair, and together the two men founded the Everest Jennings Company, the largest producer of wheelchairs in the United States. Savitz's book makes interesting reading and can be referred to for a more amplified history of the development of wheelchair sports.

Wheelchair games are now held in all areas of the country, governed by the National Wheelchair Athletic Association, which directs the national games taking place each June. From the national competition, the United States team is chosen to compete internationally in the Paralympics, which are held annually in England, with the exception of every fourth year when they are held in the country that hosts the Olympics.

Organizations dealing with specific sports include the American Wheelchair Bowling Association (membership is limited anachronistically to disabled males, although disabled women are encouraged to bowl) and the National Wheelchair Basketball Association. Sports such as archery, weight lifting, swimming, table tennis, and field events are regulated by the National Wheelchair Athletic Association. Not generally known is the fact that hand control flying has become possible since portable hand controls have been approved by the Federal Aviation Administration. There are several organizations active in this sport throughout the country. Camping is promoted by the Committee for the Promotion of Camping for the Handicapped, which will answer problems in this area. (For a listing of sports organizations, see Appendix.)

The sport of skiing has become popular with the physically handicapped. The National Amputee Skiers Association, now known as the National Inconvenienced Sportsmen's Association (3738 Walnut Avenue, Carmichael, California 95608), has as its enlarged purpose to encourage sports among the handicapped throughout the country. In Winter Park, Colorado, there are classes in skiing for amputees, operated out of the Department of Rehabilitation, Children's Hospital, Denver, Colorado 81026. The U.S. Deaf Skiers Association (2 Sunset Hill Rd., Simsbury, Connecticut 06070) plans to institute a deaf-blind skiers program.

Horseback riding for the disabled is still a new concept in America, although such programs have been run successfully for some time in Europe and Great Britain.[18] In 1969 the North American Riding for the Handicapped Association (NARHA) was founded to promote riding as therapy and recreation. The NARHA now has about 60 centers, serving over 5,000 handicapped individuals in the United States and Canada. NARHA has films, guidebooks, and training available for groups considering establishing riding programs for disabled persons. It sets standards for assuring the safety of the riders. Information can be obtained by writing to NARHA, Thistlecroft, Park Street, Mendon, Massachusetts 01756.

A leading authority on teaching the disabled to ride is John A. Davies, now associated with St. James Farm in Warrenville, Illinois. He has written "Reins of Life," on teaching the disabled to ride (available from Davies at St. James Farm, Winfield Farm, Warrenville, Illinois 60555). In 1970 the Cheff Center for the Handicapped was established to teach horseback riding to the handicapped. The booklet "It Is Ability that Counts," written by Lida McCowan, executive director of the center, is available from the Cheff Center (P.O. Box 171, R.R.1, August, Michigan 49012). It includes chapters on training horses and instructors, methods for teaching disabled individuals to ride, recommendations on special equipment, and recruiting volunteers. Two other active centers are Therapeutic Horsemanship, Inc. (Route 1, Valley Road, Pacific, Missouri 63069), and the Berkeley Outreach Recreation Program (BORP) (CIL, Berkeley, California 94704). Other centers may be located through NARHA.

Other Leisure Activities—Outdoor Recreation

Although disabled people have been participating in sports for some time, very little had been done for the furthering of other forms of recreation until, in August 1974, the President's Committee on Employment of the Handicapped and the National Recreation and Park Association cosponsored a national forum on meeting the recreational and park needs of handicapped people. In October 1976, the Architectural and Transportation Barriers Compliance Board held a national hearing, in Boston, Massachusetts, at which the same needs were reiterated. Major problems facing handicapped people in the area of recreation were listed as (1) inaccessibility of facilities and transportation; (2) public attitude; (3) failure of recreation professionals to be ambitious in creating programs; and (4) failure of politicians to commit themselves fully and to follow through.[19]

This hearing recommended further research on exploring the use of outdoor space by disabled persons, development of new equipment and programs, training of qualified recreation leaders, and the dissemination of information. Two computer-based centers now exist for information in this area (they are discussed more fully in Part III). One is TRIC (Therapeutic Recreation Information Center), Department of Recreation and Park Administration, California State Univerity, 6000 J Street, Sacramento, California 95819; and the other is IRUC (Information and Research Utilization Center), sponsored by the American Alliance for Health, Physical Education and Recreation, 1201 16 Street N.W., Washington, D.C.

During the 1977 White House Conference, the topic of leisure fulfillment for the handicapped was given a great deal of attention. Some gains have now been made in accessibility of parks, beaches, cabins, camps, trials for the blind and physically handicapped, and the use of interpreters for the deaf on guided tours. Some special areas (always a controversial topic) have been developed. One outstanding site that librarians can recommend is Will-a-Way Recreation Area for the Handicapped in Fort Yargo State Park, Winder, Georgia 30680, (404) 867-5313.

Will-a-Way is a pilot project made possible by the state of Georgia, the Federal Bureau of Outdoor Recreation, and the Department of the Interior. It includes day-use areas, swimming and fishing, and land sports such as shuffleboard, golf, and horseshoes, family cottages available to the disabled and their families, nature trails, and picnicking. A group camp with a 250-person capacity may be rented by nonprofit organizations serving the handicapped.

Today disabled people are making known their wishes not to be segregated from the general population. Evidence of the progress that has been made can be found in the 1978 edition of *Access National Parks: A Guide for Handicapped Visitors* (No. 024-005-00691-5, National Park Service, Department of the Interior, Washington, D.C., and for sale by Superintendent of Documents). Parks or monuments are described in detail with information about location, telephone numbers, architectural accessibility of visitors centers, overnight accommodations, restroom adaptations, special outdoor trails, and availability of medical services.

The guide is organized by state. A key to the sites is alphabetical with page numbers given. The general information section explains that regional maps and addresses of the regional park service offices are included at the back of the guide. Visitors should decide where they want to go and then write for maps and other information. Most of the park areas at high elevation have oxygen and first-aid equipment available. Some have clients staffed by doctors and nurses. Many have wheelchairs, some electric. Improved exhibits now include contour maps, and many parks have sensory trails and interpreters for deaf visitors. This is a valuable item for vertical files.

THE ARTS AND THE DISABLED

Since the mid-1960s, the National Endowment for the Arts has worked toward the goal of eliminating barriers, both physical and social, that prevent millions of handicapped people from enjoying the arts on a regular and significant basis. In 1975 the National Endowment, with the cooperation of Educational Facilities Laboratories (EFL), published a booklet entitled "Arts and the Handicapped: An Issue of Access." The report describes over 130 programs that eliminate architectural and attitudinal barriers in new facilities and interagency programs that enable the handicapped to participate in the arts. There is still a tremendous gap between services and need, but a great deal of progress has been made.

In 1977 EFL published a packet of material and announced the formation of the National Arts and the Handicapped Information Service, directed by Larry Molloy. Librarians serving physically disabled patrons who are interested in participating in the arts may subscribe to the service without charge and be placed on the mailing list. The project has already developed several reports and bibliographies. Information may be obtained from ARTS, Box 2040, Grand Central Station, New York, New York 10017.

Museums and Handicapped Students: Guidelines for Educators was published by the Smithsonian Institution, with a grant from the Bureau of Education of the Handicapped, HEW, Washington, D.C. (1977). It is available free of charge by writing to: Harold W. Snider, Coordinator, Programs for the Handicapped, Room 3566, National Air and Space Museum, Smithsonian Institution, Washington, D.C. 20560. The booklet surveys the literature on museum programs for handicapped students and federal legislation pertaining to access and the disabled, including access to library materials provided by the Library of Congress/National Library Services for the Blind and Physically Handicapped.

A survey of museum use indicates that over one-half of the physically disabled respondents did not visit museums because of inaccessibility, and over 90 percent of these said they would do so if museums were made accessible. The booklet offers guidelines, including improved accessibility, staff training, programming, and publicity. Special sections on the blind and the deaf are included.

TRAVEL AND TRANSPORTATION

Mobility is a way of life for modern society. Both our work and our recreation often involve travel. Travel and transportation opportunities, important for the disabled as well as for the able-bodied, and for the same reasons, have broadened tremendously in recent years. (See also Chapter 3.)

Handicapped Drivers

The collapsible wheelchair made it possible for disabled people to travel. It was some years later, however, before automobiles were adapted with special controls, enabling handicapped people to drive themselves. In May 1971 the Veterans Administration Prosthetics Center was asked to develop minimum safety and quality standards and test existing equipment. No prior efforts had been made in this area.

In March 1978 the VA published a program guide entitled *Add-on Automobile Adaptive Equipment for Passenger Automobiles.* Standards for controls are given and commercial hand or foot controls evaluated. Many controls are now available, and a listing of manufacturers is included in this section. Each disabled person has individual abilities and must make an individual decision as to what controls will work best.

Most people who are disabled, particularly young people, are now aware that part of their medical rehabilitation, or habilitation (in the case of the congenitally disabled), should have been in this area. Persons whose legs are paralyzed but who have sufficient hand control, or someone with only leg control, can be taught to operate an automobile using special equipment. Classes to train handicapped drivers are now held in many centers. Rehabilitation counselors at offices of rehabilitation should be aware of the location of these classes.

An increased interest in this area has resulted in many new developments. The Association of Driver Educators for the Disabled (ADED) was organized in August 1977 to provide continuing education for those working in the field. As the organization grows, it plans to conduct workshops and hold annual meetings. ADED publishes a quarterly newsletter, which includes reports from members across the country, articles on new developments, and announcements of upcoming meetings. Membership is $15 per year. Write to Dorothy Beard, ADED, Texas Institute for Rehabilitation, 2307 Arbor, Houston, Texas 77004.

The American Automobile Association has published a 78-page booklet entitled *The Handicapped Driver's Mobility Guide*, with descriptions of over 500 transportation services available to handicapped persons through a variety of organizations. Among the services listed are driving schools in the United States that are prepared to work with handicapped drivers and manufacturers of adaptive equipment, with names, addresses, and telephone numbers for each listing.

The University of Wisconsin at Stout sponsors a driver education program for the handicapped, plus in-service teacher education through its safety center. The center is willing to distribute its instructors' manual to anyone wishing to set up a program. Contact Safety Center, University of Wisconsin, Stout, Wisconsin, 54751.

Driving for the Physically Handicapped, a manual developed by the Department of Occupational Therapy at the University of Southern California, tells how to establish driver training programs and describes its program at Ranchos Los Amigos Hospital. It is available from Dorothy Wilson, Department of Occupation Therapy, Ranchos Los Amigos Hospital, 7601 East Imperial Highway, Downey, California 90242.

Disabled adults may come to the library for information about commercially available devices or about vans that can be adapted with automated lifts for those persons who cannot leave their wheelchairs (see Appendix).

Studies made during the 1970s have shown that state governments, which control driver licensing, do not have standard rulings for issuing licenses to disabled drivers. However, in most cases, reasonable standards are followed. If during the road test the disabled person demonstrates the ability to control a vehicle safely, licenses are issued without problems.

The handicapped driver who is planning an extended trip may wish to consult *Highway Rest Areas for Handicapped Travelers*, published by the President's Committee on Employment of the Handicapped (Washington, D.C. 20210). The committee states that since this book was first published the number of accessible rest stops has doubled. The present edition contains over 800 accessible rest areas in 48 states. They are designated, as many travelers may have noticed, by a blue and white sign bearing the international symbol of access. The committee is attempting to keep this information up-to-date with the help of the Federal Highway Administration through the state highway departments. Newly constructed highway rest areas, in compliance with new laws, must be accessible to the disabled.

Travel

There have been for some time travel guide listings for the handicapped to cities in the United States and abroad. These guides supply information about architecturally accessible hotels, motels, restaurants, and public buildings. Handy guides have appeared annually for over ten years. Tours for the handicapped, organized by people knowledgeable about problems encountered by disabled persons who wish to travel for pleasure, have also existed for a long time. But now there is much greater movement than ever before. Airlines, trains, and buses are all making accommodations for the handicapped traveler.

Louise Weiss's *Access to the World: A Travel Guide for the Handicapped* (New York: Chatham Square Press, 1977) gives recognition to the fact that the ability to travel is a matter of access to the same extent as is the elimination of architectural barriers. It is worthwhile, although not perfect; it is said to contain some inaccuracies about a number of places mentioned as accessible. Weiss has, however, done research, and presents all of the information the handicapped traveler will need to plan a trip. She describes the most recent airlines regulations for the disabled, including boarding, wheelchair handling, medical certification, and companions. Also included are lists of special diets available on all airlines, a source directory of addresses not otherwise available, and a chart listing the architectural features of many airport terminals.

Tips for bus, train, and ship travel are handled in the same thorough manner. In a chapter on automobiles and recreational vehicles, the author gives toll-free numbers to call to rent cars with hand controls from Avis, Hertz, and National. She also says that it is possible to rent a car with hand controls in Honolulu and Australia, but not in the British Isles, Europe, or Canada. Such specific information is invaluable to the handicapped traveler. Recreational vehicles or vans that can be adapted to carry wheelchairs are described, and addresses of manufacturers supplied.

Also listed are access guides for many cities in the United States and overseas. These guides are good to have in the library for the home city, as well as for such likely tourist places as New York City, Washington, D.C., San Francisco, and London. It is, however, sometimes sufficient to inform a patron that such a guide exists and is available before he or she takes a trip. This is easier than trying to keep an updated file of all city guides.

Weiss also supplies the names of travel guides that specialize in handling reservations for the disabled and lists special tours available for those wishing to travel with a group. Finally, there is advice about how to cope with health problems, tips on handling luggage, packing, special clothing, and other handy hints that will contribute greatly to the comfort of the disabled traveler.

A handy companion guide is *The Wheelchair Traveler* by Douglass R. Annand, a paraplegic.[20] He has been traveling extensively and issuing the guide for many years. A library that buys this guide should try to keep the editions updated, if not every year, at least every other year. Nothing will discourage a disabled person more quickly than outdated reference information.

Annand checks his sources personally and also lists information supplied by other trusted handicapped travelers and a variety of knowledgeable groups. Many of the subjects covered in *Access to the World* are touched upon in *The Wheelchair Traveler*, but in much abbreviated form. Its major value is its more than 3,500 listings for the 50 states, Canada, Mexico, Puerto Rico, and other areas for hotels, motels, restaurants, and sightseeing attractions for the handicapped traveler. These are coded for architectural accessibility, specifically for such features as overhead bed trapezes, support bars, restaurant accessibility, bedside telephones, bed heights, and bathroom adaptability. Most recent rates are given when they can be established.

The Department of Commerce has published a handy packet of pamphlets (write to Consumer Information, U.S. Travel Services of the Department of Commerce, Washington, D.C. 20230). The packet includes *Travel Tips for the Handicapped*, which describes briefly the Federal Aviation Administration, Amtrak, and National Bus Line regulations. Better still, it supplies the names and addresses of consumer or handicapped information persons in each airline, train, or bus line who can give the most up-to-date data on all aspects of travel for the disabled. Since things are changing so rapidly in this field, the wise librarian should have on hand these sources of information in order to advise patrons to make their own calls and find out exactly what they must do ahead of time when planning to take a trip.

The pamphlet also supplies the names and addresses of large motel chains such as Holiday Inn, Howard Johnson, Quality and Ramada inns, and the Hilton, Hyatt, and Sheraton hotels, all of which have made some adaptations for the handicapped traveler.

Some of the other titles in the packet are *Benefits of Using a Travel Agent*, *Helpful Hints for the Older Traveler*, *Traveling with Pets*, and *Helpful Information Sources*, which is a handy listing of national parks and tourism offices in the 50 states. Sometimes a search for information for the handicapped traveler turns up data for library pamphlet files that will benefit all patrons who travel, and this little packet proves the point.

Librarians who want more pamphlet information in their reference files may order *Access Amtrak*, a guide to Amtrak services for elderly and handicapped travelers (available from the National Rail Road Passenger Corporation, 955 L'Enfant Plaza S.W., Washington, D.C. 20024). The preface, stating that new Amfleet cars and turbolines are equipped to serve handicapped travelers on "most of Amtrak's short to medium distance routes" and that "over 60 stations have been built or renovated for barrier-free access," gives the impression more has been done than is actually so. The intentions are certainly there, as well as the will to comply with the equal access laws. However, close perusal indicates that of Amtrak's 524 stations, although many are barrier-free, others have barriers ranging from one curb to flights of stairs. All are scheduled for renovation and new access stations are being built. Also, although there is no entry problem to the Metroliner and to most other trains along the New York/Washington run, throughout the rest of the country, there may be as many as four steep steps to board trains. The pamphlet does state that a loading chair is being tested in the Seattle area and a hydraulic-lift chair is being tested for use at major stations.

The pamphlet describes and offers floor plans for different types of trains operated by Amtrak, the advantages and disadvantages to handicapped travelers, and what arrangements can be made. Charts of the measurements of door and aisle widths are useful. The answer seems to be to call ahead to plan a trip. Toll-free numbers are listed in all local area telephone books under Amtrak.

Access Travel: Airports (2nd ed., October 1977) is available from the Consumer Information Center, Pueblo, Colorado 81009. The format of this pamphlet is a chart listing airports all over the world and indicating their accessibility. Librarians will also find this information in *Access to the World*. However, *Access Travel* offers the charts in a much larger, more readable format, which makes them easy to machine copy. Additional copies would be a handy addition to vertical files.

Another organization formed to aid the handicapped traveler is the Society for the Advancement of Travel for the Handicapped (SATH). A nonprofit association made up of many persons and organizations associated in some way with travel for the disabled, SATH's main address is 26 Court Street, Brooklyn, New York 11242. The association issues a newsletter, and one copy, for instance, was full of information for the disabled traveler, including aid for traveling diabetics. Area chapters are being set up. The newsletter might be well worth its cost. However, librarians are asked to inquire about this directly to the organization.

PUBLIC LIBRARY PROGRAMS

Many libraries operate active outreach programs, serving disabled readers with recreational reading materials in book or alternative format under the mandate of the National Library Services for the Blind and Physically Handicapped of the Library of Congress, or with books needed for academic or other work. In addition, a number of librarians have already begun to acquire a great deal of the reference information outlined in this chapter in answer to requests.

It is not the purpose of this book to discuss outreach and like programs. Most librarians are aware that physically disabled people have the same recreational reading tastes as their able-bodied peers. Although a book may sometimes prove inspirational, in most cases disabled people are interested in well-written books that depict the human condition in all its aspects, through good fiction, nonfiction, or biography. Offering a disabled person a book about someone with a disability, unless it is in response to a request, is presumptuous and to be avoided. In addition to recreational reading, many disabled people need the library (and will be needing it more and more as they enter the marketplace in greater numbers) for professional reading materials. All of these needs can be handled easily by the professional librarian once architectural barriers are eliminated and disabled people are able to get into the buildings.

The intent of Chapters 3 and 4 is to discuss the special informational needs of the disabled. In Chapter 8, a core reference collection is suggested for public libraries.

A question very often asked by public librarians is how they can reach the disabled people who live in their communities, but who are not using the library. As with any other library user, the physically disabled person sometimes must be lured to the library with a little extra effort. Some librarians have found that after building what they consider to be an accessible library, physically disabled patrons still do not appear. In one such library, it was found that no reserved parking had been provided for the disabled.

Following are suggestions that may encourage greater library use by the physically disabled.

1. Wherever possible, when planning architectural adaptations, include disabled people on the planning team to ensure that alterations are feasible (see Chapter 5 for helpful sources of information when planning to adapt facilities).

2. Publicize. After physical adaptations have been made to the library building, a news story in the local press may spark interest.

3. Set aside two or three reserved parking spots (see Chapter 5) appropriately marked with the symbol of access or a sign stating "reserved for the handicapped." This in itself is an advertisement to the community that the library staff is aware that disabled people are part of the population and that the library is anxious to serve them.

4. A newsletter is an excellent way to publicize what the library has to offer and can be sent legitimately to all homes in the area. One of the most difficult things to find out is actual names of disabled people living within a district. It may even be a violation of privacy to do this. Moreover, it is impossible to judge to what extent an individual perceives him- or herself to be disabled. Elderly or infirm people may also benefit from some of the materials acquired or the architectural modifications made. The newsletter might mention the acquisition of some of the reference materials already suggested. In addition, an item in the local press, indicating that a special collection is being developed in this area, may bring patrons in or to the telephone.

5. Club activities sometimes bring surprising results. In one public library, the reference librarian had an interest in CB radios and started a hobby club. Four teenagers in wheelchairs arrived to attend the first meeting.[21]

6. Children's librarians will find much of the reference information in this chapter helpful in answering questions raised by the parents of disabled youngsters. In addition, efforts can be made by children's librarians to determine which special schools in their areas do not have librarians, and they can offer to develop story hours or help teachers acquire special materials. (See Part IV for specific suggestions.)

7. Above all, librarians must be aware of what can and cannot be answered by supplying a book. It is important to make sure that the patron has had appropriate medical information. For example, in the case of low back pain symptoms, books containing exercises will not help unless the specific problem has been diagnosed and the exercises prescribed or approved by a physician. Persons seeking information that is rehabilitative in nature should be referred first of all to a rehabilitation facility. If the person is disabled, the local vocational rehabilitation office should be suggested, where a rehabilitation counselor can make the proper referral.

WHERE THE MONEY IS

Many libraries are hard pressed to stay within their limited budgets and do not have the staff to send to shut-in people or to service local hospitals or nursing homes as appropriately as they wish. Deposit collections, once considered sufficient, are only the beginning when one thinks of the personal information and reading guidance services that could be rendered with proper staff and budget. In today's society, money for special projects is often raised by applying for grants, either from the public sector or private foundations. There is money available today for projects that would be of benefit to disabled people. Grantsmanship is a business, and it helps to have expert advice. If a library director, or someone else on the staff, is designated as the grant-writing person, he or she might welcome ideas for special projects for library service to disabled patrons.

Public libraries wishing to apply for government funds can do so under the Library Service Construction Act (LSCA), which, under Title 1, offers money for special projects for the handicapped.[22] The monograph *Library Programs Worth Knowing About* (September 1977), published jointly by the U.S. Office of Education, Bureau of Elementary and Secondary Education, Office of Libraries and Learning Resources, and the Chief Officers of State Library Agencies, tells about 62 projects originally funded under LSCA. Several of the projects involved services to one or another segment of the handicapped population. Either this booklet, or an update of it, should be most useful in generating ideas for special projects. Write to State and Public Library Services Branch, Office of Libraries and Learning Resources, Seventh and D Streets S.W., Room 3124, Washington, D.C., 20202.

Both the *Federal Register* and *Commerce Business Daily* list requests for proposals when money is available for special projects. If your library actively seeks government funding, both of these publications should be obtained. In addition, the publication *Federal Assistance for Programs Serving the Handicapped*, HEW Publication No. (CHD) 77-22001, Office for Handicapped Individuals (1977), is available or may have been updated. Program descriptions and sponsoring agencies are followed by a good listing of publications on grantsmanship and addresses of state special education programs, Title 20 programs, "crippled children's services," as well as state vocational rehabilitation programs and program services for the blind and visually impaired.

Money for programs for the disabled may also be available through auxiliary acts such as the Comprehensive Employment and Training Act (CETA) of 1973 (PL 93-203). Such funds might be utilized to obtain library aides to assist in special programs.[23]

Private funds are also available. The Foundation Center (888 Seventh Avenue, New York, New York 10019) analyzes and disseminates facts on philanthropic foundations. It publishes the *Foundation Directory* (annual) and *Foundation Grants Index* (annual), both offering information on the special interests of private foundations and those that might be interested in funding projects for the disabled. The Foundation Center also provides Comsearch, an annual computer printout of grants arranged by field of interest, in paper and fiche. Reference librarians at the Foundation Center in New York City and Washington, D.C., are available to provide free information, and their materials are also available at 60 cooperating libraries.

The Handicapped Funding Directory, Burton J. Eckstein, editor (Research Grant Guides, P.O. Box 357, Oceanside, New York 11572, 1978–1979) might be of help in looking for funds. It has many drawbacks as a directory; it is not comprehensive and foundations are arbitrarily chosen and listed, with only a modicum of information. Most of the material is obtainable from other publications. However, it does bring together in one book information about funding sources, associations, foundations, and federal agencies interested in funding programs for disabled people.

There are, in addition, two essays in the directory, one by R. E. Mason, which is on proposal writing, and one by Dr. Pierre Wong, on evaluation tips.

SUMMARY

There is nothing so important to disabled adults, and to the parents of disabled children, as information in all areas of daily living. Often this information is difficult to obtain. Many changes are taking place in the fields of rehabilitation engineering research and education and employment of the disabled. These changes will enable disabled people to function as active members of society. Public librarians who are the first-line information officers for the general public will be seeing more and more of this new client population. School librarians will be seeing many more physically disabled children. Institution and hospital librarians and those going into the relatively new field of rehabilitation librarianship will find it necessary to keep abreast of new advances in this fast-moving field.

NOTES

1. Sister Kenny Institute Staff, *Wheelchair Selection: More than Choosing a Chair with Wheels*, rev. ed., Rehabilitation Publication No. 713 (Minneapolis: Sister Kenny Institute, 1977).

2. Veronica Washam, *The One Hander's Book: Helpful Hints for Activities of Daily Living* (New York: John Day, 1973).

3. Elizabeth Eckhardt May, Neva R. Waggoner, and Eleanor Boettke Hotte, *Independent Living for the Handicapped and the Elderly* (Boston: Houghton Mifflin, 1974), Chapter 8.

4. Ibid., p. 211.

5. Gini Laurie, *Housing and Home Services for the Disabled: Guidelines and Experiences in Independent Living* (New York: Harper & Row, 1977).

6. Ibid., p. 11.

7. Miriam Bowar Strebel, R.N., O.T.R., *Adaptations and Techniques for the Disabled Homemaker*, 5th ed., Rehabilitation Publication No. 710 (Minneapolis: Sister Kenny Institute, 1978).

8. Judith Lannefeld Klinger, O.T.R., M.A., with the Institute of Rehabilitation Medicine, New York University Medical Center and Campbell Soup Company. *The Mealtime Manual for People with Disabilities and the Aging*, 2nd ed. (Camden, N.J.: Campbell Soup Company, 1978).

9. Susan Pflueger, "Independent Living, Emerging Issues in Rehabilitation," Institute for Research Utilization, Washington, D.C. (1977), p. 52.

10. Ibid., pp. 11–13.

11. Laurie, *Housing*, p. 373.

12. Ibid., p. 132.

13. Paul Corcoran, M.D. et al., "BCIL Report: A Summary of the First Three Years of the Boston Center for Independent Living, Inc.," a transitional living program for persons with physical disabilities, Peter Reich, ed., Department of Health, Education, and Welfare, Office of Human Development, Rehabilitation Services Administration, published by Boston Regional Medical Rehabilitation Research and Training Center, No. 7. Tufts/New England Medical Center, Boston, Mass. (1977).

14. Pflueger, "Independent Living," pp. 22, 24.

15. Ibid., p. 47.

16. St. Andrews Presbyterian College, "Mobile Homes: Alternative Housing for the Handicapped," Laurinburg, N.C., U.S. Department of Housing and Urban Development, Office of Policy Development and Research, Washington, D.C., Sudoc No. 0-235-962 (1977).

17. *Communication Outlook*, Artificial Language Laboratory, Computer Science Department, Michigan State University, East Lansing, Mich. 48824.

18. "Disabled on Horseback," in *Accent on Living* (Summer 1978).

19. Frederick A. Fay, Ph.D. and Janet Minch, M. A., "Access to Recreation: A Report on the National Hearing on Recreation for Handicapped Persons," for Architectural and Transportation Barriers Compliance Board, Department of Health, Education, and Welfare, Office of Human Development, Rehabilitation Services Administration, published by Tufts/New England Medical Center, Medical Rehabilitation Research and Training Center, No. 7, proceedings of conference held October 1976.

20. Douglass R. Annand, *The Wheelchair Traveler* (Milford, N.H.: author, updated yearly).

21. Public Library, Port Washington, New York.

22. "Grants and How to Get Them, an Update," in *American Libraries* (November 1977), based on bibliography by Sara Case for the 1977 annual American Library Association conference. (Updated by Case but not comprehensive, according to author.)

23. Ibid.

5
Barrier-Free Design
for Libraries

For too long disabled people have accepted exclusion from society simply on the basis of "not being able to get in the door." Able-bodied Americans have been largely insensitive to the fact that architectural barriers have prevented many people from participating in such life-sustaining activities as shopping, such pleasurable activities as going to the theater or a concert or traveling, and such academic activities as going to school. Many libraries, which are the source of much recreational reading pleasure as well as essential information, have been part of this dismal picture. However, librarians have begun to realize that even if Section 504 of PL 93-112 did not mandate architectural modifications under certain conditions, their public duty to a large segment of the population makes it imperative that they try to modify their premises so that disabled people *can* get in the door.

Numerous guides have been published offering information for architectural modification of public buildings, but very few discuss libraries specifically. The American National Standards Institute published its original specifications for the elimination of architectural barriers in 1961.[1] Known as ANSI Standards, they have been under revision for several years and are due for publication. Watch for them. When they appear, the National Center for a Barrier Free Environment in Washington, D.C., plans a series of conferences to explain the provisions and implications. These meetings will be designed to assist architects, designers, and others as they try to provide architectural accessibility.[2]

Schools of architecture must begin to offer additions to present courses as well as special course work in this fairly new area. Librarians who serve such schools should be compiling files now to be ready with the reference materials that will surely be requested. (See the bibliographies in Chapters 8 and 11 for help in gathering these materials. Additional specialized information for school and academic librarians can be found in Chapter 14.)

Some basic guidelines are listed here to help librarians who wish to begin modifying their facilities. Until the revised ANSI standards appear, the dimensions indicated do not represent nationally accepted requirements, but they are recommended by the National Center for a Barrier Free Environment and by the General Services Administration as generally acceptable standard measurements that have been tested through use.

Information for libraries wishing to modify facilities is required in two areas: (1) general information, which is necessary for all public buildings, such as wheelchair measurements, curb cuts, parking areas, ramps, door widths and thresholds, rest rooms, telephones and elevators, and corridor widths and floor space; and (2) specific requirements for libraries, including stack widths, reference table and carrel heights, and optimum heights for circulation desks and card catalogues.

The population for which adjustments must be made includes

1. Nonambulatory disabled; those with permanent or temporary injury with some degree of paralysis to lower and/or upper limbs.
2. Semiambulatory disabled; persons who walk with difficulty, including people using crutches, braces, walkers, amputees, people with pulmonary or cardiac ailments, and arthritics.
3. People with neuromuscular impairments, which may cause lack of control and/or faulty coordination.
4. Blind or visually impaired people.
5. Deaf or hearing impaired people.
6. Disabled people due to aging.[3]

STANDARDS FOR BARRIER-FREE DESIGN

The general information that follows is culled from the original ANSI Standards, as well as from the many guides published in recent years.

The standard model collapsible wheelchair of tubular metal construction most commonly in use is 42 inches long (see Figure 1), 25 inches wide when open, and has a fixed turning radius of 18 inches wheel to wheel and 31.5 inches from front to rear structure. Average turning space is 60 × 60 inches. A minimum width of 60 inches is required for two individuals in wheelchairs to pass each other.

In parking areas, spaces that are accessible and close to the building should be set aside and identified for people with disabilities. An area at least 12 feet wide is adequate and provides room for a disabled person to get out of the car and into a wheelchair. This is about the width of a regular parking space plus an area of approximately 4 feet next to it, preferably

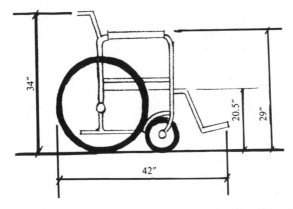

FIGURE 1. Average measurements for standard collapsible wheelchair.

crosshatched so that it is obviously designated as a "no parking" space for another car (Figure 2). There should be a passageway so that the disabled person need not wheel or walk behind other parked cars, as well as curb cuts and ramps into the building (Figure 3).

Ramps may not have a slope greater than one rise in 12 feet and must

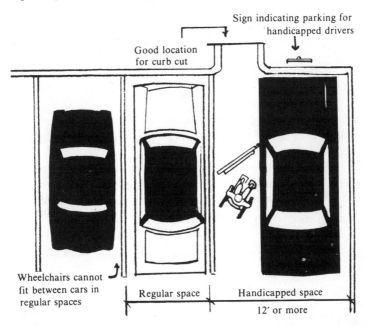

FIGURE 2. Parking for the handicapped person may be perpendicular, as above, diagonal, or parallel to the curb. For parallel parking, the curb and sidewalk on the right side of the car is preferred. Two percent of the total number of parking spaces, or a minimum of one space, should be set aside for physically disabled patrons.

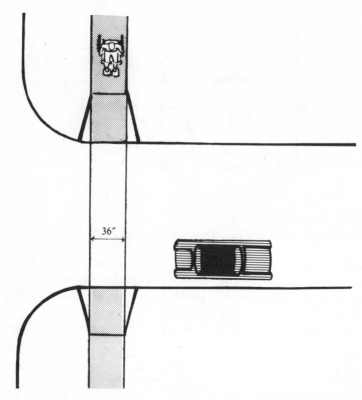

FIGURE 3. Walkways and ramps should align across the roadway. Ramps and walkway should be at least 36 inches wide; curb height should not exceed 6 inches.

have a handrail on at least one side where the rise is greater than 10 feet, as well as a level area at the top at least 4 feet square, large enough for entry by a wheelchair (Figures 4 and 5).

At least one primary entrance to the building shall be usable by persons in wheelchairs, doors to be no less than 32 inches wide, easy to operate (no heavier than 10 pounds of pressure), with a see-through panel if possible, as well as a kickplate from the bottom of the door to at least 16 inches from

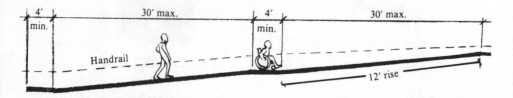

FIGURE 4. The maximum length of the ramp between platforms is 30 feet.

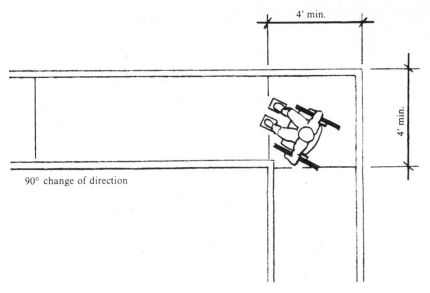

FIGURE 5. A 4-foot-square platform is needed wherever there is a change of direction on a ramp since it is very difficult to turn a wheelchair on a ramp slope.

the floor, made of a material to withstand wear and tear from bumps by wheelchair foot pedals or wheels or crutches. Thresholds should be flush with the floor, and abrupt changes in level should be avoided at the entrance. Figure 6 shows maneuverability of wheelchairs on push side of door, side approach.

Switches and controls for lights, heat, ventilation, windows, draperies, fire alarms, and all similar controls of frequent or essential use should be

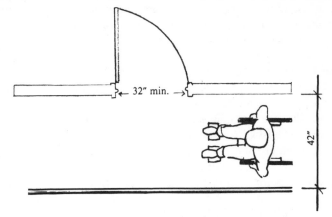

FIGURE 6. Maneuvering space on push side of door, side approach; minimum of 42 inches for corridor or walk width.

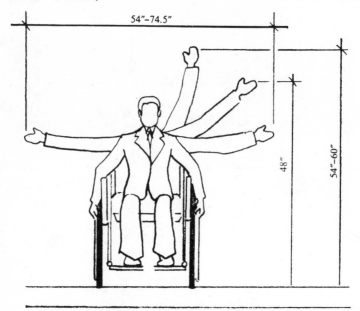

54"–74.5"

48"

54"–60"

FIGURE 7. Area of reach from a wheelchair.

placed within reach of individuals in wheelchairs (at a maximum height of 48 inches, see Figure 7). Raised letters and numbers to identify offices, reading rooms, or stacks should be placed conveniently at about 5-foot height for the use of blind persons. Doors that might lead to areas not intended for use, or dangerous, should be identified by knurled door knobs or handles. Audible and visual warning signals should be installed for blind and deaf persons. Low hanging signs, ceiling lights, and other objects that protrude in corridors or traffic ways should be avoided. A minimum height of 7 feet from the floor is recommended. Maps with raised features or letters showing locations of materials are useful for blind patrons.

In the March/April 1979 issue of *The Report*, Samuel Genensky, director of the Center for the Partially Sighted of the Santa Monica Hospital Medical Center, Santa Monica, California, and national president of the Council of Citizens with Low Vision, has written about architectural barriers for persons who are partially sighted. The two most formidable barriers, according to Genensky, are stairs and locating public rest rooms and then determining whether they are for men or women. He recommends marking 2-inch-wide strips on the leading edges of stairs, on both the runner and the riser, with a paint or nonskid material that has a color and gray value in high contrast to the color and gray value of the rest of the stairs. Rest rooms should be marked with protruding panels on the exterior face of the doors, about 2 feet square and $\frac{1}{4}$ inch thick. The men's rest room

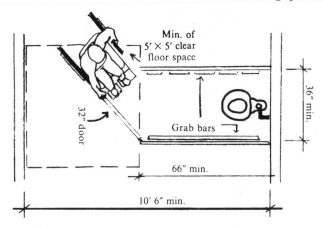

FIGURE 8. Dimensions for rest room stall, which should have grab bars on both sides.

panel should be one simple geometric shape (for example, rectangle) and the one on the women's rest room door should be a distinctly different shape (perhaps a circle). These panels should also be of distinctly different colors and gray values from each other and from the doors on which they are mounted.[4]

Rest rooms (Figure 8), telephones, and elevators (Figure 9) should be made accessible by providing appropriate space and fixtures, and in the case of elevators, audible signals, whenever possible, for blind patrons. Existing rest room stalls can, in some instances, be modified at little cost. If the stall is wide enough to accommodate a wheelchair, the door and door jams may be removed and a full curtain substituted for privacy.

LIBRARY ADAPTATIONS

In some cases, providing access to the library building and personal service thereafter may be all that a very old and inaccessible library can accomplish until adequate funding or a new building allows for greater improvements. Access to the building, or even an alternate service such as a bookmobile or home delivery of books, is all that is required by law, according to policy 3 issued by the Office of Civil Rights as one of six interpretations relating to Section 504.[5]

In many cases, however, it will be possible for libraries to improve access to reading areas, circulation desk, and book stacks (see Figure 10). The card catalogue, an essential tool, may be made accessible by lowering the base; however, removing a drawer and placing it on a low table may serve as a viable alternative. An able-bodied patron might be happy to perform this function should a librarian not be readily available. When li-

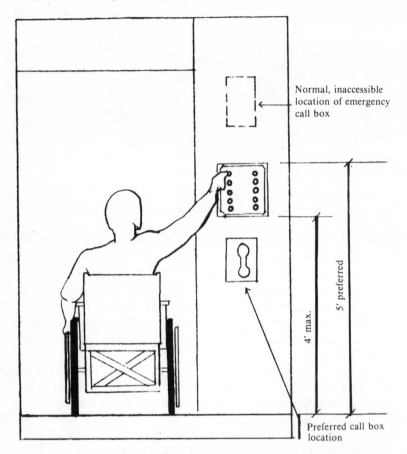

FIGURE 9. Bottom of elevator control panel should be no higher than 4 feet, with the panel top no higher than 5 feet (average highest reach from a wheelchair is 5 feet, as shown in Figure 7). Elevator controls should be pushbuttons with raised letters.

brarians realize how much more there is to library service than home delivery of books, they will certainly wish to make all the adaptations they can possibly afford to allow disabled people to take part in all library activities.

The General Services Administration, Public Building Service, in *Design Criteria: New Public Building Accessibility* (December 1977; available from the GSA Business Service Center in local areas), provides several pages of recommendations for libraries. They suggest locating card files 18 to 48 inches from the floor with a 36-inch maximum height preferred. An adjacent work surface should be 29 inches from the floor. Checkout counters and information desks should be no higher than 36 inches from the floor.

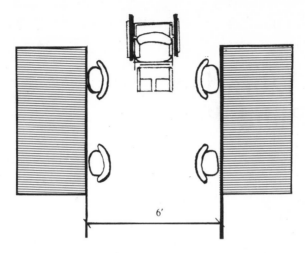

FIGURE 10. Area between library tables should be at least 6 feet for easy passage.

Tables should be 29 inches from the floor and apronless or with recessed aprons. Carrels should be 29 inches from the floor, a minimum of 30 inches wide, with a preferred width of 34 inches and a 20-inch depth.

NOTES

1. American National Standards, specifications for making buildings and facilities accessible to, and usable by, the physically handicapped, American National Standards Institute, New York, distributed by Easter Seal Society, Chicago, Ill. (1961, under revision).
2. National Center for a Barrier Free Environment, *The Report*, Washington, D.C. (Nov./Dec. 1978), p. 7.
3. American National Standards (ANSI).
4. *The Report* (March/April 1979), p. 8.
5. *Federal Register*, August 7, 1978, Office of Civil Rights policy interpretation, No. 3 of Section 504 of the Rehabilitation Act of 1973.

6

The Librarian and the Blind Patron

When I told my friend Lawrence,[1] ordinarily a humane and thoughtful person, that I was writing a paper on improving library service for the blind, he shot back: "Hanan, providing library service for the blind is like teaching a one-legged person to ski!" Well, Lawrence, it so happens that one-legged persons *do* ski, balancing themselves with tiny outrigger skis fastened to the ends of their ski poles. Moreover, even the blind can ski—not only cross-country but also downhill, relying on a trained, sighted guide who skis a few paces behind the blind skier and shouts instructions as needed.[2]

Making it possible for the blind to use libraries has several important things in common with teaching the blind to ski. To make this assertion convincing, it will be useful to take a more abstract look at the process by which a blind person can read the books in a library.

A CONCEPTUAL SCHEME FOR UNDERSTANDING ACCESS TO LIBRARIES

When sighted people try to understand what it means to be blind, they often close their eyes for a few moments or, if they are determined to make a serious effort, they even may put on a blindfold for periods up to a day. Unfortunately, this praiseworthy effort at empathy is doomed to fail, for the sighted person who incurs some difficulty in this experiment has only to

Hanan C. Selvin, Ph.D., professor of sociology at the State University of New York at Stony Brook, is the author of this chapter.

open his or her eyes or remove the blindfold. It is this very inability to leap in an instant from blindness to sight that is at the psychological core of blindness.[3]

Instead of trying to achieve such an unattainable state, it will be more useful for librarians to understand the theoretical elements of the process by which the blind, or those unable to read typical print—the dyslexics and physically injured persons unable to hold an ordinary book or turn its pages—are able to make use of the printed material in an ordinary library.

1. The *information* contained in the library, usually in the form of print
2. A *transducer*—a person, device, or system by which material intended to be perceived through one sense (here, vision) is transformed in such a way that it can be perceived through another sense (hearing or touch)
3. A *blind user* with the training and attitudes needed for effective use of the information and the transducer(s)
4. A library that can provide the necessary *support* personnel, facilities, and equipment

Fitting these four elements together in ways that will make a library truly accessible to blind users takes thought, determination, and money— the first two from both the user and the library staff and the last from the institution of which the library is a part. Some suggestions and information for the user are offered below, after which are some suggestions for the staff.[4]

The Heart of the Matter

As Robert A. Scott put it in *The Making of Blind Men,*[5] blindness is more a *learned social role* than a physical condition. Of course, only those who have the physical condition need to learn that role, but the way in which they behave and the way others behave toward them depend more on their ideas of blindness than on the physical condition itself.

If one defines blindness as a supreme catastrophe, the worst thing that can happen, then the only rational sequel is suicide. If, however, one defines blindness as a nuisance that can be circumvented or overcome with appropriate gadgetry, training, and thought, then being blind is not the worst of all possible fates. In short, life as a blind person is what one makes of it.

Getting into the "Blindness System"

The "blindness system" is all of those people, agencies, facilities, laws, and other aspects of culture and society that have to do with sight and blindness. Anyone reading this chapter has already made some contact with that system, but a more formal and prolonged contact is necessary to reap its full benefits.

Legal Blindness

Relatively slight defects in sight may deprive one of certain rights, such as a license to drive a car or pilot a plane, but the condition of being legally blind is something else again. The precise definition may be left to an ophthalmologist (medical doctor specially trained to deal with problems of vision) or optometrist (a paramedical practitioner licensed to prescribe and sell glasses), but it may be useful for those approaching legal blindness to have at least a rough idea of what it means.

There are two different sets of legally blind conditions, usually known as *visual acuity* and *visual field*. One is legally blind if one's acuity is insufficient for reading ordinary newsprint even with glasses or in the terms of the familiar fraction whose value is 20/20 for normal sight; if one's central vision is less than 20/200; or if one's visual field is less than 20 degrees.[6]

The precise measurement of visual field is difficult, but you can easily test your own visual field to see whether or not it is normal. Hold your hands about 6 inches from your ears and, while staring straight ahead, wiggle your fingers. The normal visual field is slightly more than 180 degrees. Thus, if your field is normal, you should be able to see both sets of fingers wiggling while you are staring straight ahead.

If you cannot, try the following: Hold one arm straight ahead, fully extended, with your thumb and forefinger as far apart as possible. The angle formed by the tip of your thumb, your eye (do this with one eye at a time), and the tip of your forefinger is about 15 degrees. If you cannot see both tips at the same time, you are probably well below the visual field that is legal blindness.

Unlike a decline in acuity, which is usually obvious, declines in visual field are insidious and may go undetected for many years. If you think that your visual field may be impaired, take yourself to an ophthalmologist or optometrist for a precise measurement. And don't put it off; some of the causes of blindness are easily treated, others are not, but you ought to know the score right away.

All right, then, assuming that you *are* legally blind, get a statement in writing to this effect from your ophthalmologist or optometrist. Make several copies of this letter and put the original in a safe place, preferably a bank vault.

What do you do with these documents? First, attach one to your next income tax return, and be sure to claim the additional exemption that legal blindness confers. That alone should more than pay for the cost of the visit to the ophthalmologist or optometrist. If your condition is irreversible (if there is no way in which medicine, surgery, or glasses can restore your sight to normal), have your specialist say so, and this one certification will satisfy the IRS for the rest of your life; you will not need to include it in subsequent returns.

You will need a second copy to get rehabilitation training through your state's division of vocational rehabilitation (or whatever the functional equivalent of this is called in your state). You will need a third copy to get books from Recording for the Blind, Inc., the main source of recorded textbooks and technical books, and still another copy to get reproducers and books from the National Library Service for the Blind and Physically Handicapped of the Library of Congress, which are available in each state through regional libraries and subregional libraries (see Books and Magazines later in this chapter).

Rehabilitation: The Magic Wand

The following remarks apply to those who would be able to be in the labor force except for difficulties of vision. If you are over 65 years of age, you are defined by the government as being outside the labor force and therefore not capable of vocational rehabilitation. Similarly, if you have multiple handicaps, such as motor disabilities (inability to get around by yourself) or other sensory impairments (being deaf as well as blind), you may need to be put in touch with more specialized agencies. Most social workers and counselors in agencies serving the blind should be able to refer you to such specialized agencies.

If you are legally blind, by all means go to the nearest rehabilitation agency and inquire into what can be done for you. Don't assume that you already know what can be done. You don't! I remember saying to myself before my first visit that I didn't want to have anything to do with the long white cane because *that* was an obvious symbol of blindness and I still had enough residual vision to classify myself as being "other than blind."

I was wrong on two counts. First, I underestimated the speed with which my residual vision would deteriorate to the point where even I could no longer rationalize my condition as being other than blindness. Second, I entirely misunderstood what the long cane would do for me. It does identify me as being blind, but its function is much more than stigmatizing. For one thing, it allows me to claim services that I need from the sighted people around me. Holding my cane where it is clearly visible to oncoming pedestrians, I can ask the first one to help me cross a busy street, find the right subway platform, and so on. In short, the long cane is a license to ask for the special help that the blind need and that the sighted usually provide cheerfully.

Of course, the long cane has even more important uses. Again, my own experience may be illuminating here. Although I know midtown Manhattan as well as I know the streets of Stony Brook (New York)—probably even better, since I learned the layout of Stony Brook after my sight had deteriorated appreciably—I had come to the point where simply walking down a midtown street was too dangerous. I would bump into lampposts, step off curbs inadvertently, and occasionally find myself falling down the entrance to a subway (fortunately, I was able to right myself in time).

With the long cane, properly used, none of these things troubles me any longer. In short, I am able to move about in familiar places almost as well as a sighted person. Manhattan now poses only two small difficulties for me: I must ask the help of sighted passersby to identify the number of the building that I want and I must ask for help in crossing a street.

In situations where the ambient noise level is lower, such as most small towns and cities, I am able to cross streets by listening for the sound of oncoming traffic. Unfortunately that option is not available in noisy places like midtown Manhattan. Perhaps someday the environmental movement will have quieted Manhattan down to the point where this option is open to the blind.

One last word about the long cane: You must be *taught* to use it properly. The training takes only a few weeks, but there are many important details that you cannot figure out by yourself. Indeed, many of these details are literally matters of life and death; to have to work out all of them for yourself would be far too dangerous.

There is much more to rehabilitation than the long cane. Depending on the financial condition of your state and on what you need to complete your rehabilitation and/or education, the rehab center may provide you with tape recorders, braille writers, and other tools of the trade.

More important than these gadgets, however, are the skills and ideas that you will pick up. First, there is elementary braille. Although braille is no longer as important as it was before the invention of tape recorders, and although few of the adventitiously blind (those who become blind after birth) ever become rapid braille readers, a knowledge of elementary braille can be useful in some unforeseen ways.

Take as example only the two that I use now. When I spent my 1972–1973 sabbatical leave in California without my family (my wife's job might have been lost had she taken an unpaid leave to be with me), I had small aluminum two-letter braille tags sewn into the closings of my shirts and into the lining of my ties. (These tags are available free of charge from the American Foundation for the Blind.) BR stood for "brown," BL for "blue," and so on. My shirts bore labels corresponding to their colors, but the ties, which are often too multicolored for easy identification, carried labels for the suits or jackets with which they could be worn. A great convenience!

My second use of braille is to label the many cassettes that I have on hand at any moment. I braille a one-word or two-word description onto a blank price tag, the kind that comes with a tied string loop, and fasten the tag to a rubber band, which I snap around the cassette. I have done the same to the bottles in my liquor cabinet.

In closing this section, I shall simply list a number of skills that I learned in the rehabilitation center. You should be able to figure out what these mean. In the course on skills of daily living, I learned such simple procedures as handling coins, handling paper money, dialing telephone numbers, and sewing buttons. Those who wanted it were taught how to operate sewing machines and how to make clothing. In the course on home repair, I learned to handle ordinary tools safely and to make the simplest kind of household repairs.

As one indication of what the blind can do when properly instructed, let me note that in this same part of the rehab center, men were being taught to cut wood on power saws! The instructor told me that the blind user is less likely to hurt him- or herself on dangerous machinery than the sighted user, for the blind user knows that he or she must never become overconfident and slight the safety rules.

In the homemaking class, I learned the simplest kitchen skills: how to center a pot on an electric or gas stove, how to measure hot and cold liquids, and how to cook various simple dishes. I must report that I grudgingly went along with the instruction on how to clean a bathroom mirror and how to dust furniture, skills I loftily felt I would never need. However, I reckoned without the problem of living alone in California the next year, when such skills were desirable.

Let me return now to mobility and the proper use of the long cane. My instruction included the special techniques for different environments. Thus I received special instruction on how to move safely on railroad station platforms. My instructor also came to Stony Brook several times to familiarize me with special techniques I would need at home, in the village, and at the university. When I arrived in California, I hired a local mobility instructor for one hour to teach me similar facts about my new neighborhood. It was a good investment. Now, however, I understand the procedure well enough to be able to tell any sighted person how to instruct me in a new location. Do you understand now why I titled this section "Rehabilitation: The Magic Wand"?

Reading, Writing, and Figuring

Many people who are legally blind nevertheless are able to read print. Usually, it is larger, darker, or more widely spaced than that read by the normally sighted. Thus the *New York Times* prepares a large-type weekly, which is a combination of news stories from its daily editions and features from the Sunday edition, printed in type that is three or four times as large as that used in its regular edition. Most libraries that cater to the blind have many books in similar large type, including dictionaries, encyclopedias, and other reference works. Ask your counselor or social worker about such services if you can use them.

Once your vision deteriorates beyond the level where you can read large type, you may be able to go on reading for some time, as I was, by the use of special eyeglasses and other devices, such as hand-held or stand-mounted magnifiers. This entire field is the province of low-vision specialists, who may be either ophthalmologists or optometrists—in both cases with special training. Caution: The ordinary ophthalmologist or optometrist is *not* a low-vision specialist and may well be unaware of their existence. Take my word for it; these specialists can be unbelievably helpful if your vision is in that marginal area between the normal and the totally blind.

How to Find a Low-Vision Clinic

The best advice I can think of is to telephone the department of ophthalmology at the nearest medical school or the nearest school of optometry and ask if they have a low-vision clinic or if they can recommend one in your area. I list here only the three that I know of (the first is the one I used).

The Low-Vision Clinic of the Industrial Home for the Blind, 57 Willoughby Street, Brooklyn, New York 11201.

The Low-Vision Clinic, Boston University School of Medicine, Boston, Massachusetts.

The Low-Vision Clinic, School of Optometry, University of California, Berkeley, California.

One step further down the scale of sight takes you beyond the optical low-vision aids to the electronic aids generally called "TV magnifiers." These devices generally consist of three main parts: a sliding table on which the reading material is placed; a television camera, often equipped with a zoom lens, mounted vertically above the sliding table; and a television "monitor," a television receiver that is connected by wire to the television camera.

After a few hours of instruction and practice, you will be able, in effect, to reprint the reading material in a size, brightness, contrast, and "mode" of type that pleases you. (The "mode" refers to the ability of the machine, by the flick of the switch, to change ordinary black-on-white print to white-on-black, which is much easier to read for people with many kinds of visual problems.) In other words, the image of the page that is projected on the monitor conforms to that combination of characteristics that you find easiest to read.

These machines sell from about $900 to about $1,500, depending on size, portability, accessories, and so on. As mentioned earlier, some states may pay for all or part of the cost of such a machine for further study and/or work.

At this point, we leave the realm of the visual, whether aided by optical or electronic means, and pass to that newer and still more magical realm of devices that transduce visible information into information that can be apprehended by some other sensory modality. In short, these devices change sight into sound or touch.

Perhaps the most widely used is the Optacon, a device produced by Tele-Sensory Systems, Inc., in Palo Alto, California. It consists of a fountain-pen-sized, light-sensitive device with a small wheel at its bottom, which is connected by wires to a cigar-box-sized unit. The user rolls the light sensor along a line of print, and the electronic circuitry in the other unit converts the shape of each letter into a set of vibrations in a rectangular array of tiny vibrators.

In use the device is even simpler than this description. The user runs the light sensor along the line of print with one hand and places the index finger of his or her other hand in a slot in the electronic unit. As the sensor moves along, the tiny vibrators mark the shape of each letter on the under-side of the user's forefinger. The entire unit is small enough so that the user can carry it wherever he or she needs to—into a supermarket to read labels on packages, into library stacks to find the right book, and into the reading room of a library.

Unfortunately, the speed that even a good practiced Optacon user can achieve is relatively low—seldom more than 80 words a minute, far less than a good sighted reader, but still a great improvement over most braille readers. Moreover, the Optacon has the virtue of not requiring the preparation of braille or tapes; the user can read anything that is printed in regular type.

The current price of the Optacon, including several weeks of instruction and a year's free service, is about $2,000. This is a great deal, but it will probably be reduced in time, and at least one state (Massachusetts) has bought Optacons for some of its blind trainees and the Rehabilitation Center at the University of Illinois lends Optacons to students free of charge.

The same firm that produces the Optacon has come out with a pocket-sized electronic calculator that not only has the usual visual display but also, at the press of a button, announces in words what the user is doing and what the registers show. For example, if the user presses a *2* then the *plus*, then a *3*, and then the *equal* sign, the machine will say in a surprisingly understandable synthetic speech: "Two plus three equals five point zero zero" and display 5.00 in its register. (The speech accompanies the pressing of the keys, and if the user forgets what is in the keyboard or in the registers, the pressing of a special key will cause the machine to tell him or her.) The machine sells for many times what a voiceless pocket calculator now costs. Again, competition and demand undoubtedly will reduce the price.

Most remarkable of all is the Kurzweil Reading Machine, which turns print of any ordinary style and any language into synthetic speech. The performance is mind-boggling; its design is so sensitive to the needs of the blind that there is a key that, when pressed, causes the machine to spell the last word, that is, if the user does not understand the machine's speech (probably because the word in question should be pronounced in some way that the Kurzweil Company had not encountered in its programming), the machine will spell that word, letter by letter, and then resume "normal" speech.

At this writing, most university and college libraries are still in the process of making themselves accessible to the handicapped, as required by Section 504 of the Rehabilitation Act of 1973. Although the Department of Health, Education, and Welfare has issued interpretations of the law, there has been no official statement or legal decision on what "accessibility to libraries" means. I can report, however, an unofficial opinion by a group from the regional Office for Civil Rights of HEW, who visited Stony Brook recently, that it is reasonable to interpret accessibility as requiring the purchase of a Kurzweil machine or equipment (Telesensory Systems, the producer of the Optacon, is also working on such a machine). The current model of the Kurzweil machine sells for about $20,000, depending on accessories.*
It remains to be seen whether or not the vocational rehabilitation agencies will pay most or all of this cost, just as they pay the college tuition of blind students who are preparing for some occupational goal.

Writing

One of the simplest devices used by the blind is the Marks Guide, a standard clipboard to which is affixed a movable wire guide that travels up and down the page, a line at a time, and encloses the space available for writing on one line. One simply writes or prints in the usual way until one reaches the right-hand margin indicator; one then moves the guide a line lower and repeats the process.

The typewriter may seem an improbable instrument for the blind, but the modern typewriter was actually invented *for the blind*, and touch typing was invented *by the blind*. As one indication of what a properly trained blind person can do, note that there are many blind people who earn their

---

*Author's note: The Spring 1979 issue of *The Kurzweil Report* states that Kurzweil Computer Products, Inc., has developed the Kurzweil Talking Terminal, which converts computer-transmitted, standard English text into synthetic speech. Under its leasing program, the Talking Terminal will be available for approximately $18 per week. This machine will give blind people access to the same computer information that sighted persons get through the use of CTRs (television-type screens) or computer printouts and will provide new career opportunities for visually handicapped people in fields where computers are used. This exciting device is being tested as a means of communication for people who are unable to speak and, with special control adaptations, for people who are both paralyzed and unable to speak. The Talking Terminal can generate an unlimited vocabulary without the need for linguistic programming on the part of the user. From: *The Kurzweil Report: Technology for the Handicapped*, No. 3 (Spring 1979), Kurzweil Computer Products, Cambridge, Massachusetts. Available in talking book version.

living by transcribing dictated materials. Indeed, there are even special associations of blind transcribers.

Braille can be written by either of two means. The simpler is a hand-held stylus and a "slate," a template that allows one to make the braille dots in an orderly and simple way. The stylus-and-slate method is, however, very slow, suitable for making labels but not for large amounts of brailling. For larger amounts of writing, one must turn to braillewriters, devices about the size of a typewriter, which allow one to produce braille much more quickly than with the stylus and slate. These are available for examination, trial, and instruction at most rehab centers.

Further along in specialization is a typewriter, formerly manufactured by IBM, that may still be available in some secondhand market of blind goods. With the machine, one can type braille as fast as the ordinary typist types print. Then there is the other side of IBM, the computer side. If you are a computer programmer or need to read a great deal of computer output (beyond what a sighted helper can easily do), your computing center can buy, at relatively low cost, a braille "printchain" that will operate on a high-speed printer and produce reams of braille. Yes, there are blind computer programmers.

Still in the process of development at Telesensory Systems is the Versa-Brailler, a device that combines the electric brailler with a computer terminal. With it, a blind person will be able not only to write braille rapidly and to receive computer outputs at home or in an office, but also to edit a braille text—for example, to insert additional words or to delete some part of an existing text without the necessity of rewriting the existing text.

Figuring

In addition to the slightly larger than pocket-sized "talking calculator," the current version of the Kurzweil Reading Machine can be used as a talking calculator. There is also a braille version of the standard Marchant mechanical calculator. The blind can, of course, learn to keypunch and to read braille printouts, as described above. At the other extreme, there are braille slide rules. (See also the next sections on Tools of the Trade and Books and Magazines.)

TOOLS OF THE TRADE

There is hardly any technical task, save such things perhaps as driving a car or performing surgery, that a blind person cannot do, given the right tools. Take carpentry for example. There are braille-marked carpenter's squares, levels that emit an audible signal, and many other standard and specialized tools that the blind find easy to use. Large collections are available from such agencies as

Aids and Appliances Division, American Foundation for the Blind, 15 West 16 Street, New York, New York 10011. (*Note:* You may order items on a toll-free number and charge them to your credit card number: 800-447-4700 continental United States except Illinois; Illinois only 800-322-4400.)

Aids and Appliances Division, National Federation of the Blind, 1101 St. Paul Street, Baltimore, Maryland 21202. 301-659-9314.

American Printing House for the Blind, 1839 Frankfort Avenue, Louisville, Kentucky 40206. 502-895-2405.

Howe Press, Perkins School for the Blind, Watertown, Massachusetts 02172. 617-924-3434.

Write to one or more of these institutions for their catalogues, which usually are available in either inkprint or braille; also, some have recently added recorded versions. If you are able to visit one or more, you will be enlightened by the variety of useful devices.

New devices and new sources are frequently listed in *The Braille Monitor*, the monthly magazine of the National Federation of the Blind (see Organizations of and for the Blind, later in this chapter).

A word of caution. Like the amateur photographer, the novice blind person can easily go wild over gadgets. Use restraint! You can always go back or send in a mail order, so buy only those gadgets that you have already seen and tried. This applies above all to the expensive gadgets, such as TV magnifiers, which occasionally have been sold by unscrupulous salespeople to those who literally could not use them.

In the end, you will become your own inventor of devices and procedures to facilitate your own work and leisure. For example, I was annoyed by my inability to read a printed calendar and had not acquired a braille calendar (cheap and widely available). In lieu of both, however, I figured out a way to keep the calendar for a year at a time in my head. This sounds more impressive than it is. All one has to do is to memorize each year the 12 dates of the first Monday of each month; for 1980, for instance, these are 7, 4, 3, 7, 5, 2, 7, 4, 1, 6, 3, 1. To illustrate this procedure, let me show you how to determine the day of the week for the Fourth of July and for Christmas.

1. Convert the month to its numerical equivalent; thus, July is the seventh month and December is the twelfth.
2. In the above list of 12 numbers, locate the date of the first Monday of the given month. It is 7 for July and 1 for December.
3. Since July 7 is the first Monday in July, the Fourth of July will be three days before, which is Friday.
4. For Christmas, reason this way: The first is a Monday, and the eighth, fifteenth, and twenty-second are also Mondays; the twenty-fifth will be three days after the last-named Monday, so it will be on Thursday.

Do you think that memorizing 12 numbers is particularly difficult? Surely, you know your own Social Security number and your own telephone number, which together are many more than 12 digits.

Although there is no truth to the popular notion of "sensory compensation," meaning that the loss or deterioration of one sense will somehow be compensated by a magical improvement of another, this small example should convince you that the blind can learn to make more intelligent use of their remaining senses and especially of their memories. (After inventing the calendar scheme, I discovered that someone else had done it before me, but it is nevertheless worth knowing and using.) You will be surprised by the speed with which your memory will improve.

BOOKS AND MAGAZINES

The National Library Service for the Blind and Physically Handicapped (NLS) of the Library of Congress is charged by law with providing braille books and Talking Books, as well as the machines for reproducing the latter, free of charge, to the blind and to those physically handicapped who are unable to read ordinary print (unable, for example, to turn the pages of an ordinary book).

Your local library will be able to put you in touch with the regional library or subregional library that will serve you. The arrangement varies widely from state to state. When I was in California during 1972–1973, I obtained my Talking Book reproducer from the state lending agency in Albany (New York) and my books from the California State Library in Sacramento. In New York, however, I get both from the subregional library that serves Suffolk County; it is located some dozen miles away, albeit in a direction that is unreachable by public transportation. This latter awkwardness poses no real problem, however, for a letter or phone call brings me whatever I need.

Not only are the books and the machines available free, but the books travel back and forth without postage, as indeed do large print, braille, and recorded material to and from a legally blind person. All you or your correspondent has to do is write "Free Matter for the Blind" where the stamp would go and send off your package. Unfortunately, this does not apply to ordinary letters.

I have already mentioned *The Braille Monitor* and *Talking Book Topics*. *The Braille Monitor* is available from the National Federation of the Blind (1101 St. Paul Street, Suite 412, Baltimore, Maryland 21202). The American Council of the Blind, the other large national organization of blind people, publishes the *Braille Forum* (190 Lattimore Road, Rochester, New York 14620). (Do not be misled by the word *braille* in the titles of these two newsletters. It dates from the time before inexpensive recordings were widely available. Both newsletters are published in inkprint and recorded editions as well as braille; simply specify which version you want.)

Several other magazines of special interest to the blind are *Choice Magazine Listening* (14 Maple Street, Port Washington, New York 11050) —a selection of high-quality articles and stories that were previously published elsewhere—which comes as free individual subscriptions or on a loan basis through your regional or subregional library. These are announced every other issue or so in *Talking Book Topics*. Also of note are *Dialogue with the Blind* (3100 South Oak Park Avenue, Berwyn, Illinois 60402), a magazine of general interest to the blind, including editorials, articles, and fiction; and *The Hadley Focus* (Hadley School for the Blind, Winnetka, Illinois 60093), valuable especially if you want to keep up-to-date on the Hadley School's free correspondence courses.

Unfortunately, few technical journals are available from the above sources, and they tend to be specialized journals in such fields as education and social work, in which there are many blind readers. What do I do about the *American Sociological Review*, for example, which is not available from these sources? I have worked out the following procedure. I have a volunteer, John Fraser. He has an inexpensive cassette recorder on which he records such material for me, and I have a bulk eraser with which to erase the cassettes that I have read. John records tables of contents, abstracts, and, when requested, entire journal articles. He also records university memoranda, reprints, and other "fugitive documents" that are not available elsewhere.

For longer or more technical material, I have friends in other cities who are willing to record such data from time to time. In enlisting and using such volunteers, I try to send them material that they are likely to find interesting, so that there is something in this relationship beyond simply doing a good deed for a friend.

It may seem that I have no shortage of volunteer readers, but experience has taught me that, as an active teacher and researcher, I never have too many. This is one reason why I urge librarians to take the initiative in compiling a roster of volunteer readers (discussed later).

For student papers and dissertations, cassette machines are so widely available nowadays that students who cannot buy one for their own use can easily borrow one from a friend or from a university's audiovisual center. Students who want to do their master's essays or doctoral dissertations with me understand that they will have to record them and that I will respond by sending them one or more cassettes of comments. I have prepared special instructions for such students to make the recording and commenting go smoothly.

For Talking Books, the National Library Service for the Blind and Physically Handicapped of the Library of Congress commissions agencies to hire professional actors to record the books that they select. Each actor or actress reads an entire book, and one has to experience such a reading to understand how wonderful it can be. Indeed, one of the genuinely good things about being blind (I am absolutely serious here!) is the ability to get Talking Books; the reading by a skilled reader adds a wholly new aesthetic dimension to the printed page.

The NLS sends out, free of charge, a bimonthly newsletter, *Talking Book Topics*, which carries news of the NLS and lists the new recordings. The mission of the NLS is primarily fiction and nonfiction for the general reader, not textbooks or technical monographs.

Recording for the Blind (RFB), an organization with headquarters at 215 East 58 Street, New York, New York 10022 and branches in many cities throughout the country, especially near large universities (some of the branches are Oak Ridge, Tennessee, Palo Alto, California, New Haven, Connecticut, and Stony Brook, New York), has a different mission than that of the NLS. It uses volunteers to make recordings of texts, technical, classical, or whatever other kinds of books a reader might want, but it sees its primary mission as serving students and professionals.

Like the NLS, RFB does not charge for its services. It maintains a master tape library of some 50,000 titles. When you request something that is already in the library, the master tape is run through a high-speed duplicator and a new set of cassettes is prepared for you. You may keep these cassettes for as long as you need them and then return them to RFB, where they are erased and used for another reproduced recording. Like the books of the NLS, the cassettes of RFB travel postage free in both directions, but, unlike the NLS, RFB does *not* provide the necessary machines (see below).

What about titles that are not in the master tape library? One simply sends two copies of the inkprint book to RFB, which records it, usually within a month or two, and then either returns the two books or returns one and pays you for the other. (If you elect this option, be sure to enclose a copy of your bill or receipt.) RFB needs two books so that the recording can be checked by a monitor, who holds the second copy and, in principle, catches mistakes that the reader is too busy to notice.

All in all, there are more than two dozen other organizations that record special categories of books. For example, the Jewish Braille Institute provides books in Yiddish, Hebrew, and English in both braille and recorded form. In addition, there are a few commercial organizations that prepare specialized material—for example, cassettes to which doctors or lawyers can listen while driving their cars. You can find out about both organizations from your Talking Book Library.

Reproducing, Cassette, and Other Speech Machines

The NLS provides excellent machines for reproducing its discs and cassettes. Its disc reproducer is unique, being able to play at 33⅓, 16⅔, and 8⅓ revolutions per minute. The 33⅓ is, of course, the standard long-playing record speed, and the 16⅔ speed is available on some commercial machines, but the $8\frac{1}{3}$ is unique to the NLS machine. This speed allows one hour of uninterrupted listening on each side of a 10-inch record, a pleasant length.

The NLS has announced that it will gradually shift from discs to cassettes, and it has already begun issuing books in the latter form. The cassettes are smaller, less easily damaged, and much more convenient for blind users. Moreover, almost all cassette recorders and reproducers are easily portable, and many operate on disposable or rechargeable batteries. The NLS cassette machine, which, like the disc reproducer, is loaned free and maintained free by your regional or subregional library, is excellent. You can even obtain free headphones, which are usable with the disc reproducer as well as the cassette machine and allow you to listen without disturbing others.

I am forced to note here one strong dissatisfaction with the NLS cassette reproducer. Charged by Congress with providing machines for reproducing recorded material, NLS provides a machine that, unlike commercial cassette machines, does not have a recording head. Thus the NLS has saved perhaps $5 and deprived the blind of the convenience of an additional recording device.

Although the NLS cassette machine will play cassettes recorded on most commercial machines as well as the NLS and RFB cassettes, the converse is not true. The newer cassettes made by both organizations are recorded at a special low speed of $\frac{15}{16}$ inches per second (ips), which is not available on most commercial machines at this time.

In addition to playing these cassettes, the APH (American Printing House)-modified GE cassette player (see below) will record at the $\frac{15}{16}$ ips speed also, thus allowing a great deal of material to be recorded on the four tracks of a cassette.

Perhaps the best buy for the novice cassette user is the APH-modified GE cassette machine. It has a rechargeable battery, a great convenience when you want to play or record cassettes away from a power outlet. Finally, this machine will do what apparently no commercial cassette machine will do: play four-track cassettes monaurally at the $\frac{15}{16}$ ips speed, the combination that is now standard for both RFB and NLS.

Experience, your own and that of others, will soon show you whether or not you can make use of other kinds of machines. If you do a great deal of dictating that is transcribed by a secretary, it is useful to have dictating and transcribing equipment especially adapted for these purposes. There are many brands and several modes of recording that serve interchangeably.

The one innovation that I have made is to buy a cheap cassette recorder for two special uses. Ordinarily it stays in the kitchen, on a shelf near the telephone. When I find it on the kitchen table, however, I know that it contains a message for me, and I rewind the cassette for a few seconds to play the message. Think of how much confusion this avoids! The second use for this machine is as a backup for the APH cassette machines when the latter are out for repairs.

Academics and others who write for a living and who compose their papers on the typewriter often ask how I manage to write papers without a typewriter. The procedure I have worked out is surprisingly good, but it does require a desk top full of equipment—a minimum of two cassette machines. On the left I put my NLS cassette player, on which I listen to an outline, a previous draft, or part of a book or journal article. On the right I have my American Printing House cassette player/reproducer, on which I record my new draft. When I have three working machines on hand (here is a third use for the backup machine), I use the third machine to make "running notes," reminders about points to cover in the passages immediately ahead, or anything else that comes to mind while writing. This sounds more complicated than it is, and you will be able to master the two- or three-machine arrangement with a half-hour of practice. I now find myself able to turn out papers even faster than before.

ORGANIZATIONS OF AND FOR THE BLIND

You will hardly have entered the blindness system before you discover that the nature of organizations of and for the blind is a topic of hot controversy. I list below the most important organizations and describe them briefly; I also append some of my own idiosyncratic and perhaps biased observations. Be warned of these possible biases and make up your own mind when you have all the information.

National Federation of the Blind (*NFB*) is by far the largest organization of blind people (there are only two others of national scale, discussed below) and also the most active and most belligerent. It fights everywhere and with unparalleled zeal for fair treatment of blind people. It publishes *The Braille Monitor*, which is well worth reading every month. In only one issue you will learn what the NFB is all about. In addition, the NFB has an unusually good Aids and Appliances Division; send for its catalogue. As just one example, its long cane is far better than the one I received from my rehab center. I am a member of the NFB and of the Greater Long Island Chapter of the NFB of New York. Nevertheless, I am not always in agreement with the tactics that the NFB employs, nor with the way it treats its opponents or even its former supporters who have come to disagree with it.

American Council of the Blind split off from the NFB (or vice versa) some years ago. It is much smaller and much less visible than the NFB, but, for all I know, it may do as much good work.

Blinded Veterans Association is for those who have served in the U.S. Armed Forces and are blind, whether or not the blindness is service connected. It helps all blind veterans, members or not, to get their benefits and to find employment.

American Foundation for the Blind (AFB) is the bête noire of the NFB, especially for its having spawned the National Accreditation Council for Agencies Serving the Blind and Visually Handicapped (NAC). Almost any issue of *The Braille Monitor* will tell you more about NAC than you may care to know.

Nevertheless, even if everything that the NFB says about the NAC and AFB is true, the AFB still is worth knowing about for two services: (1) its Aids and Appliances Showroom, open during normal business hours, has an excellent selection of gadgets and materials. If you live in the New York City area, be sure to visit it at American Foundation for the Blind, Inc., 15 West 16 Street, between Fifth and Sixth avenues. (2) The AFB will provide a book of coupons and an identification card that enable a blind person to take a sighted companion free of charge on railroads and buses where the fare is more than $1. There are some further qualifications, but this is the meat of it. For details write to One-Fare Travel Concession, AFB, 15 West 16 Street, New York, New York 10011. Some members of the local NFB have told me that they refuse to use this service on the ground that they don't need a companion, but I look upon it as a small and good thing that makes life slightly easier for blind people.

Almost all railroad and bus lines honor these coupons. A major exception is the Long Island Railroad, which is operated by the Metropolitan Transit Authority of New York State. This organization issues an identification card that allows handicapped persons to travel at half fare on the Long Island Railroad and on New York City subways and buses. Write to the MTA for application blanks if you are interested; you will need another copy of your certification of legal blindness.

From time to time, various activists—blind, otherwise handicapped, and "normal"—have conceived of forming coalitions of handicapped persons with different disabilities. Some of these coalitions are national, others local. I think this is an admirable idea, but others, both inside and outside the blindness system, disagree. The NFB, for example, is so adamantly against coalitions that it forbids its members to join them, as it also forbids joining the American Council of the Blind.

PUTTING IT ALL TOGETHER

As I sat with my cassette recorder in hand, pondering how to begin this section, I thought of saying: "That's all there is; there isn't any more." But, of course, there is a great deal more that I could tell you and much more that you will, or should, discover for yourself. I leave you with two requests: (1) think creatively about your blindness; look on it as a problem for research and study, and try to think up new solutions for your problems (they will be someone else's, too); (2) share your thoughts with me, whether critical, approving, or questioning. You can write to me if you wish or send me a cassette. I will reply in the mode that you have used (my standard rule for corresponding by cassettes is that I try to keep the trade balanced, but I don't promise to return the identical cassette that you send me). To keep the quality of our trade uniform, use only C-60 cassettes of voice quality. Longer cassettes cause trouble, shorter ones are uneconomical, and the high-fidelity cassettes are unnecessarily expensive.

LIBRARY EQUIPMENT AND FACILITIES

For an academic library* to equip itself properly and to provide the necessary facilities and services to accommodate blind users effectively, it is probably necessary that there is someone on the professional staff who takes the trouble to learn about the needs of the blind and to keep up-to-date on the rapidly changing technological and service situations in this area. I shall assume that there is such an informed and concerned person on the staff of each library that seeks to accommodate the blind.

The Physical Structure of the Library

Large libraries tend to have wide aisles, large entrance doors, elevators, and other such less obvious facilities as wide stack aisles. These seem to be the usual concomitance of large numbers of students, but they also serve the obvious needs of the physically handicapped. The architectural needs of the blind are less elaborate. The most obvious are a so-called braille map of the library or a set of three-dimensional models, probably located near the main entrance, so that the blind user can find the desired services and facilities.

Elevator control panels nowadays often carry braille markings to identify the button for each floor, but it has not yet become obvious to many architects and coordinators of services for the handicapped that such elevators also need some way of informing the blind user when the elevator has arrived at the desired floor. It is vexing to press the button for, say, the third floor and have the elevator stop at some intermediate floor without giving an indication of this fact.

Two simple expedients are useful here: a gong or tone that signals the number of the floor at which the elevator is about to stop and *large* braille markings in the metal frame that usually encloses the outer doors, so that the blind passenger can reach out at a standard height, probably at the level of the control panel, and feel these braille markings in order to know at which floor the elevator has stopped.

A little thought here would suggest that standard braille is too small for easy location and fast reading in this situation. Some architects and others

Author's note: Although Professor Selvin is writing specifically of his own experience with academic libraries, his suggestions obviously would apply to all libraries.

have suggested using large hemispherical bolt heads—say, one-half inch in diameter—to make the braille symbol. Moreover, given the need for speed to locate and read the floor indication before the elevator door shuts, it would probably be sensible to drop the so-called number sign and assume that the blind passenger who feels a letter E will understand that it corresponds to the fifth floor without the necessity of prefixing a number sign to the letter, the usual convention for distinguishing letters from numbers (the letters A to J, when prefixed by the number sign, correspond to the ten digits, 1, 2, . . . , 8, 9, 0).

Special Rooms for the Blind

Any hint of segregation of the blind from the sighted is likely to meet emotional resistance on the part of the blind and their friends, but the use of electromechanical or human transducers (live readers) in the presence of sighted users of the library is certain to be distracting to the latter. And no matter how much goodwill they may have, it is likely to prejudice them against the blind. It is necessary therefore to have special, reasonably sound-proof rooms for those blind users who wish to listen to recordings without the use of headphones or to work with a live reader. It is often necessary, by the way, to provide live readers where rapid interaction between the information and the blind reader is necessary—for example, in answering a questionnaire or in taking a multiple choice test or examination. Depending on the library's resources, some or all of these rooms can be equipped with the basic transducers—for example, optical magnifiers, Talking Book disc players, cassette players, compressed-speech cassette players, TV magnifiers, and reading machines.

One might expect that those machines provided free to blind and physically handicapped users by the National Library Service for the Blind and Physically Handicapped of the Library of Congress would also be available free to libraries, and this is sometimes true, depending on the willingness of the machine-lending agency in a given area to interpret the rules of the NLS broadly. Some librarians have interpreted the congressional mandate to provide machines to the blind as not being applicable to libraries that serve the blind. This seems to me an altogether indefensible, narrow-minded, and unsympathetic view; I hope that the NLS will clarify this point for libraries that try to serve the blind effectively.

Given the proclivity of many people who inhabit or pass through colleges and universities to make away with electronic equipment that is not bolted down, it behooves the thoughtful librarian to pay special attention to problems of security, even if this inconveniences the blind user, who must check out a key to the listening room while the sighted user is able to walk in and out of most parts of the library without such restrictions. Even more, there is the deplorable but all-too-often present possibility of vandalism.

Providing Special Materials for the Blind

In this section I include the partially sighted who may be able to read large-print books as well as those who are completely unable to read print without the help of special transducers. Just as a reference library provides dictionaries, encyclopedias, and card catalogues classified according to various principles (subject, author and title, serials, and so on), so it should provide at least the rudiments of such a collection for the visually handicapped. The most important element is lists of such materials in forms that the visually handicapped can use—a large-print catalogue of large-print holdings for those who can use them, a braille list of braille holdings for braille readers, and a recorded list of recorded holdings. Depending on demand, such lists may be available in more than one copy.

It will require frequent vigilance on the part of the library's specialist in the needs of the handicapped to determine when new technology makes one or more of these lists unnecessary. If, for example, everyone learns to work effectively with a reading machine and if such reading machines are available in sufficient quantities at the places where they are needed, the blind user may be able to read a printed catalogue in book form or, indeed, to use the reading machine to scan the visual display on a cathode-ray tube. The problem of working with catalogues that are in card-drawer form is likely to be temporary, since such catalogues are rapidly being replaced by computer-printed books or cathode-ray-tube displays.

In present forms, most reference books adapted to the needs of the blind are both bulky and expensive, so that this, among other factors, limits the number of reference works that can be provided in such forms for blind users. Even more than their sighted counterparts, blind users will benefit from easy access to reference librarians, either in person at the reference desk or by telephone. Similarly, they require page service to get the desired books from the library stacks and, as now provided in a deplorably small number of academic libraries, delivery service of library material to campus locations outside the library. In the same way, unusually enterprising academic libraries have provided rapid copying service—within the copyright laws, of course—from current periodicals for both sighted and blind readers.

Although I have by no means made a systematic survey of facilities for the blind in academic libraries, I am most impressed with the facilities provided by the libraries of the University of Illinois, Urbana/Champaign, and by the rehabilitation center on that campus. The center lends cassette machines and Optacons free to blind students; it takes the initiative in seeing that all required textbooks are available in recorded form *at the start of each semester*. (Given the weeks or months that it usually takes to get a new book recorded, especially in the peak periods of the summer, blind students on campuses not blessed with such sensitive organizations often have to wait several weeks after the beginning of a semester to get their recorded books, which places an unnecessary burden on them and on the sighted friends whom they must ask to read the textbooks aloud in the interim.)

I should note, by the way, that the sensitivity and intelligence of people at the University of Illinois in dealing with the handicapped are not restricted to the blind. All in all, this campus probably shows more thoughtfulness and concern than any other, at least at a large university. By way of contrast, I once heard of a university president who, on being asked by a physically handicapped member of the faculty when the campus would be made fully accessible to the handicapped, replied: "Let's get the buildings built first, and then we can worry about the handicapped."

THE LEADERSHIP ROLES OF LIBRARIANS

Perhaps the most important elements in providing adequate library services for the blind are energy, imagination, and courage on the part of the director of libraries and the library's specialists in serving the blind. In this era of tight budgets, they will have to twist arms, pound tables, and mount propaganda campaigns to get adequate budgets. (As mentioned elsewhere in this book and in this chapter, the provision of such facilities and services seems to be the clear intent of Section 504 of the Rehabilitation Act of 1973, but, pending judicial action, one can only assume that accessibility to a program implies accessibility to the library's holdings that support the program.) In this connection, it seems desirable for the director of libraries to arrange a conference with the university's legal representatives and with appropriate members of the senior administration to plan the university's response to this new and far-reaching law. Such a meeting may well have the important consequence of raising the consciousness of all parties.

In addition to pressing for the establishment, maintenance, and staffing of special facilities for the blind, such as those discussed above, librarians might well take the lead in mobilizing and coordinating other campus resources. For example, even the best cassette machines require such periodic maintenance as cleaning the recording and reproducing heads and replacing rubber drive belts—operations beyond the competence of most blind users of the library. Such tasks are part of the normal competence of audiovisual technicians, who are found in virtually all institutions of higher education. Especially when it comes to designing a new library building, it would make good sense to locate the institution's audiovisual center in the library building. In addition to meeting the occasional needs of the blind, the staff of the center might provide such services to the handicapped as replacing crutch tips, charging the storage batteries of electric wheelchairs, and making simple, emergency repairs on wheelchairs.

Perhaps the most important, and potentially the most dangerous, task for librarians is taking part in and, if necessary, organizing advocacy groups of and for the handicapped. It is one thing to have a few librarians and other people of goodwill remonstrate with an administrator; it is something else again to have the administration building picketed by a platoon of students and others in wheelchairs or using long canes or guide dogs. One newspaper picture of such a demonstration will probably be all that an administrator needs to find the necessary money to provide adequate library services for the blind. It is a fact of organization life that every administrator has some discretionary money, the amount increasing with rank.

On a less drastic level, such an organization can often provide information to architects and others in the planning of new facilities or the rehabilitation of old ones. For example, the necessity of providing an indication of the floor at which an elevator has stopped was first pointed out to the Construction Fund of the State University of New York by a blind student member of the President's Committee on the Disabled at Stony Brook. Such organizations can also provide useful mechanisms for the exchange of information between blind members of the campus community, much as is done in the self-help groups of the Vision Foundation in Massachusetts.[7]

It hardly needs to be said that everyone, including academic librarians, has more than enough work to do and, in most cases, insufficient reward for that work. Why, then, should librarians go out of their way to take on the additional tasks of determining the needs of the handicapped and trying to meet these needs? I can think of several reasons:

1. The law. The Rehabilitation Act of 1973 is not the end of the line. Congress has already amended and extended this law, and the courts are only beginning to interpret these new laws. It seems elementary prudence for an academic library to bend over backward in trying to conform to the intent of these laws without forcing the handicapped and their supporters into demonstrations and legal actions. Without presuming to be a lawyer or a judge, I will go so far as to say that I would interpret the law as *requiring* libraries to make accessible to blind students *all* readings that are assigned in the courses they take. Working with the registrar, librarians could easily ask instructors in courses for which blind students have preregistered (usually in the spring) to give them the reading lists for such courses as far in advance as possible—certainly, no later than the end of the preceding spring semester. The librarians could then order available books from such agencies as Recording for the Blind and coordinate the recording of material that is not already available.[8]

2. Humane concerns and public relations. Either of these motivations may suffice to get the library interested in the problems of the handicapped. The most effective motivations, of course, are those that originate at the top—from the chief campus officer or, in the case of multicampus institutions, from the head of the system. In this connection, organized faculty governance structures may play an important part. For example, in the

State University of New York (SUNY), the Statewide Faculty Senate requested its Committee on Library Resources to conduct a survey of the extent to which the libraries of SUNY were complying with the provisions of the Rehabilitation Act of 1973. This survey showed clearly that, except for the largest libraries, which, as noted above, unintentionally served many needs of the physically handicapped by seeking to provide a smooth flow of traffic for their many normal users, the libraries of SUNY have done precious little to comply with the law. Indeed, the survey prompted the Statewide Faculty Senate to pass a resolution urging the chancellor of SUNY to take steps to accelerate that progress, and it is good to be able to report that he has done so.

3. Benefits to the individual librarian. Apart from feelings of satisfaction from having taken an active interest in the problems of the handicapped, there are less obvious direct benefits to librarians from doing so. As Mickey Spencer, a sociologist with considerable experience in such matters, has pointed out, the benefits of warm and informed social interaction between librarians and handicapped users of their libraries are likely to be reciprocal. Many handicapped persons are interesting human beings—*not* because they are handicapped, but because they are warm and exciting human beings who happen to be handicapped.[9] Indeed, this argument is supported by a well-known sociological generalization, that people who are useful to each other tend to enjoy each other's company. Come, librarians, you have little to lose by venturing into this new area, and everyone, including you, has much to gain.

NOTES

1. Not his real name, but he will surely recognize himself.

2. Miriam Winer, "Skiing without Seeing," *Vermont Life* 33 (Winter 1978): 39–41.

3. For further speculation on the meaning of blindness to the blind and to the sighted world, see Michael A. Monbeck, *The Meaning of Blindness* (Bloomington: Indiana University Press, 1973). Although this book has the best bibliography on blindness that I have encountered, it is seriously flawed; see my review in *Contemporary Sociology* 4, no. 4 (July 1975): 441–442.

4. Much of what follows, up to the section entitled "Library Equipment and Facilities," is a revised version of my paper "How to Succeed at Being Blind," *New Outlook for the Blind* (December 1976): 420–428. Reprints of this article are available in quantity, free of charge, from the American Foundation for the Blind, 15 West 16 Street, New York, New York 10011. Those wishing to consult it in a library may be helped by learning that, beginning with the next issue, this journal changed its name to *Journal of Visual Impairment and Blindness*.

5. Robert A. Scott, *The Making of Blind Men* (New York: Russell Sage Foundation, 1969).

6. For definitions of some common visual impairments, see Anne Lesley Corn and Iris Martinez, *When You Have a Visually Handicapped Child in Your Classroom* (New York: American Foundation for the Blind, 1977), p. 23.

7. Both blind members of the academic community and librarians interested in improving library service to the blind will benefit from reading the Vision Foundation's publication *The Help Book for People with Sight Loss*. This book is available at a nominal charge in both inkprint and cassette versions from the Vision Foundation, 770 Center Street, Newton, Massachusetts 02158. This invaluable collection of ideas, sources, and agencies was compiled by people who had to ferret out these ideas for themselves. Reading it is a simple and inexpensive way to keep oneself from reinventing the wheel.

8. Although Recording for the Blind and the National Library Services of the Library of Congress both interpret their mandates as requiring service to individual blind users rather than to institutions, they will probably be willing to have librarians serve as aides to the blind, providing the name of the legally blind user when ordering books and machines.

9. Mickey Spencer, "The Politics of Disability," *Broomstick* 1, no. 6 (April 1979): 15–20. Subscription orders for *Broomstick* may be sent to San Francisco Women's Centers, OPTIONS, 63 Brady Street, San Francisco, California 94103.

7

Special Needs of the Deaf Patron

WHY DEAF AWARENESS?

Since public librarians serve people in all walks of life, I want them to share my feelings of the needs and concerns of deaf people and also the opportunities for service they can provide to them. Since I am deaf *and* a librarian, I decided to compile this handbook of information to share with public librarians.

Deafness is a frequently misunderstood handicap. Many misconceptions about deafness are still found in otherwise reputable reference books. For instance, some current general encyclopedias continue to cite sources published many years ago that do not reflect current theories or issues of deaf education. Many things have happened during the last ten years in the world of the deaf. The spread of interest in sign language among the hearing population all over the country is one instance. Another is more concern about conservation of hearing.

Webster's New Collegiate Dictionary, 1973, gives definitions of deaf-mute, dumb, and mute that are offensive to deaf people.

deaf-mute: a deaf person who cannot speak.
dumb: devoid of the power of speech (deaf and dumb from birth).

Alice Hagemeyer, librarian at the Washington, D.C., Public Library, is the author of this chapter. The chapter is taken, with permission and updating, from Alice Hagemeyer's *Deaf Awareness Handbook for Public Libraries* (D.C. Public Library, 1976).

mute, adj.: unable to speak: dumb.
mute, noun: a person who cannot or does not speak.

These words continue to be used in most current books. Nearly all deaf people can speak, but because of their inability to hear their own voices and because they are aware of their unusual sound characteristics and speech not intelligible to the general public, most do not want to use their voices at all. Only in very unusual cases does a deaf person also lack vocal cords, and such additional loss is not directly related to deafness. Absence of vocal cords does not cause deafness.

A few facts about deafness and a short list of additional readings are not enough background for a librarian who wants to effect an improvement in library services to the deaf. A few stabs at better collections or services to the deaf won't help much if you really want to provide better services to an isolated community of citizens. Few deaf users will respond to a meager library campaign, since deaf people largely are unfamiliar with the host of services that a good public library provides to hearing citizens. It is necessary for one to understand the culture and the communication of deaf people, their information needs, and their suspicion of professionals who want to do something for them—rather than with them. If you are capable of doing this and can demonstrate that deaf users are welcome in your library and not a nuisance or an embarrassment, then you will be rewarded.

Besides the needs of the deaf themselves, there are several related audiences whose interests one needs to bear in mind while building collections and planning services. They include people with hearing impairments; parents with deaf children; hearing users who want general information about deafness; users who want some good, inspirational reading; professionals working with the hearing-impaired; and last but not least important, citizens who encounter hearing-impaired persons in their own daily lives. These encounters are with clients, customers, coworkers, renters, voters, classmates, neighbors, or new in-laws. Also, because of ever-increasing noise pollution and greater longevity, many more millions of people will eventually acquire a partial or total hearing loss later in life.

Through programs held at the library, through displays on deafness in library windows, through provision of more appropriate materials, and through cooperation with mass media and other agencies, libraries can help the general public become familiar with our world—the world of silence. One never knows when deafness will impinge upon one's personal life through accident, illness, or new relationships with people in our highly mobile society. The public library can set up vibrations of information dissemination in the community as a pebble tossed into a pond sets up ripples. Some efforts will make bigger splashes than others, but, if hundreds—or thousands—of public libraries across the land act, within a short time a major improvement can be made in providing library services to the hundreds of thousands of deaf people—and the millions of hearing-impaired people—in our society.

EVERY HEARING-IMPAIRED PERSON IS DIFFERENT

I became deaf as a result of spinal meningitis at the age of three. Before the emergence of antibiotics, that crippler was a common cause of deafness to any age. My late grandfather was hard of hearing for as long as I remember. Being deaf and being hard of hearing are not the same. Hard of hearing persons usually hear well enough, with the aid of a hearing aid, to communicate with others in an almost normal way. But when a person is deaf, that is something else. I am totally deaf. No surgery can help me because my nerves were damaged. I, like thousands of other deaf people who have a hearing loss in their better ear of 80 percent or more, cannot hear spoken words even with the best amplification. I live in a different world—even from hard of hearing persons such as my grandfather.

As I was growing up, I experienced frustrations and isolation, integrating the hearing society through speech and lip reading alone. Sign language was forbidden, lest I never attain the ability to speak and read lips. So there was always a communication barrier during my growing-up years. I knew that my parents loved me and cared for me. They, like most parents when discovering deafness in their child, wanted information on deafness and needed help in understanding me in my silent world. Like many, they went to see doctors, who, themselves, often were in need of more information. Eventually, I was sent to a residential school for the deaf, where I started using sign language outside the classroom with my new friends. But I tried hard to learn by the oral method in class. I said "tried" because it was difficult to read lips completely. Even now, I probably can identify only 25 percent of English syllables on the lips and guess the rest. I never for a day in my whole life felt sorry about being deaf—only that I wished that my deafness was accepted and that hearing people would find ways to communicate with me. I did not want to be deprived of learning the many things that my sister and brother did. I am always happier when I can talk with people who write on paper, or use sign language, or any other method just to get the message across to me.

The largest percentage of hearing-impaired Americans is made up of the elderly and those who work in occupations which subject them to noise. Incidentally, my mother is among the count of the hearing-impaired population. Her sense of hearing has been on the decline for several years. After a series of operations and with a hearing aid, she is able to hear. She learned finger spelling when I was growing up.

My nine-year-old son, whom my husband and I adopted three and a half years ago, lost his hearing from spinal meningitis before he was one. He, like his new dad, who himself was born deaf, and like most other deaf persons, who were either born deaf or lost hearing during the first year of life, has been experiencing great difficulties in developing speech and language. Persons who become deaf after developing speech usually retain most of it.

Even though my son spent two and a half years in an oral school and had no knowledge of sign language before he moved into his new home with us, he had no speech and was unable to express his wishes and ideas through his gestures alone. Now he has learned sign language from his new parents and his new school has accepted the new philosophy in communication in the classroom—total communication, which means whatever it takes to get a message across and to have it properly understood, i.e., language of signs, speech, speech reading, finger spelling, reading, writing, and gestures. My son, like many other deaf children, has a basic right to communicate in order to learn and to develop his language. I have already introduced five hearing-impaired members of my family. You see each of us is different. There is no "average" deaf person. Each should be treated as an individual. Future deaf adults will probably be different from present deaf adults, in general because of presently better methods used in teaching at school, the spread of interest in learning sign language at home and in school, and the availability of registered interpreters to the deaf since early 1970.

In a public library you will meet all types of hearing-impaired persons. As you serve hearing-impaired users, you may wonder why one can speak well when the others don't, or why one does not write proper sentences while the others can write like an average hearing person, or why an elderly deaf lady, who does not know sign language, can write beautiful English.

To give you a general idea of all types, I will paraphrase Leo Jacobs's *A Deaf Adult Speaks Out.*[1]

Adventitiously deaf adults. These persons lost their hearing after they acquired language and speech, so they are probably the "elite" among deaf people. They have the best language, are usually the spokesmen for the community. These people, on the average, lost their hearing between the ages of five and twelve and completed their education in programs for the deaf, where they became acquainted with other deaf students and were introduced into their community. Persons who lose their hearing at ages older than 12 are more likely to remain with their former hearing friends and struggle along with the help of hearing aids and lip-reading practice, for there are very few of those people who have joined the community of deaf adults.

Prelingually deaf adults who come from deaf families. They had early communication and, therefore, are more likely to have better than average language, although they may have no usable speech. Since they have encountered practically no frustrations because of their deafness, they are more outgoing and at ease with other deaf persons. They also frequently become the leaders in the community.

Other prelingually deaf adults. They are the bulk of the deaf community. They come from hearing families who have had trouble communicating with them when they were little. Consequently, for the most part, they have difficulties expressing themselves in English. They have had more frustrations than the deaf adults in the first two groups, so they are for the most part less aggressive and confident.

Low-verbal deaf adults. These adults have missed a great deal of education that they should have received for various reasons, so they are almost illiterate. They may be able to sign their own names and write simple sentences, phrases, or words, but certainly not long and involved sentences; nor can they read anything but simple English constructions. They are able to express themselves with gross signs, maybe mixed with homemade pantomime. There are various reasons for their retardation: They might have been slow learners; oral failures who were kept in oral programs until they were too old to continue; went to residential schools to stagnate; or they may be members of culturally deprived families.

Products of oral programs. Many products of oral schools have found their lives to be more rewarding when they learned manual communication and joined the community of deaf adults. They were soon signing and finger spelling among the best of the manual deaf adults, but they are, for the most part, easy to distinguish because their oral schooling has left its mark on them, such as habitually mouthing when signing.

Products of public schools. Another category is those who went through regular public school programs without the benefit of interpreting services. If they are average or less in their ability, they are very likely to get very little from their public school programs, and what is worse, to have developed a lifelong habit of inattentiveness while maintaining an alert look for their teachers' benefit. Many of these persons are low verbal.

Uneducated deaf adults. We must not overlook those deaf adults who have had very few years of schooling or none at all and are, therefore, uneducated for practical purposes—indeed, at the very bottom stratum of the deaf community and therefore are objects of pity and charity. However, there are many who have been so self-reliant that they have managed to obtain an education after a fashion by themselves and have turned out to be hard-working and useful deaf citizens, although they are by necessity confined to less skilled or menial work.

Deafened adults. These are individuals who lost their hearing after they were well through their educational programs, probably due to illness, injury, war wounds, or to the debilitating effects of old age. Their late deafness does not suddenly change their makeup; in fact, the handicap does not take anything away from them except their hearing. Therefore, their problems are entirely different; they have normal speech but probably have a much greater need for hearing aids. They usually follow one of two courses of action, again depending upon the many and various factors involved in their loss of hearing: either continue in the same environment with the same circle of acquaintances with the help of a hearing aid and an acquired skill in speech reading, or gradually withdraw from their former friends into a lonely existence or into a new circle of friends who are similarly afflicted. Even though deaf, they are hearing persons in mind and spirit, and therefore leagues away from those who have been deaf since an early age.

Hard of hearing adults. It is very difficult to draw a line between them and the deaf, as there are many who are borderline cases. The hard of hearing have residual hearing which is functional; in other words, they are able to make sense out of what they hear. This has a great implication in their education and development. With amplification by hearing aids they are usually able to achieve at a more normal pace and are usually more acceptable to the hearing community. If they choose to join the deaf community, they often become leaders who are accepted by both the hearing and deaf community.

There are many other factors besides deafness and education that contribute to the makeup of deaf adults such as additional handicaps, racial problems, and religious persuasions.

We now have more prelingual deaf children than ever and the involvement of additional handicaps is greater now. Less than ten years ago, the number was much lower. Why? Due to the advances in the medical field, we have more premature children born alive. Many of them were not well developed and had a difficult time breathing at birth. Because of lack of oxygen, one or more organs was affected. Also, because of the epidemic outbreak of rubella in pregnant women during the early 1960s, many babies were born deaf.

WHAT LIBRARIANS SHOULD KNOW

Until recently, deaf people were considered burdens to society. We were thought to be hopelessly dull and had to accept whatever society offered us. We were supposed to be glad that society at least let us have an existence. Today, it is known that the deaf have normal intelligence. We have as much right as others to enjoy life to the fullest. Every library should reach out to the unreached deaf. Only in this way can the library help to enlarge our minds and our hearts and our spirits. Those who serve us are given the opportunity to learn something about us—the deaf—the forgotten people in society.

Many articles have been written on the meaning of deafness. To a few writers, deafness only means partial or complete loss of the ability to hear. Period! But, if truth be told, it means much more. Depending upon age of onset, deafness can mean additional handicaps for deaf persons: difficulties with language for those who were born deaf or became deaf at an early age; problems in communication; invisibility to almost all, except for those hard of hearing who can live normally like the hearing.

There are two groups of hearing-impaired people: (1) the deaf, who are defined as "those in whom the sense of hearing is nonfunctional for the ordinary purpose of life," and (2) the hard of hearing, defined as "those in whom the sense of hearing, although defective, is functional with or without hearing aid." For the first group, deafness is like a subculture in our society. We speak our own language and most have similar characteristics and mannerisms. In our homes, we use our own system for doorbell lights, alarm clocks that flash, baby criers that warn parents when a baby cries, and even our own telephone system. We have many types of clubs and associations on the national, state, local, and even international levels. We have our own separate churches and separate schools in our society. We even run our own insurance company. In general, deaf people enjoy being together.

To us, deafness is not a handicap. We only experience disadvantages in the hearing society. Being deaf is a challenge to us who have to live and/or deal with the hearing in the same world. Disadvantages can be reduced if everyone in the society knows sign language, uses dual-phone systems for hearing and hearing-impaired persons, and respects our deafness. It is true that people who can hear will never completely understand what it is like to be deaf no matter how hard they try. But they can learn to accept us just as we accept our deafness.

Where the term "deaf community"[2] formerly referred to deaf persons and their social, religious, and athletic activities, it now encompasses a vastly different and enlarged segment of the general public. Today the deaf community includes deaf citizens, audiologists, educators, rehabilitation counselors, ministers, psychologists, social workers, interpreters, other professionals in various disciplines, parents with deaf children, and members of the general public who are concerned about finding solutions to the inconvenience and burden that hearing loss places on many fellow citizens.

Communication

For deaf people's communication, most prefer to use sign language and/or finger spelling.

The earliest known contributor to the one-hand manual alphabet as it is widely used in the United States today was a Spaniard, Juan Pablo Bonet, who in the seventeenth century published *Simplifications of the Letters and the Art of Teaching Deaf-Mutes*. Later, Abbé Charles-Michel de L'Epee of Paris, who began to familiarize himself with the signs already in use among the deaf, corrected and enlarged the language. After the Abbé de L'Epee's death, the Abbé Sicard became the head of the National Institution in Paris, which was founded by the Abbé de L'Epee. The Abbé Sicard continued the method, which was brought to America by Thomas Hopkins Gallaudet, who visited the school, and by a young deaf man, Laurent Clerc, who had been an outstanding pupil and teacher at the institution. Gallaudet founded in 1817 the first permanent school for the deaf in the United States—the American School for the Deaf, now located in West Hartford, Connecticut.

The American Sign Language, known as Ameslan, until recently has been considered "bad English" by many who thought that it would impede the progress of deaf children in learning English. Almost all deaf adults use Ameslan. Deaf people who have deaf children naturally use it, and those children learn it easily. Such children, in turn, then pass on the standard signs to deaf children of hearing parents at school and at play. Hearing children of deaf parents learn Ameslan easily, too. For instance, my hearing daughter learned and used Ameslan easily, before she learned to speak sentences in English when she started nursery school at three years of age.

Deaf children can also learn English. They should be encouraged to enjoy reading books at an early age. Hearing people may find Ameslan difficult to learn, since they are used to saying every word and a certain pattern of grammatical construction. However, with effort, anyone can learn signed English—that is, to spell out or sign each word in correct English order, rather than signing concepts as in Ameslan. Signed English is understood by educated deaf persons and is acceptable to them, although it slows down communication for some. Some deaf people have not learned to "speak" or write English at all, so it always is very helpful for people working with the deaf to learn something about Ameslan.

You may wonder how Ameslan "works"—how it is different from signed English. Let me give you an example: "Do you like to watch television?" You can say it completely in signs and finger spelling for *each* word, but in Ameslan (if you wrote it down) it would read: "Like watch TV?" For what would be long sentences in signed English, we abbreviate, because it is boring to sign every word. Signing every word—rather than the concept—takes much longer, too. Even among some educated deaf persons, it may be difficult for them to remember "proper" word order when writing for the benefit of hearing people. Please remember that signed English is a foreign language to persons born deaf or for those who became deaf in early childhood, although some of them can write English fluently.

An issue of *Gallaudet Today* (Winter 1974–1975) has several excellent articles on communication.

When you want to speak to a deaf person, it is not necessary to exaggerate your speech, but speak slightly more slowly and more distinctly and keep the natural rhythm of speech. Also make sure the light is on your face and not behind you. Be aware that gum chewing and cigars, cigarettes, and pipes in the mouth while speaking make for difficult lip reading and slurred speech. Keep lips flexible rather than rigid.

Always talk directly, facing the person to whom you are speaking. Look into the person's eyes and use pantomime or any gestures that you feel will help. In other words, make use of all the body language available through your face, eyes, and hands. Use anything that will express the feeling or idea and will support your meaning.

Write on paper if you do not understand each other. Never show your reluctance in doing so. You offend the person if you ask him if he can read lips *after* he made his efforts in asking you in writing for something.

Most of all, be as natural as possible!

When a storyteller tells a story to hearing children, she uses her voice to describe characters, emotions, mood, and action. All of these are lost to a deaf child who sees a story simply "interpreted" by one person and told by another in a library situation. It is highly preferable that the storyteller and the story signer be one person. Furthermore, the signer must use a special kind of sign language. The size of the signs should vary with the "voice" of the character. Try to have signs with a distinct personality for each character. Let the signs move slowly, rapidly, smoothly, and so on with the action of the story. Also, the setting should be described in signs, and placement of houses, forests, and such should remain constant, as if there were a set that the action was occurring on. Facial expression, mime, and body action should be used, but with control.

In every large community there are deaf people who are good actors and storytellers. These people are accurate, fluent, and versatile in sign language. Many adult deaf people enjoy listening to these deaf storytellers from their school years to old age.

In such communities, it is not difficult to get these storytellers to tell stories or perform short plays for occasional evening programs.

Library Use by the Deaf

Most hearing-impaired and deaf people do not use their library. I have seen many remarks from my deaf friends as to why they did not use a library. Several reasons were given, such as those below:

I never did like to read. Libraries are for bookworms anyway.

I do not know how libraries operate, and I do not want to show my ignorance by asking.

There is no deaf employee who could help me. It would be much easier if I could receive assistance by sign language.

I like to go to places where my friends go. None of my friends go to the library.

Buying books and reading at home are much easier for me.

I had a bad experience at the public library once. My class was taken there by our teacher who had already told us a little about the library. She left us there so we could learn more about the library and so we could get some books. The librarians did not know what to do with us, and they seemed to lack skills in communicating and listening to us. We felt isolated and did not know how to get our needs across to them. I never went back again!

I love to read. I just never thought of going to the library to borrow books.

Oh, I did not know people could call the library for information services.

Anyway, I hate to bother hearing people to do the telephoning business for me, since the library does not have TTY.

That is the trouble with us. We, the deaf, were never trained to use our public library when young. We were never taken there, and now I am too scared to try it. You will have to help me.

They have reasons to feel that way. It is well known that most deaf students have mediocre reading skills, ranging from third- to fifth-grade level by the time most of them leave school. In order to increase the incentives for deaf persons to use the public library, more directional signs to help find services and materials should be used and special bibliographies should be prepared on such topics as high-interest, low-vocabulary books.

Library Education for Service to the Deaf

How many librarians are trained to serve the hearing-impaired? Lee Putnam, associate librarian at Gallaudet College, comments that

> service to this special group has been largely neglected by library schools. An occasional student initiated a special project. A few teachers incorporated materials in their regular courses. Until recently, however, efforts to expose library school students to the special concerns of library service for hearing-impaired people have been conspicuously slight.

> The Catholic University of America began a special program in the summer of 1975. Services to handicapped people in a variety of situations were covered; all forms of disability were included. Each student completing the requirements earned a postmaster's certificate. One course, three credits, was the "Workshop on Library Services to the Hearing Impaired." Information was incorporated in other courses, such as "Developing Library Programs to Serve Handicapped People" and the "Seminar on the Conversion of Library and Media Resources to Meet Special Needs."

> One excellent source of manpower is hearing-impaired librarians. For many years Gallaudet College offered a B.A. degree with a major in library science. Graduates are working in libraries throughout the country. Most of them are involved in cataloguing and other technical processing activities; very few work in public services. The library science major is being phased out at this time. In its place, Gallaudet will offer some basic introductory courses and support services for students who wish to pursue graduate studies.

> The number of hearing-impaired students in library schools has risen sharply in the last year or so. The University of Maryland College of Library and Information Services has been particularly receptive. These students comprise an exceptional talent pool. At the same time, they provide their hearing peers with exposure to new ideas and opportunities for informal learning.

> Gallaudet is also exploring the possibility of providing an A.A. degree. In addition, to support activities in cataloguing and acquisitions work, micrographics, indexing and abstracting, data processing, and on-line searching

seem to be areas where job opportunities will exist and deaf people will contribute.

The library profession recently made a forward step in enabling hearing-impaired librarians to have full participation in the profession. At the 1974 American Library Association Conference, membership passed a resolution calling for sign language interpreters at sessions of membership and Council. Council approved this resolution at the 1975 mid-winter meeting. Beginning with the 1975 Conference in San Francisco, hearing-impaired librarians will benefit from interpreters.

Library administrators should be aware that deaf people can perform many library tasks successfully according to their interests, motivation, and capabilities, if they are properly selected and trained. Library job opportunities should be publicized through any local educational program for the deaf and through publications serving the deaf. Contact the local rehabilitation counselor for the deaf for résumés of hearing-impaired persons qualified to perform certain jobs at the library or contact Professional Rehabilitation Workers with the Adult Deaf, Inc. (PRWAD), for more information. In a community with a considerable deaf population, consideration should be given to hiring a deaf person for public service work. Schools serving deaf students should know about library careers for them. Career counselors in such schools should know that professional library careers are open to deaf people and that a masters degree in library science is required for professional advancement.

PRWAD has some articles on employment in its journals and it also publishes *Deafness Annual*, a useful source of programs available to deaf people and a guide to where parents can obtain sign-language training.

Communication by Teletypewriter

Back to 1968, ours was among the first 12 deaf families in the Washington, D.C., area to own a teletypewriter, known as TTY. During the next few years, I kept telling my friends that I would see that my place of employment (D.C. Public Library) got one, too. For what? How often would you and two other deaf employees use it to call when you are unable to go to work? At the Government Printing Office that is understandable because they have over 100 deaf employees, but at the library, that is crazy! My friends did not know then, and deaf people in many places still do not know, that hearing people call the library for information on any subject.

The following information on TTY was written by H. Latham Bruenig, executive director of Teletypewriters for the Deaf, Inc.

More and more deaf people are communicating with each other, with relatives without hearing disabilities, and with organizations serving deaf people. This development has been nurtured by an administrative organization, Teletypewriters for the Deaf, Inc. (TDI). Using acoustic couplers interfaced between a telephone and a teletypewriter, the system has grown from 35 installations in 1968 to more than 10,000. Operating through a group of volunteer representatives, TDI coordinates the distribution of surplus teletypewriters (TTYs). Acquired from the operating companies of the American Telephone and Telegraph Company, from Western Union, International Telephone and Telegraph Company, and other sources, these are reconditioned and placed in the homes of deaf people for a modest fee. In addition to its coordinating role, TDI keeps track of its members who pay an enrollment fee and an annual membership fee. It publishes an *International Telephone Directory of the Deaf*, which is updated annually. TDI also distributes to its members a newsletter containing items of interest to the membership. Another publication of TDI is *Teletypewriters Made Easy*, a service manual covering the three most widely distributed makes of TTY.

With the growth of the network there have developed auxiliary features such as answering services whereby deaf people may reach hearing persons, news and weather services, emergency services in police departments, TTYs in department stores and businesses, hospitals and Internal Revenue Service offices, and many others. Schools, churches, vocational rehabilitation offices, and other such groups have TTYs. In recent years more modern telecommunications terminals, featuring light weight, portability, and quiet operation, have been added to the system, adding versatility to the nine or ten models of old surplus machines. An important concern of TDI is that all devices in the system be compatible with each other. For this reason "recommended practices" aimed at ensuring uniformity were distributed by TDI.

Depending on the amount of reconditioning work needed, and upon the make of interface coupler purchased, a typical TTY installation will have a one-time cost of approximately $250 and up. The more modern telecommunications terminals cost considerably more.

Below is a short list of the manufacturers of the major types of TTY equipment:

Acoustic Couplers for Interfacing with Teletypewriters
Applied Communication Corporation, P.O. Box 555, Belmont, California 94002 (Phonetype)
Essco Communications, 14-25 Plaza Road, Fair Lawn, New Jersey, 07410 (Acoustiphone)
Silent Aids Communications, P.O. Box 1727, Washington, D.C. 20001 (Sacco)

TV Type of Display
Hal Communications, P.O. Box 365, Urbana, Illinois 61801
Phonics, Inc., 814 Thayer Avenue, Silver Spring, Maryland 20910 (TVPHONE)

Rolling Screen (LED) Type of Display
Magsat Corporation, 151 Vanderbilt Avenue, West Hartford, Connecticut 06110 (Magsat)
Micon Industries, 1440 29 Avenue, Oakland, California 94601 (MCM)

Try to contact a member of the deaf community for names of TTY agents in or nearest your area. If you cannot locate one, write to Teletypewriters for the Deaf, Inc., 814 Thayer Avenue, Silver Spring, Maryland 20910.

For various reasons, many hundreds of deaf people still have not bought TTY for their homes. Therefore it is advisable for each public library to keep up-to-date information on all types of TTY equipment and a list of contact people.

Publications and Services for the Deaf

1. *Directory of Programs and Services for the Deaf,* issued each April by the *American Annals of the Deaf,* is an invaluable reference book. It includes teacher training data, a comprehensive listing of services for the deaf, up-to-date reports on research, publications on deafness, and a listing of schools, classes, and clinics for the deaf in the United States and Canada.

2. Another helpful source that should be in a public library is the Gale Research Company's *Encyclopedia of Associations.* Under "Deaf" are 29 organizations serving the deaf. The date of establishment, name of director, address, phone number, purpose, number of members, name of publication(s) if any, and annual conference are given for each organization.

   a. The American Speech and Hearing Association directory should be in public libraries. It lists the members, state associations, and members of the legislative council, as well as other information of use to members and the public. Institutions of higher learning that have accredited master's degree programs in speech pathology and audiology are also listed. The association and Gallaudet College founded Deafness, Speech, and Hearing Publications, Inc., which publishes *dsh Abstracts.*

3. Public Service Programs, established as a divison of Gallaudet College, responds to requests for service on a nationwide basis. It cooperates with the numerous professional organizations and agencies serving deaf people locally and nationally, such as National Association of Hearing and Speech Agencies, Registry of Interpreters for the Deaf, and Teletypewriters for the Deaf, Inc. The staff prepares community leadership training for deaf adults, TTY news service, and publications such as the Ladder Series Books, a series of novels and classics rewritten with reduced vocabulary. It has information programs for parents of deaf children and assists professionals in various fields—librarians, doctors, and lawyers—serve deaf citizens more effectively.

4. Media Services and Captioned Films, established by the Office of Education of the Department of Health, Education, and Welfare, is basically a loan service of captioned films through which many educational and theatrical films are made available to registered groups of deaf users. Cap-

tioned films can be shown in public libraries. Since deaf people could not use sound films, cassettes, and records, every effort to arrange captioned film showings for them should be made. You may be surprised, but in some areas there are deaf people who are still unaware of the availability of captioned films being distributed for their use. The library can publicize captioned films for the deaf in local papers and ask deaf readers to register at the library. You can help a deaf person apply for loans and make some arrangement for film showings in your meeting room at regular intervals. Theatrical films should be shown only to groups of deaf people, because of copyright restrictions, but educational films may be viewed by hearing audiences, too. No admission charge is allowed.

5. National Association of the Deaf (NAD) is the spokesman for all areas of deaf concerns. Among its interests are employment, senior citizens, interpreted or captioned programs on television, better educational opportunities, sign language, legislation, communication, and health. NAD publishes monthly *The Deaf American*, which keeps deaf people, parents, educators, librarians, vocational rehabilitation counselors, and the general public informed about deaf concerns. In *The Deaf American* are articles on humor among the deaf, sports, book reviews, film fare, foreign news about the deaf, reports from national conventions for the deaf, biographies, parents' point of view, advertisements, and much more. Every public library should have a subscription.

Among many many good articles, there are several by Robert F. Panara, professor of English and Drama at National Technical Institute for the Deaf in Rochester, New York. He is a well-known deaf writer and poet. Among his numerous works are "Deaf Characters in Fiction and Drama," "The Deaf Writer in America, from Colonial Times to 1970," and "Deaf Studies in the English Curriculum."

6. Alexander Graham Bell Association for the Deaf and Edward Miner Gallaudet Memorial Library at Gallaudet College have the two largest collections on subjects related to deafness and hearing-impaired people in the world. The collections include books, periodicals—many of them from the first issue—newspapers, yearbooks from schools of the deaf, theses and dissertations, conference reports, unpublished works, and archives. Both libraries are open to visitors.

   a. Librarians do not see enough book reviews on books relating to the deaf and deafness. Books on deafness written by well-known authors, such as Joanne Greenberg's *In This Sign* and Paul West's *Words for a Deaf Daughter*, are reviewed in well-known sources and are indexed in *Book Review Index* or *Book Review Digest*. Not all periodicals listed in *Standard Periodical Directory* under "Hearing and Speech" that include book reviews are indexed in *Book Review Digest* or *Book Review Index*. Book reviews appear in *Gallaudet Today*,

Volta Review, and *The Deaf American*. These titles should be in most public libraries. For a complete list of periodicals on hearing, deafness, or related topics, consult *Standard Periodical Directory*.

7. The bookstore at Gallaudet College has a complete publication list of books on the deaf and deafness available for sale.

8. There are films related to the deaf and deafness available at Gallaudet College for loan to libraries. Another collection of films on such subjects as total communication and documentary films aimed at acquainting the public with deafness is available for rent from Western Maryland College in Westminster, Maryland. Persons wishing to purchase, borrow, or rent films for use with deaf, as well as hearing audiences, should contact sources listed under films.

9. It is very likely that parents, on discovering deafness in their child, may call libraries for information. There are two organizations serving parents of deaf children. International Association of Parents of the Deaf is for parents to share their experiences in raising deaf children, to keep up with information concerning deaf children, and to help parents seek harmonious union with all professionals, friends, and organizations in promoting the general welfare of deaf children and youth. It publishes *Endeavor*. The other association is International Parents Organization, a section of the Alexander Graham Bell Association for the Deaf, whose aims and goals are to promote the teaching of speech and lip reading and the use of residual hearing of the deaf and to encourage research on deafness.

10. There are funds in support of service to the hearing-impaired and to the public on information about the deaf and deafness, the hard of hearing, and the deaf-blind. Lions International promotes Hearing Conservation and work for the deaf through Lionism. Quota International, Inc., an organization of professional and business women, also has projects focusing upon hearing and speech problems and deafness. Both organizations wish to extend a helping hand to hearing-impaired citizens. They may be a source of support for services to the hearing-impaired and to the public to provide information about hearing problems. They may be contacted to sponsor sign language classes, buy books and kits for children, and for support in purchasing Library Shelves on Deafness, available from the National Association of the Deaf.

11. Where can you find information for graduating deaf students who want to continue their education beyond high school? A booklet, "Guide to College/Career Programs for Deaf Students: Post-Secondary Programs," edited by E. Ross Stuckless and Gilbert Delgado, is available at no cost from the Office of the Dean of the Graduate School at Gallaudet College. In it you will find program descriptions. Among them are two national programs offered by Gallaudet College and the National Technical Institute for the Deaf. As mandated by federal law, they both serve deaf students from all of the states.

12. The cause, treatment, and prevention of deafness are the concerns of the Deafness Research Foundation. The foundation encourages young scientists to enter the field of deafness research, and it conducts public information programs on deafness. Individuals with ear disorders are encouraged to will their inner ear structures to the Temporal Bone Banks Program for Ear Reserach.

Hearing Conservation

Medical experts are concerned about the danger of people being exposed to high-intensity rock music or similar intense noise over long periods of time that may produce actual deafness in them. The Environmental Protection Agency has been attempting to reduce noise pollution at airports, in industries, and along highways.

Most workers who are subject to high-level noise, like steel workers, are now encouraged to protect their hearing by wearing earplugs or earmuffs while at work. More books and articles are appearing on the relationship between noise and hearing. Libraries should stock such materials in order to make people aware of this cause of hearing loss and thus to help conserve hearing ability.

If a person is aware of a hearing loss, he or she should visit an ear specialist (otologist or otolaryngologist). The specialist will diagnose and, if possible, treat the cause of the hearing loss. If it can't be treated, then the patient should be referred to an audiologist, a professional who specializes in hearing testing and hearing aid evaluation. The audiologist will then prescribe the aid best suited to the patient's need. Then a hearing aid dealer will take over. Better Hearing Institute is the best source of information about hearing aids. In a *Reader's Digest* reprint, "Deafness—The Silent Epidemic," which was condensed from *Lion*, Roul Tunley emphasized that the loss of hearing is the most widespread malady in the United States today and that the problem gets worse, yet many refuse to admit that it exists.

What Librarians Can Do for the Hearing Impaired

1. Look around and see what you already own—books and other materials about deafness and related topics (sign language, hearing aids, and noise pollution).

2. Contact the local teletypewriter agent for more information on a suitable machine for your library.

3. Contact Quota International, Lions International, or any charitable organization in your local community to tell them of your interest in providing service to the hearing-impaired. Service would include the ownership of a teletypewriter for deaf use in information service in lieu of telephone and building a collection of information resources on deafness in your library.

4. Establish contact with sources for free materials. Secure information on membership, subscriptions, and purchase of materials. Get your name on appropriate mailing lists.

5. Familiarize yourself with the literature on the deaf and deafness. Purchase appropriate publications and in sufficient quantity. Make displays of free materials available to the public. Consider maintaining a noncirculating reference file on deafness that would include recent periodical articles and ephemeral material.

6. Consider the hiring of qualified deaf employee(s) who will be able to do most tasks at the library along with the following jobs seldom now performed in public libraries:

 a. Teach staff on-the-job finger spelling and sign language and about the human factors that hearing people need to be aware of when communicating with the deaf.

 b. Inquire about captioned film loan service for library use and arrange film programs for registered hearing-impaired patrons.

 c. Sign books and show captioned films to the disadvantaged hearing-impaired people at local institutions (prisons and homes for the aged).

 d. Provide orientation to the hearing-impaired at the library.

 e. Get involved with the deaf community to help bring publicity from the library and to receive feedback.

 f. Help arrange a program for a class on finger spelling and sign language for people who have just become deaf or whose hearing is on the decline. People who need adjustment to hearing loss will benefit from a lecture series given by experts in the field. Quota and Lion members may be interested in such a program. A special program for hearing people who work with the deaf at regular jobs should be considered.

 g. Interpret Ameslan speaking and writing of low-verbal deaf people who call in or request in person in order to give them better service from knowledgeable librarians.

 h. Work with deaf-blind people. Many deaf people have such experience.

7. Make library resources on deafness known in your community through personal visits, brochures, annual Deaf Awareness Week, and other methods of publicity.

8. Consider the training of a staff member to become an interpreter to the deaf or consider the hiring of a worker with knowledge of sign language (for any position needed in the library) who will also be on call for interpreting service during the regular library hours. It is advisable for each library to maintain a list of local interpreters to the deaf, with their phone numbers. Such interpreters will be able to assist with library programs and also will be available for other programs or interpreting needs in the community. The Center for Continuing Education for the Deaf will be helpful

for ideas and suggestions for Adult Education programs for the deaf at your library. The center has an orientation manual for teachers of deaf adults and many other vital materials for your use.

9. Plan Deaf Awareness Week as an annual event in which everyone in the community will take part: mayor, other local government officials, business leaders, experts from hearing and speech centers, organizations serving the deaf, professional people, ear specialists, parents of deaf children, leaders and members from organizations for the deaf, Quota and Lion members, schools, celebrities and political figures who overcame their hearing loss, and many others. During that week the library could arrange events for each day, such as displays of special devices for the hearing-impaired, book readings, posters on hearing alert, and a lecture series by deaf authors or authorities on hearing and noise pollution. Offer free hearing tests during that week by a local clinic. Free mini-classes on sign language will increase people's interest in learning more about deafness.

10. Prepare a workshop at intervals for people working with or serving the hearing-impaired.

In general, services at the public library can be proposed as follows:

Children (Hearing-Impaired)
Communication kits
Signed English books
Nonverbal books
Signed storytelling
Captioned film showings and nonnarrated films[3]
Puppet and drama shows

Young Adults and Adults (Hearing-Impaired)
Dramatization and storytelling
Book club
Captioned, foreign, or nonnarrated films
Annotated bibliographies on special interests such as careers, leisure and recreation, or how-to-do-it. High interest-low vocabulary books with many illustrations should be listed. These bibliographies also will be helpful for hearing people whose second language is English
Orientation and handbooks on using their own library
Captioned videotape programs (also in sign language)
Information service via TTY

General (Professionals, Students, Interested Hearing and Impaired Patrons)
Bibliographies on the deaf and deafness
Information resources on deafness
Deaf Awareness Week
"Integrated" library programs

LSCA Funds

According to the *A.L.A. Washington Newsletter* (August 23, 1974), there is a new bilingual priority for the Library Services and Construction Act.

The basic state plan now must "set forth the criteria to be used in determining the adequacy of public library services in geographical areas and for groups of persons in the state, including criteria designed to assure that priority will be given to programs or projects which serve urban and rural areas with high concentrations of low-income families, *and to programs and projects which serve areas with high concentrations of persons of limited English-speaking ability.* . . ." "Limited English-speaking ability" is defined to mean "(A) individuals who were not born in the United States or whose native language is a language other than English, and (B) individuals who come from environments where a language other than English is dominant . . . and, by reason therefore have difficulty speaking and understanding instruction in the English language."

Public librarians should be aware of this interpretation and how it might be used to secure LSCA funds for improving services to hearing-impaired citizens.

SOME HAZARDS OF DEAFNESS[4]

You[5] start your car but don't feel the vibrations because the motor is running so smoothly. You push the starter again and step on the gas fully. The car makes so much noise that it sounds like a jet getting ready to take off. Passersby give you the "stupid" look.

While you are eating at a restaurant, the waitress asks if you care for more coffee. You reply in the negative since your cup is still half full. Later the waitress comes back and says something again. You "catch" only the word "coffee" at the end of her question and reply "yes," assuming that she is repeating her previous question—only this time she has said, "Are you through with your coffee?"

A stranger asks you for a match, directions, or something behind your back or when he does not have your attention. You, of course, do not know it and say nothing. The stranger then gives you a "dirty" look when you do see his face and you wonder why.

You judge a person to be very nice by his appearance and manners, never knowing that his voice labels him as a big phoney.

You turn around at exactly the right moment when someone calls you. That person may then scratch his head and wonder if you really are deaf. He may never know that you often look around just to make sure that no one wants you and that all is right with the world.

You take something out of your pocket. Other things come out, too, and fall on the floor without your knowing it. Later, much later, you find your-self missing keys, loose change, or something that should be in your pockets.

You go on vacation trips, visiting many interesting places, and pay for guides who tell you practically nothing since you can't understand them. Worse still are the sites that have preprepared tapes to explain interesting facts about the beautiful places you are paying to visit.

You ask someone what was said at a meeting and you usually get a shorter reply than former President Coolidge was famous for giving.

When people know you use a hearing aid they talk loud enough to be heard nearly in the next state.

AFTERMATH

Doesn't it sound challenging? Now you can start making plans in your library for services to the hearing-impaired. Then, later on, you will wonder if it is worth the effort. They may say something in their writing that you find offensive or they may seem to avoid you even though you know sign language. You will often wonder what you have done wrong!

These reactions that occur will be mostly negative and most of you may find it easier and more rewarding to work with children. That's great—and that must be done because deaf children should grow up using the public library, but deaf adults must *not* be neglected. You must try to understand their backgrounds and to accept the way they express their feelings by word and action. Many deaf adults were brainwashed as children that they must be able to speak with their voice and to read lips well enough to be accepted by the hearing society. In their own language, deaf people are very articulate and expressive, but when they must use English, communication is difficult. Most people tend to stay in a community where they feel comfortable; deaf people are no different from others. Deaf people prefer to join with other deaf people simply because they feel at ease and can communicate with other deaf people. They tend to choose to stay within their own groups and may not respond to or take advantage of the library services you are now willing to offer them.

Deaf adults have had many experiences of the hearing not understand-ing their English and being made fun of because they used "odd" expressions. Since facial expression is an important factor of their native sign language, deaf people are extremely sensitive to any inner thoughts carried by your face. They know when you are impatient, hurried, and irritable.

Communication between deaf and hearing is *not* easy at first. No one ever said it was! Both groups must learn to be patient, accepting, and under-standing with the other. Both must realize that good communication will come in time—but from the very beginning the important thing for each group to know is that each can learn from the other. The deaf must make the effort to take advantage of what the hearing world has to offer and learn from it. The hearing librarian must not have a patronizing, pitying, or condescending attitude toward the deaf. If you are to give any kind of meaningful library services at all, you must totally accept the deaf—as people. Just that; no more—no less!

It may be years before the public library can really help the deaf community. First, it will be necessary for the deaf to learn something about public libraries. My handbook *The Public Library Talks to You* (available from Alice Hagemeyer, D.C. Public Library, Washington, D.C.) can serve as an example of how public libraries can publicize their services to the deaf community. (I am indebted to many of my wonderful library and deaf colleagues for their spiritual support, encouragement, and suggestions while I worked on this and other "free" booklets. They did not charge for their contributions because they agreed that deaf awareness at the library is a vital necessity.) Both deaf and hearing people must realize the importance of what libraries can offer—education of the deaf and education of the hearing as to the meaning of deafness.

Author's note

Alice Hagemeyer's library program at the Washington, D.C., Public Library was described by her in an article in *The Deaf American*, October 1978. Although several public libraries around the country have attempted to serve their deaf patrons with special services, funded in some cases by either Library Services Construction Act (LSCA) or CETA funds, D.C. Public remains the only public library in the world with a full-time staff member on its regular budget who is devoted to serving the deaf community.

Until the mid 1970s, there was no section in the American Library Association devoted only to library needs of deaf people. In 1975, ALA began using interpreters for the deaf to sign at meetings. In 1976, a movement started, spearheaded by a group of librarians from D.C. Public, to establish a committee on library service to the deaf. In January 1978, after a great deal of preliminary work, it was recommended that a permanent unit on Library Service to the Deaf be formed within ASCLA (Association of Specialized and Cooperative Library Agencies). This agency represents a merger between ASLA (Association of School Library Agencies) and HRLSD (Health and Rehabilitative Library Service Division).

In September 1978, the Deaf Service Unit, known as the Library Service to the Deaf Section (LSDS), officially came into existence. By-laws and standards of service are still to be completed by this committee, which will be doing pioneering work in the future.

The following are scheduled 1980 publications by Alice Hagemeyer:

The Joy of Being a Deaf Person. A book dealing with deaf pride, deaf culture, and deaf heritage; heavily illustrated.

Communicating with Hearing People. A notebook based on experiences and information sharing of deaf participants in sign language classes with hearing participants at D.C. Public. It will be a resource to help deaf people communicate with the hearing world, especially at the library.

Library Service to the Deaf. A collection of Hagemeyer's speeches and papers.

The exciting field of Library Service to Deaf Patrons is truly still in its infancy. The decade of the 1980s, it can be said, will be "the decade of library service to the deaf."

NOTES

1. Leo M. Jacobs, *A Deaf Adult Speaks Out* (Washington, D.C.: Gallaudet College Press, 1974), pp. 56–60. Reprinted by permission of the author and the publisher, Gallaudet College.
2. Definition given by Council of Organizations Serving the Deaf, 1975.
3. Salvatore Parlato, *Films—Too Good for Words: A Directory of Nonnarrated 16mm Films* (New York: R. R. Bowker, 1972).
4. Adapted with permission of Roy K. Holcomb, author, and Jesse Smith, editor, of the *Deaf American*, from "95 Hazards of Deafness."
5. "You" refers to a deaf person.

8

A Core Public Library Collection

This basic collection of materials would enable public librarians to serve the informational needs of disabled people. For those who wish to add a starter collection in special education, note the starred (*) entries in Chapter 14.

REHABILITATION, GENERAL

Bowe, Frank. *Handicapping America: Barriers to Disabled People.* New York: Harper & Row, 1978. An overview of the way in which disabled Americans are handicapped. Case studies, source directories of organizations, and special government programs.

Wright, Beatrice. *Physical Disability—A Psychological Approach.* New York: Harper & Row, 1960. A classic study of the psychology of, and attitudes toward, disabled people.

REHABILITATION, MEDICINE

Biermann, June, and Toohey, Barbara. *The Diabetes Question and Answer Book.* Los Angeles: Sherbourne Press, 1974. Questions and practical answers for the diabetic and for their relatives. Appendixes include listing by state of affiliates of the American Diabetes Association. Exchange lists for foreign foods, ethnic diets, sample menus, etc.

Cooper, I. S. *Living with Chronic Neurological Disease: A Handbook for Patient and Family.* New York: Norton, 1976.

Davis, Marcella Zalewski. *Living with Multiple Sclerosis: A Social Psychological Analysis.* Springfield, Ill.: Charles C. Thomas, 1973.

Dorland. *Dorland's Illustrated Medical Dictionary*. Philadelphia: Saunders, 1974. An excellent medical dictionary.

Klinger, Judith L. *Self-Help Manual for Arthritis Patients*. New York: The Arthritis Foundation, 1974.

Schmidt, J. E. *Paramedical Dictionary: A Practical Dictionary for the Semi-medical and Ancillary Medical Professions*. Springfield, Ill.: Charles C. Thomas, 1973.

REHABILITATION COUNSELING

Goldenson, Robert M., ed.-in-chief, Dunham, Jerome R., and Dunham, Charles S., assoc. eds. *Disability and Rehabilitation Handbook*. New York: McGraw-Hill, 1978. With many contributors; a tremendous compendium of information, medical definitions of disabilities, definitions of health science professions concerned with rehabilitation, civil rights, and consumerism, independent living, educational programs, vocational rehabilitation, psychosocial aspects of disability, environmental barriers, recreation, statistics, organizations interested in the disabled, listings of perodicals and directories, government programs, sources of information. No mention of rehabilitation libraries or of rehabilitation librarians.

INDEPENDENT LIVING

Accent on Information—AOI, service of Accent on Living. A computerized retrieval system for information on helpful devices, commercial equipment, and how-to-do-it problems.

Aids and Appliances. Catalogue from the American Foundation for the Blind. Annual.

Beasley, Mary Catherine, Burns, Dorothy, and Weiss, Janis. *Adapt Your Own: A Clothing Brochure for People with Special Needs*. University, Ala.: University of Alabama, Division of Continuing Education, 1977.

Bowar, Miriam T. *Clothing for the Handicapped: Fashion Adaptations for Adults and Children*. Publication no. 739. Minneapolis: Sister Kenny Institute, 1977. Good item for vertical files. Solutions to problems of adapted clothing for the disabled. Alterations of clothing for the able-bodied suggested, patterns offered as well as a source directory.

Bruck, Lilly. *Access: The Guide to a Better Life for Disabled Americans*. New York: Random House, 1978. A book of consumer services for the disabled that serves truly to place them in the mainstream of society. Invaluable information as to where and how to obtain products, the civil rights of disabled, travel tips, recreation.

Chasin, Joseph, and Saltman, Jules, eds. *Home in a Wheelchair*. Washington, D.C.: Paralyzed Veterans of America, 1977. General advice for anyone buying or building a house—grade of land, ramps, car ports or garages, door widths, handles, special environmental systems for the interior, kitchen, laundry, storage design, floor coverings, bathrooms and bedrooms, chairlifts, elevators, easy opening windows.

————. *The Wheelchair in the Kitchen*. Washington, D.C.: Paralyzed Veterans of America, 1973. Good kitchen layouts, optimum counter heights, wheelchair measurements and turning radius, design of all equipment, laundry room ideas. Kitchen helpers such as tools for grasping items beyond reach. Suggestions for remodeling old layouts. What to look for when apartment hunting. Safety tips. Bibliography.

Cleo Living Aids. Catalogue. Physical therapy, occupational therapy, and rehabilitation equipment, treatment tables, parallel bars, whirlpools, many professional items such as traction equipment, wheelchairs, shower chairs, toilet seats, trapezes, etc.

Everest & Jennings Catalogue. Everest & Jennings, Inc.

Fashion-Able. Rock Hill, New Jersey. Catalogue of clothing for the disabled.

Gilbert, Arlene E. *You Can Do It from a Wheelchair.* New Rochelle, N.Y.: Arlington House, 1973. Author has multiple sclerosis and four children to take care of. How-to information of a very practical nature for the disabled about all aspects of daily living and doing.

Hale, Glorya, ed. *The Source Book for the Disabled.* New York: Paddington, 1979. Illustrated guide to more independent living.

Independent Living for Handicapped Individuals: Sources of Information. Clearinghouse on the Handicapped, Room 338D, H. H. H. Building, Department of HEW, Washington, D.C. 20201. Spring 1979. Lists types of independent living facilities available nationally. Plan is to update periodically.

Klinger, Judith Lannefeld, ed. *Mealtime Manual for People with Disabilities and the Aging,* 2nd ed. Ronks, Pa.: Campbell Soup Co., 1978.

Laurie, Gini. *Housing and Home Services for the Disabled: Guidelines and Experiences in Independent Living.* Hagerstown, Md.: Harper & Row, 1977. An excellent book in the field of adaptations of interiors for independent living for the disabled. Accounts of different life-styles and factual information as to where the field of independent living stands. Information about group homes, apartment clusters, long-term residential homes, mobile homes, HUD assisted housing, independent living with attendant care.

Lowman, Edward, and Klinger, Judith Lannefeld. *Aids to Independent Living: Self-Help for the Handicapped.* New York: McGraw-Hill, 1969. Expensive, but well worth the money. It is the latest and most definitive catalogue of devices for independent living for the disabled. The authors are on the staff of the Institute of Rehabilitation Medicine, New York University Medical Center. Useful for groups who work with the disabled without benefit of medical centers, such as general practitioners, public health nurses, occupational and physical therapists, vocational counselors, as well as disabled people themselves. Each category is expanded by the inclusion of bibliographies of agencies and periodicals. At the end of the book is a list of equipment sources with addresses and priecs. Emphasis is on mail-order availability, thus making many devices available to people who lack access to distributors in large metropolitan areas.

May, Elizabeth E., Waggoner, Neva R., and Hotte, Eleanor B. *Independent Living for the Handicapped and the Elderly.* Boston: Houghton Mifflin, 1974. An updated version, but still retains some outdated bibliography. However, it is worth buying for library shelves because of some practical information in areas of clothing for the handicapped and for some of the appendixes, which contain addresses of organizations and some current source materials.

Prentke Romich Company. Prentke Romich markets electronic aids for severely handicapped persons. Includes nonverbal communication aids, environmental control systems, education aids. Equipment hard to find anywhere else.

Preston. Same materials as *Cleo*; also markets perceptual educational training and testing materials, teaching resources, large knobbed puzzles, balance activities, playground equipment, and more.

Sammons, Fred, Inc. *Be OK: Self-Help Aids*. Brookfield, Ill. Professional and institutional catalogue, orthotics, wheelchair accessories, homemaking, hygiene, dressing, and eating.

Schweikert, Harry A., Jr. *Wheelchair Bathrooms*. Washington D.C.: Paralyzed Veterans of America, n.d. Complete directions for designing a bathroom to accommodate wheelchairs. Measurements of room, equipment of all kinds.

Sister Kenny Institute. *Educational Materials Catalog*. Minneapolis, 1979. Monographs in areas of daily living as well as audiovisuals. Nursing care after stroke, as well as general rehabilitation nursing care. Extremely valuable material.

Strebel, Miriam Bowar. *Adaptions and Techniques for the Disabled Homemaker*, 5th ed. Publication no. 710. Minneapolis: Sister Kenny Institute, 1978. Information about simple devices and adaptions that can be used by the disabled homemaker.

Washam, Veronica. *The One-Hander's Book*: *Helpful Hints for Activities of Daily Living*. New York: John Day, 1973.

BARRIER-FREE DESIGN

American National Standard: Specifications of Making Buildings and Facilities Accessible to, and Usable by, the Physically Handicapped. New York: American National Standards Institute, Inc. (distributed by Easter Seal Society, Chicago, 1961). Currently under revision.

Cary, Jane Randolph. *How to Create Interiors for the Disabled: A Guidebook for Family and Friends*. New York: Random House, 1978. Cary is a home furnishing and building editor. Practical information about remodeling techniques, diagrams and instructions for ramps, kitchens, and bathrooms, doors and windows, furnishing and arranging rooms. Useful products and materials. Suppliers' names and prices; individuals and organizations.

General Services Administration, Public Building Service. *Design Criteria: New Public Building Accessibility*. December 1977. Standards for architectural modification of public buildings. Requests for copies should be directed to the GSA Business Service Center in your area.

Kliment, Stephen A. *Into the Mainstream: A Syllabus for a Barrier-Free Environment*. Publication no. 210-826/5043. American Institute of Architects, Rehabilitation Services Administration, Department of HEW, 1976; for Sale by the Superintendent of Documents. Legislation, minimum standards, resources, both printed and audiovisual, listing of societies, agencies, and other helpful organizations.

Montalvo, Alfredo, project director, and Weitzman, Mark Ross, corporate project coordinator. *Bathroom Facilities: Accommodating the Physically Disabled and the Aged*. A Research and Design Project, Program in Industrial Design, School of Art, University of Michigan, Owens-Corning Fiberglass Corp., 1977. Design of a bathroom for physically disabled and elderly people. Bibliography.

National Center for a Barrier Free Environment. *Opening Doors: A Handbook on Making Facilities Accessible to Handicapped People*. Prepared for Community

Services Administration, Washington, D.C., n.d. Minimum accessibility standards, suggestions for paying for the project, additional sources for information, sources for international symbol of access.

National Easter Seal Society for Crippled Children and Adults. *Current Materials on Barrier-Free Design.* Chicago. Bibliography, current issue.

National Library Service for the Blind and Physically Handicapped, Reference Service. *Bibliography on Architectural Barriers.* 1976.

TRAVEL

Access Amtrak, A Guide to Amtrak Services for Elderly and Handicapped. Washington, D.C.: National Railroad Passenger Corp., 1977. Some provisions have been made on Amtrack trains for handicapped travelers, but many trains and stations are still not barrier-free.

Access: National Parks: A Guide for Handicapped Visitors. Publication no. 024-005-00691-5. Washington, D.C.: National Park Service, Department of the Interior, 1978. Available from Superintendent of Documents. Parks are listed by state and accessible areas noted.

Access Travel: Airports, 2nd ed. Pueblo, Colo.: Consumer Information, 1977. Much of this data will be found in the Weiss book, but this pamphlet offers the charts of accessible airports in a much larger, more readable format.

American Automobile Association. *The Handicapped Driver's Mobility Guide.* Descriptions of over 500 transportation services available to handicapped persons through a variety of organizations, including driving schools, manufacturers of adaptive equipment with names, addresses and telephone numbers for each listing.

Annand, Douglass R. *The Wheelchair Traveler.* Milford, N.H.: the author, yearly editions. This well-known travel guide, written and issued yearly by a world-traveling paraplegic, includes 2,000 listings in 49 states, Canada, and Mexico of accessible motels, restaurants, and sightseeing areas. Annand also lists the cities for which the National Easter Seal Society has issued guides. He offers helpful hints about making travel easier for the disabled, such as how to narrow your wheelchair for those "slightly too narrow" doorways, how to handle air travel, how to summon medical aid, etc.

Atwater, Maxine H. *Rollin' On: A Wheelchair Guide to U.S. Cities.* New York: Dodd Mead, 1978. Itineraries for Chicago, Honolulu, New York, Philadelphia, San Diego, San Antonio, San Francisco, and Washington, D.C. Three- to six-day sightseeing tours with precise details as to how to get around in a wheelchair. Information is also given on other major cities. A novel and useful idea and a good reference work for the wheelchair traveler.

Aviation Public Services Division, Newark International, LaGuardia, and Kennedy International Airports. *Facilities and Services for the Handicapped.* New York. Terminals, parking, car rentals, rest rooms, other services, maps of each airport designating accessible areas and services.

European Highways E1 and E4: Motel Guide for the Disabled. New York: International Society for Rehabilitation of the Disabled. The International Society for

Rehabilitation of the Disabled has member organizations in 65 countries. This pamphlet is published by the subcommittee of ISRD, International Committee on Technical Aids, Housing, Transportation, which is housed by the Swedish Institute for the Handicapped. It is an early attempt to list motels aˡɔng Highway 1 (London–Palermo) and Highway 4 (Lisbon–Helsinki).

Evergreen Travel Service, Inc. 19429 44 Street West, Lynwood, Washington. Tours for the disabled, blind, and retarded. Brochures available in braille. Information on request.

Handi-Cap Horizons. 3250 East Loretta Drive, Indianapolis, Indiana. Organized tours for the handicapped. Newsletter listing future tours will be sent for a small fee for subscription.

1978–79 International Directory of Access Guides. Rehabilitation World. Spring/ Summer 1978 issue, vol. 4, nos. 1, 2, or available separately from Access Guide, Rehabilitation International USA.

Lockhart, Freda Bruce. *London for the Disabled.* London: Ward, Lock, 1967. Lockhart, well-known film critic, broadcaster, and victim of multiple sclerosis, has been wheelchair-bound for some years. She has compiled a directory of London shops, hotels, restaurants, galleries, museums, libraries, churches, theaters, transportation, etc., accessible to the handicapped.

Pan American Tours for the Disabled. Information can be obtained at local Pan American ticket offices or write: Larry J. Chadwell, Sales Coordinator, Pan American World Airways, 1219 Main Street, Houston, Texas 77002.

President's Committee on Employment of the Handicapped. *Highway Rest Areas for Handicapped Travelers.* Washington, D.C. Over 800 accessible rest areas in 48 states. These areas are designated by a blue and white sign bearing the international symbol of access.

Rambling Tours. P.O. Box 1304, Hallandale, Florida. Guided tours for disabled travelers. Severely disabled persons requiring physical care may bring an attendant or request tour directors to provide one for a fee, which will be agreed upon in advance. A newsletter is issued about past and future tours and will be sent upon request.

Reamy, Lois. *Travelability: A Guide for Physically Disabled Travelers in the United States.* New York: Macmillan, n.d. Developments within the travel industry that have resulted in greatly expanded travel opportunities for persons with mobility limitations. Suggestions for planning trips, state-by-state listing of guides to barrier-free travel, medically related questions, etc.

Sath News. Society for the Advancement of Travel for the Handicapped. Brooklyn, New York. A membership organization for travel agencies, publishers, and others interested in travel for the disabled.

Weiss, Louise. *Access to the World.* New York: Chatham Square Press, 1977. An up-to-date, comprehensive source of information, the first book of its kind. Well worth purchasing for reference for disabled people wishing to travel.

Women's Committee, President's Committee on the Employment of the Handicapped. *A List of Guidebooks for Handicapped Travelers.* This directory lists guidebooks prepared for cities in the United States and includes a section on foreign cities.

SEX AND THE DISABLED

Bregman, Sue. *Sexuality and the Spinal Cord Injured Woman.* Booklet 726. Minneapolis: Sister Kenny Institute, 1975. This is a practical pamphlet in which 31 spinal cord injured women speak frankly and explicitly about their sexual relationships. It was written for physically disabled women and the health professionals who work with them.

Eisenberg, M. G., and Rustad, L. C. *Sex and the Spinal Cord Injured: Some Questions and Answers.* Publication no. 051-000-00081-1. Washington, D.C.: Superintendent of Documents, rev. March 1975. This pamphlet includes information on the effects of spinal cord injury on sexual functioning in both the male and the female, and deals with specific concerns such as loss of sexual functioning and other problems, sexual alternatives, marriage, divorce, and children.

Gregory, Martha F. *Sexual Adjustment: A Guide for the Spinal Cord Injured.* Bloomington, Ill.: Accent on Living, 1974. This paperback was written by a woman who is experienced as a counselor as well as a marriage partner. It concerns the ability to perform in relation to the self-esteem of the handicapped person and his/her partner.

Mooney, T. O., Cole, T. M., and Chilgren, R. A. *Sexual Options for Paraplegics and Quadriplegics.* Boston: Little, Brown, 1975. Written by a spinal cord injured person and two physicians as a guide to techniques. The text and photographs show that disabled people can lead sexually fulfilling lives.

Toward Intimacy: Family Planning and Sexuality Concerns of Physically Disabled Women. Task Force on Concerns of Physically Disabled Women. New York: Human Sciences Press.

Within Reach: Providing Family Planning Services to Physically Disabled Women. Task Force on Concerns of Physically Disabled Women. New York: Human Sciences Press, 1978. Complements *Toward Intimacy.* Describes the specifics of implementing the long-denied sexual and contraceptive rights of disabled women. Provides guidelines to providers of health care services.

PERIODICALS

(Starred entries indicate publications by disabled people.)

*Accent on Living. Raymond C. Cheever, pub. and ed. Bloomington, Illinois. Quarterly.

*The Deaf American. National Association of the Deaf. 814 Thayer Avenue, Silver Spring, Maryland. 11 issues a year.

Disabled USA. President's Committee on Employment of the Handicapped. Washington, D.C. Monthly.

*Green Pages. Newsmagazine for the Disabled. 614 West Fairbanks Avenue, Winter Park, Florida. Quarterly.

Informer. Information Exchange, Office of the Secretary, Office of Human Development Services, RSA, Department of HEW. Prepared by the Information Exchange Program, Arkansas Rehabilitation Research and Training Center (RT-13), University of Arkansas and Arkansas Services. Free.

Journal of Visual Impairment and Blindness. American Foundation for the Blind. 15 West 16 Street, New York, New York.

*Paraplegia News. Paralyzed Veterans of America and National Spinal Cord Injury Foundation. 935 Coastline Drive, Seal Beach, California. Monthly.

Programs for the Handicapped. Department of HEW, Office for Handicapped Individuals. Washington, D.C. Monthly or more often. Apply.

Rehabilitation Gazette (formerly *Toomey j Gazette*). Gini Laurie, ed., 4502 Maryland Avenue, St. Louis, Missouri. Annual. Must apply.

Volta Review. Alexander Graham Bell Association for the Deaf. 3417 Volta Place N.W., Washington, D.C. Monthly except June, July, and August.

NEWSLETTERS

American Foundation for the Blind Newsletter. American Foundation for the Blind, Inc., 15 West 16 Street, New York, New York.

In the Mainstream. Mainstream, Inc. 1200 15 Street N.W., Washington, D.C. To report on the progress of affirmative action for the handicapped.

National Rehabilitation Information Center (NARIC). *The Pathfinder: Your Guide to Information Resources and Technology in Rehabilitation.* 6 times a year. Washington, D.C.

On Your Own. Continuing Education in Home Economics. P.O. Box 2987, University, Alabama. Monthly.

The Report. National Center for a Barrier Free Environment. Seventh Street and Florida Avenue N.E., Washington, D.C. Bimonthly. Offers up-to-date information on nationwide developments in making the environment accessible to the disabled. Valuable.

DIRECTORIES

American Foundation for the Blind. *Directory of Agencies Serving the Visually Handicapped in the United States,* 19th ed. New York, 1975. A state-by-state listing of services on the state and local levels with supplementary lists of specialized agencies and organizations (of professional workers and councils of agencies for the blind, federal agencies, guide dog schools, medical research organizations, national consultative voluntary organizations, resources for reading and educational materials), useful directories, and organizations with an interest in the blind.

Association of Rehabilitation Facilities. *ARF Membership Directory.* Washington, D.C. Annual. Lists institutional member (facilities) along with group associate members and individual members. Also included is a listing of services that each facility offers. Lists officers and board of directors, ARF chapters, and ARF committees and chairpeople. Published annually in May.

Clearinghouse on the Handicapped. *Directory of National Information Sources on Handicapping Conditions and Related Services.* Washington, D.C.: Office for Handicapped Individuals, Department of HEW, 1976. The directory contains abstracts on 225 national organizations providing information services to handicapped persons or about handicapping conditions, and 45 federal agencies and programs that serve handicapped individuals or provide benefits and assistance. Single copy requests accepted from programs providing information services with enclosed self-addressed mailing label. Other requests and additional copies available from Superintendent of Documents.

Gollay, Elinor, and Bennett, Alwina. *The College Guide for Students with Disabilities.* Cambridge, Mass.: Abt Associates, 1976.

National Spinal Cord Injury Foundation (formerly the National Paraplegia Foundation). *National Resource Directory: A Guide to Services and Opportunities for Persons with Spinal Cord Injury or Disease and Others with Severe Physical Disabilities.* Newton Upper Falls, Mass., 1979. Valuable information on all aspects of medical and vocational rehabilitation, as well as independent living, sexuality, agency addresses, journals, and newsletters. Listing of pamphlets on spinal cord injury, paraplegia, and quadriplegia.

Plus Publications, Inc. *Handicapped Americans Reports: A Guide to Organizations, Agencies and Federal Programs for Handicapped Americans.* Washington, D.C., n.d. An extremely useful guide with addresses and telephone numbers of national organizations which deal with the disabled. Includes federal offices and programs, committees of the U.S. Congress, associations and organizations, and foundations that are sources of funds and information. Will be updated periodically.

Selected Federal Publications Concerning the Handicapped. Publication no. (OHD) 77-22005. Washington, D.C.: Department of HEW, Office of Human Development Services, Office for Handicapped Individuals. Government publications in areas of education, employment, housing, legislation, travel, Social Security, statistics, etc.

U.S. Rehabilitation Services Administration. *Directory of State Divisions of Vocational Rehabilitation.* Washington, D.C. Annual. A listing of professional personnel in state divisions of vocational rehabilitation. A similar list is available of state agencies for the blind (*Directory of State Agencies for the Blind*).

PART III

The Special Rehabilitation Library

9

History and Philosophy
of Rehabilitation

Most disabled people need a variety of services from birth to adulthood. This is generally called *rehabilitation*, defined as a process through which a disabled person reaches his or her highest level of self-sufficiency. It calls for a team approach, and librarians only now are becoming part of the team. The idea of librarians serving the disabled must, of course, become a reality wherever disabled people are to be found. The first two sections of this book dealt with information that could be placed effectively in all public and school libraries serving disabled users. This section will develop the concept of rehabilitation librarianship as a profession within the general health science field. Rehabilitation professionals need trained librarians to support their work. Rehabilitation and librarianship must be brought together to utilize the acquisition, organization, and retrieval skills of the professional librarian in order to improve information delivery systems to disabled patrons and to the professionals who serve them.

Rehabilitation librarians do not need to become rehabilitation counselors. However, they do need enough background to enable them to understand the goals of the professionals in the rehabilitation field, to evaluate the body of rehabilitation literature that now exists, to be able to retrieve the information being generated in ever-increasing quantities, and to deal with these materials in an organized fashion. Students need to receive this special training in library school if they wish to enter the field. In addition to including general library service to the disabled as part of their core curricula, library schools should initiate specialized courses in rehabilitation librarianship within the health science curriculum.

Rehabilitation librarianship is a new concept in the field of library service to the disabled. Librarians are needed in all types of rehabilitation facilities. They must have the information and referral skills that will enable them to function as useful members of the rehabilitation team and to serve a disabled clientele.

TYPES AND FORMS OF REHABILITATION

For the congenitally disabled, the process of attaining the highest level of self-sufficiency might better be defined as "habilitation." It is achieved through a combination of medicine and therapy, education, and vocational training. The goal of rehabilitation is the greatest degree of independence for each disabled person. But the word *independence* means different things to different people. For some, independence may mean education, vocational training, and a job as a productive member of society. For the severely disabled, it may mean a sheltered workshop with opportunities to socialize with others. For some, it may mean work at home and/or simply to achieve an independent living situation.

Medical rehabilitation has come of age in the past few decades, giving the disabled the chance to minimize the destructive effects of disability, whether it is the result of disease or accident, congenital, or the consequence of deterioration because of age. Rehabilitation medicine seeks to restore normal functioning to the greatest possible degree.

Medical rehabilitation may take place in a comprehensive rehabilitation hospital or in a center that specializes in the treatment of a special disability, such as spinal cord injury, burns, strokes, or other conditions. Special departments include physical, occupational, and speech therapy, recreation, psychology, social work, prosthetics and orthotics, and rehabilitation counseling. An important department in many such facilities is "activities of daily living" (ADL). This is a simulated apartment living area in which a patient can learn to execute the daily tasks that will allow him or her to function independently. Rehabilitation units in general hospitals function in conjunction with the medical departments to provide consulting services. For example, a rehabilitation specialist might teach an amputee proper care of his or her stump after an operation.

Wheelchairs are important aids to self-sufficiency and are made by technicians according to the physician's prescription. All parts of the wheelchair can be modified to meet the needs of the user. The kind of brakes and materials to be used, as well as the type of back, seat, and wheels, are specified by a physician.

Vocational rehabilitation can be defined as a series of actions moving toward a goal. The goal can be full-time or part-time competitive employment, sheltered or voluntary work, self-employment, homebound employment, housekeeping and independent living, or any combination of these life adjustment activities. The purpose is to develop disabled persons' abilities to their highest functioning levels. Training or retraining or education may be part of the process.

The *rehabilitation agency* is a facility that provides or secures services for the rehabilitation of vocationally disadvantaged persons. The services of such an agency include coordinating and counseling and one or more of the following: evaluating, work adjustment, physical or occupational therapy, the fitting and use of prostheses, and job placement.[1] Rehabilitation agencies may be public, state-supported, voluntary local units in hospitals, the Veterans Administration, insurance companies, sheltered workshops, rehabilitation centers, or speech and hearing clinics.

"*Rehabilitation centers* are agencies which may be independent or part of a hospital which provides an integrated program of medical, psychological social and vocational services for rehabilitative purposes."[2]

A *sheltered workshop* may be loosely defined as "a nonprofit organization that provides employment to handicapped persons and that is certificated by the wage and hour division of the Department of Labor, as covered by special minimum-wage provisions for at least some of the handicapped persons employed at the organization."[3] The Vocational Rehabilitation Act Amendments of 1968 substitute "rehabilitation facility" for "workshop." To the layperson or librarian looking for information, these differences in definition can be confusing. Often a rehabilitation facility provides comprehensive services that include those provided by rehabilitation agencies, as well as transitional or long-term employment for the severely disabled in sheltered workshop-type settings. In many cases remedial education is also provided.

A BRIEF HISTORY OF PROGRESS

In the United States there was little or no interest in the rehabilitation of the physically disabled before the nineteenth century. Originally considered to be the responsibility of their families, disabled persons became the early nineteenth-century inhabitants of asylums and poor houses. Historical attitudes were influenced by a mixture of inherited ideas. From the Greeks came the notion that the physically impaired were inferior; from the Hebrews, the belief that the sick were being punished by God. The Christian concept that ministering to the handicapped leads to the acquisition of moral virtue vied with the Calvinistic assumption that the absence of material success resulting from disability was evidence of lack of grace and with the Darwinian theory of survival of the fittest. All these concepts were balanced against the pre-World War I faith in the progress of mankind through science and technology.[4] At the end of the nineteenth and early twentieth centuries, there was a mixture of attitudes consisting of some forms of social welfare with a growing interest in primarily medical and physical restoration.[5]

During the years between 1870 and 1920, medical science made great progress in developing the means of preventing disease and disability and offering hope for the cure and rehabilitation of disabled people. In 1899 the Cleveland Rehabilitation Center established the first formal rehabilitation program in the United States. All rehabilitation was medically oriented and aimed for the best possible physical recovery.

In 1912 the U.S. Public Health Service was established. The emphasis on preventing disease for the masses rather than on a social medical program that would be concerned with the individual seemed to indicate the feeling that the twin objectives of sanitation and immunization would eventually eliminate disease entirely.[6]

Religious Groups and Health and Social Organizations

Religious groups also made significant contributions. The Salvation Army came from England in 1879 with social programs to bring welfare relief as they preached the gospel. Goodwill Industries, established in 1902 by Edgar James Helms, a Methodist minister in Boston, developed the idea of hiring unemployed persons to repair and renovate clothing and materials donated by the public. Workers were paid with funds from the sale of the refinished products. In 1918, the Board of Missions of the Methodist Church took over Goodwill, emphasizing a sheltered workshop program for the physically handicapped. B'nai B'rith, a welfare and education organization developed by American Jews in 1843, developed rapidly during the late nineteenth and early twentieth centuries. Its present programs in vocational guidance and its sponsorship of nondenominational vocational training centers for the handicapped developed during the early years of this century.[7]

The immigrants of the late 1800s were predominantly Roman Catholic, and the American Catholic church of this period became the church of the city, the worker, and the immigrant. The papal encyclical *Rerum Novarum* of 1891 pointed out social ideals and responsibilities that supported the social views of many Americans.[8]

In 1881 the American Red Cross was established, sponsoring an Institute for Crippled and Disabled Men in New York City and Braille Transcriptions for the Blind. The Braille Transcriptions were later turned over to the Library of Congress. In 1904 the National Tuberculosis Association was founded, followed by the National Association of Mental Health, founded in 1909 by Clifford Beers, a former inmate of mental institutions. In 1919 came the Easter Seal Society, originally a local organization in Ohio affiliated with local Rotary Clubs.[9]

Within a 30-year period, 1890–1920, the immigration, urbanization, and industrialization of America necessitated that the federal government take an interest in citizens' rights, including the health of the individual. By the end of the nineteenth century, industry had accepted the view that when an employee was injured or killed, the employer was responsible if negligence could be proven. Many states began to accept judicial decisions in this area, and in 1910 the first Workmen's Compensation law was passed in New York State.[10] Many other stated followed suit in the next decade. Although the concept of rehabilitation for return to work was not included in the original laws, many people supporting the legislation also believed in vocational rehabilitation.

Industries, realizing that profits were at stake, went on to develop industrial medical programs for workers. Doctors and nurses began to work in industrial settings, and the professions of industrial medicine and industrial nursing were born.

Jane Addams, in 1889, established Hull-House in Chicago, where she developed the casework approach to help individuals adjust to their environment. She pushed for the first eight-hour-day laws for women, the first state child labor laws, and the first juvenile court, and she was a strong backer of reform in education, where her ideas supported those of John Dewey.[11]

Vocational Rehabilitation

During the early years of the twentieth century, influenced in part by developments in western Europe and in part by American social welfare reform, the emphasis on purely medical rehabilitation of the disabled began to change. The growing idea that physical rehabilitation was not enough and that people needed to be trained or retrained if at all possible for some form of productive activity marked the beginning of the vocational rehabilitation movement.

In 1918 the U.S. government initiated a vocational rehabilitation program for World War I veterans.[12] This program emphasized the development and purchase of prosthetic appliances. Although the goal was reemployment and the program did include some vocational training, the major emphasis was on physical restoration. Today the Veterans Administration is still very active in the fields of prosthetic and orthotic research. Its products are only available to veterans; however, many VA designs are given to commercial engineering firms for development and sale to the civilian disabled. Here, a breakdown in the communication system often prevents the civilian disabled from being aware of where these products are to be found or even that they exist.

The success of the initial veterans' program led to the passage of the first federal law for rehabilitation of civilians, the Vocational Rehabilitation Act of 1920 (PL 236).[13] In some cases this law had been preceded, and later followed, by enabling legislation in two-thirds of the states. At this time the National Rehabilitation Association was established, and objectives began to form for the development of the profession known today as rehabilitation counseling. The case method technique was adopted from the social work field. Early emphasis left no doubt that the program was to be vocationally oriented, and disabled people were to be trained only if they demonstrated employability. Emphasis was on vocational training rather than on higher education. The financial benefits of helping the disabled become contributing members of the working society rather than public charges were obvious. This philosophical concept prevailed through the 1960s and, in many state offices of vocational rehabilitation, it prevails today.

Early critics of the act included rehabilitation medicine pioneers such as Henry H. Kessler of New Jersey, who felt that excluding medical rehabilitation was a mistake. Such cooperation as did occur was due to initiative taken by individual state agencies with physicians, clinics, volunteer agencies, and other organizations.

As the program developed, and remains today, it is a cooperative venture between federal and state governments, with the federal government providing funds and leadership to state and regional programs administered locally. Any disabled person is entitled by law to take advantage of this service, and upon application will be assigned a rehabilitation counselor. Early legislation makes no mention of funding to disabled people while in training. This concept developed in 1933 as part of Franklin D. Roosevelt's New Deal. People on relief who received vocational rehabilitation services also were provided living expenses while they were in training.

The Social Security Act of 1935 provided a large increase in grants to the states, as well as an increase in funding for the federal administration budget.[14] In 1940 Congress increased the appropriation to the states, and provision was made to extend services to the severely handicapped not eligible before—those either homebound or employed in sheltered workshops. Residents of institutions were not mentioned. Redefinitions of this philosophy continue to have repercussions today as Congress considers funding for new types of independent living arrangements being pioneered mainly by young adults with severe disabilities.

It is a point of interest that early rehabilitation services were developed for people with orthopedic disabilities. As will be seen, in the development of education for handicapped children, exactly the reverse process occurred; as a result, services for orthopedically disabled children were the last to be developed in the field of special education.

In 1940, for the first time, a program for paying living expenses for handicapped people participating in a rehabilitation plan was made available to the state agencies. World War II had a great effect on the growth of the vocational rehabilitation movement. In 1943 a new and separate agency, known as the Office of Vocational Rehabilitation, was established and a federal act known as the Barden-LaFollette Act (PL 113) was passed.[15] This legislation, in addition to greater expansion of existing services, provided for the first time for the vocational rehabilitation of the mentally handicapped.

In 1945 Congress passed a joint resolution that established the President's Committee on Employment of the Handicapped, and many states followed suit by forming governor's committees. Promotional materials were developed by these organizations in a program of information and education of the public in positive attitudes toward the employment of handicapped people, emphasizing abilities rather than disabilities.

In 1951 Mary E. Switzer was named director of the Office of Vocational Rehabilitation in the Federal Security Agency. Two years later Dwight D. Eisenhower appointed Oveta Culp Hobby as secretary of the new Department of Health, Education, and Welfare. Switzer conceived a greatly enlarged plan for vocational rehabilitation, and her ideas were strongly supported by Nelson Rockefeller, then undersecretary to Secretary Hobby.[16] Public Law 565, called the Vocational Rehabilitation Amendments of 1954, became law on August 3, 1954.[17] For the first time, funds were authorized to train doctors, nurses, physical therapists, occupational therapists, social workers, and rehabilitation counselors to meet the needs of an expanded rehabilitation program. Funds were also authorized for research and demonstration projects.

For many years the only educational qualifications for rehabilitation counselors had been a standard college education and some experience in the social service field. Now graduate degrees were becoming available for the new profession of rehabilitation counseling. Public Law 565 recognized the shortage of personnel for this rapidly expanding field and authorized a training program to provide funds for short-term special courses and long-term degree training.

Rehabilitation in the 1960s

During the 1960s, three key events contributed to a tremendous period of growth in the rehabilitation movement. First, the Vocational Rehabilitation Amendments of 1965 were passed unanimously by Congress, providing for a substantial increase in federal funds and also broadening the base of service to include people with "socially handicapping conditions" as determined by a psychologist or psychiatrist. It also provided special grants for the construction and operation of sheltered workshops and other rehabilitation facilities.[18]

In 1967 the Department of Health, Education, and Welfare was reorganized, and the Social and Rehabilitation Service Division was established to emphasize the rehabilitative nature of many of the department's welfare and health programs. John W. Gardner, then secretary of HEW, appointed Mary E. Switzer to head this new unit. In addition to the new Rehabilitation Services Administration, the Children's Bureau, Administration on Aging, Medical Services Administration (Medicaid), and Public Welfare Assistance Payments Administration were consolidated into the new Department of Social Rehabilitation Services.[19]

In 1968 Congress passed the Vocational Rehabilitation Amendments.[20] One important goal added was the authorization of funding for work adjustment centers for the disadvantaged.

Rehabilitation Act of 1973

The year 1973 was significant in the history of rehabilitation in the United States. The Ninety-third Congress passed a set of rehabilitation amendments that completely recodified the Vocational Rehabilitation Act as originally passed in 1920 and subsequently enlarged in 1943, 1954, 1965, 1967, and 1968. The two major thrusts of the act were to place emphasis on expanding services to the most severely handicapped individuals, and place the responsibility for the ultimate rehabilitation of the disabled squarely on the shoulders of society as a whole. The ultimate effect of this far-reaching legislation has yet to be felt, but in time it will and must result in improving the quality of life for all disabled people and bringing them into the mainstream of society.[21]

The major features of PL 93-112 are:

1. It established within HEW a Rehabilitation Services Administration and delegated to its commissioner the responsibility for administering all aspects of the program. This original setup has since been modified and is still in a state of flux. (For current structure, see Chapter 10.)

2. It requires state agencies to develop individualized written rehabilitation programs on all clients, paralleling the development of Individualized Educational Plan (IEP) for disabled children under PL 94-142.

3. It directs that a comprehensive study be undertaken of the role of sheltered workshops in the employment and rehabilitation of handicapped individuals.

4. It directs that vocational rehabilitation services be directed especially to clients with the most severe handicaps, including individuals with spinal cord injury, older blind, underachieving deaf, and migratory farm workers.

5. It authorizes funding for an expanded research and demonstration program to develop methods to provide services and training to the severely handicapped; these programs are to include rehabilitation research, rehabilitation engineering research, and spinal cord and end state renal disease research.

6. It established the Helen Keller Center for the Deaf-Blind as a national center for rehabilitation and training of clients as well as for research.

7. It directs that the secretary of HEW establish a central clearinghouse for information and resources and spearhead the development of a coordinated information and data retrieval system. This mandate is of direct interest to librarians, as it will serve to make assessible to them, in machine-readable form, all of the medical and vocational rehabilitation information that has heretofore not been indexed completely.

The bill was originally written with five titles. Title 5, in four sections, is the most well-known to the general public, and Section 504, in particular, may well prove to be a revolutionary breakthrough, a benchmark for all the disabled people of this country.

Section 501: Provides for the hiring of disabled federal civil service employees, under an affirmative action program.

Section 502: Establishes an Architectural and Transportation Barriers Compliance Board.

Section 503: The "affirmative action" clause provides that any company with federal contracts in excess of $2,500 must employ qualified handicapped individuals.

Section 504: States as follows: "No otherwise qualified handicapped individual in the United States, as defined in Section 7(6), shall, solely by reason of his handicap, be excluded from participation in, be denied the benefits of, or be subjected to discrimination under any program or activity receiving Federal financial assistance."[22]

Section 7(6) defines the term *handicapped* as "any individual who (a) has a physical or mental disability which for such individual constitutes or results in substantial handicap to employment and (b) can reasonably be expected to benefit in terms of employability for vocational rehabilitation services. . . ." The following year, in Section 111(a) of the Rehabilitation Act Amendments of 1974 (PL 93-516), Congress amended the definition of handicapped individual for purposes of Section 504 and the other provisions of Titles 4 and 5 of the Rehabilitation Act so that the definition is no longer limited to the dimensions of employability. For purposes of Section 504, a handicapped individual is defined as "any person who (a) has a physical or mental impairment which substantially limits one or more of such person's major life activities, (b) has a record of such an impairment, or (c) is regarded as having such an impairment." This makes it clear that Section 504 was intended to forbid discrimination against all handicapped individuals, regardless of their need for or ability to benefit from vocational rehabilitation services.

Was Congress aware, when these words were written, what a far-reaching effect they would have? Had the costs, in both architectural and program adaptation, been determined and provided for? Possibly not. On April 28, 1977, Joseph A. Califano, secretary of HEW, issued the regulations for Section 504, which had been written into law in 1973.[23] During the four-year interim, severely disabled individuals had lobbied and eventually demonstrated in Washington, D.C., to insist that regulations for the implementation of this law be issued. Califano stated that the delay was due to lack of explicit guidance as to the full meaning of the law.

Although the law limits compliance to recipients of federal funds, the American way of life ensures that most schools, universities, libraries, businesses, and even museums are recipients of some federal funds in the form of grants of some kind. The Califano regulations, limited so far to recipients of HEW funds, provide:

1. That all new facilities must be barrier-free.
2. Programs in existing facilities must be made accessible.
3. Employers must hire the handicapped if reasonable accommodations can be made.

4. Handicapped children must receive free education appropriate to their needs (see also PL 94-142).
5. Colleges and universities must make reasonable modifications in academic requirements when necessary to ensure full educational opportunity.
6. Educational institutions and other social service programs must provide auxiliary aids, such as readers in school libraries or interpreters for the deaf, to ensure full participation of handicapped persons.
7. All recipients of HEW funds must complete within one year a self-evaluation process, in consultation with handicapped individuals and organizations, to determine which of their policies and practices need to be changed to ensure equal opportunity for handicapped Americans.

As interpreted in the regulations, Section 504 became the "equal access" law, and the word *access* the catchword for the 1970s, to describe what disabled people want—access to education, employment, recreation and travel, and independent living opportunities. Books have been written using the word *access* in the title, and the 1970s will be known as the time when the United States granted equal access to a normal life, under the law, to the disabled people of this country.

On August 14, 1978, four policy interpretations were issued by the Office of Civil Rights of the Department of HEW to interpret further the department's regulations issued under Section 504 of the Rehabilitation Act of 1973. These regulations have direct bearing on libraries, which are mentioned as an example.

Here the policy interpretation of "program accessibility" is expanded to allow flexibility in selecting means of compliance. Extensive structural changes are therefore not necessary if other methods can be found to make services available to the mobility-impaired. Libraries, for example, may deliver books by bookmobile or special clerical aide to an "alternate site." The regulations go on to say that priority should be given to methods that offer handicapped and nonhandicapped people programs in equivalent settings.

A knowledge of the range of resources—professional reading guidance, periodical reading rooms, information and referral services, and other facilities offered by the typical library—should make plain the paradox implicit in these two statements. It is hoped therefore that librarians will not be satisfied with the option of alternative service mentioned in these regulations and will recognize that physically disabled people need access, to the greatest extent possible, to the library premises.

In November 1978, President Carter signed the Rehabilitation Amendments entitled "Rehabilitation, Comprehensive Services and Developmental Disabilities Amendments of 1978" (PL 95-602).[24] The amendments reauthorize old programs and establish several new ones.

Title 1. Provides basic state grants for vocational rehabilitation services and also includes a provision that information and referral services should be provided in all state rehabilitation agencies. This provision has direct importance to the library field since many state rehabilitation agencies do not have rehabilitation libraries.

Title 2. Established a national institute of handicapped research.

Title 3. Authorizes additional supplementary services in the rehabilitation field.

Title 4. Provides for the establishment of a national council of the handicapped to include the disabled consumer as well as rehabilitation professional representatives.

Title 5. Strengthens Title 5 of the 1973 act with the following modifications:

1. Courts may allow attorney's fees to the prevailing parties in discrimination suits under the Rehabilitation Act. This will encourage private lawsuits under this act.
2. Section 504, the antidiscrimination section, which prevents those agencies receiving federal funding from discriminating against the disabled, is extended to include federal agencies.
3. An interagency coordinating council is established to prevent duplication of effort in enforcing Section 504.
4. The authority of the Architectural and Transportation Compliance Board (A&TBCB) is expanded to include jurisdiction over communications barriers and the authority to provide technical assistance in the area of accessibility.

Title 6. Establishes a program to provide public service jobs for disabled individuals, and also expands the Projects with Industry program (discussed later in this chapter).

Title 7. Authorizes special programs for individuals with severe handicaps or developmental disabilities including the development of special centers for independent living.[25]

Much of the funding for these amendments has not yet been authorized.

THE PROFESSION OF REHABILITATION COUNSELING

No qualifications for counselors were set up during the early history of the rehabilitation movement in the United States. In the late 1920s, the concept of aiding the disabled to find employment was called vocational guidance. Professional staff members in vocational rehabilitation met for the first time in a sectional meeting at the Annual Conference of the Society for Vocational Education in Buffalo, New York, in 1923. At that time the National Civilian Rehabilitation Conference was established by leaders from the state/federal rehabilitation agencies. In 1925 this organization began operating independently and had its first annual meeting in Cleveland, Ohio. In Memphis, Tennessee, at its 1927 conference, the name of the organization was changed to the National Rehabilitation Association (NRA).[26] Its objectives were to further agreement upon the principles and practices in the field of rehabilitation; promote communication between the various agencies in the field; educate the general public as to the importance of the civilian rehabilitation movement; and set up a mechanism through which the views of the membership might be expressed.[27]

At the NRA's second national conference in 1924, in Washington, D.C., the first statement on qualifications for rehabilitation agents (counselors) was recorded:

1. Interviewing applicants
2. Setting up feasible plans of rehabilitation
3. Supervision of training
4. Job placement
5. Soliciting funds for areas not covered
6. Securing cooperation of individuals and agencies

The kind of person needed to carry out these duties was someone with a liberal education, a graduate of a standard college, who had "tact, common sense, good judgment, a good sense of humor, and some experience in social service work."[28]

By 1930 there was an obvious pattern developing for a profession of rehabilitation counseling, and the idea further refined that one person should deal with the disabled person as a client who is in need of direction. During the middle and late 1940s, a more sophisticated view of rehabilitation counseling emerged. In the 1944–1945 annual report of the Federal Security Agency, one section showed the agency's growing concern for trained professional staff: "since counselling is the one service extended to disabled people directly by the State Rehabilitation Agency. As such, counselling becomes the very core of the Rehabilitation process around which all other services revolve."[29]

In-service training by state agencies was recommended, and short-term institutes and workshops developed through extension divisions of the colleges and universities. By 1949 nearly every state rehabilitation agency had adopted "rehabilitation counselor" as the title for workers serving disabled people.[30]

In 1954 the passage of PL 565 provided for the Federal funding of higher education programs for rehabilitation practitioners. It was generally agreed that the curriculum should be anchored in schools of social work or psychology or educational psychology and draw on general course content in these areas for a large part of its curriculum. No specific guidelines or standards for the degree were developed at that time.

Today the rehabilitation counselor is called upon to perform many functions. To ensure the effectiveness of the rehabilitation process, a "client-centered" approach must be used and the talents of all types of professional workers utilized—physicians, nurses, occupational, physical, and speech therapists, psychologists, vocational evaluators, and many others.[31]

The rehabilitation counselor must try to coordinate and integrate all the other professional information. The counselor must be able to develop possible job opportunities, modified work opportunities, or opportunities for self-employment. He or she must be able to interpret tests to clients, help them with personal problems, understand the contributions of the related disciplines and the functions of the sheltered workshop, as well as other types of rehabilitation facilities. All of this service is performed in many counseling facilities, both public and private, for the most part without benefit of library or information services or staff librarians to help the counselor track down hard-to-locate services or general information for the client's best possible adjustment to living. Such an adjustment is the prerequisite to possible employment readiness.

Rehabilitation counseling is a young profession. Like other, older professions, it is now beginning to question whether the rehabilitation generalist can handle the entire job or whether efforts need to be made to analyze the counselor's jobs with an eye toward restructuring and developing new career ladders in favor of support personnel.

Client Assistance Projects

One experiment in supplementary aid to disabled clients was a program developed in 1974. During the 1970's, it became apparent that disabled clients were, in many cases, not benefiting from the new information being made available in the fields of rehabilitation engineering and job modifications, and from the many new programs and opportunities opening up in the world of work and also in higher education. Colleges and universities had been working for two decades in a limited way, and more recently in a more active and positive way, to improve access to buildings and programs for the disabled (see Part IV).

A lack of communication also often existed between counselor and client. Counselors in many cases were overworked and lacking in support personnel. There was an acute need in the field of information, and that need was not, and is still not, being met by professional information specialists or librarians, who themselves in most cases are unaware of specialized sources, unable to provide help in traditional library facilities, and unprepared for jobs (should they ever exist) in rehabilitation facilities where they could develop much needed rehabilitation reference libraries.

The vacuum was filled in 1974 by a pilot project first authorized by Congress under the Rehabilitation Act of 1973, which provided for an ombudsman, an advocate, within the state rehabilitation agency, who would, while respecting the client/counselor relationship, assist clients with personal problems. Success in the initial projects has led to an expansion of the program. Clients have become more committed to their own rehabilitation because they understand the system better. Agency procedures have been influenced, and communications with community agencies have been improved. There are now over 20 such projects across the country.[32]

Although the client assistance program performs a function separate and distinct from that of delivery of information only, client advocates themselves could benefit from having sources of information more readily available so that they could provide services to clients more efficiently and with greater knowledge of resources.

Professional Organizations

During the 1960s, a number of professional organizations pertaining to rehabilitation counseling came into existence as divisions of professional associations. The National Rehabilitation Counselling Association (NRCA) is a division of the National Rehabilitation Association. The American Rehabilitation Counselling Association (ARCA) is a division of the American Personnel and Guidance Association (APGA). The American Psychological Association (APA) includes a Rehabilitation Counselling Association and Division 22, Psychology of Disability.[33] These organizations reflect the multifaceted nature of the rehabilitation counseling role. The NRCA grew out of the vocational rehabilitation tradition. The ARCA is oriented toward vocational education, reflecting the principal purpose of its parent organization as an educational vocational guidance organization. APA's division is more closely affiliated with the psychological aspects of counseling.

By 1977 the leadership of NRCA and ARCA recognized the need for closer ties between the two organizations, which represent the majority of counselors practicing the relatively new profession of rehabilitation counseling. Combining their newsletters, they began to issue a joint publication called the *NRCA/ARCA News Report.*[34] A joint task force to promote rehabilitation counseling as a profession was established in the summer of 1978 during the APGA convention to further the association of the two organizations and promote joint professional activity. Also during that convention the American Mental Health Counseling Association was accepted into the APGA. Members of this group are predominantly trained counselors working in mental health centers.

Rehabilitation Counseling and Counselor Certification

In summer 1969, a group of rehabilitation professionals met to discuss the need for accreditation of master's degree programs in rehabilitation counseling education. After two years of planning, the Council of Rehabilitation Education (CORE) was formed, and incorporated in 1972, with representation from the five major rehabilitation organizations: ARCA, NRCA, ARF, Council of State Administrators of Vocational Rehabilitation, and the National Council on Rehabilitation Education.

A commission for standards and accreditation included members from other disciplines and agencies relating to counseling, as well as from consumers. Performance of graduates is assessed and standards are revised by survey after five years to reflect additional competencies. Funding assistance is provided by the Rehabilitation Services Administration. .

By summer 1978, CORE had accredited over two-thirds of eligible programs (40) and was considering 16 more. CORE also sponsored a task analysis of rehabilitation counselor functions and developed a manual specifying the functions of master's level rehabilitation counselors.

Inquiries about this program may be addressed to CORE, Rehabilitation Institute, Southern Illinois University, Carbondale, Illinois 62901.

Another step in the establishment of credentials for the profession of rehabilitation counseling was taken in the mid-1970s with the creation of the commission on rehabilitation counselor certification. It is composed of the principal rehabilitation organizations. Certification is awarded after an examination based on the standards set for rehabilitation education. Rehabilitation counselors who have been practicing for some time before standards were set up are awarded certification under a "grandfather clause."

A librarian working in the field of rehabilitation, a public reference librarian, or a school librarian serving a guidance department, who has been asked for information, would be able to find pertinent data from the above professional organizations.

SHELTERED WORKSHOPS

The sheltered workshop plays an important role in the vocational rehabilitation of the severely disabled. In 1974 Greenleigh Associates was contracted by HEW to conduct a congressionally mandated evaluation of sheltered workshops in the United States. Entitled *The Role of the Sheltered Workshop in the Rehabilitation of the Severely Handicapped*, the study originally appeared in three volumes, which was condensed into a single-volume format.[35] The Greenleigh study was a benchmark in the sheltered workshop program in that it summarized and evaluated the state of this movement as it has developed in the United States.

The successful workshop must be concerned with the interests of its clients. At the same time it must create a viable business enterprise if a work atmosphere is to be maintained. The successful workshop is able to balance these two elements.

Although the first sheltered workshop in the United States opened in 1838, the greatest growth in this movement has occurred from the 1960s on. The Greenleigh study concentrates its statistical data therefore on workshops starting operation in 1964. Workshops for the blind are much older than that. Reportedly, by the second quarter of 1975, there were 2,766 certificated workshops, both for the blind and nonblind and the physically and mentally handicapped.[36] Four out of five workshops are operated by voluntary, nonprofit organizations and associations. Most have working relationships with state offices of vocational rehabilitation, which usually involve the provision of services to clients on a fee basis. There is therefore an interdependent relationship between the government and the agencies that operate workshops.

Standards

An institute in Bedford Springs, Pennsylvania, in 1958 pioneered in setting standards in the workshop field. Since then, many standards have been adopted. State rehabilitation agencies must have such criteria to guide their selection of those workshops from which they will purchase services for clients and to whom they will provide grants for improving or expanding facilities and services. The National Committee on Sheltered Workshops and Homebound Programs was organized at the Cleveland Conference of Social Work in 1949. It was later founded as an independent association and its name changed to the National Association of Sheltered Workshops and Homebound Programs (NASWHP). In 1952 the Association of Rehabilitation Centers was established.[37] The International Association of Rehabilitation Facilities, now called the Association for Rehabilitation Facilities, has replaced both NASWHP and ARC, and ARF now represents all types of rehabilitation facilities in one major organization.

The Association of Rehabilitation Facilities (ARF)

The Association of Rehabilitation Facilities is the only organization that represents rehabilitation facilities of all types in the United States today. It has more than 600 members, although unofficial estimates indicate about 2,000 more existing facilities. Some of these, however, are very small shops with just a few people, and these remain unlisted.

ARF has begun to computerize its mailing list. It has also started to identify as many agencies as possible by cross-referencing the nationwide facilities of such large organizations as Goodwill Industries, the National Easter Seal Society, and United Cerebral Palsy. ARF publishes a membership directory, which is updated annually (available from ARF, 5530 Wisconsin Avenue, Suite 955, Washington, D.C. 20015). The association has moved toward standardization by using the same program services categories as currently used by the Commission on Accreditation of Rehabilitation Facilities.

The Commission on Accredition of Rehabilitation Facilities (CARF)

Rehabilitation facilities were in operation for many years before an effort was made to develop national standards. This was a natural order of progress, since operational procedures need to be developed before an attempt can be made to standardize them. Representatives from rehabilitation facilities, state and local governments, labor, and the general public met prior to the issuance of the first set of standards by the Rehabilitation Services Administration in 1966. These were revised in 1969 and again in 1971.[38] The RSA also supported the work of CARF, a nonprofit organization established by the American

Hospital Association, the Association of Rehabilitation Facilities, Goodwill Industries, the National Association for Hearing and Speech Action, National Easter Seal Society, and NRA for the purpose of setting standards.

Agencies wishing to be accredited by CARF must apply and be examined to determine if they meet the criteria. Listings of newly accredited agencies are carried in the newsletter *CARF Report* (issued by CARF, 2500 North Pantamo Road, Tucson, Arizona 85715). The latest standards manual is available from CARF. Standardization is important to the state offices of rehabilitation, which place clients for a fee and supply funding for projects to rehabilitation facilities of all kinds.

VOCATIONAL REHABILITATION, PRACTICES, AND PHILOSOPHIES

In the vocational rehabilitation movement, many terms are used that should become familiar to anyone wishing to work in the field as part of the professional rehabilitation team. Prevocational evaluation, work evaluation, work adjustment and job placement, and on-the-job training (OJT) are all used to define the testing and training given to a client in any type of training facility. Sheltered workshops can be of a transitional type in which the client is offered the opportunity to perform in a work adjustment setting in order to achieve good work habits and performance, attitudes, and knowledge of the world of work itself.[39]

When a realistic goal has been reached (with the emphasis on *realistic*), the client is given job placement in the regular labor market, or, if this is not possible and a plateau has been achieved, he or she will be referred to a long-term or permanent workshop situation. Many severely disabled people reach their ultimate potential by functioning in such a long-term setting. There is a need for periodic reevaluation as philosophies in the labor market continue to change.

The Redkey Study

A study of the sheltered workshop field in the 1970s was the subject of a significant paper by Henry Redkey, based on his lecture in 1973 to inaugurate a rehabilitation lecture series at the University of Wisconsin, Stout.[40] This paper summarized the current state of thinking about sheltered workshops. Based on a tour of European countries to investigate sheltered workshop programs for the handicapped, it offers valuable insights into vocational rehabilitation and the sheltered workshop movement.

According to Redkey, workshops have become more and more dependent on state rehabilitation agencies for funding, usually on a project grant basis to provide primarily for related professional services rather than for work. The drawbacks to this type of funding are that the money runs out and the shop must then look for new funds to support staff overhead that has built up.[41]

Although no rehabilitation program can be lifted in whole or even in large part and transplanted to another country, many interesting ideas emerged from Redkey's trip to Europe as outlined in his study. In a look at rehabilitation and sheltered workshop programs in countries such as Denmark, Sweden, the Netherlands, and Poland, Redkey points out similarities and differences and makes suggestions for the improvement of facilities in the United States.

Denmark and Sweden have what Redkey calls "cradle-to-grave systems," with the difference that Denmark employs a social service approach, with rehabilitation work primarily done by social workers. Most sheltered workshops are privately operated and are much like those in the United States. However, in Denmark, all sheltered employment is subsidized by the state through a system of pensions, which all disabled people receive on a graded formula basis, and also by reimbursement of operating expenses. An "enclave system," in which groups of handicapped workers are placed in a private factory under the supervision of sheltered workshop staff, has been very successful.

In Sweden, rehabilitation is heavily oriented toward employment, much like the American vocational rehabilitation program. Sweden now recognizes the need for better sheltered employment and more attention to social and medical rehabilitation. It has also experimented with a program to subsidize private employers to hire the handicapped, but has achieved only limited success. In Sweden's Archives program, handicapped people work in public institutions such as museums. This offers employment to highly skilled, severely disabled persons.

In Poland, all sheltered employment is done in cooperatives in which the workers have some voice in the management. The difference between an ordinary labor cooperative and a disabled labor cooperative is that 75 percent of the employees in the latter are disabled. About one-third of employed disabled people are in cooperative workshops. The most severely disabled are employed at home. Wages are often on a piecework basis, but hourly rates are also used. They approximate those of able-bodied workers except in the case of the homebound, which is strictly piecework. It must be kept in mind that Poland is still moving into an industrial system. A very large proportion of workers, including the disabled, have limited education; therefore, factory work must be the choice for a great many.

The Netherlands has a well-developed program for employment of the disabled. This highly industrialized country of 13 million people has about four and one-half million in the work force. The handicapped are considered part of that force, and everyone has the right to work. The labor department screens and counsels the disabled, and those who cannot be placed in private jobs are referred to social employment consisting of industrial workshops, "open-air projects," and "clerical projects." The first and third do subcontracting with private industry, as well as prime manufacturing, and office work for public agencies. The open-air projects are of a public nature, mostly in municipal parks. Wages are based on a percentage, depending on productivity.

Redkey makes several recommendations for the future of sheltered employment in the United States. He feels that we need to separate permanent or extended employment from transitional workshops, which should be operated in connection with comprehensive work evaluation centers. Concepts that could be learned from other countries include the Dutch social employment approach, including the open-air concept, the co-op approach in Poland, the Archives program in Sweden, and the enclave idea in Denmark. A normal wage, with specific modifications, as in Holland, could be paid. Major funding must come from the federal government with administration by state and local agencies. Standards for operation should allow for different types of systems.

Redkey notes that sheltered workshops are only one type of employment in a whole spectrum of active living and working situations for disabled people.

The Vash Study

Redkey's conclusions take on an even deeper significance when viewed in conjunction with "Sheltered Industrial Employment," written by Carolyn Vash, Ph.D., as one of a series of four monographs.[42] The series title, *Emerging Issues in Rehabilitation* (1977), is published by the Institute for Research Utilization, 719 Delaware Avenue S.W., Washington, D.C. The four papers synthesize major research findings and report on innovations of current concern to vocational rehabilitation professionals.[43]

Vash's paper concerns work opportunities for people with severe disabilities who cannot fit easily into positions. This, after all, is what rehabilitation is all about. Vash points out that she is not only a vocational rehabilitation professional but also, as a severely disabled person herself, a consumer of services. Just as the independent living movement, as described in Chapter 4, seeks to help severely disabled individuals live in the mainstream of society, Vash views the entire spectrum of opportunity in the marketplace with an eye toward breaking down the artificial barriers, sometimes primarily attitudinal, that stand between the severely disabled adult and the potential work opportunity afforded him or her.

This highly significant monograph should be read by anyone wishing to become an information specialist in the field of employment of the disabled. Vash has brought together the philosophies of Redkey and others writing during the 1970s. She deals with the history, background, and changing concepts of wages versus welfare. The paper describes some of the principal projects now in operation in the United States and puts forth exciting new concepts that could and should be implemented during the 1980s.

Vash explains that the word *shelter* traditionally has been used for a job situation that must conform to the special physical needs of a disabled worker. However, there are many new ways of thinking in which job modification is used in normal work settings to met the needs of workers who are not necessarily disabled, but for whom some adjustment must be made so that other life obligations can be met. This type of adjustment is generally called an "accommodation." According to Vash, therefore, "accommodation is something an employer provides to enable a worker to perform up to standards. Shelter is something the employer provides for selected employees who are unable to meet the standards."[44]

We are living in a time of modifying jobs to meet the needs of workers, rather than asking workers to make all the adjustments. This is the employment aspect of equal access. Architectural modification of the work place, modification of the work area, use of modern technology to aid in modification of work tools, typewriters, telephones—all of this is now being attempted in new programs that will, with the indispensable help of the spread of information about them, expand in the 1980s. "Mainstreaming" in the work place, according to Vash, can take place to any number of degrees in an ascending scale of levels, from homebound or totally sheltered employment, to semi-integrated units in mainstream industry with significant accommodation or shelter, through full integration in industry with some accommodation, to competitive employment with no accommodation or shelter.[45]

Using Wright's distinction between disability and handicap, Vash points out that in this instance she is dealing with all types and degrees of disability, but with only one handicap—vocational.

The United States citizen with a disability is now protected legally from discrimination in employment (see Chapter 3).

Vash summarizes available information about the innovative programs in Europe, the United States, and Australia in the various stages of semi-integrated and integrated employment. The literature about these programs should be a part of any rehabilitation library so that counselors can be kept informed about the types of opportunities available to their disabled clients.

As industry in the 1970s began to play a more important role than ever before in employment of the disabled, the concept of on-the-job training in the world of real work was recognized as a viable way to create realistic job opportunities with real possibilities for success. This concept has been pioneered in the special education field, where real work experience is made a part of the day for students in vocational education programs. In the rehabilitation field, experiments in the early 1970s originated in California, where Ranchos Los Amigos Hospital created job slots for disabled people within the staff itself. Later, the city of Sante Fe Springs, working with Ranchos Los Amigos, established a work experience program.[46]

A national effort in the 1970s is the Projects with Industry (PWI) program, funded by RSA, working through the state vocational rehabilitation agencies and utilizing community resources. PWI opens up job training opportunities in both unskilled labor and highly skilled professional work. Disabled people placed in industry receive the continued support of rehabilitation counselors to ensure that they are given all the information they and the employer need to make realistic job and work area modifications when necessary.

One of the first dozen PWIs funded was an outgrowth of a new concept in medical and vocational rehabilitation pioneered by the Insurance Company of North America (INA) during the 1960s. A series of regional offices was set up throughout the country, staffed by rehabilitation coordinators and rehabilitation nurses. The teams worked together with medical personnel to obtain an early evaluation of a patient who was a victim of accident or injury. The determination of cost of rehabilitation, wherever possible, was made to include vocational retraining with the objective of productive reemployment. The cost of rehabilitation, borne by the insurance company, was in all instances more economically sound for the company than a large payment to a client for a lifetime of inactivity. For the client, the value was self-evident.

The rehabilitation activities in INA were taken over by a separate subsidiary called International Rehabilitation Associates (IRA), which is able to contract services to other insurance companies as well as to INA clients. IRA, funded as a PWI, conducts a placement program for severely disabled persons with insurance claims by developing a nationwide pool of potential employers of disabled workers.

The Jacksonville Restaurant Association in Florida sponsors a PWI to fill a serious personnel shortage in restaurant jobs. Both IBM and Goodwill Industries sponsor PWIs. And the city of Los Angeles, defined as an industry, has created a city OJT project using CETA funds.[47] A prospective PWI, reported by Vash, is to be sponsored by the AFL-CIO to bring organized labor into this program.

Vash's reflections on the future include financial issues concerning the cost factor in sheltered employment, unionization, marketing, and federal subsidies. Greater development of mainstreaming in employment requires more work in the area of job development and an expanded role for the rehabilitation engineer in helping with work site and machine modifications. An example is the "talking calculator," which has opened up new occupations for the blind. Other accommodations to be explored are flex-time and job sharing.[48]

In deploring irrelevant training for jobs that do not exist, Vash states that the problem here is a need for accurate information on job and labor markets. No one in the rehabilitation network knows where the jobs exist, and they cannot add the task of digging out this information to all their other professional counseling and training roles.[49] It is imperative that NARIC, described in Chapter 10, include information on what innovations in the job field have been tried and failed and which have been successful. Rehabilitation counselors must begin to receive this information through new rehabilitation library services.

Vash's monograph concludes with an examination of the philosophical implications of the question "which is the better way . . . welfare or wages?" Her conclusion is that whether or not it costs money should not be a deciding factor because if disabled people are working, regardless if the accommodation or shelter costs the employer money or if there is a need for government subsidy, they are no longer being supported on the welfare roles. Vash recommends that cost studies should determine just how much the consumer will bear in terms of increased costs for merchandise before subsidies are instituted. A knowledge of the general philosophies of work and the disabled, as put forth by such people as Redkey and Vash, are important to anyone planning to work in the rehabilitation information field.

Study on the Homebound

The severely handicapped homebound have been identified in the Rehabilitation Act of 1973 as a priority population for service. This has important implications for state rehabilitation agencies. Severely handicapped homebound clients have not received appropriate rehabilitation services over the years. They will, however, make up a large percentage of clients served in the future because of legislation, advances in medical science and rehabilitation engineering, and new philosophies in job modification, as well as new modes of transportation and the demands of the severely disabled homebound themselves.

Rusalem (1974) estimates that there are more than two million disabled Americans who are homebound, each one an individual and each one different from the others.[50] A significant document developed to aid in promoting service to this group is "The Rehabilitation of the Severely Handicapped Homebound" (June 1977). The Fourth Institute on Rehabilitation Issues, held in Dallas, Texas, included a study group on this topic, and this report is an outgrowth of their work. It is available from the Arkansas Rehabilitation Research and Training Center, University of Arkansas, or from the National Oklahoma Clearinghouse, Stillwater, Oklahoma.

Recognizing the fact that there is no one model rehabilitation homebound program to meet the needs of all clients or all rehabilitation agencies, the report endeavors to develop training guides to assist counselors in instituting programs for the handicapped homebound. It details programs already developed in many areas of the country and suggest models for homebound employment, as well as possibilities for bringing clients out of the home whenever possible by utilizing the most recent advances in all areas of rehabilitation.

Typical homebound employees, their jobs, and disabilities are listed.

Suggestions are offered for taking advantage of existing information about the Small Business Administration, which is underutilized by handicapped persons who might wish to operate a small business. This organization furnishes very personal counseling, as well as loans, for this purpose. Further information is available from the Small Business Administration, Washington, D.C. 20416; see also SBA's Pamphlet OPI-6 SBA, "What It Is . . . What It Does"; and Pamphlet OPI-18 SBA, "Business Loans." Job modification, job placement, staff training, sample workshops, and available materials are also included in this very complete and valuable report from the Texas study group. It should be made available to rehabilitation counselors in all types of rehabilitation facilities.

SUMMARY

Disabled people need a great variety of services from birth to adulthood. The field of service to this large segment of our population has developed rapidly since the late 1950s.

It is necessary that the library profession develop a new field of professional service as part of the health science field, to be called rehabilitation librarianship, and to begin to prepare library students who wish to serve in this special field with the information they will need. This would encompass a background in the field of rehabilitation as well as an understanding of the psychological and physical nature of various disability groups, an understanding of attitudes involved in working with the disabled, and a knowledge of the types of information needed by the disabled and the professionsals who serve them.

The rehabilitation profession needs to be made aware that all types of rehabilitation facilities need properly trained librarians to acquire, organize, and retrieve rehabilitation information. Rehabilitation librarians will in time become valuable members of the rehabilitation team.

NOTES

1. James F. Garrett and Edna S. Levine, *Rehabilitation Practices with the Physically Disabled* (New York: Columbia University Press, 1973), p. 14.
2. Ibid.
3. Greenleigh Associates, Inc., *The Role of the Sheltered Workshop in the Rehabilitation of the Severely Handicapped*, 1st printing, July 1975, 2nd printing, November 1976, p. 8.
4. Garrett and Levine, *Rehabilitation*, p. 6.
5. Ibid.
6. John G. Cull, Ph.D., and Richard E. Hardy, Ed.D., *Vocational Rehabilitation: Profession and Process*, American Lecture Series in social and rehabilitation psychology (Springfield, Ill.: Charles C. Thomas, 1972, 1975), p. 14.
7. Ibid., pp. 18–19.

8. Ibid., p. 18.

9. C. Esco Obermann, Ph.D., *A History of Vocational Rehabilitation in America* (Minneapolis: Denison, 1965), p. 105.

10. Obermann, *History*, p. 120.

11. Cull and Hardy, *Vocational*, p. 20.

12. Garrett and Levine, *Rehabilitation*, p. 7.

13. PL 236, 66th Congress, Washington, D.C., June 2, 1920, Vocational Rehabilitation Act.

14. Obermann, *History*, p. 270.

15. PL 113, 78th Congress, Washington, D.C., 1943, Barden-LaFollette Act.

16. Obermann, *History*, p. 311.

17. PL 565, 83rd Congress, Washington, D.C., August 3, 1954, Vocational Rehabilitation Amendments of 1954; also, Obermann, *History*, p. 316.

18. PL 89-333, 89th Congress, Washington, D.C., 1965, Vocational Rehabilitation Amendments of 1965.

19. Cull and Hardy, *Vocational*, p. 49.

20. PL 90-391, 90th Congress, Washington, D.C., July 7, 1968.

21. PL 93-112, 93rd Congress, Washington, D.C., September 26, 1973, Rehabilitation Act of 1973.

22. Ibid.

23. *Federal Register*, May 4, 1977.

24. PL 95-602, 95th Congress, Washington, D.C., November 6, 1978.

25. *In the Mainstream* 3, no. 4 (Nov./Dec. 1978), Mainstream, Inc., Washington, D.C.

26. Obermann, *History*, pp. 354–358.

27. Cull and Hardy, *Vocational*, p. 34.

28. Ibid., p. 35.

29. Federal Security Agency, Annual Report, Washington, D.C., U.S. Government Printing Office (1945), p. 154.

30. Cull and Hardy, *Vocational*, p. 153.

31. Ibid., p. 67.

32. Leslie B. Cole, "Ombudsman in Vocational Rehabilitation Process," in *American Rehabilitation*, U.S. Department of Health, Education, and Welfare, Rehabilitation Services Administration, Washington, D.C.

33. Cull and Hardy, *Vocational*, p. 141.

34. The *NRCA/ARCA News Report*, joint publication of the American Rehabilitation Counseling Association and the National Rehabilitation Counseling Association, Singer Career Systems, Rochester, N.Y.

35. Greenleigh, *Sheltered Workshop*.

36. Ibid., p. 19.

37. Obermann, *History*, p. 109.

38. *Standards for Rehabilitation Facilities and Sheltered Workshops*, rev., Department of Health, Education, and Welfare, Social Rehabilitation Services, Rehabilitation Services Administration, Washington, D.C. (1971).

39. Cull and Hardy, *Vocational*, p. 505.

40. Henry Redkey, "A Way of Looking at Sheltered Workshops for the 1970s," Rehabilitation Lectures Series, Menomonie, Wis., University of Wisconsin, Stout, Vocational Rehabilitation Institute (December 1975).

41. Ibid., p. 3.

42. Carolyn L. Vash, Ph.D., "Sheltered Industrial Employment," in *Emerging Issues in Rehabilitation*, Institute for Research Utilization, Washington, D.C. (December 1977).

43. Ibid.

44. Ibid., p. 1.

45. Ibid., p. 2.

46. Ibid., p. 50.

47. Ibid., p. 52.

48. Ibid., p. 60.

49. Ibid., p. 61.

50. H. Rusalem, "The Characteristics and Rehabilitation Experience of Homebound Applicants for State Vocation Rehabilitation Agency Service," a Monograph of the Programmatic Research Project on the Rehabilitation of Homebound Persons, New York, N.Y., Federation of the Handicapped (1974).

10
Rehabilitation Today

As the decade of the 1970s began the field of rehabilitation encompassed all of the public and private agencies that had dealt with disabled individuals throughout American history—private rehabilitation hospitals and public Veterans Administration hospitals, private rehabilitation centers and sheltered workshops, some run by the earliest private organizations in the field such as Goodwill Industries and the Easter Seal Society. The federal government presided over a large network of vocational rehabilitation offices, administered through the individual state governments operating a network of local offices.

PRESENT STRUCTURE OF THE FIELD

It is always difficult to offer an up-to-date description of a government agency. Changes are made often to keep up with newly emerging needs and to streamline services for greater relevance and efficiency. A state of flux exists in the entire area of rehabilitation of the disabled. This is encouraging because it indicates that the field is changing, growing, and offering better and more efficient service.

In endeavoring to meet new needs, the federal government reorganized the offices concerned with the disabled. Plans announced on February 16, 1978, integrate handicapped-related programs under an expanded Rehabilitation Services Administration in the Department of Health, Education and Welfare. Rehabilitation Services Administration is one of five programs administered under the Office of Human Development Services

(OHDS). The other four are Administration on Aging, Administration for Public Service, Administration for Native Americans, and Administration for Children, Youth, and Families. The Architectural and Transportation Barriers Compliance Board, which had reported directly to the assistant secretary for human development, is now included under the expanded Rehabilitation Services Administration.

A department within RSA has direct responsibility for supervising the state offices of vocational rehabilitation, which are known under various names depending on the individual state: department of rehabilitation, department of vocational rehabilitation, office of vocational rehabilitation, and so on. These departments are funded by the federal government with monies earmarked for client service, utilized in a network of local offices staffed by rehabilitation counselors working directly with disabled clients. The state offices of vocational rehabilitation operate local branches, which serve disabled people—physically, mentally, or emotionally handicapped— in their immediate communities, either county, city, or other regional designation. Any disabled person with a substantial employment handicap who can become employable within a reasonable period of time may be eligible.

The emphasis here is in the guidelines. Actually this original mandate has been broadened considerably so that funding for higher education where the person qualifies, regardless of whether or not it will lead to employment, is now offered. Employment may be defined as competitive or sheltered employment or homemaking, and these interpretations have been broadened to include the achievement of some form of independent living and also an attempt to employ all manner of new technologies to enable the severely physically and mentally handicapped to become employable in some fashion. Recent guidelines mandate a new emphasis on service to the most severely disabled. For these reasons, rehabilitation counselors need up-to-date information more than ever before. The only people not served by the Office of Vocational Rehabilitation (OVR) are those with visual impairments, who are served by a separate network in most states.

The services offered by the offices of vocational rehabilitation include:

1. Individual counseling and guidance to determine interests and aptitudes
2. Medical examinations and other evaluative services to determine the nature and degree of disability, remaining abilities, need for treatment, and work potential
3. Physical rehabilitation where needed
4. Instruction, training, and/or education to provide living and vocational skills
5. Special transportation where needed
6. Interpreter services for the deaf
7. Individual job placement and follow-up

Expenses for some services are on a shared basis with the client. The OVR works closely with departments of mental hygiene, social service, and labor, the Workmen's Compensation Board, health and correction facilities, and many public and private voluntary service agencies. Handicapped persons may apply to the OVR office nearest their homes by letter, phone, or in person. Local offices are listed in the telephone book; see Appendix for state listings.

In addition to the departments of vocational rehabilitation administered by the individual states, there is a rehabilitation network of federal offices organized in ten regions throughout the United States, Puerto Rico, and the Virgin Islands (see Appendix). These offices are the local monitoring agencies of federal government monies. The states spend the dollars allocated to them, but must report on that money to the regional RSA office.

For facility and program improvement, such as greater service to the homebound, independent living projects, and the like, the state sets priorities based on need and the regional office sets up the peer review process on them.

Certain specific projects, such as Projects with Industry (PWI), are originated directly at the federal level and continue to be administered by the federal government, although the region is kept informed.

Training monies are made available in three ways:

1. Directly from the federal government
2. Through the regional RSA office
3. Through the state vocational rehabilitation department, which has some small amounts of money for training grants

In 1973 the Office for Handicapped Individuals (OHI) was established by law in the Office of Human Development of HEW. Congress created this office as a staff resource for the office of the secretary of HEW, its purpose being to provide a coordinating and information focus to the department's efforts on behalf of the handicapped. Through the reorganization of departments since this office was created, it now functions within an expanded RSA.

The goals of OHI are long term. It works to encourage governmental planning, evaluation of programs, and improvement in information resources among service providers and handicapped individuals. It now has the task of implementing the recommendations developed during the 1977 White House Conference on Handicapped Individuals and, most particularly, of establishing a national clearinghouse on information to respond to inquiries and to serve as a resource to organizations that supply information to and about the disabled.

The clearinghouse is interested in forging a network among information providers on national, state, and local levels. As a first step in identifying and coordinating services to the disabled, OHI developed a directory, which was published in December 1976[1] (available from the Superintendent of Documents), entitled *Directory of National Information Sources on Handicapping Conditions and Related Services*. A conference called by OHI in Washington, D.C., in June 1977, and attended by representatives of many of the organizations listed in the directory, explored the various ways in which networking might be achieved. The directory lists 181 national organizations that concern themselves in some way with the disabled and also explains the federal government's structure as it existed at that time. Although far from complete, this source directory would be of help to librarians who serve the disabled in any capacity.

A SPECIAL REHABILITATION RESEARCH NETWORK

In 1961 Congress initiated a network of rehabilitation research and training centers, funded in the budget for vocational rehabilitation and administered by RSA.[2] These centers, which pioneered in research in physical and rehabilitation medicine, have done significant work, and their programs have been expanded. There are now 19 centers, 12 specializing in medical rehabilitation, 3 in vocational rehabilitation, 3 in mental retardation, and 2 in deafness rehabilitation. Continued funding by Congress has been the result of the effectiveness of their work, and they are organized in the ten RSA regions. Their goal is to explore every means for medically rehabilitating the adult disabled and to devise new methods for rehabilitation counseling, work evaluation, and training and placement in jobs.

Some major contributions of the medical centers are research on rehabilitation of aphasia patients by New York University, the hemophilia research being conducted at the University of Southern California, the research on Harrington Rod procedures for spinal deformity at Baylor College of Medicine, research in communication devices at Tufts University School of Medicine/New England Medical Center Hospital/Boston and Trace, Wisconsin, and many others.

The rehabilitation research and training centers at the universities of Arkansas, West Virginia, and Wisconsin, Stout, are designed as vocational centers to conduct programmatic research and training in psychosocial and vocational areas of rehabilitation, including work adjustment and work placement. Their primary function is to develop methods to be used by vocational rehabilitation agencies in order to respond effectively to the vocational needs of the severely handicapped.

Three of the 19 centers focus their efforts on the habilitation of the developmentally disabled, terminology now being used to identify the mentally retarded: at the University of Wisconsin in Madison, the University of Oregon in Eugene, and Texas Tech University in Lubbock. Their work has centered upon experiments in group home living, work/study programs, and vocational training for severely retarded people. RT-17 at New York University is responsible for the rehabilitation of deaf persons, and RT-23, at the University of California at San Francisco, is concerned with deafness and mental health rehabilitation.

Since 1955 there have been projects in what is now called rehabilitation engineering. These projects were part of a governmentwide effort in prosthetics and orthotics, in which the Rehabilitation Services Administration joined with the Veterans Administration, Department of Defense, and others in a coordinated effort. As more agencies, especially NASA, became involved, it was obvious that a network of rehabilitation engineering centers was needed. In 1972 the RSA established the first of these centers at the Rancho Los Amigos Hospital in Downey, California, and at the Moss Rehabilitation Hospital in Philadelphia, Pennsylvania.[3] Six more centers have been established. Three international centers, established in 1973, are in Ljubljana, Yugoslavia; Poznan, Poland; and Cairo, Egypt. Each center has developed a core area of research on a problem related to rehabilitation that might be solved through engineering and related scientific expertise.

Thus, since 1972, a new profession has emerged and been defined. Thousands of engineers and health professionals have committed their careers to rehabilitation engineering, and their efforts have brought a large number of new devices, techniques, and equipment to the disabled. The application of sophisticated microminiature electronic techniques has already had a major impact on the quality of life for the disabled population, and the promise for increased vocational effectiveness and improved life-style is unlimited. The work of these centers ranges from electrical stimulation techniques and sensory aids for the blind to biofeedback experiments and artificial joints.

A series of small regional rehabilitation research institutes was also funded during the 1960s and 1970s. Each of the five serve two of the ten regions set up by RSA. They are located at the School of Social Work, Columbia University, New York City; George Washington University, Washington, D.C.; the School of Education, University of Michigan at Ann Arbor, Michigan; the Center for Social Research and Development, University of Denver; and Portland State University, Oregon.

The primary aim of these centers is to provide technical assistance to those agencies concerned with vocational rehabilitation of the disabled in federal, state, and local rehabilitation agencies and to improve the ties between labor and management and community rehabilitation facilities in order to increase employment options for the disabled.[4]

The Rehabilitation Act of 1973 (PL 93-112) made provision for the establishment of a national center for deaf-blind youth and adults. Headquarters for this facility, which had operated on a smaller scale as a function of the Industrial Home for the Blind, was dedicated in October 1976.[5] The main building, in Sands Point, Long Island, New York, was named in memory of Mary E. Switzer.

The center consists of three modern buldings on a 25-acre site and provides facilities for housing and training for up to 50 deaf-blind individuals. Seven additional offices are located at Philadelphia, Atlanta, Chicago, Dallas, Denver, Seattle, and Glendale, California. All are involved in seeking out and training deaf-blind persons for possible job placement, and they also assist local agencies in services to the deaf-blind. The Sands Point center's research department is involved in developing and field-testing communication aids and devices such as the tele-braille communications system and the tactile speech indicator, now in the early stages of commercial production. Information about them can be obtained from the Sands Point center. Also being established at Sands Point is a computerized national register of deaf-blind persons.

The center has a library, staffed by a professional librarian who is building a collection of materials in the field of deaf blindness. The book *Audiological Evaluation and Aural Rehabilitation of the Deaf-Blind Adult*, by Lynne C. Kramer, M.S., Roy F. Sullivan, Ph.D., and Linda M. Hirsch, M.S., is scheduled for publication in 1979. The center publishes a newsletter called the *Nat-Center News* (available from Helen Keller Center, 111 Middle Neck Road, Sands Point, New York 11050). Its editor, Robert J. Smithdas, is director of community education at the center. Smithdas, who has been deaf and blind since before the age of five years, is a graduate of the Perkins School for the Blind in Watertown, Massachusetts, and St. Johns University. He earned his master's degree at New York University. He has written eloquently of the special isolation caused by the loss of both sight and hearing and of the neglect that deaf-blind people have, until very recently, experienced in society.[6]

The research of this center and its branches is linked to the research network, and its offices are therefore listed on the chart in the Appendix.

In 1976 at a national conference, all of these centers—the rehabilitation research and training centers, the rehabilitation engineering centers, and the regional rehabilitation research institutes, as well as the Helen Keller Center—formed themselves into the Association of Research and Training Centers.[7] Nine hospitals specializing in spinal cord injury were integrated into the system.

A problem facing all of the centers is one that challenges all research organizations—making sure their work is properly publicized so that the results will reach the disabled, for whom it is intended. For this reason, *The Informer*, a quarterly magazine, is published by the Information Exchange at the Arkansas Research and Training Center in Region IV. Available on a subscription basis, this magazine, while extremely useful, is only a start in the monumental task of cataloguing, indexing, and disseminating information about all of the monographs, reports, and audiovisual training materials produced by the centers. An annual of research abstracts, a training directory, and an audiovisual directory are also produced by the network and are available from RSA in Washington, D.C.

Although many of these centers employ librarians to maintain libraries that serve mainly as resource centers for their own professional staff, in far too many instances the persons so designated are not trained and certified by the library profession. Called information specialists, they often are considered by the centers to be clerical staff members. In such instances, the libraries take on the character of information clearinghouses, whose major purpose is to store and distribute their own publications within the network. There is a great need for members of the library profession to project a stronger image as information and referral officers, so that the directors of rehabilitation research facilities will perceive the advantages inherent in hiring professional librarians as important members of their staffs.

In the early 1970s another network of service, called Regional Rehabilitation Continuing Education Programs (RRCEPS), was established to meet the continuing education needs of rehabilitation professionals. Fourteen training offices were set up across the country in each of the HEW rehabilitation services administration regions. Staff members of these agencies are professionals, trained to understand the needs of rehabilitation counselors. Periodic meetings with state agency directors and with members of professional organizations such as NRA, NRCA/ARCA, and NCRE are held and committees formed to help RRCEPS with specific training needs. Workshops are generally organized throughout the region, training packages developed, and annotated bibliographies prepared. Special medical aspects packages are prepared according to need.

Some of these continuing education programs maintain resource libraries, which are made up of training modules developed by the various RRCEPS. The RRCEPS are oriented toward providing training in job counseling skills and are performing a valuable job in providing continuing education and orientation for the professoinal rehabilitation counselor. Recent studies within these units are indicating that counselor training programs abound with courses related to counseling theory, but pay little attention to everyday administrative problems that come up during a typical workday.[8]

Similar studies need to be undertaken to develop programs that will equip counselors to deal with the everyday living problems of their clients. To do this, resource libraries, which consist of professional training materials, should be expanded to include information on daily living needs (as outlined in Chapter 4), as well as a more realistic picture of the actual job availability market, as recommended by Caroline Vash.

Private Organizations

Many private organizations contribute to the work of advocacy and information for and about the disabled; some were established early in the century and others were formed during the 1970s. It is not possible to list all of the agencies concerned in some way with serving the disabled, although many of them are mentioned in other chapters of this book. (See Appendix for addresses.) The services of some of the principal agencies (of particular interest are the more recently established ones in such fields as dentistry, recreation, and driving) are described briefly. (For some of the following descriptive material, the author is indebted to the OHI directory.)

The National Easter Seal Society for Crippled Children and Adults, founded in 1919, is the nation's oldest and largest voluntary health agency serving the disabled. Easter Seal societies adapt their services to specific community needs and administer their programs through some 2,000 separately incorporated affiliates. These local offices operate rehabilitation and treatment centers, sheltered workshops, home employment services, resident and day camps, hospitals, and mobile and home therapy units. Among the services offered are physical, occupational, vocational, and speech therapy, physical and vocational evaluation, psychological testing and counseling, home and sheltered employment, special education programs, social clubs, day and residential camping, transportation and referral, and follow-up programs.

In an effort to find causes, cures, and prevention for crippling, the Easter Seal Research Foundation makes grants to finance investigation in those fields that directly relate to the needs of Easter Seal clients. The foundation finances initial exploration of a promising idea or a small pilot study, which could lead to broader financing if findings are justified. Since its beginning in 1956, the foundation has made grants totaling more than $4 million to universities, medical schools, hospitals, and other research institutions.

The National Easter Seal Society publishes a wide variety of pamphlets and technical reports as well as reprints of articles from its professional journal, *Rehabilitation Literature*, which originates in its national office at 2023 West Ogden Avenue, Chicago, Illinois 60612. Bibliographies in areas such as vocational rehabilitation, books about the disabled and architectural barriers, periodicals in the field of rehabilitation, and other related topics are published and updated periodically. An annual publications catalogue, available free of charge, describes all Easter Seal publications. Direct community services are described in the *Directory of Easter Seal Services for the Disabled.* An annual *Easter Seal Directory of Resident Camps for Persons with Special Health Needs* is available from the national office at a nominal cost.

At national headquarters in Chicago, the Easter Seal Library and Information Center houses a collection of materials related to individuals with handicapping conditions. The collection consists of over 4,000 monographs and 40,000 reports, pamphlets, reprints, and miscellaneous items filed by subject in over 100 pamphlet file drawers. The library receives 600 periodicals, including 250 major professional journals. This organization answers requests from the public and professional staff in both the rehabilitation and special education fields, with emphasis on the handicapped child. Information is provided free of charge; however, fees are charged for some of the publications. Local Easter Seal offices are listed in telephone directories.

One of the greatest needs for disabled persons who wish to be active functioning members of society is a barrier-free environment. In 1974 the National Center for a Barrier Free Environment was established by a National Conference on Barrier Free Design. The conference called for the establishment of a central agency to coordinate efforts to make the United States free of architectural barriers and to improve the accessibility of mass transportation. Founding members of the center are the American Institute of Architects, Disabled American Veterans, Gallaudet College, Goodwill Industries of America, Inc., National Congress of Organizations of the Physically Handicapped, National Easter Seal Society for Crippled Children and Adults, National Paraplegia Foundation, National Rehabilitation Association, Paralyzed Veterans of America, Inc., and the President's Committee on Employment of the Handicapped.

Membership dues are the primary source of funds for the center. It acts as a central coordinating agency for all groups concerned with elimination of architectural barriers. A national clearinghouse of information provides service to designers, legislators, disabled people, the professionals who serve them, and the lay public. It assists businesses, schools, and others affected by legislation to adapt their facilities and make them accessible to the handicapped. It also initiates and assists in drafting model legislation and codes.

The center publishes a newsletter called the *Report*, which notes activities in this area all over the United States. This publication has been placed on a subscription basis. The center also provides information free of charge, sending brochures, pamphlets, fact sheets, bibliographies, indexes, and abstracts.

Librarians receiving inquiries from businesses, schools, homeowners, and others wishing to modify and adapt their facilities for the disabled may wish to contact the National Center. (For some specific sources of architectural information, see Chapters 8 and 11.)

The National Clearing House of Rehabilitation Materials is part of the Rehabilitation Counselor Training Program at Oklahoma State University. Since 1962, it has disseminated such materials as abstracts, monographs, articles, final reports, booklets, audio and videotapes, and slide presentations in the areas of rehabilitation and special education to professionals in the field. Professionals working in rehabilitation and related fields are asked to notify the Clearing House about newly developed materials. Some materials are also originated by the Clearing House. All items received are listed in *MEMO*, distributed quarterly to rehabilitation professionals. Those wishing the Clearing House to take over the distribution of their materials must deposit approximately 100 copies with them. Items for sale or distribution free of charge by the author or institution originating them will be so listed. Changes in status of these items (such as selling monographs in a second printing rather than distributing free of charge) must be reported and will be announced in a future issue of *MEMO*. There are some materials available for loan, and fees are sometimes charged for the loan of films or other audiovisuals. The Clearing House will also answer inquiries by phone or letter and make referrals to other sources.

The National Congress of the Physically Handicapped, Inc., was founded to coordinate the work of its 45 member organizations of the physically handicapped in the United States on the national, state, and local levels. It acts as a clearinghouse and library for publications by or about physically handicapped people. Some of these publications are the 125 periodicals published by member organizations or their affiliates.

The National Congress provides general information and referral services, responding to letter or telephone inquiry. It distributes brochures, pamphlets, and fact sheets, as well as its own newsletter, upon request. Lay inquiries are usually referred to direct service providers. Librarians may use this service, but its primary value is to organizations of the physically handicapped. There is a charge for the newsletter, but other information is free.

One of the practical medical rehabilitation problems facing disabled people and the parents of disabled children is the care of teeth. Many dentists are not familiar with the manner in which various orthopedic disabilities react on the structure and condition of the teeth. Reference librarians or librarians working in special facilities who are asked for this type of referral should be aware of the National Foundation of Dentistry for the Handicapped (NFDH).

The Academy of Dentistry for the Handicapped incorporated the foundation in 1974 primarily to develop a campaign of concern, designed to decrease future dental needs of the disabled by furthering educational campaigns to control the incidence of oral disease among them. A model project operating in Colorado is being followed throughout the country. It operates in special schools, sheltered workshops, residential facilities, and nursing homes. NFDH seeks to involve dentists with organizations that give service to the handicapped. It has developed units that seek to identify dentists and clinics providing service to the disabled.

Preventive Dental Care for the Handicapped Child, an audiovisual presentation developed by the foundation, is available for loan in both film and videotape format. Other audiovisual presentations are being developed to instruct dentists and auxiliary personnel in the nature of disabilities. Information is provided free of charge to anyone. Rental fees are charged for the audiovisual materials.

The National Foundation/March of Dimes was originally founded in 1938 by Franklin Roosevelt as the National Foundation for Infantile Paralysis. Since that time, its scope has grown to include all birth defects, and its name has been changed to reflect that growth; 2,500 chapters nationwide are listed in local telephone directories.

The goal of the National Foundation is to prevent birth defects, and numerous programs in medical research and education are funded toward this end. The March of Dimes built and largely supports the Salk Institute in San Diego, California, a research organization that carries on research in molecular genetics, reproductive biology, immunology, virology, the growth of normal and cancerous cells, the central nervous system, and the origins of life. The foundation is also funding a research and education center—the March of Dimes Center for Nutrition, Genetics and Human Development in memory of Dr. Virginia Apgar—at Columbia University, which will provide a central facility for research into birth defect prevention.

Information about birth defects is provided to the general public and professionals. The foundation has available for distribution upon request brochures, pamphlets, fact sheets, bibliographies, indexes and abstracts, and prepared materials. It publishes a newsletter and permits on-site use of its library. Latest scientific findings on birth defects are transmitted to schools of medicine and nursing and other medical centers, hospitals, and health professionals. It has developed 16mm color films for the use of medical and health personnel, and many educational materials have been prepared for public broadcast.

The foundation publishes the *International Directory of Genetic Services*, a comprehensive listing of medical centers in the United States and other countries that provide genetic counseling; the *Birth Defects Atlas and Compendium*, the first book to standardize names and descriptions of nearly 800 congenital anomalies; and *Syndrome Identification*, an international journal on congenital disorders. Information on all these programs and publications may be obtained by calling or writing foundation headquarters in White Plains, New York.

The National Institute of Rehabilitation Engineering (NIRE) is a private, nonprofit organization, founded to serve the severely physically handicapped, utilizing current technology. The institute is not a primary rehabilitation facility. It specializes in seeing people who have already been through regular rehabilitation programs, but who need devices and/or techniques to help them function. NIRE provides patient evaluation on a highly individualized basis. Devices developed by NIRE include electronic speech aids, modified wheelchairs, specially equipped cars and vans, self-care aids, kitchen, clothing, and sexual aids, writing and communication aids, and special self-employment setups.

NIRE is a member organization; however, any lay or professional person may request information. Telephone or letter inquiries will be answered and referrals made. The literature available includes brochures, pamphlets, fact sheets, prepared bibliographies, and films and other audiovisuals, mainly in its area of expertise. On-site use of NIRE's holdings is permitted.

Brief inquiries are answered free of charge. Fees for direct services are levied on a sliding scale.

The National Spinal Cord Injury Foundation is a voluntary health agency. It encourages research on all aspects of paraplegia; refers individual paraplegics to the best available sources of care; publishes a magazine called *Paraplegia Life*; distributes brochures, pamphlets and fact sheets; prepares bibliographies; and permits on-site use of its holdings. It also sponsors seminars and conferences. The foundation has 53 chapters nationwide and makes small incentive grants in support of research. Local chapters provide some direct services, and handicapped individuals are the most frequent inquirers. It is estimated that there are 150,000 spinal cord injured people in the United States and 7,000 more each year injured in automobile, diving, and other accidents; 85 percent of these are males between ages 18 and 25.

Paralyzed Veterans of America is a national organization founded in 1947 and chartered by Congress in 1971. It is charged with the responsibility of representing veterans in their claims before the Veterans Administration. PVA is a federation of autonomous local chapters, which join with the national organization in an attempt to improve veterans' benefits and achieve such goals as barrier-free design.

PVA's services to veterans include overseeing hospital and rehabilitation treatment, locating suitable housing, encouraging driver education programs and adapted mass transportation, adjudicating claims before federal, state, and local agencies, and supporting legislation to assist all disabled individuals. PVA also has a research foundation to review requests for funding and award grants, particularly in the area of spinal cord research.

Publications issued by PVA include *Paraplegia News*, a monthly magazine; pamphlets on adaptation of kitchens and bathrooms for wheelchair use; and a travel guide called *When Turning Wheels Stop*, listing accessible restaurants, motels, and other facilities. Other information is provided free of charge. Write to the national headquarters (see Appendix) or contact a local office, which may be listed under a slightly different name, such as Eastern PVA in New York City.

Rehabilitation International USA (RIUSA) is an independent national voluntary organization that offers assistance to disabled persons worldwide by providing a link between the United States rehabilitation community and rehabilitation activities in other countries. RIUSA is the United States affiliate of Rehabilitation International, established in 1922. It is an excellent resource for information about rehabilitation and special education facilities in other parts of the world. Professional persons wishing to visit agencies similar to their own in other countries may take advantage of this information service. Librarians receiving reference questions of this type can make referrals to RIUSA and be assured that their clients will receive the information needed plus letters of introduction and such.

RIUSA publishes *Rehabilitation World*, a quarterly journal, available with membership in RIUSA or on subscription. It maintains a film library in the area of rehabilitation, which is available for rental. Since 1975 it has been publishing a film catalogue of its holdings.

RIUSA is a membership organization, although anyone may request information, which is supplied free of charge. Its library holdings consist of back copies of its own publications, approximately 50 international journals, and publications acquired through exchange, as well as films. Special files and directories of international film producers and distributors have been developed. As an affiliate of Rehabilitation International, RIUSA has access to the Rehabilitation Information Center at Heidelberg, Germany. It is anticipated that this service will be computerized. A new project for RIUSA is the development of a travel service in the United States for disabled visitors from foreign countries.

The Sister Kenny Institute is a comprehensive center providing rehabilitative care to patients with physical disabilities. It was established in 1941 by Elizabeth Kenny, an Australian nurse who had a great influence on the treatment of polio. In 1975 it merged with Abbott-Northwestern Hospital Corporation.

Sister Kenny provides a full range of therapy to patients and supplements its direct services with public and professional education. It is a source of information in the areas of training of personnel working with the handicapped, housing, transportation, activities of daily living, equipment, and special devices and aids.

The institute disseminates information by responding to letter or telephone inquiry, by referrals to other information centers or to direct service providers, and by sending brochures and pamphlets and providing films and other audiovisuals. The Sister Kenny Institute has an extensive publications program and is a major producer of rehabilitation materials. Hard-to-find information in the field of rehabilitation nursing is available. The institute originally aimed materials particularly at the health professional. However, new publications are geared to meeting the needs of educators, patients, and their families.

A catalogue of publications and audiovisuals is available on request. The Kenny stroke multimedia series consists of several presentations on various aspects of stroke rehabilitation programs and is available on 16mm film, slides, or 35mm filmstrips.

Sister Kenny offers continuing education courses, workshops, and seminars for professional health workers, provides consulting services, and maintains a speaker's bureau. Information is available on request. Direct services are provided to patients referred by physicians or other qualified personnel. Fees are on a sliding scale according to a patient's ability to pay. No patient is refused care due to lack of funds.

To serve persons with severe speech impairments, TRACE Research and Development Center for the Severely Communicatively Handicapped, formerly known as the Cerebral Palsy Communication Group, is located at the University of Wisconsin. Its goal is to provide severely physically handicapped, speech-impaired individuals with some form of communication.

A number of centers in the United States and abroad are working to develop devices in this area, and exciting breakthroughs are taking place. To coordinate research in this field, TRACE Center maintains files of projects at other institutions in the area of nonvocal communication, techniques, and aids. A device called the Autocom, developed by the center, is being field-tested. TRACE answers inquiries, makes referrals, and sends literature upon request. Its publications include *Master Chart and Listing of Nonvocal Communication Aids; Annotated Bibliography of Communication Aids;* and *Communication Outlook*, a newsletter about new developments in communication aids and techniques. This quarterly publication, published in conjunction with the Artificial Language Laboratory of Michigan State University, is available from the Artificial Language Laboratory, Computer Science Department, Michigan State University, East Lansing, Michigan 48824.

The American Association for the Advancement of Science, Project on the Handicapped in Science, is an interesting prototype for possible similar projects in other professional fields. Think of the opportunities that could be opened to qualified disabled people if all professional organizations began to develop activities in this area!

Established by a group within the American Association for the Advancement of Science, the project is designed to explore the barriers that deter disabled people from participation in education and employment opportunities for science. It develops programs to improve the opportunities for science education to handicapped youth, to train science educators, and inventory science resources for disabled students. Accessibility to professional meetings is a special objective, and the association hopes to encourage greater active professional participation on the part of disabled members. Tapes on many scientific subjects are made available to disabled scientists. Reference services are provided to lay and professional inquirers. Information on careers in science is made available to interested disabled students, who will also be referred to an individual in the association related to his or her career choice and a scientist with a similar disability, who can give advice and support.

The American Coalition of Citizens with Disabilities was formed in 1974 and is staffed by persons with disabilities. It is composed of five major groups: American Council of the Blind, National Spinal Cord Injury Foundation, PVA, National Association of the Deaf, and TTYs for the Deaf, Inc., plus 20 smaller organizations. These groups have joined to coordinate and improve communication within groups of people with physical and mental handicaps. They provide information on education, employment, transportation, health, and activities of daily living. In addition, the organization acts as an advocate for disabled people by testifying on legislation. It provides an information service and makes referrals.

Just One Break (JOB) was founded in 1949 by Eleanor Roosevelt, Orin Lehman, and Bernard Baruch, and was incorporated in New York City in 1952. Its original purpose was to assist disabled veterans returning from World War II in rejoining the work force. Its services were later expanded to aid all handicapped adults in achieving employment in business and industry. No fees are charged, and JOB has a placement rate of 50 percent.

Although JOB's principal activities are in the greater New York Area, it distributes information about its operations nationwide to rehabilitation facilities and educational institutions. It conducts research and demonstration projects in the area of placement of the disabled. JOB answers telephone and mail inquiries, refers inquiries to other information centers, and provides brochures, pamphlets, and fact sheets. Studies have been conducted on the placement of the emotionally disturbed and of disabled persons living in poverty areas. Other studies are planned on the placement of cancer-cured patients and of the blind and partially sighted.

One outstanding rehabilitation research library is located at the Institute for Crippled and Disabled in New York City. It was established in 1917, with the official name of the Bruce Barton Memorial Library. The library houses 6,000 books, 2,500 bound periodical titles, and 76 drawers of vertical file materials in the major subject areas of rehabilitation of the physically and mentally handicapped, general medicine, phychiatry, physical and occupational therapy, sensory feedback therapy, and orthotics and prosthetics. It also includes materials on vocational evaluation, work adjustment, rehabilitation counseling, psychiatry, psychology, social work, speech pathology and audiology, attitude training, and rehabilitation research.

The library also maintains two special collections. The Douglas C. McMurtrie Rehabilitation Collection specializes in the early history of rehabilitation, and there is also a microfiche collection of 4,000 research reports funded by the Social Rehabilitation Service. Indexes and abstracts provide access to these research documents. The library serves a large professional population and is also open to the public.[9]

The Institute for Crippled and Disabled (ICD) in New York City was originally founded in 1917 to help disabled soldiers restructure their lives. Central to the ICD program are vocational rehabilitation services, which include evaluation, skills training, counseling, and job placement. It operates as an outpatient center and, in addition to vocational rehabilitation, offers medical services, including diagnosis and treatment, physical and occupational therapy, biofeedback training, and speech and hearing therapy. Social adjustment services offer special programs for the brain-damaged, mentally retarded, and emotionally disturbed. The only group not served is the blind.

A new service of ICD is the Service Programs for the Aging (SPA) Center for Developmental Aging, a program designed to work with elderly persons who are experiencing mild to severe degrees of confusion and disorientation. Emphasis will be placed on improving functional capacities for independent daily living, as well as increasing a sense of personal worth. The primary objective of this program is to enable the participants to remain in the community by providing the rehabilitative services that are needed for them and their families.[10]

This is an incomplete listing of some of the important organizations offering service to the physically disabled. Professional rehabilitation organizations such as the Association of Rehabilitation Facilities have been mentioned earlier. There are new and interesting organizations in many areas concerning the disabled. Librarians pursuing information in specific areas should use some of the source material in this text to contact these organizations or their local affiliates.

Additional Information Resources

It becomes apparent that a wealth of information exists to help disabled individuals solve many of their problems. The local information situation, however, is still very uneven, characterized particularly by the lack of information sources in most rural areas. Information that does exist in metropolitan areas is often hard to track down. General community information and referral centers do not specialize in information for the handicapped, but they sometimes do have some relevant data. Although hospitals and/or libraries might seem to be obvious suppliers of information regarding the handicapped, in general they are not equipped to do so.

It is interesting to note how many times the word "clearinghouse" appears when listing organizations. These attempts, by many of the organizations that serve the disabled, to establish comprehensive sources of information are a first step in controlling the information explosion that has taken place in the field of service to the disabled in the 1970s.

The obvious answer to the problem of access to information about all of the latest developments in this fast-moving field lies in a computerized information retrieval network. Partial attempts in this direction have already been made. One such model, called SCRIP, initially a cooperative enterprise started by a coalition of several state organizations for the handicapped in New Jersey, is now a New Jersey state program. SCRIP demonstrates that a computerized information file on available services and facilities can be effective.

A limited amount of medical information on disabilities is available through Medline; however, this contains only data covered in the medical journals. Special education information is stored in the ERIC network and also indexed more specifically in *Exceptional Child Education Resources* (formerly *Exceptional Child Education Abstracts*) and *Closer Look*, the federal clearinghouse of information on exceptional children. These education networks are discussed in Part IV.

The editor of the magazine *Accent on Living* operates a computerized retrieval system called Accent on Information (AOI). AOI's files include approximately 2,400 items selected from books, periodicals, brochures, commercial catalogues, and other information on new products and services of interest to the physically disabled. This information deals specifically with activities of daily living, and answers are specially adapted to the needs of the person submitting the request. A charge is made for this service but is waived for disabled individuals who cannot afford to pay.

Persons sending questions to AOI should be as specific as possible about the subject or problem area on which they need information and about the nature of their disability. Inquiries may be addressed to Accent on Information, P.O. Box 700, Department I, Bloomington, Illinois 61701.

Another computer-automated information retrieval system is the Information and Research Utilization Center (IRUC), sponsored by the American Alliance for Health, Physical Education and Recreation (AAHPER). The center began operation in 1972 as a demonstration project supported by the Bureau of Education of the Handicapped, Office of Education, HEW. Information is collected and abstracted about programs, activities, methods, research, personnel preparation, and other pertinent data about adapted physical education, recreation, and therapeutic recreation for individuals with physically disabling conditions.

IRUC also has a certain amount of general information on disabling conditions, education, health, activities of daily living, special devices, and psychological services. It answers inquiries, makes referrals to other organizations, and permits on-site use of its materials. IRUC's data base is updated several times per year. It may be used at a base price for batch retrievals with additional costs for special searches. Contact IRUC, 1201 16 Street N.W., Washington, D.C. 20036.

The Therapeutic Recreation Information Center (TRIC) (Department of Recreation and Park Administration, California State University, 6000 J Street, Sacramento, California 95819) is a computer-based, information-

acquisition, storage, retrieval, and dissemination center specifically concerned with published and unpublished materials related to recreation service to ill, disadvantaged, disabled, and aging persons. The original TRIC
data base was developed in 1971 at Columbia University and encompassed
the period 1965–1970. It moved to the University of Waterloo in Ontario,
Canada, and was updated in 1974.

TRIC supplies abstracts of materials on therapeutic recreation, and
describes its system as the largest computer-automated data bank in this
field. Currently the data base contains approximately 3,500 abstracts and
citations, which are being updated. It is hoped that the system will be updated on an annual basis. On-site library materials are available. Rates for
printouts will be quoted upon request.

Other more general computerized sources of information include the National Technical Information Service operated by the federal government,
which abstracts all federal technical reports, including those in the field
of disability, and the abstracts on research available from the Smithsonian's
Science Information Exchange. Other attempts at service, directed more
specifically at the disabled user, are community hot lines. In some states,
such as Illinois and New York, a hot line for the handicapped has been
established, which can be called for reference information.

In 1975 the Rehabilitation Research and Training (RR and T) Center
at George Washington University, Washington, D.C., undertook a feasibility
study for a National Rehabilitation Information Center.[11] The study was
supported by funds from the Rehabilitation Services Administration of
HEW, and the results were published in June 1975. Its major recommendation was the ultimate establishment of a National Rehabilitation Information Center (NARIC), which would have as its principal purpose the
acquisition, storage, and indexing of all resources being generated by the
RR and T network and all other projects funded by RSA, as well as a core
collection of relevant commercially generated materials. The report acknowledged the fact that there is no central repository of rehabilitation information. Although it stated that this information center would interface in
some way with the clearinghouse at OHI, it did not make entirely clear
how duplication of service would be avoided.

In October 1977 the Rehabilitation Services Administration made a
five-year grant to establish a National Rehabilitation Information Center,
to be located in Washington, D.C. The center is a joint project of the graduate
department of library science at Catholic University of America and the
Institute for Information Studies, Inc., a private, nonprofit organization
headed by Elizabeth Pan. The director of the center is Judith J. Senkevitch.
It is particularly significant to the library field that the center has been
established under the wing of a library school and that the director is a
librarian. The center's basic goal is to improve information delivery to the

rehabilitation community. It will house all RSA-generated research reports, as well as other significant books, journals, and conference proceedings relevant to vocational rehabilitation.

In June 1978 a second conference on the topic of networking was held in Washington, D.C. It was attended by representatives of many members of the rehabilitation research network. Again, as at the 1977 conference, the small number of librarians in attendance reflected the small number working in the rehabilitation field. At both conferences the topic of networking was explored, and at the end of the 1978 conference a committee was appointed to study further steps in the possible development of a data base in the area of rehabilitation. Recommendations were formulated and submitted to NARIC, which has been making great progress toward establishing such a national rehabilitation data base. Reporting on this progress in the April 1979 issue of the *Bulletin of the American Society for Information Science*, Director Senkevitch describes NARIC's work:[12]

> It must be clearly understood that NARIC's primary mandate is to disseminate the findings and research results of the funded programs operating under the governance of the Rehabilitation Services Administration. The Center now has a library of approximately 4,000 RSA research reports, monographs and audiovisual packages, 1,000 rehabilitation reference books, and 150 periodical subscriptions in the field of rehabilitation. The catalog is maintained in an on-line storage and retrieval system, using an IBM 370 computer. Bibliographies have been generated in a number of areas, and this listing will be furnished on request. Individual reference questions are handled through searching NARIC's resources, as well as related data bases such as ERIC, NTIS, MEDLARS, and Psychological Abstracts. At the present time these searches are conducted through a commercial data system and there is a charge for them. Although anyone may use NARIC, most of the collection is oriented toward professionals in the area of rehabilitation.

Beginning in March 1979, access to NARIC's computerized system was provided to a limited number of organizations through Bibliographic Retrieval Services, Inc. (BRS), and by September 1979, it was anticipated that NARIC's data base would be open for full public use by anyone having access to a computer terminal. It is anticipated that a large portion of the collection will be made commercially available as an indexed packaged set of microfiche through Microfilming Corporation of America, a subsidiary of the *New York Times*.

NARIC now has the beginning of a rehabilitation network, but some work remains to be done. Area centers already exist in special fields all over the country. These centers, which could bid for contracts to enable them to join the computerized central system, include

Oklahoma Clearinghouse

National Center for Law and the Handicapped (legal)

Research centers on deafness and developmental disabilities

Work evaluation and job development centers

Research Engineering centers

TRIC and IRUC—both recreational information centers

AOI-ADL information in an existing small information retrieval system

American Printing House for the Blind

Helen Keller Center for the Deaf/Blind

All of these components are not a part of the RSA research network, but all could be brought together under the umbrella at NARIC with the cooperation of the Information Clearinghouse of OHI.

In addition, a center might have to be set up (or NARIC could do this in Washington) to index and abstract all the rehabilitation and related journals, which are at present not completely indexed anywhere. Medline does some on a spot basis, ERIC does the special education journals. No one does all of them. This would include *Developmental Disabilities Abstracts*, as well as journals for the blind and the deaf.

In some way, the area centers would have to include the monographs and newsletters, which are now coming out in large numbers and are not recorded anywhere, and so impossible to retrieve.

We have an overall need to bring rehabilitation and librarianship together, to make use of the information retrieval search skills of the trained librarian in serving the information needs of the rehabilitation counselor, who is the first line of communication with the disabled client.

It is to be hoped that such a complete clearinghouse, with one computerized data base, soon will be on its way to fruition. Information about NARIC and its services can be obtained from NARIC, Judith J. Senkevitch, Director, P.O. Box 136, Catholic University of America, Washington, D.C. 20064.

REHABILITATION LIBRARIANSHIP AS A PROFESSION

Opportunities for establishing rehabilitation libraries can be found at:

1. The state level, where some states have already pioneered in the establishment of libraries to service the state departments of vocational rehabilitation
2. The local level, where all vocational rehabilitation offices could benefit by having a trained librarian on the staff
3. In all rehabilitation facilities
4. In rehabilitation hospitals
5. In Veterans Administration hospitals
6. In regional offices of the rehabilitation research network
7. In all private organizations dealing with the disabled that do not yet

have a trained librarian on the staff, including advocacy parent organizations that deliver services to disabled children

Chapter 11 is an annotated bibliography that could be used by the librarian setting up a small rehabilitation library collection. Further development of the collection would, of course, reflect the special needs of the facility in which the library functions.

The following suggestions for programming are only a start. Each librarian will find many ways to serve professionals and clients.

Hospital and Institution Libraries

Until recently, hospital and institution librarians concerned themselves with two types of service: recreational reading for patients and scientific informational services to the medical and other professional staff. By adding information to their files in the fields of activities of daily living, prosthetics and orthotics, and other areas of need, and by including some of the rehabilitation literature as annotated in Chapter 11, hospital and institution librarians will expand their areas of usefulness one hundredfold to the patients and to the rehabilitation professionals.

Rehabilitation Libraries

For libraries in rehabilitation centers and facilities, a full professional collection of books, journals, and research monographs and newsletters should be supplemented by whatever specialized materials are needed at the specific work site. For organizations operating on government and private grants, the library should include the *Federal Register, Commerce Business Daily*, and other sources on how to write and acquire grant money.

If the rehabilitation facility is active in the field of placement, and for all vocational rehabilitation state and local offices, the collection should include information about the availability of appropriate job opportunities for disabled clients. The latest research results in the field of rehabilitation engineering are important for the collection, so that counselors will be aware of all new technological modifications that will assist in job productivity.

The rehabilitation librarian should scan periodicals constantly for new materials that must be acquired to keep the collection up-to-date. Articles on subjects of interest to particular professional staff members should be circulated as needed. Newsletters from all of the research and national centers should come into the library. Some of the most valuable, such as *The Informer, The Report, Programs for the Handicapped, Amicus, Main-stream* (there are two of these from two separate groups), and some of the newsletters put out by the more active state governor's committees should be received and scanned for information. Individual librarians will treat newsletters according to individual preference. Some will wish to file for at least a year. Others will circulate them and then discard after perusal.

Sending out a newsletter of one's own from the library is an extremely good way to publicize holdings and give information to professional staff who are sometimes too busy to do as much reading as they would like. If your library is a state facility, this newsletter could be circulated to all rehabilitation facilities and OVR branches in the state that do not have libraries of their own.

Each library should have a file of the principal research monographs that are the result of current research being generated by the research network. If the rehabilitation facility is active in the field of placement, the librarian can play an active role on the rehabilitation team by supplying information to industry in the fields of job and work site modification so that employers and disabled employees may take advantage of the latest research in the field of rehabilitation engineering to ensure that disabled workers will have the benefit of all new technological modifications to assist them to be productive on the job. Information such as travel and transportation and telephone modifications, which can be found in Chapter 4, will also be of use to the disabled person on the job.

Direct service to the client in the rehabilitation facility may be less likely than it would be in a school or public library. However, the librarian should be prepared to offer information as requested pertaining to all of the daily living needs discussed in Chapter 4. The librarian should make sure that professional personnel have told clients about the availability of such information in the library.

All rehabilitation librarians should be in contact with NARIC, the National Rehabilitation Information Center. Appropriately placed terminals will in time maintain contact with it so that each of the rehabilitation regions will be adequately served.

SUMMARY

The decade of the 1970s witnessed great changes in the lives of disabled people who are entering the mainstream in greater numbers than ever before. During this time, an information explosion has reflected the work being done in all areas of rehabilitation—medical, engineering, and vocational —and in education to make this participation possible.

Libraries that operate information and referral services and wish to serve their disabled clientele need to become aware of the variety of information resources that exist in this field. A National Rehabilitation Information Center, at the Catholic University Graduate School of Library Science, has made a start in the vast project of centralizing and indexing a great number of existing materials. The fact that this is a library-oriented project represents an encouraging forward step in the integration of the fields of library science and rehabilitation. It should help to make the development of rehabilitation librarianship as a professional specialization a viable reality.

NOTES

1. Clearinghouse on the Handicapped, Office for Handicapped Individuals, Department of Health, Education, and Welfare, *Directory of National Information Sources on Handicapping Conditions and Related Services*, Washington, D.C. (1976).

2. Information Exchange Program, *The Informer*, Arkansas Rehabilitation Research and Training Center, University of Arkansas, 6, no. 2 (February 1977): 4.

3. Joseph E. Traub, "Rehabilitation Engineering: A Program of Research, Evaluation, Training and Service," in *American Rehabilitation* 2, no. 4 (March–April 1977): 19.

4. Sheila H. Akabas, Ph.D., "Jobs through Technical Assistance," in *American Rehabilitation* 2, no. 4 (March–April 1977): 20.

5. PL 93-112, Section 305 (a).

6. Robert J. Smithdas, Litt. D., "Lest We Forget," in *Nat-Center News* 9, no. 2 (January 1979).

7. Information Exchange Program, *The Informer*, Arkansas Rehabilitation Research and Training Center, University of Arkansas (December 1976).

8. Regional Rehabilitation Continuing Education Programs, *Newsletter*, Region 2, State University of New York at Buffalo.

9. Helen Stonehill, librarian, Bruce Barton Memorial Library, Institute for Crippled and Disabled, New York, N.Y., description (unpub. 1978).

10. Institute for Crippled and Disabled *ICD News* 13, no. 2 (Winter 1977–1978): 9.

11. Rehabilitation Research and Training Center, George Washington University, "A Feasibility Study for a National Rehabilitation Information Center," Washington, D.C. (1975).

12. Judith J. Senkevitch, "Toward a National Rehabilitation Data Base," in *Bulletin of the American Society for Information Science* 5, no. 4 (April 1979).

11

A Model Rehabilitation Library

The collection on the following pages represents a basic library in the fields of medical and vocational rehabilitation. Such a library would be of use in any type of rehabilitation facility. Any library must be a living, breathing organism and must reflect the needs of the people it serves. For example, a library in a rehabilitation hospital will need to place a slightly more medical emphasis on its collection, while a library in a vocational rehabilitation center will need more rehabilitation counseling and job opportunity materials.

In addition to the specialized materials listed here, the librarian might wish to acquire a general basic collection in the areas of anatomy and physical medicine, psychology, sociology, economics, and other related general topics, according to the professional needs of the user population. Much of this material should also be made available to library school students where the curriculum includes course work in rehabilitation librarianship or library service to the disabled.

A good deal of the valuable up-to-date information in the field of rehabilitation, which is of real practical use to disabled people and to the professionals who counsel them, is available in fugitive materials, such as pamphlets and monographs. It would be impossible to list all of them here. Many of the organizations mentioned throughout this book publish such materials. The librarian wishing to establish a rehabilitation library might use this suggested basic bibliography as a starting guide and continue to build the collection by sending for the publication catalogues of the voluntary rehabilitation organizations and reading the basic rehabilitation journals to locate new publications.

Until recently, these methods, combined with word of mouth, were the only ways of locating new materials. It was extremely difficult to learn about the new research reports being generated by the Rehabilitation Research Network. It was important that a national information network in the field of rehabilitation be established, and this was done by NARIC, the National Rehabilitation Information Center (P.O. Box 136, Catholic University of America, Washington, D.C. 20064). Access to NARIC by computer terminal would be extremely useful to a librarian setting up a library in a rehabilitation center. However, it cannot take the place of a basic library on the premises.

It is always difficult to recommend cataloguing procedures for a special library. The author has found, through years of experience, that neither the Library of Congress system nor the Medical Cataloging system is entirely successful for books in the field of rehabilitation. In addition, managing the extensive vertical files that accumulate as pamphlets and monographs are acquired becomes increasingly difficult if a simple alphabetical subject heading system is used.

During the late 1950s, Doreen Portal developed a rehabilitation filing system under a research grant through the University of Colorado. For a librarian starting a new library, if all materials and books, as well as vertical file materials, were catalogued according to this system, it should prove very satisfactory. All rehabilitation libraries should be using the same system so that interlibrary loan could be facilitated.

The Portal system was modified by Laura A. Edwards, and the shorter version was published in "Establishing a Research Utilization Specialist in a State Vocational Rehabilitation Agency," Commonwealth of Virginia, Department of Vocational Rehabilitation, May 1974.

The areas covered in this collection include

Rehabilitation, General

Rehabilitation, Medicine

Rehabilitation Counseling

Independent Living

Barrier-Free Design

Travel

Recreation

Sex and the Disabled

Periodicals

Newsletters

Directories

Sources for Audiovisual Materials

This model rehabilitation library collection should be considered in conjunction with the core collection for public libraries in Chapter 8. Thus Chapters 8 and 11 represent a basic collection in medical and vocational rehabilitation. The core collection in Chapter 14 covers the area of special education; however, there is a great deal of overlap in the usefulness of material. Therefore school librarians, library schools offering course work in library service to exceptional children, and education departments with special education courses may be interested in much of the information in this chapter and in Chapter 8, as well as in Chapter 14.

REHABILITATION, GENERAL

Bolton, Brian. *Introduction to Rehabilitation Research.* American Lecture Series no. 945. Springfield, Ill.: Charles C. Thomas, 1974. Summarizes the current status of psychological measurement principles and practices in the evolution of disabled clients.

Cobb, A. Beatrix. *Medical and Psychological Aspects of Disability.* Springfield, Ill. Charles C. Thomas, 1973. Cobb's objective is to relate the medical aspects of each disability to its social, psychological, and vocational aspects. Helping rehabilitation counselors to develop a medical and psychosocial vocabulary will improve their in-depth understanding of the total rehabilitation process.

————. *Special Problems in Rehabilitation.* Springfield, Ill.: Charles C. Thomas, 1974.

Cull, John G., and Hardy, Richard E. *Rehabilitation Facility Approaches in Disabilities.* Springfield, Ill.: Charles C. Thomas, 1975.

————. *Rehabilitation Techniques in Severe Disability: Case Studies.* American Lecture Series in Social and Rehabilitation Psychology. Springfield, Ill.: Charles C. Thomas, 1974. Case studies point up special problems in rehabilitation of certain groups of individuals.

————. *Understanding Disability for Social and Rehabilitation Services.* American Lecture Series in Social and Rehabilitation Psychology. Springfield, Ill.: Charles C. Thomas, 1973.

Garrett, James F., and Levine, Edna S., eds. *Rehabilitation Practices with the Physically Disabled.* New York: Columbia University Press, 1973. A broad discussion of rehabilitation, encompassing physical, psychosocial, and vocational techniques.

Goble, R. E. A., and Nicols, P. J. R. *Rehabilitation of the Severely Disabled.* Vol. 1. *Evaluation of a Disabled Living Unit.* Vol. 2. *Management.* New York: Appleton, 1971. Evaluation of physical impairments and personality and intellectual assessment, provision of appliances, social and welfare services.

Wright, George N., and Trotter, Ann Beck. *Rehabilitation Research.* Madison: University of Wisconsin, 1968. Old but classic; can be used as a benchmark in understanding where rehabilitation has come from. Covers neurological, physically disabled, mentally retarded, speech and hearing, homebound, aging, rural, and sensory.

REHABILITATION MEDICINE

Barnes, Marylou, and Critchfield, Carolyn A. *The Patient at Home: A Manual of Exercise Programs, Self Help Devices, and Home Care Procedures.* Thorofare, N.J.: Charles B. Slack, 1971.

Bobath, Berta. *Adult Hemiplegia: Evaluation and Treatment*, 2nd ed. London: Heinemann, 1978. Up-to-date guide in medical rehabilitation, treatment of adult hemiplegia.

Boroch, Rose Marie. *Elements of Rehabilitation in Nursing: An Introduction.* St. Louis: Mosby, 1976. To help the nursing profession to understand today's nursing care, encompassing membership as part of a rehabilitation team. Chapters on supportive equipment and sexual functioning. Appendixes include equipment resource list and questions for a health history.

Bulletin of Prosthetics Research. Washington, D.C.: Rehabilitative Engineering Research and Development, Department of Medicine and Surgery, Veterans Administration, Fall and Spring. SuDoc, Stock no. 051-000-00130-3.

Burke, D. C., and Murray, D. D. *Handbook of Spinal Cord Medicine.* New York: Raven Press (first published in Great Britain, Macmillan), 1975. A pocket book for resident and house directors with no previous experience with spinal cord injury. Good for medical schools and nursing staffs and schools. Basic and thorough. Treatment, sexual effects, nursing care, rehabilitation, etc.

Commission for the Control of Epilepsy and Its Consequences. *Plan for Nationwide Action on Epilepsy*, vol. 1. Publication no. (NIH) 78-276. Washington, D.C.: Department of HEW, Public Health Service, National Institutes of Health. An impressive compendium of information about epilepsy and action of all kinds to control the disease and rehabilitate for participation in society. This is the summary report. In addition to volume 1, there are appendixes (Vols. 2 through 4) that offer documentation of all input, research analyses, budget computations, and cost benefit projects. Copies of these volumes are available upon request from the Office of Scientific and Health Reports, National Institute of Neurological and Communicative Disorders and Stroke.

Davidson, Roslyn. *Rehabilitation Administrative Procedures for Extended Care Facilities.* Springfield, Ill.: Charles C. Thomas, 1973.

Dean, Russell J. N. *New Life for Millions: Rehabilitation for America's Disabled.* New York: Hastings House, 1972.

Donahoo, Clara A., and Dimon, Joseph H., III. *Orthopedic Nursing.* Boston: Little, Brown, 1977. Up-to-date information on orthopedic nursing care and medical rehabilitation.

Downey, John A., ed. *Physiological Basis of Rehabilitation Medicine.* Philadelphia: Saunders, 1971.

Feller, Irving, and Jones, Claudella Archambeault. *Nursing the Burned Patient.* Ann Arbor, Mich.: National Institute for Burn Medicine, 1973.

Ford, Jack R., and Duckworth, Bridget. *Physical Management for the Quadriplegic Patient*. Philadelphia: Davis, 1974. Manual for the use of paramedic students, nurses, and therapists who work with traumatic quadriplegic patients.

French, John D., and Porter, Robert W. *Basic Research in Paraplegia*. Springfield, Ill.: Charles C. Thomas, 1972. Medical and historical account of research in this field.

Friedmann, Lawrence W. *The Psychological Rehabilitation of the Amputee*. Springfield, Ill.: Charles C. Thomas, 1978. Useful to medical, rehabilitation, social, and mental health professionals who work with amputees.

Hardy, R. E., and Cull, J. G. *Counseling and Rehabilitating the Cancer Patient*. American Lecture Series. Springfield, Ill.: Charles C. Thomas, 1975. Medical information, psychological implications, therapeutic work with patients, psychosexual aspects, case studies in vocational rehabilitation.

Hirschberg, Gerald G., Lewis, Leon, and Vaughan, Patricia. *Rehabilitation: A Manual for the Care of the Disabled and Elderly*, 2nd ed. Philadelphia: Washington Square, 1976. All aspects of rehabilitation of patients with specific impairments.

Ince, Laurence P. *The Rehabilitation Medicine Services*. Springfield, Ill.: Charles C. Thomas, 1974. Treatment of physically disabled adults and children is dealt with in terms of the interaction of all professional services that make up the rehabilitation team—physical therapist, occupational therapist, speech pathologist, audiologist, psychologist, social worker, rehabilitation counselor, nurse, recreational therapist. A book for all health care professionals.

Kaplan, Paul E., Materson, Richard, and Season, Edwin H. *Physical Medicine and Rehabilitation: Continuing Education Review*. New York: Medical Examination Publishing Co., 1977.

Krusen, Frank H., Kottke, Frederic, and Ellwood, Paul M., Jr. *Handbook of Physical Medicine and Rehabilitation*, 2nd ed. Philadelphia: Saunders, 1971. Patient evaluation, psychological and vocational assessment, principles of therapy, rehabilitation for activities of daily living and rehabilitation of persons with specific disorders. Chapter on education of physicians and other professionals in the field of rehabilitation.

Larson, Carroll B., and Gould, Marjorie, eds. *Orthopedic Nursing*. St. Louis: Mosby, 1974. Good chapter on rehabilitation aspects of orthopedic nursing.

Licht, Sidney, ed. *Rehabilitation and Medicine*. Baltimore, Md.: Waverly Press, 1969. Contributions by many specialists in the fields of physical and occupational therapy, rehabilitation nursing, psychology, vocational evaluation, and rehabilitation of specific disabilities.

————. *Stroke and Its Rehabilitation*. Baltimore, Md.: Waverly Press, 1975. History and pathology of stroke, physical rehabilitation, nursing care, mental and social problems, and rehabilitation potential of the stroke patient.

Macdonald, Elizabeth M., MacCaul, G., and Mirrey, L., eds. *Occupational Therapy in Rehabilitation: A Handbook for Occupational Therapists, Students, and Others Interested in this Aspect of Reablement*. Baltimore: Williams & Wilkins, 1970.

Nichols, P. J. R. *Rehabilitation Medicine: The Management of Physical Disabilities*. Woburn, Mass.: Butterworths, 1976.

Pierce, Donald S., and Vernon, H. Nickel, eds. *The Total Care of Spinal Cord Injuries.* Boston: Little, Brown, 1977. Team approach to treatment of patients with spinal cord injury. Covers every aspect of patient care.

Rosenstein, Solomon N. *Dentistry in Cerebral Palsy and Related Handicapping Conditions.* Springfield, Ill.: Charles C. Thomas, 1978. All aspects of dentistry for patients with cerebral palsy.

Rusk, Howard A. *Rehabilitation Medicine,* 4th ed. St. Louis: Mosby, 1977. Medical rehabilitation principles and clinical applications. Developments in research and experience in training the disabled homemaker, handling speech problems, prescribing prostheses and orthotics. Photographs, case studies, and charts.

Sarno, John E., and Sarno, Martha Taylor. *Stroke: The Condition and the Patient.* New York: McGraw-Hill, 1969. For families and friends of people who have had strokes.

Sine, Robert, Liss, Shelly E., Roush, Robert E., and Holcomb, David J. *Basic Rehabilitation Techniques: A Self Instructional Guide.* Germantown, Md.: Aspen Systems Corp., 1977. For the medical rehabilitation team concerned with total rehabilitation of the disabled. Primarily for the nursing care professional to improve the quality of rehabilitation nursing care.

Stryker, Stephanie. *Speech after Stroke: A Manual for the Speech Pathologist and the Family Member.* Springfield, Ill.: Charles C. Thomas, 1978. Structured practice material for helping the asphasic patient recover speech skills lost through brain injuries commonly referred to as strokes.

Tabers. *Cyclopedic Medical Dictionary.* Philadelphia: Davis, 1972.

Vukovich, Virginia, and Grubb, Reba D. *Care of the Ostomy Patient.* St. Louis: Mosby, 1973. Information for the hospital staff, as well as on counseling and care of the dying patient. Home nursing, counseling for rehabilitation, psychosocial, sexual, making use of community resources.

Williams, Paul C. *Low Back and Neck Pain: Causes and Conservative Treatment.* Springfield, Ill.: Charles C. Thomas, 1974.

Zankel, Harry T. *Stroke Rehabilitation.* Springfield, Ill.: Charles C. Thomas, 1971. Comprehensive guide to rehabilitation of the adult following stroke.

REHABILITATION COUNSELING

Backer, Thomas E. *New Directions in Rehabilitation: Outcome Measurement.* Emerging Issues in Rehabilitation Series. Washington, D.C.: Institute for Research Utilization, 1977. One of a set of four monographs, synthesizes major research findings on innovations of current concern to vocational rehabilitation professionals. Annotated bibliography.

Bolton, Brian, ed. *Handbook of Measurement and Evaluation in Rehabilitation.* Baltimore: University Park Press, 1976. Summarizes current status of psychological measurement principles and practices in the evaluation of disabled clients.

Bolton, Brian, and Jaques, Marceline E. *Rehabilitation Counseling: Theory and Practice.* Baltimore: University Park Press, 1978. Thirty-four articles on rehabilitation counseling, for courses in the rehabilitation counseling curriculum. Also a background reference for rehabilitation practitioners. Chapters come from the *Rehabilitation Counseling Bulletin*, official publication of the American Rehabilitation Counseling Association.

CARF Standards Manual on Accreditation of Rehabilitation Facilities. Tucson, Ariz.: CARF, n.d. Provides authoritative source for use in establishing standards to evaluate rehabilitation facilities. Guidelines for the establishment of new facilities and an educational resource for in-service training of executives and program administration personnel as well as students in formal educational programs for rehabilitation facilities administrators.

Christopher, Dean A. *Manual Communication*. Baltimore: University Park Press, 1976.

Cull, John G., and Colvin, Craig R. *Contemporary Field Work Practices in Rehabilitation*. American Lecture Series Publication no. 833. Springfield, Ill.: Charles C. Thomas, 1972. Intended as a text for the rehabilitation counselor who is finishing a master's degree and is preparing to enter an internship in rehabilitation, and as a basic orientation for the newly employed counselor whose training and experience are in an area other than vocational rehabilitation. Included are 27 field-work exercises and an extensive appendix.

Cull, John G., and Hardy, Richard E. *Counseling and Rehabilitating the Diabetic*. American Lecture Series. Springfield, Ill.: Charles C. Thomas, 1974. What diabetes is; information on youth program counseling, services, psychological aspects, rehabilitation care of child diabetics, case studies.

————. *Rehabilitation Techniques in Severe Disability: Case Studies*. American Lecture Series in Social and Rehabilitation Psychology. Springfield, Ill.: Charles C. Thomas, 1974. Case studies of persons with mental retardation and epilepsy, visual impairment, diabetes and diabetes with blindness, spinal cord injury, deaf, amputation, cancer, rheumatoid arthritis, drug abuse, cardiovascular disease, and pulmonary disabilities.

Davis, Marcella Z. *Living with Multiple Sclerosis: A Social Psychological Analysis*. Springfield, Ill.: Charles C. Thomas, 1973.

Dorken, Herbert. *Perspectives in National Health Insurance and Research Utilization*. Emerging Issues in Rehabilitation Series. Washington, D.C.: Institute for Research Utilization, 1977. Research findings and innovations in the field of insurance and rehabilitation. Annotated bibliography.

Goldenson, Robert M., ed.-in-chief, Dunham, Jerome R., and Dunham, Charles S., assoc. eds. *Disability and Rehabilitation Handbook*. New York: McGraw-Hill, 1978. With many contributors, a tremendous compendium of information, medical definitions of disabilities, definitions of health science professions concerned with rehabilitation, civil rights, and consumerism, independent living, educational programs, vocational rehabilitation, psychosocial aspects of disability, environmental barriers, recreation, statistics, organizations interested in the disabled, listings of periodicals and directories, government programs, sources of information. No mention of rehabilitation libraries or of rehabilitation librarians.

Greenleigh Associates, Inc. *The Role of the Sheltered Workshops in the Rehabilitation of the Severely Handicapped*. New York, 1975. The overall purpose of this study was to ascertain the effectiveness of sheltered workshops in the rehabilitation, training, and placement of the severely handicapped and what changes are needed to provide more employment opportunities within and outside the sheltered workshop system.

Hardy, Richard E., and Cull, John G. *Educational and Psychosocial Aspects of Deafness.* American Lecture Series. Springfield, Ill.: Charles C. Thomas, 1974. A practical compendium of articles that offer information for rehabilitation counselors, social workers, psychologists, teachers, and others working with deaf people. Psychology, types of hearing loss, living problems, services, working with parents of deaf children, case studies, rehabilitation and vocational adjustment, a review of important research in the field, the deaf student in colleges and universities.

_____. *Severe Disabilities: Social and Rehabilitation Approaches.* American Lecture Series in Social and Rehabilitation Psychology. Springfield, Ill.: Charles C. Thomas, 1974. A collection of articles by experts in the field, this book treats the problems of specific disabilities.

_____. *Vocational Evaluation for Rehabilitation Services.* American Lecture Series in Social and Rehabilitation Psychology. Springfield, Ill.: Charles C. Thomas, 1973. This book contains studies on work evaluation and adjustment, counseling, and testing.

Huffman, Jeanne, et al. *Talk with Me: Communication with the Multi-Handicapped Deaf.* Sacramento: Joyce Motion Picture Co., California State Department of Health, 1975.

Jenkins, William M., Anderson, Robert M., and Dietrich, Wilson L. *Rehabilitation of the Severely Disabled.* Dubuque, Iowa: Kendall/Hunt, 1976. Role of the rehabilitation counselor, vocational evaluation, work adjustment, medical and psychosocial problems of the spinal cord injured, nursing aspects and rehabilitation of the disabled.

Levitan, Sar A., and Taggert, Robert. *Jobs for the Disabled.* Baltimore: Johns Hopkins University Press, 1977. A very specific work, this book attempts to apply performance standards to the vocational rehabilitation effort, taking into account the realities of the labor market, but recognizing that the field of vocational rehabilitation offers individual treatment and the belief that despite noneconomic benefits, those with problems deserve help. Presents vocational rehabilitation as part of the larger picture of the field of manpower.

McDaniel, J. *Physical Disability and Human Behavior,* 2nd ed. New York: Pergamon Press, 1976. Classic work; attitudes toward the disabled, emotional factors in illness and disability, perceptual problems, the factor of motivation in the rehabilitation process.

Malikin, David, and Rusalem, Herbert. *Vocational Rehabilitation of the Disabled: An Overview.* New York: New York University Press, 1969. A basic introductory text for the training of rehabilitation personnel in the various professional work areas. The book contains 14 chapters, each contributed by an eminent professional in the subject field covered. Addressed to rehabilitation counselors, physicians, social workers, psychologists, therapists, and other professionals in the field, as well as students and teachers.

Marinelli, R., and Orto, D., eds. *Psychological and Sociological Impact of Physical Disability.* New York: Springer, 1977. A collection of articles published in the 1970s.

Martin, Rolland A. *Occupational Disability: Causes, Predictions, Prevention.* Springfield, Ill.: Charles C. Thomas, 1975. Information for insurance companies, workmen's compensation, administrative legislators, employers, and labor leaders. Points up need for disability prevention and active rehabilitation.

Materials Development Center. *Suggested Publications for Developing an Agency Library on Work Evaluation and Work Adjustment,* 6th ed. Menomonie, Wis.: Stout Vocational Rehabilitation Institute, University of Wisconsin-Stout, 1974.

_____. *VEWAA-CARF Vocational Evaluation and Work Adjustment Standards with Interpretive Guidelines and VEWAA Glossary.* Menomonie, Wis.: Stout Vocational Rehabilitation Institute, University of Wisconsin-Stout, n.d. In addition to standards and guidelines, a glossary and definition of 140 terms related to the profession and practice of vocational evaluation and work adjustment.

_____. *Work Evaluation and Adjustment: An Annotated Bibliography.* 1975 Supplement. Menomonie, Wis.: Stout Vocational Rehabilitation Institute, University of Wisconsin-Stout, 1974. References supplement a comprehensive bibliography (1974) published by the center on the literature in work evaluation and vocational adjustment.

_____. *Work Evaluation and Adjustment: An Annotated Bibliography, 1947–1977,* Menomonie, Wis.: Stout Vocational Rehabilitation Institute, University of Wisconsin-Stout.

Moses, Harold A., and Patterson, C. H. *Research Readings in Rehabilitation Counseling.* Champaign, Ill.: Stipes, 1973. This anthology of 54 readings includes four papers reprinted from rehabilitation literature. The importance of the production and utilization of research is stressed.

Nagi, Saad Z. *Disability and Rehabilitation: Legal, Clinical and Self-Concepts and Measurement.* Columbus: Ohio State University Press, 1970. Examines the criteria on the basis of which disability is measured. Rehabilitation potential assessed and eligibility for benefits determined. Good in terms of historical value.

Obermann, C. Esco. *A History of Vocational Rehabilitation in America.* Minneapolis: Denison, 1967. A history of the development of rehabilitation services in America. Valuable as a documentary of how far we have come in the evaluation of how far we still have to go.

Porter, Edgar B. *Guidelines for the Rehabilitation of Hearing Impaired Persons.* Silver Spring, Md.: National Association for Hearing and Speech Action, n.d. Information on medical, communication, psychological, social, and vocational rehabilitation of the hearing-impaired. Anatomy of the human ear. Glossary of terms.

The Rehabilitation of the Severely Handicapped Homebound. Arkansas Rehabilitation Research and Training Center, University of Arkansas, Fourth Institute on Rehabilitation Issues, May 31, June 1–2, 1977, Dallas, Texas. Report from study group. Up-to-date information and philosophy on rehabilitation of the homebound.

Renetzky, Alvin, ed. *Directory of Internships, Work Experience Programs, and On-the-Job Training Opportunities.* Thousand Oaks, Calif., 1976. Very valuable reference. Check for new edition.

Rice, Carl O. *Calculation of Industrial Disabilities of the Extremities and the Back*, 2nd ed. Springfield, Ill.: Charles C. Thomas, 1968. An abridgment of the first edition, which outlines basic principles in calculating loss of use of parts of the body in terms of industrial cost.

Roessler, Richard, and Bolton, Brian. *Psychosocial Adjustment to Disability*. Baltimore: University Park Press, 1978. Summarizes results of research at Arkansas Rehabilitation Research and Training Center. Designed to serve as a manual in rehabilitation counseling courses, special education training programs, and other health-related programs. Physical, psychiatric, intellectual, and social disabilities covered, with special emphasis on the severely disabled and a separate chapter on spinal cord injured. Training packages and research reports listed in reference can be obtained from the publisher's office, Arkansas Rehabilitation Research and Training Center, Hot Springs Rehabilitation Center, or from the Oklahoma Clearinghouse.

Routh, Thomas A. *Rehabilitation Counseling of the Blind*. Springfield, Ill.: Charles C. Thomas, 1970. Suggestions advanced are for working with blind clients in an effort to help them help themselves to a better life—not as blind, handicapped people but as dynamic human beings. The author's treatise is that the blind person should be placed in a training situation or in an employment opportunity leading to full social and economic adjustment. Concerned only with blind people as seen in a counseling relationship.

Rusalem, Herbert. *Coping with the Unseen Environment: An Introduction to the Vocational Rehabilitation of Blind Persons*. New York: Teachers College Press, 1972. An introduction to the vocational development and rehabilitation of blind persons, intended for the general rehabilitation worker with minimal preparation and experience in this specialized field who needs a better understanding of blind persons and their problems.

Rusalem, Herbert, and Malikin, David, eds. *Contemporary Vocational Rehabilitation*. New York: New York University Press, 1976. Addresses controversial topics and ideas currently surrounding the field of vocational rehabilitation. Contributing authors examine the changing role of federal-state government agencies, the emergence of career development theory, the rise of the consumer, new approaches to vocational evaluation, counseling the mentally retarded, assessment training, placement, and changing client population.

Safilios-Rothschild, C. *The Sociology and Social Psychology of Disability and Rehabilitation*. New York: Random House, 1970.

Sanders, Richard M. *Behavior Modification in the Rehabilitation Facility*. Carbondale: Southern Illinois University Press, 1975. Case studies illustrating how behavior modification was used to enable clients to be more readily employable.

Schein, Jerome D., and Delk, Marcus T., Jr. *The Deaf Population of the United States*. Silver Spring, Md.: National Association of the Deaf, 1974. A national study (the first in 40 years) of characteristics of deaf people. A valuable reference work covering size of deaf population, civil status, family composition, occupations, and economic status. Many appendixes list organizations, construct of research, questionnaires used, etc.

Stubbins, Joseph, ed. *Social and Psychological Aspects of Disability: A Handbook for Practitioners*. Baltimore: University Park Press, 1977. A valuable book on the sociological and psychological aspects of disability. Deals with such diverse topics as body image and sexuality, as well as architectural barriers and civil rights.

Vash, Carolyn. *Sheltered Industrial Employment.* Emerging Issues in Rehabilitation Series. Washington, D.C.: Institute for Research Utilization, 1977. An extremely valuable work concerning the future of sheltered employment.

Wright, George N., ed. *Epilepsy Rehabilitation.* Boston: Little, Brown, 1975. In collaboration with the Epilepsy Foundation of America and the University of Wisconsin, Madison Regional Rehabilitation Research Institute. Nature of epilepsy, psychosocial aspects, rehabilitation counseling, job placement services, case studies.

INDEPENDENT LIVING

Battelle Columbus Laboratories for Office of Policy Development and Research, Department of Housing and Urban Development. *Study and Evaluation of Integrating the Handicapped in HUD Housing.* Stock no. 023-00419-4. For sale by the Superintendent of Documents. May 1977. Documentation for the increased cost of construction necessary to make rental housing accessible to handicapped persons with differing degrees of disabilities. Useful references.

Bertelsen, Jean B., bibliographer. *Small Group Homes for the Handicapped and Disabled: An Annotated Bibliography.* Stock no. 023-000-00458-5. Department of Housing and Urban Development. For sale by Superintendent of Documents. June 1977. Residential needs, alternative living situations, case studies, handbooks, and manuals for establishing and operating small group homes, law, etc.

Cadell, Kay. *Natural Creations.* Lubbock Tex.: Textile Research Center, Texas Tech University. Patterns for adaptive clothing.

Clothing to Fit Your Needs. Ames: Iowa State University, n.d.

Copeland, Keith. *Aids for the Severely Handicapped.* New York: Grune and Stratton, 1974. Oriented toward British services, but a good account of environmental control units and special typewriter systems for the disabled that have been developed in England, such as the Possum systems available in this country. This work has been used as a reference by the communications engineering groups in this country. Worth purchase by rehabilitation engineering libraries. Contains some prints for electronic circuits.

Disabled Living Foundation. Publishes material on clothing, adapted equipment, and special devices.

Handee for You, Fashions for the Handicapped. Lowville, N.Y.: C. O. Smith, n.d.

Kaamenetz, Herman. *The Wheelchair Book.* Springfield, Ill.: Charles C. Thomas, 1969. Although this is not a recent book, there is nothing else like it. Describes wheelchairs and other indoor vehicles for the disabled, their parts, usage, including wheelchair transfers, wheelchair sports, clothing for wheelchair users.

Larson, Maren R., and Snobl, Daniel E. *Attendant Care Manual, Rehabilitation Services.* Marshall, Minn.: Southwest State University, 1978. An extremely detailed outlining of the duties of an attendant. Definitions of disabilities, discussion on sexuality of the disabled, activities of daily living, sources of information.

Leinenweber, Inc., 69 W. Washington, Chicago, Ill. Menswear fashions adapted for wheelchair use, n.d.

National Center for Law and the Handicapped, Inc. *Community Living for the Disabled: A Selective Annotated Bibliography.* Washington, D.C., n.d.

Olson, Sharon C., and Meredith, Diane K. *Wheelchair Interiors.* Chicago: National Easter Seal Society for Crippled Children and Adults, 1973.

Plfueger, Susan. *Independent Living.* Emerging Issues in Rehabilitation Series. Washington, D.C.: Institute for Research Utilization, 1977. Major findings in the field of independent living. A valuable, up-to-date summary of the state of the field, which is offering new options to the disabled in their living arrangements. Good bibliography.

Rehabilitation Equipment, Inc. 1556 Third Avenue, New York, N.Y.

Rehabilitation for Independent Living: A Selected Bibliography. Washington, D.C.: Center for the Family American Home Economics Association, Women's Committee, President's Committee on Employment of the Handicapped, 1978. Bibliography of materials in all areas of independent living, such as devices, clothing, travel, cooking, special materials for people with specific disabilities such as blindness, arthritis, diabetes, deafness, paraplegia, and hemiplegia. Items are numbered and addresses for sources given at the end.

Rehabilitation Products. American Hospital Supply Corporation. 2020 Ridge Avenue, Evanston, Illinois.

Resource Catalog for Independent Living. San Francisco: Disabled Student Service Center, San Francisco State University, 1977. A good catalogue of adaptive devices, offers addresses of suppliers, manufacturers, and distributors. Some bibliographic references to articles and books relating to independent living. Names and addresses of agencies and organizations interested in the disabled.

Richardson, Nina K. *Type with One Hand.* Cincinnati, Ohio: Southwest, 1959. A very useful teaching or self-teaching tool to enable a one-handed person to learn to type. Instructions are given for left-handed or right-handed typing.

Robinault, Isabel. *Functional Aids for the Multiply Handicapped.* New York: Harper & Row, 1973. Listing of prostheses and orthotics.

Sister Kenny Institute. *Wheelchair Selection: More than Choosing a Chair with Wheels,* rev. ed. Minneapolis, 1977. For the person who will live in a wheelchair, the chair becomes an extension of the body. This monograph describes different types of chairs for adults and children, types of chair cushions, listings of manufacturers, how to select chairs for agencies.

Sullivan, Richard, et al. *Telephone Services for the Handicapped.* Monograph no. 37. New York: Institute of Rehabilitation Medicine, New York University Medical Center, n.d. This manual is directed toward the disabled person seeking ideas for adapting his or her telephone.

Thompson, Marie McGuire. *Housing and Handicapped People.* Washington, D.C.: President's Committee on Employment of the Handicapped, 1976. Federal legislation, housing in other countries, options, recommendations.

————. *Housing for the Handicapped and Disabled: A Guide for Local Action.* Washington, D.C.: National Association of Housing and Redevelopment Officials, 1977. Action guide to serve as a resource for states and local communities wishing to provide noninstitutional housing arrangements for the disabled.

Walton, Kathy M., Schwab, Lois O., Cassat-Dunn, Mary Ann, and Wright, Virginia K. *Independent Living Techniques and Concepts: Level of Use vs. Importance to Independent Living as Perceived by Professionals in Rehabilitation.* Lincoln: Department of Human Development and the Family College of Home Economics. University of Nebraska, 1978. Independent living skills are important for optimum living for disabled people. This manual emphasizes the training of professional individuals to deal with the need for the development of independent living skills as part of the rehabilitation process.

Yost, Anna Cathryn, Schroeder, Stella L., and Rainey, Carolyn. *Home Economics Rehabilitation: A Selected, Annotated Bibliography.* Columbia: University of Missouri, 1977. For home economists in the field of rehabilitation and the disabled and their families. Limited primarily to the problems of adults. Some books of general information for background. Master's theses and doctoral dissertations seldom included anywhere else. Audiovisual materials, source directory.

BARRIER-FREE DESIGN

Access America: The Architectural Barriers Act and You. Pamphlet. Washington, D.C.: Architectural and Transportation Barriers Compliance Board, 1977. Instructions for filing complaints about guilty buildings.

Access to America 1976: A Compendium of Federal and State Legislation Pertaining to the Removal of Environmental Barriers Affecting Persons with Mobility Limitations. Ferndale, Mich.: Michigan Center for Barrier-Free Environment. An updated summary of statutes and codes pertaining to curb cuts, license plates, polling places, and the elimination of architectural and transportation barriers. Information listed alphabetically by state.

Architectural Barriers Removal Resource Guide. Publication no. (OHDS) 79022006. Washington, D.C.: Office for Handicapped Individuals and Architectural and Transportation Barriers Compliance Board, Department of HEW. Indications as to where funding can be obtained and which publications are available through various agencies of the federal government to assist those wishing to eliminate barriers.

Architectural and Transportation Barriers Compliance Board. *Resource Guide to Literature on Barrier-Free Environments: With Selected Annotations.* Washington, D.C., 1977. Annotated bibliography of available literature in the fields of architectural modifications for the disabled. Covers homes, public buildings, medical facilities and hospitals, rehabilitation centers, schools, colleges and universities, and work settings; also outdoor site development, recreational facilities, transportation, aids and devices, attitudes toward the disabled. Appendixes of related periodicals and organizations.

Asher, Janet, and Asher, Jules. *How to Accommodate Workers in Wheelchairs.* Washington, D.C.: President's Committee on Employment of the Handicapped, reprinted from *Job Safety and Health,* October 1976. Modifying the work space for the handicapped worker. Sources of further information having to do with bioengineering, job accommodation, and general architectural standards.

Barrier-Free Design: The Law. Vol. 1, 1976, *Federal Law, New York City, New York State;* Vol. 2, 1978, *Federal Law, New Jersey, Connecticut, Pennsylvania.* New York: Eastern Paralyzed Veterans of America. Legislative codes.

Coons, Maggie, and Milner, Margaret. *Creating an Accessible Campus.* Association of Physical Plant Administrators of Universities and Colleges, with a grant from Exxon Education Foundation, 1978. Program and building accessibility on college campuses. Special space considerations include a short section on the library. Instructional aids include special hardware for the blind.

Cotler, Stephen, and DeGraff, Alfred H. *Architectural Accessibility for the Disabled of College Campuses.* Albany, N.Y.: State University Construction Fund, 1976. Updated architectural criteria for providing realistic accessibility to the physically handicapped on campus. Sight and hearing disabilities included, plus all buildings and outdoor facilities on college campuses. Two pages on libraries and library resources.

Division of Rehabilitation, State of Washington, Seattle. *Job Ready.* Produced by the Easter Seal Society for Crippled Children and Adults of Washington, Access-Abilities Unit, March 1978. Basic architectural adaptations plus work site modifications. Washington State laws as well as related federal legislation.

Goldsmith, Selwyn. *Designing for the Disabled*, 3rd ed. New York: McGraw-Hill, 1977. A good overview. Precise details on architectural requirements in all types of buildings, public as well as private homes for physically disabled, including blind and deaf. Measurements in inches and feet as well as meters and centimeters.

Harkness, Sarah P., and Groom, James N., Jr. *Building without Barriers for the Disabled.* New York: Whitney Library of Design, 1976. Architectural needs of the blind, deaf, orthopedically impaired, site development (outdoors, transportation, interiors, metric conversion).

Mace, Ronald I. *Accessibility Modifications: Guidelines for Modifications to Existing Buildings for Accessibility to the Handicapped.* Raleigh, N.C.: Barrier Free Environments, Inc., 1976. Site modifications, plus cost analysis and related legislation.

New Jersey Department of the Treasury, Division of Building and Construction. *Barrier Free Design Regulations.* July 15, 1977, plus supplement, 1979. Regulations for architectural adaptations according to New Jersey State building codes.

Nugent, Timothy J. *The Problem of Access to Buildings for the Physically Handicapped.* Champaign-Urbana: Rehabilitation Education Center, University of Illinois, 1978. History of the movement toward removal of barriers, minimum standards, films, bibliography.

Paralyzed Veterans of America. *An Architectural Barrier Is. . . .* New York, n.d. Pamphlet about minimum standards, tax deduction incentives, community development grants, and other suggestions for methods to remove barriers.

―――. *Building Design Requirements for the Physically Handicapped.* New York, n.d. Set of drawings with minimum requirements for wheelchairs.

President's Committee on Employment of the Handicapped. *Guilty Buildings.* Washington, D.C., n.d. Information in concise form―the laws, minimum standards, sources for further information.

Progressive Architecture. New York: Reinhold, April 1978. Entire issue devoted to barrier-free design and how architecture can respond to the needs of the disabled. Articles on designing for the blind, accessibility for the orthopedically disabled, a playground for children and others.

Redden, Martha Ross, Fortunato-Schwandt, Wayne, and Brown, Janet Welsh. *Barrier-Free Meetings: A Guide for Professional Associations.* AAAS Publication no. 76-7. Washington, D.C.: American Association for the Advancement of Science. Compiled by the project on the handicapped in science. A valuable idea that should spread to other professions. The committee is also active in counseling disabled students who wish to go into the profession.

Rehabilitation Institute of Chicago. *Open House: Preparing a Successful Home Environment for the Wheelchair User.* Chicago, n.d. Concise pamphlet with instructions on making homes accessible.

Rehabilitation International. *Barrier Free Design: Report of a United Nations Expert Group meeting.* New York, n.d. Accessibility requirements for special groups. Information as to efforts in other countries. An international bibliography. Information not available in other publications.

Salmon, F. Cuthbert. *The Preparation of Orientation and Mobility Maps for the Visually and Physically Handicapped.* Stillwater: School of Architecture, Oklahoma State University, 1977. Description of a method for the production of tactual maps for the use of the handicapped. Extremely useful idea for college campuses.

Tica, Phyllis L., and Shaw, Julius A. *Barrier-Free Design: Accessibility for the Handicapped.* Publication no. 74-3. New York: Institute for Research and Development in Occupational Education, Center for Advanced Study in Education, Graduate School and University Center, City University of New York, 1974, in cooperation with the New York State Education Department, University of the State of New York. Architectural specifications for the disabled as related to New York City buildings codes.

U.S. Department of Housing and Urban Development, Office of Policy Development and Research. *Barrier Free Site Design.* Publication no. 023-000-00291-4. For sale by the Superintendent of Documents. Legislation, measurements, and requirements for outdoor facilities such as curb cuts, ramps, etc. Pools, benches, bikeways. Bibliography.

Velleman, Ruth A. "Library Adaptations for the Handicapped," *School Library Journal*, October 1974. Description of a school library adapted to serve physically disabled students.

Veterans Administration, Department of Veterans Benefits. *Handbook for Design: Specially Adapted Housing.* Washington, D.C., 1978. All architectural measurements, plus safety considerations and metric measurements.

Wachter, Peter, Lorenc, John, and Lai, Edward. *Urban Wheelchair Use: A Human Factors Analysis.* Chicago: Access Chicago, Rehabilitation Institute of Chicago, 1976. Specifications for urban environment—curb cuts, ramps, washrooms, section on transportation, elevators, doors, bibliography.

TRAVEL

The Disabled and the Elderly: Equal Access to Public Transportation. Washington, D.C.: President's Committee on Employment of the Handicapped, 1975. Legal references.

Schuler, Janet, ed. *Access Travel Bulletin*. Washington, D.C.: Ability Tours, Inc. Announcing a travel service for the disabled called Ability Tours, Inc., established 1975, to expand travel opportunities for the handicapped, their families, and friends. Latest issue.

Transportation for the Handicapped, Selected References. Bibliographic List N. 8. Washington, D.C.: Department of Transportation, Office of Administrative Operations, Library Services Division, April 1975.

Veterans Administration. *Add-On Automobile Adaptive Equipment for Passenger Automobiles*. New York, n.d. Standards for automobile controls for disabled people. Listing of manufacturers.

RECREATION

American Alliance for Health, Physical Education, and Recreation. *Making Physical Education and Recreation Facilities Accessible to All: Planning, Designing, Adapting*. Washington, D.C., 1977. Adapting swimming pools, outdoor recreation areas, camps and trails, playgrounds. A section on transportation and travel. Appendixes include pertinent journals, suppliers of physical education and recreation equipment, organizations with information on architectural accessibility, audiovisual materials. Good source of other monographs in field.

American National Red Cross. *Adapted Aquatics: Swimming for Persons with Physical or Mental Impairments*. Garden City, N.Y.: Doubleday, 1977. A textbook for Red Cross instructor courses in adapted aquatics and a resource for all persons working with the handicapped in swimming programs.

Davies, John A. *Reins of Life*. Warrenville, Ill.: Winfield Farm, n.d. About teaching the disabled to ride horseback.

Guttman, Sir Ludwig. *Sports for the Adult Disabled*. Bucks, England: HM & M Publishers, 1976. Includes the physically disabled, blind, deaf, cerebral palsied. History of the development of wheelchair sports for paraplegics, quadriplegics, and amputees.

Kraus, Richard. *Therapeutic Recreation Service, Principles and Practices*, 2nd ed. Philadelphia: Saunders, 1978. Recreational programs for the ill and disabled. Both institutional and community settings. Behavior modification, sensory training, mainstreaming the disabled, and other new areas have been added to this edition.

McCowan, Lida. *It is Ability that Counts*. August, Mich.: Cheff Center for the Handicapped, n.d. Includes chapters on training horses and instructors and methods for teaching disabled individuals to ride, recommendations on special equipment, and recruiting volunteers.

Mainstreaming Handicapped Individuals: Parks and Recreation Design Standards Manual. Springfield, Ill.: Department of Conservation. A manual to assist in making parks usable by the handicapped. For additional copies, contact Silas P. Singh, Chief, Program Development, 405 East Washington Street, Springfield, Illinois.

Overs, Robert P., O'Connor, Elizabeth, and DeMardo, Barbara. *Avocational Activities for the Handicapped: A Handbook for Avocational Counseling*. American Lecture Series. Springfield, Ill.: Charles C. Thomas, 1974. Compendium of games, sports, and hobbies and evaluations of use by types of disabilities.

Savitz, Harriet M. *Wheelchair Champions: A History of Wheelchair Sports.* New York: Crowell, 1978. A history of the development of wheelchair sports by a member of the National Wheelchair Athletic Association.

Sherrill, Claudine. *Adapted Physical Education and Recreation: A Multi-Disciplinary Approach.* Dubuque, Iowa: William C. Brown, 1978. Heavily weighted toward therapeutic exercises rather than sports. Chapter on dance therapy, one on aquatics for the handicapped, separate chapters on the blind and the deaf, orthopedically impaired, neurologically impaired, physical characteristics, and appropriate physical activities.

Shivers, Jay S., and Fait, Hollis F. *Therapeutic and Adapted Recreational Services.* Philadelphia: Lea & Febiger, 1975. Oriented toward the adult disabled. Chapters on physical disabilities, mental and neurological problems, geriatric problems, camping, games and sports, performing and graphic arts.

Stein, Thomas A., and Sessons, H. Douglas. *Recreation and Special Populations,* 2nd ed. Boston: Allyn & Bacon, 1977. Collection of articles on recreation for the physically disabled, mentally ill, young adults and adult offenders, mentally retarded, alcoholic and drug addicted, sensory impaired, and economically deprived.

SEX AND THE DISABLED

Chigier, E., ed. *Israel Rehabilitation Annual.* Special issue: "Sex and the Disabled." Vol. XIV, July 1977, Tel Aviv, Israel. A collection of articles written by specialists from all over the world in the area of sexuality and the physically disabled.

Chipouras, Sophia, Cornelius, Debra, Daniels, Susan M., and Makas, Elaine. *Who Cares? A Handbook on Sex Education and Counseling Services for Disabled People.* Washington, D.C.: Sex and Disability Project, George Washington University, 1979. An excellent study offering information on counseling about sex for disabled people. Excellent references provided. Literature summaries, books, organizations, audiovisual/tactile resources, bibliographies.

Division of Continuing Education, University of Alabama. *Human Sexuality: The Handicapped, the Aging (A Resource Guide to Printed Materials).* January 1978. An up-to-date bibliography.

Enby, Gunnel. *Let There Be Love: Sex and the Handicapped.* New York: Taplinger, 1975.

Heslinga, K. *Not Made of Stone: The Sexual Problems of Handicapped People.* Springfield, Ill.: Charles C. Thomas, 1974. This is not just another book on sexual techniques or the joys of physical relationships. It contains much scientific and detailed information relating to the physiology of the human reproductive system and impairments that may affect it, as well as chapters on genetics, sexual education, adult sexuality, and marriage and family planning.

Johnson, Warren R. *Sex Education and Counselling of Special Groups: The Mentally and Physically Handicapped, Ill and Elderly.* Springfield, Ill.: Charles C. Thomas, 1975. The need for information in this heretofore neglected area is recognized. Guidelines for sex education and counseling are offered; deals with specific sex-related behaviors.

Veterans Administration Hospital. *Sex and the Handicapped.* Cleveland, Ohio: Veterans Administration, 1974.

PERIODICALS

This list of English-language periodicals is not intended to be exhaustive, but it does include those that are generally considered relatively important and useful. Periodicals circulating locally or within a state, except in a few instances, have been omitted. Starred (*) entries indicate publications by disabled people.

American Annals of the Deaf. Conference of Executives of American Schools for the Deaf, 5034 Wisconsin Avenue N.W., Washington, D.C. Bimonthly.

American Archives of Rehabilitation Therapy. American Association for Rehabilitation Therapy, P.O. Box 6412, Gulfport, Mississippi. Quarterly.

American Corrective Therapy Journal (formerly *Journal of the Association of Physical and Mental Rehabilitation*). American Corrective Therapy Association, 4015 Broadway, no. 21, Houston, Texas. Bimonthly.

American Journal of Occupational Therapy. American Occupational Therapy Association, 6000 Executive Blvd., Suite 200, Rockville, Maryland. 8 issues a year.

American Journal of Physical Medicine. Williams & Wilkins Company, 428 East Preston Street, Baltimore, Maryland. Bimonthly.

American Rehabilitation. Rehabilitation Services Administration, Superintendent of Documents, Washington, D.C. Bimonthly.

Amicus. National Center for Law and the Handicapped, 1235 North Eddy Street, South Bend, Indiana. Bimonthly.

Archives of Physical Medicine and Rehabilitation. American Congress of Rehabilitation Medicine, 30 North Michigan Avenue, Chicago, Illinois. Monthly.

ASHA. American Speech and Hearing Association, 9030 Old Georgetown Road, Washington, D.C. Monthly.

Braille Book Review. National Library Services for the Blind and Physically Handicapped, Library of Congress, Washington, D.C. Bimonthly.

British Journal of Disorders of Communication. Longman Group, 43–45 Annandale Street, Edinburgh EH7 4AT, Scotland. Semiannual.

Bulletin of Prosthetics Research. U.S. Veterans Administration, Prosthetics and Sensory Aids Service, Washington, D.C. Irregular.

Calipe. Canadian Paraplegic Association, 153 Lyndhurst Avenue, Toronto, Ontario M5R 3A2, Canada. Quarterly.

Canadian Journal of Occupational Therapy. Canadian Association of Occupational Therapists, 4 New Street, Suite M19, Toronto, Ontario M5R 1P6, Canada. Quarterly.

Cleft Palate Journal. American Cleft Palate Association, 311 East Chicago Avenue, Chicago, Illinois. Quarterly.

*COPH Bulletin. National Congress of Organizations of the Physically Handicapped, 7611 Oakland Avenue, Minneapolis, Minnesota. Quarterly.

DAV Magazine. Disabled American Veterans, P.O. Box 14301, Cincinnati, Ohio. Quarterly.

DSH Abstracts. Deafness, Speech and Hearing Publications, American Speech and Hearing Association, 9030 Old Georgetown Road, Washington, D.C. Quarterly.

Excerpta Medica, Section XIX: Rehabilitation and Physical Medicine. Excerpta Medica Foundation, 228 Alexander Street, Princeton, New Jersey. Monthly.

Family Health. American Medical Association, 535 North Dearborn Street, Chicago, Illinois. Monthly.

Geriatrics. Lancet Publications, Inc., 4015 West 65th Street, Minneapolis, Minnesota. Monthly.

Health Services Reports. Department of Health, Education, and Welfare, Health Services and Mental Health Administration, 5600 Fishers Lane, Rockville, Maryland. Monthly.

Hospital Literature Index. American Hospital Association, 840 North Lake Shore Drive, Chicago, Illinois. Quarterly.

Human Communication. Glenrose Hospital, 10230 111 Avenue, Edmonton, Alberta, Canada. 3 issues a year.

International Rehabilitation Review. International Society for Rehabilitation of the Disabled, 210 East 44 Street, New York, New York. Quarterly.

Journal of the American Medical Association. AMA, 535 North Dearborn Street, Chicago, Illinois. Weekly.

Journal of Applied Rehabilitation Counseling. National Rehabilitation Counseling Association, 1533 K Street N.W., Washington, D.C. Quarterly.

Journal of Bone and Joint Surgery (American edition). American Orthopaedic Association, 10 Shattuck Street, Boston, Massachusetts. 8 issues a year.

Journal of Chronic Disease. Pergamon Press, Fairview Park, Elmsford, New York. Monthly.

Journal of Dentistry for the Handicapped. Academy of Dentistry for the Handicapped, 1240 East Main Street, Springfield, Ohio. Semiannual.

Journal of Gerontology. Gerontological Society, 1 Dupont Circle, Washington, D.C. Quarterly.

Journal of Health and Social Behavior. American Sociological Association, 1722 N Street N.W., Washington, D.C. Quarterly.

Journal of Occupational Medicine. Industrial Medical Association, 150 North Wacker Drive, Chicago, Illinois. Monthly.

Journal of Rehabilitation. National Rehabilitation Association, 1522 K Street N.W., Washington, D.C. Bimonthly.

Journal of Rehabilitation of the Deaf. Professional Rehabilitation Workers with the Adult Deaf, 814 Thayer Avenue, Silver Spring, Maryland. Quarterly.

Mainstream. Magazine of the Able-Disabled. Able-Disabled Advocacy, Inc., 861 Sixth Avenue, Suite 610, San Diego, California. Monthly.

Medical World News. McGraw-Hill, 1221 Avenue of the Americas, New York, New York. Weekly.

Orthotics and Prosthetics. American Orthotic and Prosthetic Association, 1440 North Street N.W., Washington, D.C.

*Ostomy Quarterly. United Ostomy Association, 1111 Wilshire Boulevard, Los Angeles, California. Quarterly.

Paraplegia. International Medical Society of Paraplegia, 43–45 Annandale Street, Edinburgh EH7 4AT, Scotland. Quarterly.

Paraplegia Life. National Spinal Cord Injury Foundation, 369 Elliot Street, Chicago, Illinois. Quarterly.

Parks and Recreation. National Recreation and Park Association, 1601 North Kent Street, Arlington, Virginia. Monthly.

Perspectives in Long Term Care. American Medical Association Council on Medical Service, 535 North Dearborn Street, Chicago, Illinois. Quarterly.

Physical Therapy. American Physical Therapy Association, 1156 15 Street N.W., Washington, D.C. Monthly.

Physiotherapy. Chartered Society of Physiotherapy, 14 Bedford Row, London WC1R 4 ED, England. Monthly.

Physiotherapy/Canada. Canadian Physiotherapy Association, 469 Stanstead Crescent, Montreal 305, Quebec, Canada. 5 issues a year.

Psychological Abstracts. American Psychological Association, 1200 17 Street N.W., Washington, D.C. Monthly.

Rehabilitation. British Council for Rehabilitation of the Disabled, Tavistock Square, London WC1H 9LB, England. Quarterly.

Rehabilitation Counseling Bulletin. American Rehabilitation Counseling Association, 1607 New Hampshire Avenue N.W., Washington, D.C. Quarterly.

Rehabilitation Digest. Canadian Rehabilitation Council for the Disabled, 242 St. George Street, Toronto, Canada.

Rehabilitation in Australia. Australian Council for Rehabilitation of Disabled, Bedford and Buckingham Streets, Syndey N.S.W., Australia. Quarterly.

Rehabilitation in Canada. Department of Manpower and Immigration of Canada, 305 Rideau Street, Ottawa, Ontario K1A, 0J9 Canada. 3 issues a year.

Rehabilitation in South Africa. South Africa Department of Labor, Private Bag X117, Pretoria, South Africa. Quarterly.

Rehabilitation Literature. National Easter Seal Society for Crippled Children and Adults, 2023 West Ogden Avenue, Chicago, Illinois. Monthly.

Rehabilitation Psychology. American Psychological Association, P.O. Box 26034, Tempe, Arizona. Quarterly.

Rehabilitation Research and Practice Review. Arkansas Rehabilitation Research and Training Center, Fayetteville, Arkansas. Quarterly.

Rehabilitation World, 112 East 23 Street, New York, New York. Quarterly.

Rheumatology and Rehabilitation (formerly *Rheumatology and Physical Medicine,* and incorporating *Annals of Physical Medicine*). British Association for Rheumatology and Rehabilitation (formerly British Association of Physical Medicine and Rheumatology), 7–8 Henrietta Street, London, WC2E 8QE, England. Quarterly.

S.A. Cerebral Palsy Journal. National Council for the Care of Cripples in South Africa, National Cerebral Palsy Division, 15 Eton Road, Parktown, Johannesburg, South Africa. Quarterly.

Scandinavian Journal of Rehabilitation Medicine. Almquist and Wiksell Periodical Company, P.O. Box 62, S-101 20, Stockholm 1, Sweden. Quarterly.

Sexuality and Disability. Human Sciences Press, 72 Fifth Avenue, New York, New York. Quarterly.

Sight-Saving Review. National Society for the Prevention of Blindness, 79 Madison Avenue, New York, New York. Quarterly.

Talking Book Topics. National Library Service for the Blind and Physically Handicapped, Library of Congress, Washington, D.C. Bimonthly.

Therapeutic Recreational Journal. National Therapeutic Recreation Society, 1601 North Kent Street, Arlington, Virginia. Quarterly.

Vocational Evaluation and Work Adjustment Bulletin. Vocational Evaluation and Work Adjustment Association, 1122 Haley Center, Auburn University, Auburn, Alabama. Quarterly.

Vocational Guidance Quarterly. National Vocational Guidance Association, 1607 New Hampshire Avenue N.W., Washington, D.C. Quarterly.

NEWSLETTERS

ADA Forecast. American Diabetics Association, 18 East 48 Street, New York, New York. Bimonthly.

All-o-Grams. Affiliated Leadership League of and for the Blind of America, 1211 Connecticut Avenue N.W., Washington, D.C.

American Lung Association Bulletin (formerly *National Tuberculosis and Respiratory Diseases Association*), 1740 Broadway, New York, New York. 10 issues a year.

ARCA-NRCA News Report. Joint publication of American Rehabilitation Counseling Association and National Rehabilitation Counseling Association, 1522 K Street, Washington, D.C. Semiannual.

The Blue Sheet. Governor's Commission for the Handicapped, 6 Loudon Road, Concord, New Hampshire.

Cancer News. American Cancer Society, 219 East 42 Street, New York, New York Semiannual.

CARF Report. Newsletter of the Commission on Accreditation of Rehabilitation Facilities, 2500 North Pantano Road, Tucson, Arizona.

Communication Outlook. International Action Group for Communication Enhancement, Artificial Language Laboratory, Michigan State University, and TRACE Center for the Severely Communicatively Handicapped, University of Wisconsin. Dealing with newest developments in the field of application of technology to the needs of persons with communication handicaps due to neurological or neuromuscular conditions. Quarterly.

Crusader. United Cerebral Palsy Associations, 66 East 34 Street, New York, New York. Bimonthly.

Disability Law News. Newsletter of the Disability Law Center, SALA (Senior Adults Legal Assistance), 624 University Avenue, Palo Alto, California.

Easter Seal Communicator. National Easter Seal Society for Crippled Children and Adults, 2023 West Ogden Avenue, Chicago, Illinois. Bimonthly.

GIA News. Goodwill Industries of America, Inc., 9200 Wisconsin Avenue N.W., Washington, D.C. Newsletter of one of the largest and oldest rehabilitation industries.

Governor's Committee on Employment of the Handicapped. State of Washington. An excellent newsletter focusing on both state and national issues for the disabled. Staff also prepares excellent special reports available on request.

Handicapped Americans Reports. Plus Publications, Inc., 2626 Pennsylvania Avenue N.W., Washington, D.C. Biweekly. Subscription correspondence: Handicapped Americans Reports, P.O. Box 64014, Baltimore, Maryland. Valuable up-to-date legislative information covering all areas of concern to the disabled.

Hearing and Speech News. National Association of Hearing and Speech Agencies, 814 Thayer Avenue, Silver Spring, Maryland. Bimonthly.

IAL News. International Association of Laryngectomees, 219 East 42 Street, New York, New York. Bimonthly.

ICD News. ICD Rehabilitation and Research Center, 340 East 24 Street, New York, New York.

ICTA Inform. Rehabilitation International, Ibsengatan 14, Blackeberg, Stockholm. An international rehabilitation newsletter that reports on activities in all countries; very valuable information.

Impact. Newsletter of the University of Nebraska, Independent Living Project, Department of Human Development and the Family, Lincoln, Nebraska. Artificial speech aids, special clothing, and much more.

The Independent. Center for Independent Living, Inc., 2539 Telegraph Avenue, Berkeley, California. Quarterly (available on cassette).

IRUC Briefings. American Alliance for Health, Physical Education and Recreation, 1201 16 Street, Washington, D.C.

The Kurzweil Report. Technology for the Handicapped. Kruzweil Computer Products, 264 Third Street, Cambridge, Massachusetts.

Materials Development Center Newsletter. Stout Vocational Rehabilitation Institute, University of Wisconsin–Stout, Menomonie, Wisconsin. The center publishes materials in the area of work evaluation and adjustment to work for the physically disabled. These are announced in the newsletter.

Mobility Review. Mobility on Wheels, Inc., 1712 Glendon Avenue, Norfolk, Virginia. Newsletter of a nonprofit organization in Virginia. State and national legislation and other information.

Muscular Dystrophy News. Muscular Dystrophy Association of America, 1790 Broadway, New York, New York. 3 issues a year.

Nat-Cent News. Helen Keller National Center for Deaf-Blind Youths and Adults, 111 Middle Neck Road, Sands Point, New York.

The National Center for Law and the Deaf Newsletter. Seventh Street and Florida Avenue N.E., Washington, D.C. Newsletter about legislative matters affecting the deaf.

National CF News Bulletin. National Cystic Fibrosis Research Foundation, 3379 Peachtree Road N.E., Atlanta, Georgia. Irregular.

National Clearinghouse of Rehabilitation Training Materials. Oaklahoma State University, 115 Old S.D.A. Building, Stillwater, Oklahoma. Listing of materials published nationwide in the field of rehabilitation. Indicates where materials may be obtained and whether or not they are free of charge.

National Spokesman. Epilepsy Foundation of America, 1820 L Street N.W., Washington, D.C. Monthly.

Newsletter. Industrial Social Welfare Center, Columbia University School of Social Work, 622 West 113 Street, New York, New York. The center is funded in part as the Regional Rehabilitation Research Institute, Region II, and in part by the National Institutes of Health.

Newsletter for Industry. Affirmative Action for Handicapped People, 235 Bear Hill Road, Waltham, Massachusetts. Articles geared toward helping industry comply with affirmative action regulations of Sections 503 and 504 of the Rehabilitation Act of 1973. Articles cover definition of the disabled, written affirmative action plans, hiring handicapped job applicants, job accommodations, training supervisors to work with the disabled, etc. Valuable.

Ohio Libraries Reach Out to the Handicapped. Eunice Lovejoy, Library Development Consultant, Services to the Handicapped, State Library of Ohio, Columbus, Ohio. A good mix of local and national information on new materials and activities, which would be useful to public libraries reaching out to the handicapped.

Open Window. National Shut-In Society, Inc., 225 West 99 Street, New York, New York. Monthly.

The Pathfinder. Your guide to Information Resources and Technology in Rehabilitation. National Rehabilitation Information Center (NARIC), Washington, D.C. 6 times a year.

Professional Report. National Rehabilitation Counseling Association, 1522 K Street N.W., Washington, D.C.

Rehab Briefs. Rehabilitation Research Institute, College of Health Related Professions, University of Florida, Gainesville, Florida. Special topic briefs, independent living, sexual problems, sheltered workshops, and much more. Free mailing list.

Remarques. Ohio Governor's Committee on Employment of the Handicapped, 4656 Heaton Road, Columbus, Ohio. State and national information for the disabled.

RP Foundation Newsletter. National Retinitis Pigmentosa Foundation, Inc., Rolling Park Building, 8331 Mindale Circle, Baltimore, Maryland.

Washington Report. American Foundation for the Blind, Inc., 15 West 16 Street, New York, New York. Bimonthly. Inkprint and braille. Reports congressional activity on legislation affecting blind persons and those who work with the blind.

DIRECTORIES

American Annals of the Deaf. Directory issue (April or May of each year). Washington, D.C.: Conference of Executives of American School for the Deaf.

American Board for Certification in Orthotics and Prosthetics. *Registry of Certified Facilities and Individuals in Orthotics and Prosthetics.* Annual. Washington, D.C.: American Orthotic and Prosthetic Association. A state-by-state listing of prosthetic and orthopedic appliance facilities. The list of persons is alphabetical by last name, showing type of certification and residence address.

American Medical Association. *Directory of National Voluntary Health Organizations and Survey of State Medical Association Committees Concerned with Rehabilitation.* Chicago, Illinois.

American Personnel and Guidance Association. *Directory of Approved Counseling Agencies.* Washington, D.C.: American Personnel and Guidance Association.

Association of Medical Rehabilitation Directors and Coordinators. *Annual Directory.* Association of Medical Rehabilitation Directors and Coordinators. Houston, Texas.

Eckstein, Burton J., ed. *The Handicapped Funding Directory.* Oceanside, New York: Research Grant Guides, 1978–79. Brings together in one book information about funding sources: associations, foundations, and federal agencies interested in funding programs for disabled people.

Hermann, Anne Marie C., and Walker, Lucinda. *Handbook of Employment Rights of the Handicapped: Sections 503 and 504 of the Rehabilitation Act of 1973.* Washington, D.C.: Regional Rehabilitation Research Institute on Legal and Leisure Barriers, George Washington University, 1978. A complete legal guide about disabled employee rights under the law. Appendix lists regional offices of federal contract compliance programs.

Materials Development Center. *Suggested Publications for Developing an Agency Library on Work Evaluation and Work Adjustment,* 6th ed. Menomonie, Wis.: Stout Vocational Rehabilitation Institute, University of Wisconsin-Stout, 1978.

National Congress of Organizations of the Physically Handicapped. *Roster of Organization of the Physically Handicapped and Their Chapters,* 2nd ed. Minneapolis: National Congress of Organizations of the Physically Handicapped, 1970. Also available is the mimeographed COPH Roster of Publications, 1969 edition, listing periodicals for and by physically handicapped people.

National Easter Seal Society for Crippled Children and Adults. *Directory.* Chicago. Annual.

National Foundation. *International Directory of Genetic Services.* White Plains, N.Y., n.d.

Office of Handicapped Individuals. *Federal Assistance for Programs Serving the Handicapped.* Washington, D.C., 1978. Program descriptions and sponsoring agencies, listing of publications on grantsmanship and addresses of state special education programs, state vocational rehabilitation programs, and programs serving the blind and visually impaired.

People-to-People Program. Committee for the Handicapped. *Directory of Organizations Interested in the Handicapped.* Washington, D.C., 1976. An expansion and revision of the first edition, published in 1960. Contains agencies as well as information on the utilization of volunteer workers and international programs. Intended mainly for distribution abroad to promote the exchange of information on techniques and procedures for rehabilitation and employment of the handicapped.

President's Committee on Employment of the Handicapped. *Membership Directory*. Washington, D.C., 1977. Alphabetical listing of executive committee members, associate members, advisory council, members of the President's Committee (organizations and individuals), governor's committees members.

Rehabilitation International. *Compendium on the Activities of World Organizations Interested in the Handicapped*. New York, n.d. Biennial. Published for the Council of World Organizations Interested in the Handicapped.

Rehabilitation Services Administration. *Ready Reference Guide: Resources for Disabled People: A Handbook for Service Practitioners and Disabled People*. Washington, D.C.: Office of Human Development, 1977. Valuable listing of organizations, both government and voluntary, that offer services to the disabled. All types of services covered.

Wasserman, Paul, and Bossart, Jane K. *Health Organizations of the United States, Canada, and Internationally: A Directory of Voluntary Associations, Professional Societies and Other Groups Concerned with the Health and Related Fields*, 4th ed. Ann Arbor, Mich.: Edwards Brothers, 1977. Gives information on location, officials, purpose and objectives, and programs and activities of more than 1,400 organizations, societies, foundations, associations, and other nongovernmental bodies. Includes classified listing of the national, regional, and international organizations, which is arranged under the subject matter that relates to their activities and functions.

SOURCES FOR AUDIOVISUAL MATERIALS

American Foundation for the Blind, New York, New York, films about blindness. AV Publications Office, Sister Kenny Institute, 1800 Chicago Avenue, Minneapolis, Minnesota.

American Hospital Association and Hospital Research and Educational Trust, Resource Catalogue, publications and audiovisual products, current edition, 840 North Lake Shore Drive, Chicago, Illinois.

Audiovisual aids directory of the Rehabilitation Research and Training Centers, audiotape, film slides, videotape, rev. ed., June 1975, Rehabilitation Services Administration, Office of Human Development, Department of HEQ, Washington, D.C.

Library of Congress, Film Reference Guide for Medicine and Allied Services (annual). Catalogue of Motion Pictures and Film strips, U.S. Government Printing Office, Washington, D.C.

National Audiovisual Center, a catalogue of U.S. government-produced audiovisual materials, General Services Administration, Washington, D.C.

National Medical Audiovisual Center, motion picture and videotape catalogue, National Library of Medicine, Department of HEW, National Medical Audiovisual Center, Atlanta, Georgia.

President's Committee on Employment of the Handicapped, Washington, D.C., rehabilitation movies, listing on request.

Region Two Regional Continuing Education Program Media Library, 480 Christopher Baldy Hall, SUNY at Buffalo, New York.

Rehabilitation International USA, Rehabilitation Film Library Catalogue and International Rehabilitation Film Review Catalogue, 20 West 40 Street, New York, New York.

Rehabilitation Research and Training Center no. 9, rehabilitation training materials study (lists AV catalogues, etc.), George Washington University, Washington, D.C.

Veterans Administration, Central Office Film Library, 810 Vermont Street N.W., Washington, D.C.

PART IV

School and University Libraries

12

History of
Special Education

The field of school librarianship offers a unique challenge in today's educational picture. As the emphasis shifts toward more instructional materials to enrich the teaching program, the expanded school library media center becomes indispensable to the complete academic development of the student. With this change in curriculum methods has come the realization that the child who, for physical reasons, has been educated on a home instructional program or in a special class without access to such a center has been deprived of a vital part of his or her educational experience.

The school library media specialist has a triple role in service to the physically disabled student. The traditional functions of reading guidance, teaching library skills, and creative media work with students are supplemented by important information services to teachers to aid them in understanding student disabilities and acquaint them with sources for any special curriculum materials needed for classroom work. The third role, and a significant one, is that of information specialist for the parents of disabled students, to help them locate the information they need to cope with daily living requirements, educational expectations, and the vocational future of their children.

The next two chapters deal with school library media service to physically disabled children and young adults and those with special health problems. To convey an understandable picture, a brief history of the development of educational opportunities for physically disabled children and a description of the field of special education will be followed by the pattern of legislation by the federal government traced up to and including PL 94-142. Signed by President Gerald Ford in 1975, this law has had a significant and far-reaching effect on the future education of all disabled children. Library media services in special education has been a parallel development and will be documented here.

BACKGROUND

Thomas Jefferson proposed a bill for a widespread system of education as early as 1776. Many years passed before his vision was realized, and the United States developed a system of free public education. It was not until the twentieth century, however, that this educational opportunity was extended in some measure to handicapped children and youth, and only in the 1970s has the principle of a full and equal education for exceptional children begun to be implemented nationwide.

Unlike the rehabilitation movement, which began with the rehabilitation of the orthopedically disabled, the earliest efforts to educate disabled children involved those who were deaf and blind. By the mid-1800s, the training school concept had taken hold in France, patterned after Edward Seguin's residential or training school model. In America the first residential school for the deaf was organized in Connecticut in 1817 by Thomas Hopkins Gallaudet. It was known as the American Asylum for the Education and Instruction of the Deaf and Dumb.[1] The name is a measure of how far we have come in our attitudes toward different individuals. The school at Hartford exists today as the American School for the Deaf. In 1829 the first training school for the blind, the New England Asylum for the Blind, was established by Samuel Gridley Howe. This became the Perkins School, which remains an outstanding facility in the education of blind and deaf/blind children.

By the end of the Civil War, 20 state schools had been established under the Department of Health and Social Welfare, rather than the Department of Education. With this influence, they were structured as residential programs. Many of these residential schools are often still the only programs serving exceptional children.

By acts of Congress, Gallaudet College for the Deaf, established in Washington, D.C. (1864), and the American Printing House for the Blind, in Lexington, Kentucky (1879), were named national centers. These two were the only such centers administered by Congress until 1965.

Orthopedically handicapped children began to receive medical attention long before any provision was made to educate them. In the medical field, children with obvious physical defects received earlier attention than children with other handicaps. In the area of education, this trend did not carry over. Schooling for the physically handicapped child who could not attend regular classes lagged behind special schooling for other handicapped groups.

The concept of education for physically handicapped children was introduced in 1863 by James Knight when he established the Hospital for the Ruptured and Crippled in New York City, insisting that the children there receive academic and religious education. Gradually, social scientists became aware of the economic and social advantages in educating these children rather than providing a lifetime of care in custodial institutions.

Between 1897 and 1922, many crippled children's hospitals and convalescent homes were established that incorporated Knight's ideas. One of the most famous is the Massachusetts Hospital School at Canton, established in 1904 by Edward H. Bradford. This was the first training school for handicapped children in the United States, and today it has a fine long-term rehabilitation program for severely handicapped youngsters. The first state crippled children's hospital facility was in St. Paul, Minnesota, established in 1897 by Arthur J. Gillette.

In 1910 the Widener School and Hospital for Crippled Children was opened in Philadelphia by DeForest Willard, himself a polio-paralytic. The Widener School is today Philadelphia's school for disabled children. The Peabody Home for Crippled Children in Boston was founded during this early period by Bradford, and in 1915 Michael Hoke opened the Scottish Rites Hospital in Atlanta, the forerunner of the chain of crippled children's institutions operated by the Shriners, an organization that has been particularly active in this field.

By 1951 there were 82 hospitals and 91 convalescent homes for crippled children in this country. Five times as many of these institutions were built by private organizations as by government agencies.[2] Although these hospitals and homes professed to combine vocational training and academic education with medical care, the emphasis was, of necessity, placed upon physical rehabilitation. Vocational training in sheltered situations tended to be emphasized at the expense of good academic education. Today, even in the most outstanding physical rehabilitation centers in this country, there continues to be some disparity between medical care and school curriculum.

By 1899, 100 large cities had special education classes of some kind. Among the pioneering localities were Boston, Chicago, New York, Cleveland, Providence, Detroit, and Milwaukee.[3] The first public school class for orthopedically handicapped children was opened in Chicago in 1899.[4] It eventually became the Spaulding High School, which is still in existence and is one of the few academic programs on the high school level for orthopedically disabled students. Chicago has led in the field of education of the handicapped, with four special schools, including Spaulding, and fine special facilities for disabled students at the University of Illinois. These facilities have been duplicated in a growing number of universities since the late 1960s.

By 1911 many large city school systems had established special schools and special classes for handicapped children, and a number of states began to subsidize special programs by paying the excess costs of maintaining special classes. In 1919 the National Easter Seal Society for Crippled Children and Adults was founded (see Chapter 10), focusing attention initially on orthopedically disabled children and gradually including children with all types of handicaps. Volunteer groups have always been a part of American history, and following World War II, groups organized by parents, with a membership primarily although not restricted to parents, came into being. Before that, parents had tended to hide the existence of handicapped children and neglected to educate them. Now the personal involvement of the parents resulted in a special type of dedication not found in many other volunteer groups.[5]

The existence of some local parent groups can be traced back before the 1930s—the National Society for Crippled Children and Adults began with parent involvement. The major thrust of the movement, however, came in the 1940s and 1950s with the organization of such groups as the National Association for Retarded Children and the United Cerebral Palsy Association.[6] Local groups developed informally as gatherings of people sharing a common problem. They came together to help their children and to help themselves by providing each other with psychological support. Public education was not accepting its responsibility toward many groups of these children. There were too few institutions with all types of handicapped individuals placed together and not enough medical research.

Parent groups began to sponsor and encourage a wide diversity of activities, including education (originally through private schools and finally through the public school systems) and the establishment of teacher training programs. Other types of projects included sheltered workshops, vocational training centers, diagnostic facilities, parent education, preschool and postschool facilities, research, therapy, and medical services.[7]

Parent groups organized according to specific types of handicaps, some of them established in the 1970s (osteogenesis imperfecta and arthrogryposis). Most of these groups have published excellent pamphlets for the information of the general public. (See Chapter 2 for addresses of parent organizations and listings of materials.)

Originally, conflicts between parents and professionals prevented cooperation because parents lacked confidence in the professionals. However, the skills of professional fund raisers, teachers, and others were needed by the parents, and so the original conflicts were ultimately overcome. Parents have retained control of the organizations for the most part, with the professionals acting as consultants. Attitudes are much more positive today, with parent groups sponsoring scholarships to train professionals and fund professional research projects.

Parent groups operate on federal, state, and local levels without conflict. As voters and taxpayers, they have used their pressure group powers to effect changes within the system. Parent groups were instrumental in the establishment of presidential advisory committees such as the President's Committee on Mental Retardation and the President's Committee on Employment of the Handicapped. They have been actively involved in the legislation that reflects new concerns for the rights of the handicapped.

Several issues must be discussed in years to come. One is the coordination of groups versus working alone. Cooperation between parent groups and public and private agencies concerned with education, social work, rehabilitation, and employment of the disabled is imperative to avoid fragmentation of services.

In the 1920s the United States established a division of special education in the Federal Bureau of Education, with Elise Martens as its first director.[8] With great persistence, Martens encouraged the states to enact legislation to aid disabled children. The states in varying degrees, had displayed some concern for the education of the handicapped since the early days of the nation's history. During the decade 1910–1920, the first states had enacted statutes making education of the handicapped a requirement, the pioneers being New Jersey (1911), New York (1917), and Massachusetts (1920).[9] In practice, however, admission to the public schools was allowed only if it did not inconvenience the majority or overburden the taxpayer.

Under the influence of Franklin D. Roosevelt, the Social Security laws of 1935 included $3 million to aid the states in developing programs for physically handicapped children. A special division was established in the Children's Bureau in the Department of Labor and later transferred to the Department of Health, Education, and Welfare.

In 1943 the Barden-LaFollette bill extended vocational rehabilitation to adults of work age. In many states this service was made available to children two years prior to the legal work age, with vocational rehabilitation counselors making contact with the students through the schools.

In 1958, although gains had been made in the education of disabled children, fewer gains were made for the orthopedically handicapped and those with special health problems than for any other group. Only one-fourth of the disabled children in the country between the ages of 5 and 17 were receiving an appropriate education. The rest were receiving either minimal home instruction or none at all or were institutionalized. Moreover, the overwhelming number of those children enrolled in special programs—83 percent—were being served on the elementary level. Very few opportunities existed for disabled high school students to receive an appropriate education.[10]

With the growth of special education in this century has come a variety of alternative facilities. The first answer to the challenge came with the residential school, which still offers the solution to complete 24-hour care for disabled children. Educational programs in these facilities are in many instances still minimal. However, residential schools for the deaf and the blind, often state-run, do offer effective educational programs. Current trends in residential care are toward smaller facilities, with the children located closer to home to encourage weekend and vacation visits with the family, and even eventual placement in the public school.[11]

Day school instruction has become increasingly popular since the 1950s. There are private schools in some states, run with state support, schools run by parent groups or organizations such as Easter Seal and United Cerebral Palsy, some run by the states, and some administered by public school systems.[12] Day school institutions take many forms, as listed below.

1. Special education classes housed in regular schools.
2. Special schools for handicapped children or for special categories of handicaps.
3. Cooperative services available on a regional basis where children are transported to the school for all or part of the day.
4. Resource rooms in schools where children go for special instruction geared to their handicaps.
5. Itinerant teachers who go from school to school to teach and tutor children and serve as consultants to classroom teachers, often bringing special materials. Itinerant services often include teachers of the blind and deaf and such special personnel as speech therapists.
6. Mobile facilities whereby vans with special equipment and special education teachers visit schools to provide diagnosis, consultation, in-service training, new materials and equipment, and actual teaching of some children.
7. Homebound instruction. Until the latest legislation, severely orthopedically disabled children have been on home instructional programs. These "hidden youngsters" are served by a teacher for the homebound, who visits the home a few hours per week, a method also employed with those students temporarily incapacitated. The difference is that the able-bodied, temporarily ill student returns to the classroom after a few weeks or months, while the disabled child is on a permanent home instructional program, never to see a classroom, never to participate in a school pageant, never to socialize with other children, never to experience an art or a music class, and never to see a school library media center. Students never have the opportunity to participate in science laboratory experiments, and none has a physical education program.

TEACHER PREPARATION

As education began to develop as a profession, the preparation of teachers for the education of handicapped children started first as a series of special courses and summer sessions and finally with acceptance into the colleges and universities as departments of special education. The first professional programs were in residential settings. Gallaudet College began courses in teacher training in 1891. Samuel Gridley Howe included teacher training in his residential institutions for the blind.

Early college courses included a three-course sequence in mental retardation begun at the University of Pennsylvania in 1897; a course entitled "The Education of Defectives" at New York University, beginning in 1906; and one at Columbia University called "The Psychology and Education of Exceptional Children" in 1908. By the end of the 1940s, 175 institutions were offering special education preparation, 77 of them with an integrated curriculum or sequence of courses and 12 with special education departments or bureaus and serving at least three different areas of exceptionality.[13]

Sequences of courses were most often reported in the areas of mental retardation, speech, and hard of hearing. Most of the staff were part-time practitioners, working with exceptional children. Federal funding in this area during the 1960s established training grants for teachers, first for the deaf and then for all disability areas. In 1963 the establishment of the Division of Handicapped Children and Youth in the Office of Education sparked the development of training and research in special education. Research and development centers were established in major universities, focusing on early childhood education, learning characteristics of handicapped children, curriculum and materials development, and innovations in teacher education.[14]

Recent concerns about staff have centered upon questions of qualifications, the quality of teachers in the field, the uniqueness of each child, and the fact that teachers are not being educated to meet the educational needs of all disabled children. Teachers of exceptional children are expected to be competent to teach all children. Similarly, future preparation of all teachers will have to include knowledge about teaching exceptional children. A general broadening of the base of knowledge, a cross-culturization, is coming about whereby teachers are being prepared to teach in many new and innovative settings and to meet the needs of all kinds of children with all kinds of physical, mental, and learning disabilities.

Understandably, there is a new emphasis on the expansion of instructional materials centers, where library/media specialists with a knowledge of materials needed for the teaching of exceptional children will take a much more active role in the preparation and training of and assistance to teachers of exceptional children.

In-service courses for older special educators as well as regular classroom teachers are now being offered to ensure teacher accountability, lend continued support to teachers working in a changing environment, and upgrade children's learning. The library/media profession is mirroring this type of much needed activity with workshops in many areas of the country.

All of these movements, however, do not indicate the complete elimination of specialization in the teaching of specific disability groups, as there will always be some children in need of highly specialized help. The dilution of this special knowledge should be guarded against even as knowledge about all areas of disability is broadened to inclusion in all teacher preparation courses.

Until the present time, teacher preparation for work with orthopedically disabled children has remained inadequate. Most staff members in special education departments, as well as most texts, exhibit little or no information about many of the disabilities defined in Chapter 2. Knowledge about these children needs to be included in teacher preparation courses, and librarians serving education departments should provide some of these materials for this purpose.

Many disabled adults are beginning to take a more active role in society, and many of them have much to offer in terms of personal experience. As college students, guest lecturers, members of professional organizations, and conference participants, they are contributing in greater numbers than ever before. Their potential should not be ignored.

RESEARCH

Research influences exceptional children and their parents. Medical research has reduced the number of children in danger of blindness from retrolental fibroplasia. It has discovered methods for treating some disorders such as the birth defect phenylketonuria (PKU) and has provided a means for early identification of some congenital disorders, such as hemophilia and muscular dystrophy, by means of amniocentesis. Polio was virtually eliminated by the invention of the Salk vaccine, while the numbers of spina bifida children surviving birth increased with the advent of antibiotics and certain procedures followed in the early weeks of life. The nature of the special education population changes, therefore, based on medical advances.

In the field of psychology, the development of special testing methods, such as the Illinois Test of Psycholinguistic Ability (Kirk, McCarthy, and Kirk, 1968) has led to special instructional programs and techniques.[15]

Special education research is still in its infancy. Most of the advances have been made since the late 1950s. A major contribution comes from Samuel A. Kirk, under whose leadership the Institute for Research on Exceptional Children at the University of Illinois became a significant center.[16]

Public Law 83-531, the Cooperative Research Act of 1957, was the first law that earmarked federal funds for research relating to the education of handicapped children (entirely with mentally retarded children).[17] In 1963, PL 88-164 authorized research and demonstration projects related to the education of all categories of exceptional children, and this research support has continued to expand.

The Bureau of Education of the Handicapped is the agency primarily responsible for funding education research on the handicapped. The National Institute of Mental Health, the National Institute of Neurological

Diseases and Stroke, the National Institute of Child Health and Human Development, and the Rehabilitation Services Administration are other agencies that have also supported such research.

In addition, some professional and parent organizations devoted to single groups of disabled children have financed research. The Council for Exceptional Children has made a large contribution for publication of research monographs, articles in *Exceptional Children* magazine, and support of federal legislation.

There are now five research and development centers located at the universities of Indiana, Minnesota, and Oregon and Columbia and Yeshiva universities. The types of research activity at these centers include (1) the development and evaluation of a social learning curriculum for the mentally retarded, (2) facilitation of language and communication abilities of handicapped children under the age of nine, (3) the development of direct classroom intervention procedures for homogeneous groups of behavior-disordered children, (4) studies of the classroom application of basic learning research, and (5) modular and computer-assisted instruction for teachers of handicapped children.[18] There are also efforts to evaluate the efficacy of mainstreaming programs, as well as several projects in early education of handicapped children.

Future major research needs include learning how exceptional children process information so that teachers can program more effectively for these students. Educational outcomes extending into the adult life of the handicapped also need to be studied as part of a program of longitudinal research. Better testing methods must be devised that will more accurately test the intellectual capacities of disabled children.

Teachers and researchers need to understand each other. Teachers need training in the interpretation of research results. Researchers need training to be able to present the results of their research in understandable language.

The Council for Exceptional Children (CEC) (1920 Association Drive, Reston, Virginia 22091) is the professional organization to which most educators in the field of exceptional children belong. It was founded in 1922 and has 54 state federations and over 950 local chapters. Its principal purpose is the advancement of the education of exceptional children and youth. It cooperates with all organizations interested in the education of exceptional children and promotes standards for professional personnel. Its official journal, *Exceptional Children*, publishes articles on the latest educational research in this area. *Teaching Exceptional Children*, another journal published by CEC, offers practical ideas to the classroom teacher working with exceptional children. *Insight* is the CEC monthly newsletter, which contains information on state and federal legislation, programs, and services. Other publications include books, monographs, nonprint media, and other resources for professional growth and development.

The council has 12 divisions: Association for the Gifted, Council for

Administrators of Special Education, Council for Children with Behavioral Disorders, Council for Educational Diagnostic Services, Division for Children with Learning Disabilities, Division of Mental Retardation, Division of Early Childhood Education, Division of Children with Communication Disorders, Division on the Physically Handicapped, Homebound, and Hospitalized, Division for the Visually Handicapped, Partially Seeing, and Blind, Teacher Education Division, and Division on Career Development.

A major function of CEC is the sponsoring of an annual international convention and of regional topical conventions and conferences for educators and other professionals in the field.[19] Although CEC's user age group is the 0–21-year-olds, much of their information is also applicable to the adult disabled. For a description of CEC's information service operation, see page 265.

Many professional groups have indicated a desire and interest in forming subgroups to develop instructional materials for use with exceptional children. For example, in 1972 the Association for Special Education Technology was formed as a special interest group within the Association for Educational Communications and Technology. The aims of ASET are to stimulate improvement in instructional materials and the development of new materials and new technology within the field of special education, to identify and publish the unique instructional needs of disabled children, and to foster cooperation between special education and instructional technology groups.[20] A tremendous growth in the development of educational technology makes it imperative that items of particular use with exceptional children be identified and their potential use publicized. Information is disseminated through the monthly newsletter, the *ASET Report*.

In March 1978, vol. I no. I of the *Journal of Special Education and Technology* was issued by ASET. Its stated purpose is "to provide a vehicle for information, reports of research and of innovative practices regarding the application of education technology toward the development and education of exceptional children." Issued twice yearly as a beginning, the journal is now available with a membership in ASET or to nonmembers for a fee. A new vehicle for publicizing events in the relatively new field of educational technology as they relate to exceptional children, this journal will be a valuable addition to others in the field of special education.

LEGISLATION

Since the 1950s and accelerating since the late 1960s, a consumer movement, led by organizations of parents of handicapped children and more recently by the handicapped themselves, has forced action with regard to the education of exceptional children. Many state legislatures responded with laws making educational opportunity for the handicapped mandatory, breaking away from the custodial care philosophy that had characterized schooling for the handicapped to provide substantive learning experiences. Today almost all states have adopted mandatory education statutes for the handicapped.[21] An appropriate education for every disabled child is regarded as an inalienable right just as for every other citizen. These laws, in many instances, include additional provisions such as the training of special education personnnel and the acquisition of needed facilities and materials. In addition, 20 states now have laws that also mandate education for disabled children of preschool age.[22]

Since the mid-1960s, the federal government has significantly increased its support of education for handicapped children. In 1965 the Elementary and Secondary Education Act was passed. Title 1 of this act included coverage of the handicapped. Major amendments gave greater emphasis to special education. The first of these, PL 89-313, provided support for the education of handicapped children in state-operated schools and hospitals and, in a special provision in some states, in private, state-supported schools. The second, PL 89-750, added Title 6 to ESEA, which established the Bureau of Education of the Handicapped and the National Advisory Committee on the Handicapped.

In 1972 the Fleischmann Committee of New York, after a two-year study, published a forward-looking and prophetic report pinpointing special education needs and proposing means for identifying and diagnosing problems. Many of its recommendations have been incorporated into the "child-find" requirement of PL 94-142.[23]

The Education of the Handicapped Act, PL 91-230, passed in 1973 and amended by PL 93-380 in 1974, provides a comprehensive federally funded program of service to disabled children. Public Law 91-230, Sections A through G, provides for the strengthening of educational services to exceptional children (Part B), early education for disabled children and centers for deaf/blind children and their parents (Part C), the recruitment of educational personnel and the dissemination of information on educational opportunities for the disabled, and the preparation of teachers and support personnel such as physical education and recreation teachers (Part D), the promotion of research in curriculum areas (Part E), the provision of media services and captioned film loans (Part F), and provision for research in the establishment of model centers for children with specific learning disabilities (Part G). Part A of this law deals with general provisions and definitions.[24]

Public Law 93-380, the Educational Amendments of 1974, authorized greater aid to the states and supported the principle of placing disabled children in the least restrictive educational environment, commensurate with their needs. It also specified due process requirements, protecting the rights of disabled children and requiring the states to develop plans setting forth how and when each expects to achieve the desired goals.

In November 1975, PL 93-380 was broadened by the enactment of an even more significant measure, the Education for all Handicapped Children Act, known as PL 94-142.[25] The new bill calls for a massive expansion of the authorized levels of the basic state grants program. Public Law 94-142 is unique in that it makes a very specific commitment to the broadening of educational opportunity to exceptional children. Unlike other federal education laws, it has no expiration date. It sets forth as a national policy the proposition that education must be extended to handicapped persons as their fundamental right.

Public Law 94-142 has four major purposes:

1. To guarantee the availability of special education programming to handicapped children and youth who require it.
2. To ensure fairness and appropriateness in decision making about providing special education to handicapped children and youth.
3. To establish clear management and auditing requirements and procedures regarding special education at all levels of government.
4. To assist state and local governments through the use of federal funds.[26]

Public Law 94-142 revises only Part B of the Education of the Handicapped Act. The other components, Parts A and C–G, remain unchanged and continue in operation. Many of the requirements of PL 94-142 were stated in the Education Amendments of 1974. All programs under these acts are administered through the Bureau of Education of the Handicapped under the Office of Education.

Handicapped children are defined by the act as "mentally retarded, hard of hearing, deaf, orthopedically impaired, other health impaired, speech impaired, visually handicapped, seriously emotionally disturbed or children with specific learning disabilities who, by reason thereof, require special education and related services."[27] The two requirements for child eligibility are does the child have one or more of these disabilities, and does the child require special education and related services. Not all disabled children require such services. Many of them are able to attend regular school programs without program modification.

Under PL 94-142, an Individualized Educational Program, IEP, must be prepared for each disabled child in an educational district by the agency currently providing educational services for the child. A committee on the handicapped, made up of a teacher or administrator of special education, a psychologist, a physician, and a parent advocate, must approve the plan.

IEPs must include:

1. A statement of the child's present level of education performance.
2. A statement of annual goals, including short-term instructional objectives.

3. A statement of the specific educational services to be provided to such a child and the extent to which the child will be able to participate in the regular educational program.
4. The projected date for initiation and anticipated duration of such services.
5. Appropriate objective criteria and evaluation procedures and schedules for determining on at least an annual basis whether instructional objectives are being achieved.[28]

The IEP is a management device only, and the teacher cannot be held accountable should the child fail to achieve the anticipated academic growth. Methods are set up that give the child's parents the right of approval of the plan and the right to judicial review if they do not find it satisfactory. Availability of an education for every child in the district between the ages of 3 to 21 must, if federal funds are to be continued, be guaranteed by September 1980.

The provisions of PL 94-142 must be seen in conjunction with Section 504 of the Rehabilitation Act of 1973. Since Section 504 sets forth the civil rights of all handicapped Americans, it also applies to all handicapped children with respect to public education. The 1977 publication "PL 94-142 and Section 504—Understanding What They Are and Are Not" by Joseph Ballard (Government Relations Unit, CEC, 1920 Association Drive, Reston, Virginia 22091) offers an in-depth explanation of the requirements of these two related pieces of federal legislation. The final regulations for PL 94-142 were published in the August 23, 1977, issue of the *Federal Register*. HEW and the Office of Civil Rights (OCR) regulations for Section 504 of PL 93-112 are in the *Federal Register* of May 4, 1977, and August 14, 1978, respectively. Additional regulations from other departments are still being issued.

Public Law 94-142 has been called the "mainstreaming" law. Although it is true that many more disabled children than before will be placed in regular classrooms, the concept of appropriate placement in "the least restrictive environment" continues to be the intent of the law, and special classes will not disappear altogether. Mainstreaming is meant to serve especially in those areas where children have not been receiving an appropriate education or any education at all.

The mandate given to the states under this law was to locate all disabled children within their jurisdiction by 1979 and to provide suitable educational services by September 1980. Monies were provided for this purpose. Most states therefore instituted what is generally called a "child-find" program.

As a result of these activities, child-find coordinators have identified two age groups where the largest numbers of unserved children seem to exist— birth to 5 years old and 16 to 21 years old. This was to be expected. There has always been a lag in services to parents of disabled infants, who find very few places to turn for advice until the children reach school age. In recent years, some infant and preschool programs for disabled children in private agencies and hospitals have begun to fill this gap in services.

Since the majority of special programs for disabled children have been on the elementary level, the disabled teenager for the most part has had to fit into a regular high school program or revert to home instructional service. Disabled adults are entitled to a rehabilitation counselor to help them prepare for the future, but the age at which this service begins varies from state to state. Often the office of vocational rehabilitation begins contact with disabled high school students. However, between the ages of 14 and 16 and for all practical purposes between the ages of 16 and 21, an acute gap in service and advice still exists in many areas of the country. Contact with the office of vocational rehabilitation during these years is haphazard and spotty.

As a result of child-find activities, school districts are also beginning to realize the inadequacy of educational service to youngsters in extended care and private residential facilities.

The 1976 annual report of the National Advisory Committee on the Handicapped states that approximately one-half of the nation's eight million handicapped children of school age are still without an appropriate education. About one million are excluded from the public school system entirely. All of these youngsters are therefore still without school library media services.[29]

In May 1973 the Rand Corporation in Santa Monica, California, published the first of two studies for HEW, entitled *Services for Handicapped Youth: A Program Overview* by James S. Kakalik et al. (May 1973). The report was the product of 22 months of evaluation of federal and state programs to assist handicapped youth. While the first report is a comprehensive account of federal and state programs for service to mentally and physically handicapped youth, the second, published in 1974, is entirely devoted to future policies to improve delivery of services to children with hearing or visual handicaps.

The 1973 study grouped programs into areas according to five different types of agencies that administered them: health, welfare, education, vocational rehabilitation, and mental health and retardation. Since nothing of this scope has been undertaken since the Rand study, it must be considered useful in providing a benchmark when discussing statistics of services being provided to handicapped children by the early 1970s.

The Rand report estimated approximately nine million handicapped youths, ages 0 to 21, in the United States in 1970, the definition of handicapped being the same as the definition used for federal legislation. In the field of special education, although the Rand study supports the estimates of the National Advisory Committee report of 1976 in terms of numbers of handicapped children served, it is pointed out that this service is very uneven. Although it estimated that 59 percent is the average of children served, some of the estimates are as low as 36 percent. Extreme variation across the states resulted in a variation in the percentages of service, from less than 20 percent to more than 90 percent.[30]

The study states that expansion of service to children now unserved will require much more than dollars. Incentives need to be found to broaden the types of handicapped children served. As the population changes, there will be new needs for changes in teacher training and school curriculum. The study speaks prophetically about the need to identify the unserved, such identification programs now being put into effect with the child-find requirement of PL 94-142.

SPECIAL EDUCATION LIBRARIANSHIP

Against this brief background, let us now trace the development of library service to exceptional children. Reports about work in this area do not exist before the 1950s; however, the years since have seen some growth.

By 1957, a few areas of the country were reporting on the establishment of special school library services for handicapped children. Most of these services were in elementary schools where modified classes had been provided, but the groups first to be served for the most part were the deaf and the blind, not the orthopedically handicapped.[31]

During this time, in regular school programs new instructional materials in programmed format, nonprint materials such as realia, recordings, filmstrips, sound filmstrips, cassettes and tapes (video and audio), microforms, film loops and films, and the hardware to accommodate all of the new software made it necessary for school librarians to become school library/ media specialists and to enlarge their school libraries into library media centers or instructional materials centers.

Earliest efforts toward use of these new media in the education of disabled children was in the education of the deaf. Blind children, too, began to benefit from new types of recorded formats for their text materials.

Orthopedically and mentally handicapped children were the last to be served by the library media field. Until recently, children in special classes continued to be deprived of school library services, and many special schools did not have library media centers. Sadly, in many cases they still do not have such facilities. In some cases, the materials are there, but without the services of certified library media specialists.

During the late 1960s and early 1970s, sophistication of educational technology has resulted in the development of new methods of dealing with children with varying disabilities. Teaching staff and other professionals concerned with the education of exceptional children, as well as parents, have become cognizant of the fact that the trained library media specialist, aware of where special materials can be obtained, is a valuable member of the educational team.

The Implications of Mainstreaming

Public Law 94-142 mandates that exceptional children must be educated in the "least restrictive environment." The language of the law has been widely interpreted to mean that many more disabled children than before will be educated together with their able-bodied peers; hence, the word *mainstreaming* has become fashionable in educational circles. Effective mainstreaming cannot occur without a tremendous amount of support service from auxiliary members of the educational team. It must be stated in no uncertain terms that almost all disabled children need some sort of auxiliary help from school nurses, physicians, physical and speech therapists, learning disability teachers, and school library/media specialists. The term *individualized instruction* has come to be used as a means for meeting the special educational requirements of exceptional children. Both regular teachers and school administrators will need to acquire a thorough understanding of the philosophies of special education.

Within this framework, the dissemination of information is extremely important. Teachers are apprehensive about the possibility of having students with problems with which they will not know how to deal. Information will be needed on the physical nature of disabilities, how to change attitudes of staff and students toward disabled children, how staff can acquire the knowledge needed to touch exceptional children, information for support services, and information for parents of disabled children. The library/media center may be considered the logical place to begin mainstreaming efforts.

Where is this information to be found? Fortunately for school librarians, the 1960s marked the beginning of many educationally related data bases in the United States.[32] In 1964 the Educational Resources Information Center (ERIC) program was established with ten clearinghouses around the country. It was set up as an information network to acquire, select, abstract, and index, for the purpose of storage, retrieval, and dissemination, all significant and timely reports in education-related areas. It now consists of a coordinating staff in Washington, D.C., and 16 clearinghouses, each responsible for a special area, located at universities or professional organizations around the country. A monthly abstracting index, *Research in Education (RIE)*, announces recently acquired reports. Documents are available in either hardcover or microfiche at many libraries and other educational centers around the country. Subscriptions to *RIE* are available from the U.S. Government Printing Office.

Since August 1972, ERIC has been under the National Institute of Education (NIE). *RIE* was unable to incorporate articles appearing in periodicals and journals; therefore a second publication, *Current Index to Journals in Education (CIJE)*, was developed, devoted exclusively to periodical literature. *CIJE* currently indexes more than 700 publications. The *Thesaurus of*

ERIC Descriptors is used for indexing all documents in the ERIC and *CIJE* systems. The *ERIC Thesaurus* can be obtained from Oryx Press, 3930 Camelback Road, Phoenix, Arizona 85018. A reprint service is now available from University Microfilm International for many of the journals indexed in *CIJE*. *CIJE* may also be subscribed to from Oryx Press.

COUNCIL FOR EXCEPTIONAL CHILDREN, INFORMATION SERVICE

A major activity of the Council for Exceptional Children includes operation of the CEC Information Center and ERIC Clearinghouse on Handicapped and Gifted Children. Under this program, dating from 1966, English-language literature on the handicapped and gifted is indexed, abstracted, and stored for rapid retrieval in ERIC and *CIJE*. The collection includes over 20,000 books, journals, articles, curriculum guides, conference reports, research reports, and other materials. All of these items would be retrieved during a search of both indexes. CEC also maintains a data bank of state and federal laws and regulations and litigation involving handicapped and gifted children.[33]

From the beginning, under the conditions of its original grant from the Bureau of Education of the Handicapped (BEH), the CEC Information Center had a broader responsibility than did other ERIC clearinghouses. It was committed to documenting all professional literature on the subject of exceptionality whether it was published or unpublished, fugitive or accessible. It also was mandated to develop information products and services that would address information needs. Instructional materials for use by the children are not included. Related areas include early childhood, disadvantaged children, vocational and career education, physical education and recreation, and other curriculum areas.

ECER

Part of the CEC Information Service has been the development of the ECER data base. ECER includes all citations submitted to the ERIC system on education of handicapped and gifted children, plus items that go beyond the ERIC scope.[34] This includes dissertations, nonprint media, and copyrighted documents that deal with the education of exceptional children. The extensive coverage of ECER distinguishes it from all other data bases. Therefore, if you are looking for information on any aspect of children with handicapping conditions, ECER will give the most comprehensive coverage. *Exceptional Child Education Resources* (formerly *Exceptional Child Education Abstracts*) is the print index and abstract for the ECER data base. It is a quarterly, and the fourth issue of each year includes a commulative index for the entire volume year.

Beginning with vol. 9, no. 1 (Spring 1977), two new sections were added to ECER. One lists recently completed doctoral dissertations in special education. The other contains a listing of nonprint resources that are directly applicable to the training of special education personnel.[35]

These data bases are excellent resources for school library/media specialists serving teachers and auxiliary personnel concerned with exceptional children.

Closer Look (P.O. Box 1492, Washington, D.C. 20013) is a private organization funded by the Bureau of Education of the Handicapped, Department of Health, Education, and Welfare. It was established by legislation in Elementary and Secondary Education Act 1968 amendments and is now operated by a group of parents of disabled children. Closer Look is a national information center established to help parents of handicapped children and young adults locate educational programs and other special services and resources. Areas covered include general information about handicapping conditions, education, recreation, activities of daily living, and civil rights legislation.

Closer Look helps parents who want to organize parent groups, supplies information packets, and helps plan state and local conferences. It answers inquiries by phone or letter, makes referrals, sends brochures, pamphlets, or fact sheets, prepared bibliographies, abstracts and indexes, and publishes a newsletter. Information focuses on the birth to 21 age group, but there is no age cutoff on any disability.[36]

Common Sense from Closer Look is a newsletter, published twice each year, providing an update on new legislation and directing parents to new resources. Single copies are available free of charge from Closer Look. *Practical Advice to Parents: A Guide to Finding Help for Handicapped Children and Youth* (June 1974) was one pamphlet published by Closer Look for parents seeking services for their disabled children.

In 1964, through the Office of Education, Bureau of Education of the Handicapped, a network of national special education instructional media centers was established whose activities were directed toward increasing instructional options for the education of children with handicapping conditions. In 1969 these centers merged with the federally sponsored Regional Media Centers for the Deaf to become the SEIMC/RMS network. This network consisted of 14 regional centers in the 50 states, Puerto Rico, and the Virgin Islands. An arm of the network was the Council for Exceptional Children's Information Center, which was also the ERIC Clearinghouse on Handicapped and Gifted Children.

Between 1974 and 1976, in an effort to improve services further, this network was reorganized into 13 Area Learning Resource Centers (ALRC), 13 Regional Resource Centers (RRC), 4 specialized offices, and coordinating offices for each. The 13 regions again encompassed the United States, Puerto Rico, and the Virgin Islands. While the ALRCs developed and provided educational media and materials, the RRCs provided diagnostic assessment and prescriptive services to all children with handicapping conditions. The specialized offices worked in four specific areas—the visually handicapped, the deaf, the mentally retarded, and one for audiovisual materials. Coordinating the efforts of the ALRCs and RRCs were the National Center on Educational Media and Materials for the Handicapped (NCEMMH) in Ohio and the coordinating office for the regional resource centers, respectively.[37]

The NCEMMH also operated a National Information Storage and Retrieval system relating to child-directed instructional materials (NIMIS), which could be accessed through the regional ALRCs and the specialized offices.

At the end of September 1977, the ALRC regional centers were phased out and merged into the regional resource centers, with emphasis on the implementation of PL 94-142. The new plan called for exceptional children to be serviced with special materials as needed to support them in the educational setting that has been determined best suited to their individual needs.

Some of the activities and services of the former 13 area learning resources centers have been discontinued. Others have been merged with those of the 13 regional resource centers. An up-to-date list of the regional resource centers can be obtained by sending a stamped self-addressed business envelope to Elwood L. Bland, Chief, Learning Resources Branch, U.S. Office of Education, Bureau of Education of the Handicapped, LRB 4849, Donahoe Building, Sixth and D Streets S.W., Washington, D.C. 20202 (see also Appendix).

The four specialized offices were also closed as of August 31, 1977. However, two new offices have taken over some of their functions. Similar services to those formerly offered by Specialized Office Two are now being performed by the Media Development Project for the Hearing Impaired, University of Nebraska, 318 Barkley Memorial Center, Lincoln, Nebraska 68583. In addition, the Audio-Visual Center, Indiana University, Bloomington, Indiana 47401, has continued to operate as a materials distribution center, as a subcontract to the conference of Executives of American Schools for the Deaf.[38]

Until the creation of NIMIS, there was no centralized system for organizing information about curriculum materials that have worked well with disabled learners. NIMIS is a computer-based, on-line interactive retrieval system, specifically developed for the purpose of assisting teachers, parents, and other educators to locate information about instructional materials in the field of special education. It provides descriptive information covering over 35,000 instructional media and materials for a nationwide audience. These include child-use materials, teacher training materials, evaluation materials, and experimental materials. Three-fourths of the entries are for nonprint materials such as instructional kits, films, videocassettes, filmstrips, games, toys, or transparencies.

The educational materials with which NIMIS is concerned are directed to children with a wide range of disabilities, including the visually handicapped, orthopedically disabled and health impaired, and multihandicapped. Material has been fed into NIMIS through the three specialized offices. Printed bibliographies are updated periodically, and the data base may be accessed through the local or state RRC offices. A thesaurus of descriptors to facilitate requesting information is available in a publication called *Instructional Materials Thesaurus for Special Education*, third edition, available from the Ohio State University Press, 2070 Neil Avenue, Columbus, Ohio 43210.

In September 1977 the federal contract for the NCEMMH was not renewed, and the NIMIS data base was moved to the National Information Clearinghouse for Special Education Materials (NICSEM) at the University of Southern California. NCEMMH is continuing to operate under the auspices of the Ohio State University College of Education. Its executive director is Thomas M. Stephens, chairman of the Faculty for Exceptional Children and executive director of the center. Publications of this center include the *National Catalog of Films in Special Education* (second edition), New York State Education Department, ALRC, Albany, New York, and NCEMMH (1977).

In early 1978 *The Program Tree*, a newsletter issued by NICSEM at the University of Southern California, introduced its services via three initial issues. Funding for this center by the Bureau of Education of the Handicapped began October 1, 1977. Its major task was to continue the development of NIMIS I. NIMIS II/NICSEM includes:

1. A master catalogue of special educational materials for the NIMIS I data base in microfiche and book form.
2. Indexes organized by handicapping conditions as well as staff training materials in microfiche and book form.
3. A catalogue of special education nonprint media from the NICSEM data base in microfiche and book form.

In September 1978 another newsletter, called *Frankly Speaking*, was introduced by NICSEM for quarterly publication. It solicited information on curriculum materials, either teacher-made or commercial, that have been successful in work with exceptional children. To receive this newsletter, address the editor of *Frankly Speaking*, NICSEM-USC, University Park-RAN, Los Angeles, California 90007.

Data entry for the new NIMIS II base has begun. Over 1,000 entries were put into the data base as of September 30, 1978. The NICSEM Master

Catalogs and Indexes include over 35,899 entries from the NIMIS I data base, organized according to learner objectives to aid in selecting materials to implement IEPs. For the special educator or school librarian wishing to access these materials, the procedure would be to go through the local regional resource office. In addition, the NIMIS I data base can be accessed commercially through Lockheed Information Systems in Palo Alto, California, and Bibliographic Retrieval Services in Scotia, New York, for a standard fee.

The account of changes in the structure of the instructional materials network for exceptional children may seem confusing to those not familiar with the way federal contract awards work. However, the services provided by this network are continuing on some basis, in some structure, nationally, and within each state. As with the field of rehabilitation, the proliferation of services, while confusing at present, serves to emphasize that the field is growing rapidly and consequently is experiencing growing pains at the expense of logical organization. Library/media specialists therefore must inform themselves of the particular setup in their own states or regions. For example, in New York State, the Special Education Instructional Materials Center (SEIMC) network was never phased out completely, but continues to exist, administered by the Special Education Department in Albany, through the Boards of Cooperative Educational Services (BOCES), which are designated as ASEIMCs (Associate Centers). In addition, the RRC network is added to the resource setup. Other states or regions, however, have retained only the RRC network.

The NIMIS data bases I and II are now only available on-line through Southern California and may be accessed through local RRC offices.

A more extensive summary of the above information is contained in an excellent article in *Top of the News*, entitled "Selecting Materials for the Handicapped: A Guide to Sources" by Henry C. Dequin.[39]

SUMMARY

The field of special education in the United States has developed from its early beginnings in the nineteenth century to a network service, including private and state-supported schools, resource rooms and special classes in regular schools, itinerant teacher services, and home instruction. By 1976 only one-half of all disabled youngsters, ages 0 to 21, were being given adequate educational services.

Legislation has mandated that child-find procedures be intensified and each handicapped child located and provided with an education "in the least restrictive environment." This mandate has been delegated to the states by virtue of the fact that they receive federal funds.

The role of the school librarian in the education of exceptional children, until recently, has been minimal. The advent of nonprint media and new curricula in special education and information networks, as well as the development of the position of library media specialist in the field of special education, have served to fill this need to some extent. However, there still exists a great gap between library service to disabled and able-bodied students in terms of availability of recreational reading, storytelling, library skills instruction, and professional and parent information. Both in regular schools, where numbers of exceptional children will be appearing for the first time, and special schools, which will continue to exist, it will become increasingly important for school library media specialists to develop an understanding of the abilities and disabilities of exceptional children and a knowledge of where to find professional materials for the staff and informational materials for the parents. School library media specialists can perform an invaluable service to classroom teachers by acquiring knowledge about special curriculum materials that have become available for disabled children in ever-increasing quantities by establishing a link, through their state or regional RRC, with NIMIS and with Closer Look, with groups of parents interested in specific disabilities, and with ECER.

As exceptional children enter the mainstream of education in growing numbers and begin to participate in regular school programs, librarians will also be called upon to adjust their own attitudes and programs to welcome them as an integral part of the student body.

NOTES

1. Barbara Aiello, "Especially for Special Educators: A Sense of Our Own History," *Exceptional Children* 42 (February 1976): 246.

2. Ruth A. Velleman, "School Library Service for Physically Handicapped Children; An Account of the Library Program at the Human Resources School, Albertson, N.Y." (Master's thesis, Palmer Graduate Library School, C.W. Post College of Long Island University, Brookville, N.Y., 1964), pp. 3–8.

3. Willard Abraham, "The Early Years: Prologue to Tomorrow," *Exceptional Children* 42 (March 1976): 333.

4. Velleman, "School Library Service," p. 6.

5. Leo F. Cain, "Parent Groups: Their Role in a Better Life for the Handicapped," *Exceptional Children* 42 (May 1976): 432–437.

6. Ibid.

7. Ibid.

8. Velleman, "School Library Service," p. 7.

9. Abraham, "Early Years," p. 333.

10. Velleman, "School Library Service," p. 13.

11. National School Public Relations Association, *Educating Children with Special Needs: Current Trends in School Policies and Programs* (Arlington, Va., 1974), p. 23.

12. Ibid.

13. Frances P. Connor, "The Past is Prologue: Teacher Preparation in Special Education," *Exceptional Children* 42 (April 1976): 369.

14. Ibid., p. 371.

15. Herbert J. Prehm, "Special Education Research: Retrospect and Prospect," *Exceptional Children* 43 (September 1976): 10–18.

16. Ibid.

17. Ibid.

18. Ibid.

19. Clearinghouse on the Handicapped, Office for Handicapped Individuals, *Directory of National Information Sources on Handicapping Conditions and Related Services* (Washington, D.C., 1976), pp. 92–94.

20. John J. Opperman, "Growth and Impact of the Association for Special Education Technology," *Illinois Libraries* 59 (September 1977): 523–525.

21. National Advisory Committee on the Handicapped, *The Unfinished Revolution: Education for the Handicapped*, 1976 Annual Report, Departtmment of Health, Education, and Welfare, Office of Education (Washington, D.C., 1976), p. 3.

22. Ibid., p. 4.

23. New York State Commission on the Quality, Cost and Financing of Elementary and Secondary Education, *The Fleischmann Report: A Report on the Quality Cost and Financing of Elementary and Secondary Education in New York State*, vols. I, II, III, "Children with Special Needs," Chapter 9 (1972).

24. National School Public Relations Association, *Educating Children with Special Needs*, pp. 20–21.

25. PL 94-142, 94th Congress, Washington, D.C., November 29, 1975.

26. Joseph Ballard, "Public Law 94-142 and Section 504—Understanding What They Are and Are Not," (Reston, Va.: The Council for Exceptional Children, 1977), p. 1.

27. Ibid., p. 1.

28. PL 94-142.

29. National Advisory Committee on the Handicapped, *Unfinished Revolution*, p. 1.

30. James S. Kakalik et al., *Services for Handicapped Youth: A Program Overview* (Santa Monica, Calif.: Rand Corporation, May 1973), p. 17.

31. Velleman, "School Library Service," p. 12.

32. Donald K. Erickson, "Exceptional Child Education Resources: A One-of-a-Kind Data Base," *Illinois Libraries* 59 (September 1977): 519–523.

33. Ibid.

34. Ibid.

35. Ibid.

36. Clearinghouse on the Handicapped, *Directory of National Information Sources*, p. 81.

37. Joan Miller, "Regionalized Support Services for Personnel Involved in the Education of the Handicapped," in *The Special Child in the Library*, Barbara H. Baskin and Karen H. Harris, eds. (Chicago: American Library Association, 1976), pp. 165–168.

38. Henry C. Dequin, "Selecting Materials for the Handicapped: A Guide to Sources," *Top of the News* 35 (Fall 1978): 59, 60.

39. Ibid., pp. 57–66.

13

Libraries Serving Students with Special Needs

The special nature of the problems of exceptional children makes it imperative to have an increasing degree of communication among the educational disciplines that deal with their development. The traditional practice of educating school librarians separately from teachers, preschool teachers separately from elementary school teachers, and secondary school personnel separately from everyone else must be somewhat modified because the exceptional teenager and adult are products of their childhood experiences, and their learning problems stem from the infancy period. A degree of integration of disciplines would be beneficial to all children. Teachers and librarians must understand the total child—normal or exceptional—and how he or she learns before they can educate the child successfully.

In line with this imperative, the ramifications of PL 94-142 have been far-reaching in the encouragement of this type of interdisciplinary activity. In one year, journals in such diverse professional fields as home economics, art education, and school guidance carried articles about how the implementation of this law will affect school programs in each subject area.

The fact that many physically disabled children will be appearing in the regular school population and that many others will, in their special school situations, be required to have a richer education—similar to that of their able-bodied peers—will inevitably result in changes in the field of school library service. School library/media specialists are frequently without the background to acquire the materials and develop programs for these children. New challenges will have to be faced. Librarians will need to expand their own knowledge about areas of exceptionality, deal with the attitudes of their staff, students, and themselves, and find sources of special materials needed by this new population.

It is very difficult to offer statistics—since they do not seem to exist—that show the extent to which disabled children have in the past had access to school library services. Indeed, the 1973 Rand study (see Chapter 12) does not even mention library service as one of the broad range of services offered to exceptional children. School library service to exceptional children has seemed very sparse until recently. Many well-known schools for exceptional children do not have school libraries, although many more than previously have some sort of media service. Although there has been growth in school library service since the 1950s, first in high schools and later in most elementary schools, schools and special classes in the field of special education have either not been able to afford or have not seen the importance of school library service for these children.

Physically disabled children have the same range of intellectual capacities as their able-bodied peers, yet 1976 statistics have indicated that roughly one-half of these children were being deprived of an education.[1] Educational opportunity was uneven, with some states providing much more than others. The education available was often a few hours of home instruction per week. A report written in the early 1960s, showing that the emotional adjustment of severely handicapped college graduates was virtually normal and demonstrably better than that of disabled high school graduates, highlighted the great importance of schooling to the highest possible level commensurate with intellectual ability.[2] The need was especially great for high school programs for the disabled, offering career education and vocational training, as well as college preparation.

The education of orthopedically disabled children ranked lowest among the disabilities surveyed in terms of service, and consequently in terms of school library programs. Those in the school library field are sure that in addition to the group experience provided by school attendance, a school library is indispensable to the academic progress of a student and that its absence can stunt the intellectual development of children who must be educated at home.

THE HUMAN RESOURCES SCHOOL PROGRAM

The Library Media Center at the Human Resources School (where the author serves as head librarian) is discussed here as a demonstration model for library service to orthopedically disabled children. Situated in Albertson, New York, Human Resources School is one of three components of the Human Resources Center, a private, nonprofit organization serving the physically disabled. It also includes Abilities, Incorporated, a work demonstration center for physically disabled adults, and the Human Resources Research and Program Development Center. Abilities, Incorporated was founded in 1952 by Dr. Henry Viscardi, Jr.

Human Resources School offers a tuition-free education yearly to more than 200 physically disabled children. Chartered by the Board of Regents of the State of New York, it provides a full academic curriculum and extra-curricular program to previously homebound children from infancy through high school.

Founded in 1962 as an experimental program for 20 physically disabled children, the school expanded quickly. The children had average or above-average intelligence and disabilities stemming from brain damage (such as cerebral palsy); special health problems like hemophilia; orthopedic disabilities like spina bifida, osteogenesis imperfecta, and arthrogryposis; and neuromuscular disorders such as muscular dystrophy, dysautonomia, and dystonia. There were also children with congenital anomalies and those who had experienced crippling diseases and accidents that produced paraplegia and quadriplegia. (The physical nature of these disabilities and the emotional and social problems faced by these children and their families are discussed in Chapters 1 and 2.)

All of the children had been receiving home instruction in their own school districts. Because of meager instruction and a great deal of time spent in hospitals, most of them were reading below grade level and had read very little before coming to Human Resources School. In the spring of that first year, the author began to develop the nucleus of a school library. Books were housed at one end of the classroom and in the small research library at the Human Resources Center. In the fall of 1963, with 600 books on hand and the help of a local public library, the initial library program was launched. It consisted of rudimentary library skills lessons and a weekly story hour for the primary grades. A field trip to the local public library showed the children how the books were shelved and introduced them to reference materials. At the end of the school term, the children filled out an interest inventory. The results, confirming the author's own intuition, showed that these youngsters were very much like their able-bodied peers. Television viewing ranged from six hours a week to six hours a day for the most handicapped, with the majority averaging two hours a day. Favorite radio programs included all of the prominent disc jockeys. The boys collected baseball cards. Leisure-time activities mentioned most frequently were reading, swimming (in the center's specially equipped pool), sewing, making models, painting, playing musical instruments, playing chess, listening to records, and playing ball. Knowing the children personally lent special poignancy to some of their answers. The little girl who said her favorite activity was walking did her walking on two artificial legs, and the little boy who loved to play baseball could only swing along on crutches.[3]

The story of the designing of the new school building, which was erected in 1964, is told by its founder, Henry Viscardi, in his book *The School.*[4] The design of the school library and its program were described by the author in "A Library for the Handicapped," an article appearing in *School*

Library Journal.[5] The original library was a warm, carpeted interior room at the heart of the school. Special features included a wood-burning fireplace for story hours, a picture window overlooking a greenhouse, a lowered card catalogue, and accessible shelves and tables. Ten years later, the original library was more than doubled in size and transformed into a library/media center. Architectural features of this facility were described in "Library Adaptations for the Handicapped."[6]

School librarians may refer to Chapter 5 for assistance in library design, although the architectural library requirements described there are primarily for public and university libraries. A description here of the architectural features of the Human Resources School Library may offer some ideas that will be helpful primarily to school librarians who are asked to adapt their facilities or contribute ideas to the design of new ones.

In designing the library, one objective was to demonstrate that disabled children do not need extensive adaptations of the normal environment to function successfully. Necessary adaptations are based upon the fact that many disabled students are in wheelchairs and have trouble reaching the lowest as well as the highest library shelves. High-pile carpeting, narrow doors, steps or door sills, and a cluttered floor plan impede the mobility of wheelchairs.

In designing the expansion of the original library, the wood-burning fireplace was retained as a focal point and the picture- and easy-book collection was located next to it in multicolored, three-foot-high, free-standing picture-book shelving. The picture window, which offers a view of the greenhouse, gives the library an open atmosphere, a feeling that is important to children who spend much of their time at home.

Since the size of the library more than doubled with the expansion, we were able to remodel it into a large L-shaped space to create a true library/media center. The new area was wide enough to enable us to combine perimeter wall shelving with three free-standing units 15 feet apart, thus creating alcoves for multilevel individualized and group work. Each alcove has a library table, 29 inches high, apronless and without pedestals. With a large wheelchair population, many students remain in their own chairs and, therefore, each table has only one-half the usual number of chairs. Near the fireplace a 23-inch high table with low stools accommodates both primary-age students who use smaller wheelchairs and older students who are undersized because of various disabilities. A height of 5 feet for book shelves enables students in wheelchairs to reach almost all of them. Where space limitations force libraries to exceed this standard, disabled people are able to adjust realistically by asking for assistance. Students in wheelchairs also find it difficult to reach the lowest shelves. Therefore, the aisle shelving used at Human Resources School is T-base, which is obtainable from all standard library suppliers.

Occasionally a disabled student needs to use a special standing box, an exceptionally small table, or some other special piece of equipment. The librarian can work with administrators, parents, and medical staff to provide such items for special needs.

The most important piece of equipment in the library is the card catalogue, a 12- or 15-drawer cabinet on a wood or aluminum frame base. At Human Resources School, to make the card catalogue low enough to be completely accessible to students in wheelchairs, each section rests on a special 16-inch-high base, which were made to order by a library furniture supplier. Four units in a square formation serve the needs of the library/media collection. When this is done, of course, space can become a problem. However, complete accessibility of information in the card catalogue to handicapped students is a must and can only be achieved by consistent use of the 16-inch base for each additional unit of the card catalogue.

Expanded library space allowed us an additional storage area for our extensive hardware and software media collection. Software is stored in standard commercial cabinets and open record cases. The only unusual features are low bases without crossbars for cabinets to make them completely accessible. One 12-foot-long wall has specially built walk-in cabinets to house all media hardware, such as 16mm projectors and video equipment. Shelving provides space for smaller items like filmstrip and filmloop projectors, cassette and reel-to-reel tape recorders and record players. Although only some students in wheelchairs are able to wheel 16mm projectors to classrooms, most can check out and carry smaller pieces of equipment.

To display periodicals with the greatest possible accessibility, wall panels with extending individual periodical holders have been hung at optimum height to suit the special needs of our population. To conserve space and for easy access, back issues of periodicals are stored on microfiche. Standard microfiche readers with average-to-high lens magnification can be used easily by students who have full or partial hand use. Two-drawer lateral files, which are most accessible to students in wheelchairs, house vertical file material.

Paperback books are stored on racks, commercially obtainable, and the books are accessible because each section revolves independently. The media area of the library is equipped with four wet carrels. Commercially made, they were purchased in 48-inch widths rather than the usual 36 inches to allow comfortable leg space for students in wheelchairs. They would also serve to accommodate special equipment such as braillers for blind students and specially equipped typewriters for youngsters with such disabilities as cerebral palsy. The lights in the media area are banked to allow sections of the room to be darkened for film showings. A roll-down screen serves the area. A book and media production area is equipped with apronless counters and a sink in the corner with a cutaway area below it to allow access for wheelchairs.

The floor is covered with an institutional-grade tackless acrylic carpet, which has a tight weave (looped through the back) and a thick jute backing. No padding is used, and the carpet is cemented to the floor. The floor covering is most advantageous to both the wheelchair population and those ambulatory students who use crutches and braces. For libraries without carpeting, a nonskid vinyl floor covering is desirable.

Thresholds consist of metal strips with gripper edges to provide level entrances into the library. Doors are lightweight and have see-through panels, lever handles (rather than knobs), and kickplates. Lowered light switches accommodate a wheelchair population.

With a group of disabled students, those who are ambulatory are asked to aid those in wheelchairs and students with good hand control help those with minimal hand use. Group research can best be handled by removing the drawers of the card catalogue and placing them on the tables to avoid a crush of wheelchair traffic.

Minimal architectural and room adaptation plus common sense will enable disabled students to participate in library activities that might otherwise be inaccessible to them. Many of these suggestions could be incorporated into any traditional school library without too much expense.

Nature of the Population

Beginning with the work of the well-known Swiss child psychologist Jean Piaget, new discoveries have expanded our knowledge of the ways in which children learn. Throughout the early sensory-motor period and the beginning of abstract reasoning, the child's emotional and intellectual development depends jointly upon the experiences with which he or she is presented and a reconstruction of the world he or she sees.[7]

Some physically disabled children do not move around freely in their world and consequently may fail to learn directionality or to acquire a sense of their own position in space. This may lead to serious deficiencies in the areas of form and depth perception. In addition, disabilities involving the central nervous system, such as spina bifida and dysautonomia, sometimes produce minimal brain damage. Added to the normal results of deprivation among physically disabled children is the realistic fact that 3 percent of all children in the United States are estimated to have what are now considered to be learning disabilities. Little is known about causes and much research still needs to be done in this area. We do know, however, that many of these youngsters have average or above-average intelligence, but they experience reading and math problems, trouble with writing, and have short attention spans and poor listening skills. Since physical disability and learning disability are not mutually exclusive, it is entirely possible for both conditions to be present simultaneously, and this is true of some of the children at the Human Resources School. The primary learning disability may then cause a secondary emotional problem because the youngster realizes that he or she cannot accomplish as much or as rapidly as other children. Hyperactivity, anger, and refusal to attempt the task are all products of the accumulation of failure for a learning disability (LD) child, and this will be exacerbated for the child who is also physically disabled.[8] For all of these reasons, the exceptional child may need special perceptual motor training in the early learning years.

Socially, the exceptional child suffers from a lack of exposure to the world. Usually, he or she is not able to play with other children and is seldom taken out of the home, thus developing a general social immaturity, often a high degree of introspection, and even withdrawn behavior. Thus, the disabled child is doubly disadvantaged, both intellectually and socially, when he or she starts to learn to read or handle mathematical concepts. Disabled children are capable of normal emotional development. In many instances, however, parental attitudes toward them tend to be more extreme (either overprotective or rejecting) or confused than toward other children, and this has a great deal to do with their ultimate life adjustment. Parental handling, rather than the nature or extent of the disability, is the most significant factor contributing to the degree of emotional stability or instability of the disabled child.

The Collection

We believed originally, and continue to believe, that the reading and leisure-time interests of our students are very similar to those of their able-bodied peers. Accordingly, our book collection has been developed to include the very best standard and new materials in the areas of fiction, nonfiction, biography, and reference. There are, however, elements of exceptionality in our population that lead to certain adaptations. Books about the disabled are purchased only when they have literary merit, since our students are quick to sense inaccuracies and insincerity in this sensitive area. A ratio of fiction to nonfiction slightly larger than the average school has made it possible to supply much of the students' leisure reading material and compensate for a somewhat lower usage of public libraries. A large reference section allows us to check out reference books overnight or for weekends.

Rapid growth of the paperback book business has also been of great assistance. A collection of approximately 1,000 paperbacks, inexpensive, lightweight, and easily handled by students with upper extremity weakness, has proved very popular. Nonfiction and elementary level fiction books are catalogued and shelved with the hardcover books. On the secondary level, a paperback bookrack for fiction draws an appreciative public. A paperback book collection on the elementary level is used to send home with those youngsters who are not yet ready for the responsibility of checking out the hardcover books and, in general, to supplement the regular book collection.

Our student body includes a few students with limited or no vision, whose primary disability is orthopedic. Large-print books and tapes are added to the collection for these students. Tapes for textbook materials are obtained upon request of the teaching staff from Recording for the Blind in New York City. The Industrial Home for the Blind, a local depository for materials from the American Printing House for the Blind, loans the school large-print text materials for the same purpose.

Some of the students require a longer than average period of time to develop their learning skills. Widespread reading retardation was at first attributed only to the fact that many of the original students had been receiving homebound instruction. In addition, a considerable amount of school time was (and still is) lost because of prolonged hospital stays. Although these factors are important, it also became obvious, as already stated, that sensory deprivation plays an important role in reading development. To compensate for the reading deprivation of many of the students, a large number of high-interest, low-vocabulary books have been purchased, using a variety of sources. (Publishers catalogues are one readily available source; individual libraries will have different needs in this area.)

The original library collection included perceptual training materials such as those from Teaching Resources and Developmental Laboratories, which were housed centrally in the library media center. As Human Resources School grew in size, these items were placed in K-3 and developmental classrooms so that they were readily available to classroom teachers on a daily basis.

Because of the broad range of abilities on any given grade level, the student book collection—except for a picture and easy-reading book corner—has not been divided between the elementary and secondary schools. The combined book collection enables all students to progress at their own rates, avoiding a feeling of inadequacy in those who work below their chronological age groups.

The media collection includes a full complement of 8mm films, film-loops, sound and silent filmstrips, recordings, cassettes, and study prints in all curriculum areas. These materials are catalogued and color coded and cards are filed in the card catalogue with the book collection cards.

An important part of the library is a full professional special education collection for the use of the school staff, which includes books, journals, newsletters, and vertical file materials in the areas of physical disabilities and special curricula for disabled children. (Chapter 14 offers a bibliography for a starter collection of this type.) Included in the professional library are books, journals, newsletters, and vertical file materials for the use of the children's parents, who, during parent meetings, are encouraged to ask for information in all areas of living and management of their children at home. Knowledge of community and national resources and services available to the disabled enables us to answer reference questions from both staff and parents. A file of field trips to adapted facilities, as well as information about adapted college campuses, and much of the information contained in Chapter 8 round out the professional files.

The Library Program

The library program at Human Resources School was developed in the belief that a school library is indispensable to the total academic progress of its students and that one of the serious disadvantages of a home instructional program is the absence of professional reading guidance and the lack of diversified library materials in both print and nonprint formats. The aims of the school library media program are the encouragement of reading, the provision of a variety of learning materials in all subject areas, the utilization of many forms of media to develop creative ability, and the teaching of library skills.

To this end, we have developed a rounded library program at Human Resources School, specially tailored to the population. One rather widespread problem we have discovered is that parents find it difficult to bring children to the public library. We try to encourage this and offer information as to the accessibility of the various libraries in our area. There are other factors besides architectural barriers, however, that cause parents of disabled children difficulty in transporting them to various activities, not the least of which is that the children may be tired. Loss of sleep is not uncommon with some children, such as those with muscular dystrophy, who must be turned over several times a night. It is also difficult to transport wheelchairs and give equal attention to other siblings.

For these reasons we have tried to make our school library program on the elementary level a combination school and public library program. Although the library is always open for research on a flexible scheduling basis in such curriculum areas as social studies and science, to offer a complete service we schedule one library period per week from nursery school through the sixth grade. During this period, the children report to the library for 20 to 30 minutes of activity, usually a story hour. This is followed by a book selection session during which the librarian is joined by the classroom teacher to offer a high degree of individual reading guidance. Such individualization is necessary because some youngsters work on or above grade level, while others work below their levels and require special help in selecting reading materials.

The students at Human Resources School have always enjoyed their story hours, which do not differ greatly from those offered to able-bodied children. Disabled youngsters who are mainstreamed should be given the opportunity to attend regular storytelling sessions. Often it is not possible to measure the positive effects of exposure to good literature on many youngsters until years later. High school students have said that they remember specific books read to them during story hours when they were in elementary school.

Disabled children are not anxious to read about people with disabilities. However, when a disabled character in a book is presented in a positive way, they are quick to notice and respond. One good example is *Moon Man* by Tomi Ungerer.[9] In this story about the Moon Man who comes to earth, his return to the moon, after a series of adventures, is engineered by a group of learned scientists. A board meeting is attended by a distinguished-looking gentleman in a wheelchair. The obvious message is that although he is physically disabled, he is obviously mentally able and occupationally active. Kindergarten students at Human Resources School who were read this story for the first time noticed the man in the wheelchair before the librarian picked up on it! This type of positive portrayal is most welcome at all levels by people who work with disabled children.

In addition to the use of good literature during story hours, an attempt is made to reach each child in a special way. To do this, the librarian often structures story hours to build upon concepts introduced in the classroom and by speech and learning resources teachers, and to broaden the knowledge of the world for the children.

Slow-learning older children, too old for picture books but with very short attention spans and immaturities, are often reached with books about emotions. When kindergarten and first-grade classes show problems in interpersonal relationships, our school psychologist and teachers like to use books about friendship. The ever-popular *Curious George Goes to the Hospital* by H. A. Rey, and other books about hospital, clinic, and doctor visits, are in constant use with disabled children, who must spend so much of their time in these environments.

Disabled children often live in a very restricted physical world. So, story hours are organized around books about other countries or cities, supplemented by films, sound filmstrips, and music pertaining to these cultures. Middle elementary children reading below grade level do well with these kinds of programs. All middle elementary groups enjoy hearing books about other cultures.

The large collection of recordings, sound filmstrips, and 8mm films that enliven our story hours come from such creative houses as Weston Woods and Coronet. Records that our children's librarian find useful in the primary story hour program include: Learning Basic Awareness through Music, Children Dance with Partners, Body Space Perception through Music, and Motor Skills Development through Music from Stallman-Susser Educational Systems, Inc. (P.O. Box AL, Roslyn Heights, New York 11577); Folk Song Carnival, Getting to Know Myself, and Learning Basic Skills through Music from Education Activities, Inc. (Box 392, Freeport, New York 11520); Adventures in Rhythm from Scholastic Records; Free to be You and Me, and Marlo Thomas and Friends from Arista Records (1776 Broadway, New York, New York 10019); and Tom Glazer, Activity and Game Songs from CMS Records, Inc. (14 Warren St., New York, New York 10017).

Storytelling techniques for physically disabled children do not differ appreciably from those used for their able-bodied peers. One helpful hint, however, is that children with minimal brain damage respond in an overwhelmingly positive way when a character in the story is given his or her name. This identification is very great and often serves to keep the child from wandering off, or brings him or her back to the group and encourages active participation.

A creative media program is directed by the Human Resources media librarian and cuts across all grade levels in the school. His work includes stories developed as animated cartoon films by elementary groups; a science fiction animated film (starring a life-sized papier-mâché dinosaur and the Human Resources School Hewlett Packard computer), which was created by an eighth-grade group; videotapes done each year by twelfth-grade social studies classes on "you are there" twentieth-century American history topics; and important staff observations of specific children or groups of children, via videotape, which are executed at the request of the school physician and/or psychologist.

Working together with the junior high school and high school science teachers, the media librarian created a slide/lecture consisting of a series of slide photographs illustrating our adapted science curriculum for physically disabled youngsters. The adapted laboratory facilities, techniques in working with students, use of volunteers, and modifications of curriculum were detailed, and the resulting slide show was presented at several science conferences and colleges with special education programs. Funds are being sought for the development of a new film on physical education for the disabled, which will illustrate the same points of modification of instructional area, the role of volunteers, techniques of handling physically disabled students, and adaptation of curriculum in a recreational program. This film would update *Therapy through Play*, developed some years ago at Human Resources School and still being loaned out constantly nationwide to schools interested in special education. The lack of up-to-date audiovisual materials in this field makes it imperative that we develop such educational films and slide shows for other curriculum areas in the school.

A computer terminal in the library media center makes use of our own Hewlett Packard 2000F computer. Terminals are also located in specific classrooms for individualized use. Programs are projected on CTRs (television-type monitors) and incorporate lessons in many subject areas. A great deal of teacher-made materials are utilized to provide individualized reinforcement. A catalogue library system for all computer-based programs consists of on-line display listings as well as hard copy printouts.

Library media centers are sometimes defined as instructional materials centers. In the case of a school such as Human Resources, this definition applies in its truest sense, as the media librarian is concerned with bringing to the attention of the staff special instructional materials for disabled students. In addition, the searching out and acquisition of hardware especially adapted for the use of physically disabled students (for example, special "spastic bars" on typewriters for students with limited hand use) is the primary responsibility of the media librarian.

On the secondary level, the use of the library is extremely flexible. Group instruction in advanced reference is offered anywhere from the seventh to the tenth grades, depending on the scholastic ability of the groups involved. The seniors are also informed of the types of reference materials made available to their parents and assured that they are free to return and consult the librarian should this information be required in the future.

It has always been the policy of the library to work with the business, guidance, and health departments to acquaint high school students with sources of career information. We supplement the *Occupational Outlook Handbook* with books, pamphlet materials, and the SRA (Science Research Associates) Occupational Exploration Kit and WORK (Widening Occupational Roles) Kit.[10]

Recent trends in education have reflected an increase in awareness of the need for an early start in career education. How much more important is this concept for disabled youngsters, who have difficulty in preparing themselves for the world of work, and for disabled females in particular, who are at the bottom of the work heap because they must cope with the disability of a physical handicap and face possible discrimination because they are female. Human Resources School is pioneering in career education models with the fifth and sixth graders, and the library has acquired such items as *Career World* magazine and the newspaper *Real World*, both published by King Features. DLM materials on careers include *The Career Card File* and *Accepting Individual Differences*. Scholastic, Coronet, BFA, Sunburst, and Jim Handy are media firms that have published useful career-awareness multimedia kits. A career-awareness series of activity books was published by Incentive Publications (Nashville, Tennessee) in 1977. Many more materials are now available in this rapidly developing field.

An important function of the library is to support special grant activities with the acquisition of appropriate materials. The librarian continually peruses the professional literature for information to this end.

Teachers are provided with materials in all curriculum areas, and the library staff solicits their requests and suggestions for purchase and apprises them of new research findings in areas of special education, suited to their field of expertise. Reports are obtained, often on microfiche, where they are deemed of interest. Basic reference tools and a selection of special education periodicals are read by the librarians so that special articles can be brought to the attention of individual staff members. These journals, as well as special newsletters, are listed in Chapters 8, 11, and 14.

Working with Parents

A very important aspect of the Human Resources School Library program is direct contact with the parents of the students. Most of these parents need a tremendous amount of support, which is offered through individual and group discussions with the school psychologist and other professional personnel. Each year, the library media staff sets up a display of special materials at the traditional parent open house, and more importantly, whenever there is a meeting of parents who are new to the school. This display is supplemented with a talk by the librarian to point out specific materials to the parents and to state that she is always available to answer reference questions. The same information is offered each year. Often, a parent who has heard this talk for a number of years will really "hear" it for the first time when the information becomes pertinent to the particular situation in that home. It is important, therefore, that the message is repeated often for these parents who are faced with the tremendous responsibility of bringing up disabled children.

Materials range from supportive literature to specialized books and materials in the areas of prosthetics and orthotics, wheelchair, bathroom, and kitchen design, travel information, recreation, dentistry for the handicapped, and much more (see Chapters 8 and 14).

Dealing with the Death Concept and Sex Education

Many of the children at Human Resources School have terminal disabilities, such as muscular dystrophy of the Duchenne type. Very few school years go by without the death of one or more of our students. Some of these deaths are expected; others are quite sudden and unexpected. The library staff has learned to purchase supportive literature in this area (see Chapter 14). Such books, however, are never put out on general display at parent nights. It is felt that some of the parents are not yet ready to cope with this concept as it relates to their own children. A certain amount of sensitivity is required to know when such books may be offered. Generally, we wait until they are requested, or we suggest to the psychologist or the physician that this literature is available.

Dealing with the concept of death is most difficult for those students with terminal disabilities, most of whom, by the time they reach adolescence, are aware of their own diagnosis. Sometimes younger children are afraid that "the same thing will happen to them," although they may not have a terminal disability at all. For younger children, books like *The 10th Good Thing about Barney*, by Judith Viorst,[11] and *The Accident*, by Carol Carrick,[12] are sometimes useful to stimulate discussion about feelings in this area.

Human Resources School has a health program that has evolved from the health study *Individualized Health Incentive Program Modules for Physically Disabled Students for Grades Kindergarten through Twelve.*[13] As part of this program, sex education is offered to our junior high and high school students, taught by our former school nurse. Special information about sex and the handicapped is kept on hand in the library (for a bibliography of sources in this area, see Chapters 8 and 11) for the use of the health teacher, physician, psychologist, and guidance counselor. Students seldom approach the librarian directly for this information. However, when requested, it is freely given. Of course, the general nonfiction section of the library contains many books on puberty, reproduction, childbirth, and so on, and children are encouraged to take these books home at an early age. It is recognized, however, and the fact dealt with, that disabled children have different physical growth rates than their able-bodied peers, and often their sexual needs differ from the norm.

SCHOOL LIBRARIANS: WHAT CAN THEY DO?

Exceptional children are being placed in regular school programs in greater numbers than ever before. Librarians in these schools are frequently without the background to deal with the needs of these children. The librarian is confronted with a new challenge and an opportunity to extend service to groups that have in the past been excluded from the library. Librarians must expand their own knowledge of the nature of exceptionality and its implications for the learning process.[14]

Architectural barriers must be eliminated wherever possible. Although the school librarian must work within the framework of the school and is dependent on the administration for cooperation, the law is now on the side of making facilities accessible. It is the obligation of the professional person involved to attempt to make facilities and programs available if there is a disabled student who can benefit from the service.

Architectural adaptations for blind students are well described in the article "Designing Desirable Physical Conditions in Libraries for Visually Handicapped Children" by Edith C. Kirk in *The Special Child in the Library*.[15] In her article "The Hearing Impaired Child in the Library" (in the same collection), Sister Doris Batt offers physical library adaptations for deaf and hearing-impaired children.[16]

Children with hand impairments may require tapes or recordings. Automatic page turners are available, but they are expensive and seldom operate efficiently. In some cases, special reading stands may be required. Traditional audiovisual equipment must be evaluated by the librarian; bulk, weight, portability, amplification, magnification, and ease of operation become important variables when considered for use with exceptional children.[17]

Physical Disabilities

Possible physical problems encountered by the librarian will cover a broad range, depending on specific disabilities, and these cannot be lumped together. In general, however, the librarian must deal with excessive fatigue, the frequent need to report to the nurse for medication, or simply the problem of mobility or accessibility.

More specifically, the nature of the disability will dictate the type of problems that can be expected. Chapter 2 defines many of the disabilities that will be seen in the schools in greater number than ever before. Those definitions should be read in conjunction with the following pages, which describe some limitations that will directly affect library use and the librarian.

Children with osteogenesis imperfecta are generally small in stature. Parents are often overprotective because they fear fractures. At special schools, these children tend to identify with each other and are clannish. Usually the disability does not directly affect their intelligence, which sets them apart from disabled children with learning problems. A distinctive facial characteristic makes them easily identifiable to professional staff and to each other. As these children grow older, their condition is apt to stabilize and the fear of breaking bones diminishes. The wheelchair basketball team at Human Resources School often has many members with osteogenesis imperfecta, and they are anything but cautious in their movements. Low tables are useful for these students into their teen years. However, they are very resourceful and are able to flop out of their wheelchairs and use the floor to look at books or take notes. With a positive attitude, children with this condition can easily become part of the library program.

Arthrogryposis, a congenital disability of the joints, can affect just the upper or the lower extremities with varying degrees of severity. Limitations in the library would involve inability to reach shelves or to carry books, and the student with hand limitations might not be able to handle media or write independently without some sort of adjustment. Often all that is needed is to tape a paper to a table and adjust a pencil. This disability is purely physical. It does not affect intelligence and children perform entirely within normal ranges.

The muscular disabilities include many subgroups, all of which affect the muscles to varying degrees. The most common that affects children (predominantly male) is the Duchenne type, which is progressive and terminal. Its onset is anywhere from four to ten years of age, and children generally start their education in regular school programs. Sometime during the elementary years, the child begins to walk with a sway back, continually falls down, and finally requires a wheelchair. This often causes great trauma. A period of denial causes them to resist special schooling where it is indicated. Each step of the way is difficult for muscular dystrophy children, as diminishing strength causes them to fall down when ambulating. The need for a wheelchair is seen as a failure on their part and causes guilt feelings that perhaps they should have been able to walk longer. In most special schools, the use of a wheelchair is a status symbol. Not so for MD children, who go through all the stages of terminal illness—denial, anger, depression, and, finally, acceptance. Sexuality in the males is a problem because while they are not lacking in sensation, there is little opportunity for fulfillment.

Children with muscular dystrophy may exhibit a wide range of intellectual ability, but because the peripheral nervous system is affected they are often poor in academic performance. Motor limitations cause inability to perform in school without a great deal of help, and emotional adjustments to the different stages of the disability may further affect academic performance. Children with muscular dystrophy control their environment by means of the many legitimate physical demands they must make on their parents. Human Resources School psychologist Dr. Ronald Friedman, who handles many of these children and their families, suggests counseling of parents, but very careful handling of children so as not to shake up their defense systems or interfere with their dreams and fantasies for the future. "Since they may have difficulty in dealing with reality," states Dr. Friedman, "it is often better not to remove their fantasies." However, he adds that muscular dystrophy children, like all children, require that realistic academic and social goals be expected of them.

MD children generally have been placed in special school programs or on home instruction. But with the new emphasis on mainstreaming, efforts will undoubtedly be made to retain these students in school. Academically they will be able to achieve in a normal manner until such time as extreme weakness makes it impossible for them to continue in class on a regular basis. Physically they will begin to require electric wheelchairs when they are no longer able to push themselves, and then the help of an aide in taking out books, writing assignments, and so on. Their hands will have to be positioned so that a book can be held open. A great deal of physical attention must be given for students with advanced muscular dystrophy to keep up with their work. Sometimes a student's position must be changed very often, or his or her head must be propped up. Books may have to be placed on reading stands. With sufficient physical help, however, students are able to function with some success.

Children with postpoliomyelits symptoms, paraplegia, or quadriplegia will be able to function with whatever muscle power they have. What is lost cannot be regained, but the conditions are not terminal. Some of the accommodations for muscular disabilities in the way of help may have to be made for them.

Children with spina bifida may manifest the same physical characteristics as paraplegics, quadriplegics, and children with postpolio symptoms, with the additional problem of loss of sensory input. The student must be watched since sensory loss may mean lack of awareness of an injury to a foot or leg. Children with spina bifida exhibit a wide range of intellectual ability. Some children have average to above-average intelligence. However, the presence of hydrocephalus at birth, which causes brain damage, can result in learning problems. Children with spina bifida often show a pattern of what is called "cocktail chatter." Since they spend much time with adults, their verbal ability appears to be high, but it is characterized by stereotyped phrases and a superficial understanding of language concepts. Therefore, care must be taken not to misinterpret their intellectual ability.

Some evidence indicates that the girls tend to be somewhat neurotic and introverted as children, but do outgrow this. The boys become aggressive as they get older, and they find outlet in physical activity, which becomes somewhat excessive at times.

Sexual development is more difficult for the males than for the females, since the males must wear a collecting device as they get older. This tends to mar the sexual image. In addition, not much is known about the sexual performance of males with spina bifida. Females with urinary devices seem not to have the same emotional difficulties with body image.

Because of incontinence in early childhood, these children have not been mainstreamed to any great extent. However, new methods of emptying bowel and bladder mean that children with spina bifida require less nursing care during the day and are able to be placed in regular school programs. Their library performance will be similar to that of their able-bodied peers. Hand usage will be good, and if architectural adaptations are made, they will have no trouble integrating into the regular library program.

The physical manifestations of cerebral palsy vary widely, as does intellectual ability. In the past, children with mild forms of this neurological disorder have been mainstreamed occasionally. Cerebral palsy may be the most severe of the physical disabilities seen in the schools. Many emotional and social problems exist for the cerebral palsied youngster. Low on the scale of employability, low in acceptance by other disabled people, they have difficulty in maintaining a positive male or female image and are often thought of as asexual. While marriages have taken place, even with the use of live-in attendants when necessary, they have been, and still are apt to be, uncommon. People who are severely palsied require a great deal of physical care, thus causing problems of resentment among siblings. Often they are taken to be younger than they are because of communication problems, as many cerebral palsied people have unclear speech. Because they are unable to express their feelings fully, intelligence and other capabilities often remain locked inside.

Parental and school attitudes and the intelligence and determination of the student have usually governed the decision to mainstream a child. Since the largest group of physically disabled children have cerebral palsy, most special schools have been made up in large part of students with this disability. And since approximately 75 percent of children with cerebral palsy have some mental retardation resulting from brain damage, the programs in these schools, in general, have been academically weak. Bright, severely physically disabled youngsters with cerebral palsy, as well as other physically disabled children, have suffered, therefore, from a lack of academic opportunity. Public Law 94-142 will, in some measure, offer all children more appropriate opportunities.

Accommodating the cerebral palsied child in the library may require a great deal of physical adjustment, with the help of an aide to handle books, other students to take duplicate notes, and, above all, a positive attitude in terms of attempting to understand the speech patterns of the child. This can be done once the librarian realizes that these children do not mind repeating over and over again, and it is acceptable behavior to let them know that you do not understand. In the case of students with exceptionally poor speech or none at all, further adaptations may have to be made in the form of communication boards or one of the new types of electronic communication equipment.

One of the less common neurological disorders is dysautonomia. It results in a childlike appearance, and those affected seem younger than their years. Sometimes they look mildly retarded. Parents often are overprotective, and the children learn to be manipulative. They tend to underreact or overreact to situations, and any type of change is a difficult adjustment for them. Within the family there is sibling rivalry and resentment. Siblings may be carriers of the disorder, which can be passed on to their children. Since the symptoms involve all of the functions of the autonomic nervous system, these children may have poor balance, scoliosis, erratic body temperature control, respiratory control, and cardiac rates, and poor sensory input. One or more of these symptoms can be present in any one individual. Students can be ambulatory, may be short in stature, or may have a severe enough form of the disease to be in a wheelchair. With appropriate architectural modifications, these students should be able to function in a regular school setting with proper medical supervision. Librarians working with them should be made aware of problems that may occur at any time, such as dizziness, inability to breathe properly, and unawareness of injury to a limb. The librarian should be able to summon medical help when it seems indicated. Educationally, these children show a delayed development, but they are capable of working within the normal academic range with some individualized help.

Children with dwarfism have a problem of body image, not so much during their elementary years, but more so as they get older and enter high school. *Everything* in the world is too high. Sometimes they have trouble walking distances and must use walkers or wheelchairs. Job possibilities largely depend on the willingness of employers to make architectural adjustments. Developing normal concepts in the area of sexuality is difficult, more so for males than females, who are generally able to project an image of femininity with their smallness.

In general, disabled children usually lack social experience and, therefore, are more immature and unworldly than their able-bodied peers. Many disabled children have high verbal ability and low performance, which may be characterized by perceptual problems or simply the inability to perform fine motor tasks as quickly as nondisabled children. The task of coping with a disabled child in the home and at school is highly complex. It is imperative that from birth families receive guidance to help them manage this stressful situation at home and that educators and other professionals be trained to work with these children at school.

Library media specialists can play a role in assisting other staff members to understand these disabilities by acquiring pamphlet materials listed in Chapter 2. Teachers, nurses, and other professional personnel will benefit from this information. In addition, *Physically Handicapped Children: A Medical Atlas for Teachers*, edited by doctors Eugene E. Bleck and Donald A. Nagel, would be a most useful acquisition.[18] It describes many of the physical disabilities with which disabled children will enter the schools. The medical terminology is simple and educational, and classroom procedures are detailed. The 1978–1979 edition of the *Yearbook of Special Education* also includes information on some of the physical disabilities about which so little has been written in the past.[19]

School librarians will also need to include in their professional collections some of the books listed in Chapters 8 and 14 for the information of both staff and parents of disabled students.

LIBRARY SERVICE TO BLIND AND VISUALLY IMPAIRED STUDENTS

Integration of the blind or visually handicapped child into regular class programs also requires special effort. Some helpful materials will acquaint the librarian with many sources of information to offer to teachers and other professionals seeking guidance.

In May 1978, the American Foundation for the Blind published *Guidelines for Public School Programs Serving Visually Handicapped Children* by Susan Jay Spungin. Dr. Spungin feels very strongly that there will be a great need for knowledgeable support personnel to help comply with PL 94-142, and the purpose of her publication is to encourage administrators of programs serving visually handicapped children to utilize such personnel effectively. The report was published for the U.S. Office of Education, Department of Health, Education, and Welfare, and is available from the Foundation without charge. It is complete, presenting information about facilities, funding, programs, types of personnel needed to serve the children, teacher responsibility, testing, special equipment, and special skills. A copy of this guide in the library will be of great value to the administration and to all staff members.

A companion pamphlet, also published by the American Foundation for the Blind and available from them without charge, is *When You Have a Visually Handicapped Child in Your Classroom* by Anne Lesley Corn and Iris Martinez (1977). It covers, in simple terms, types of visual impairments, how the visually handicapped child can be made to feel comfortable in the classroom, what special devices will be needed, and what additional skills must be provided by support personnel such as itinerant teachers.

Integrating the Visually Impaired Student into the Classroom, by Jane Milnes (published in 1974 by the Special Education Division of the Department of Instructional Services, Fairfax County Public Schools, 10700 Page Avenue, Fairfax, Virginia 22030), is also available without charge. This pamphlet is somewhat more detailed in its discussions of specific curricula in the areas of reading, language arts, mathematics, science, social studies, music, art, and physical education, in terms of what techniques are needed to remedy the motor and perceptual difficulties of the visually handicapped child. A valuable bibliography lists curriculum materials in all areas.

Mainstreaming Preschoolers: Children with Visual Handicaps; A Guide for Teachers, Parents, and Others Who Work with Visually Handicapped Preschoolers is one of a series developed by the staff of Contract Research Corporation, Education and Human Development, Inc., for the Department of Health, Education, and Welfare and for sale by the Superintendent of Documents[20] (see Chapter 14 for additional titles in this series). This detailed study tells educators how visual handicaps affect the learning of three- to five-year-old children and how to deal with these manifestations. A bibliography, as well as listings of professional, parent, and other organizations, is most valuable. In particular, a chart of normal development, infancy through six years of age, will prove helpful to school psychologists who will be seeking information in this area. Librarians in all schools should acquire the whole series.

Visually handicapped children present some special problems that can be helped by a knowledgeable librarian. In *School Library Journal*, December 1978, John F. Henne, an elementary school library media specialist, wrote a useful article describing methods that can be used with visually impaired children in the library.[21] Visually handicapped students should participate in all library media activities. Henne points out that blind children can enjoy films when someone describes what is taking place on the screen and that most visually handicapped students will be able to see much of the action if they sit close enough. Rear projection screens are ideal as they allow children to get as close as necessary without blocking the image.

In part four of *The Special Child in the Library*, Jean D. Brown describes additional storytelling techniques for blind children who benefit just as all children do from story hours.[22]

Reference materials present a problem because braille or large-type dictionaries and encyclopedias are very expensive and require a great deal of shelf space. Closed circuit television systems are recommended by Henne as an alternative. However, the price, although coming down, is out of the range of most school libraries.

In special schools for blind and visually impaired children, the card catalogue is often brailled on one side and in large print on the other. Unless schools are prepared to make this modification, and unless there is a good deal of material available in alternate format in the library, visually handicapped students will need individualized assistance in doing work that involves library research. As a rule it will be necessary to have auxiliary personnel if blind and visually handicapped children are to participate in regular classes in the library.

Special Materials

Special curriculum materials in braille, large print, and recorded format, as well as reading aids, equipment, and supplies such as note paper and Braillon for blind and visually impaired students, are available through the American Printing House (APH) for the Blind (P.O. Box 6085, Louisville, Kentucky 40206). This is the oldest national agency serving the blind in the United States. It was founded in 1858 and designated as a national center by an Act of Congress in 1879. It is legally mandated to supply materials for children in educational settings who are legally blind, meaning those who have 20/200 vision or less in the better eye, after correction. This definition of legal blindness, under which the APH must function, is outdated compared to what we now know about the many visual problems affecting school children. However, quotas are set up based on how many children in each state meet this requirement. Each state may purchase materials for legally blind students who are registered with the state education agency. Although it is possible to purchase materials from the American Printing House for visually handicapped students, the federal mandate to supply materials applies only to the legally blind.

A central catalogue maintained by the American Printing House is a compilation of their own materials produced in recorded form, braille, or large print, as well as materials listed in the catalogue of Recording for the Blind in New York City. This organization (described more fully in Chapter 6) will record anything if sent two copies of the text and maintains a library of over 48,000 text tiles, available to anyone who cannot read conventional print. This would also include certain physically disabled students. A compatible 8-track tape player is necessary to use their recorded materials.

State agencies should be able to help librarians wishing to obtain financial assistance for purchase of appropriate machines. Because of PL 94-142, the local school districts will probably be obligated to sustain this cost, whether the child is in regular school or in a special facility.

All American Printing House materials are obtained in each state through local educational outlets, and copies of the central catalogue are available locally through state agencies that serve blind children. The American Printing House will be happy to acquaint librarians with the closest local source if there is a question about where it is located. Many local agencies, such as the Industrial Home for the Blind in New York, will produce books in large print, much of the time utilizing volunteer help, where such books are not available. These books will usually be produced in 14-point print or larger for those visually impaired students needing these materials.

Parents should be told about the National Library Service for the Blind and Physically Handicapped of the Library of Congress, which traditionally provides recreational reading materials for the print handicapped. By law this now includes, in addition to children who are blind or visually impaired, those who cannot use their hands or, because of neurological impairments, cannot read traditional print materials. The availability of this service, through the local public library, should be made known. Certification by a school official such as the librarian, the teacher, or an administrator, or by medical personnel or an eye specialist, is needed to obtain this service. Although these materials are used specifically in the home situation, where appropriate, duplicate equipment is often placed in a school setting.

LIBRARY SERVICE TO DEAF AND HEARING-IMPAIRED STUDENTS

Deaf and hearing-impaired students who enter regular school programs will represent a very great challenge to the librarian, who may recognize many of the same emotional difficulties and family problems exhibited by orthopedically disabled children. Naturally, hearing-impaired children encompass a broad range of disability levels, from the mildly hard of hearing child who is able to function with a hearing aid that amplifies sound and makes use of residual hearing, to the hearing-impaired child with a sensory-neural deficiency that cannot be helped by amplification since sound reception is fragmented. Children who experience hearing loss from birth to the language development period are considered prelingually deaf; the person whose hearing loss occurs later in life is called adventitiously deaf. By the age of five, the profoundly or severely deaf child is already at a disadvantage, and headstart programs for preschool deaf children, developed in recent years, have recognized this fact. The average hearing child brings 5,000 words to kindergarten; the deaf child usually has no language when he or she goes to school.

Education of the deaf has been divided, and is still divided today, over which method of instruction is best. The aural/oral method, advocated by the Alexander Graham Bell Association (which publishes a great deal of material on deafness), as well as the journal *Volta Review*, used to be followed by many schools for the deaf, and it is still followed today by the reputed Clarke School in Northampton, Massachusetts, among others. The *Smith College Alumnae Quarterly* (Northampton, Massachusetts, Spring 1979 issue) carried an account of the training of teachers in the aural/oral method, which the school favors. This philosophy teaches that in order to function in society, deaf children must acquire speech and lip reading techniques, as well as reading and writing abilities. The method teaches lip reading and makes use of residual hearing in each student to the optimum degree.

In more recent years, the total communication method has gained acceptance with many educators of the deaf who have found that only 30 to 40 percent of words can be perceived by lip reading. The rest must be guessed. Since we require a 70 percent ability to read speech in order to function, the deaf person is at a great disadvantage when using lip reading. Total communication advocates use a combination of methods, depending on what is best for each child; amplification of hearing, lip reading, signing and finger spelling, as well as gestures and body movements. It is interesting to note that Ameslan, the sign language used by deaf adults, has been used with some success with autistic children and with brain damaged children. It has also been used to attempt communication with apes.

The schools for the deaf pioneered in their use of a great deal of media, and media centers are maintained by almost all of these special facilities. There was, until quite recently, little use of print materials in library media centers. Now, however, it is widely accepted that deaf children can benefit from high-interest, low-vocabulary materials, which help their reading skills by providing stimulating reading on appropriate reading levels.

A fine article entitled "Helping Hearing Impaired Students," by Mary Jane Metcalf, appeared in the January 1979 issue of *School Library Journal.*[23] Metcalf, referring to the reading retardation generally present in severely deaf children, explains that they learn primarily by sight, and concepts must be presented in visual format for children to understand them. Abstract concepts and words with multiple meanings are difficult for them to comprehend. Library books should contain controlled vocabulary, simple syntax, and clear and illustrative pictures. Storytelling is most effective when many visual materials are used. Similarly, library skills must be presented in visual format, one concept at a time. Among the books that Metcalf particularly likes are the Scholastic Sprint and Action books, which contain high interest and low vocabulary as well as good, clear illustrations.

Librarians working with deaf children who do not have the communication skills necessary for effective storytelling are advised by Alice Hagemeyer (see Chapter 7) to look for a deaf person from the community who has acting and storytelling skills. While someone could sign a story told by a librarian, it is not as effective as if the storyteller and the signer are the same person. Special instructional techniques in storytelling for deaf children are detailed by Patrick Huston in *The Special Child in the Library*.[24]

Captioned films for the deaf and hearing-impaired is a service of the federal government. Information about this program can be obtained by writing to Captioned Films and Telecommunications Branch, Bureau of Education of the Handicapped, U.S. Office of Education, Washington, D.C. 20202.

The National Technical Institute for the Deaf (NTID) was created by PL 89-36, enacted June 8, 1965. This legislation provided for the establishment of a postsecondary technical educational facility to prepare deaf young adults for successful employment. The Rochester Institute of Technology (RIT) in Rochester, New York, was selected for the site. Current plans include the establishment of a national center on Employment of the Deaf at RIT. The center's major functions will include job development, a computerized career-matching system, and research and training services.

BRINGING IN THE PARENTS

One of the basic provisions of PL 94-142 is the Individualized Education Plan (IEP), which was described in Chapter 11. Regulations for the preparation of this individualized plan include recognition of the parent as an official member of the educational team in order to plan the best possible education for the disabled child. To a greater extent than ever before, school professionals must work with parents and allow them an influential voice in determining what is best for their children. The library media specialist will be in a position to render an important service in trying to find information that will help parents and staff to understand each other better.

School librarians must recognize that parents are not a homogeneous group. They have different educational, cultural, and ethnic backgrounds and will need different types and levels of information.[25] In addition, parents require different kinds of information at different stages in their children's lives. Although they are different individuals, most parents do share fear, frustration, disappointment, and other difficulties in child rearing beyond that experienced by parents of nonhandicapped children. Often they have encountered ignorance among doctors and educational personnel. Stages of denial, guilt, and a search for help sometimes turn into militance. School personnel are, therefore, in need of professional information to assist them in handling conferences with parents responding with a wide range of emotional differences to extremely difficult situations.

Some of these thoughts are expressed by Elizabeth J. Webster in *Counseling with Parents of Handicapped Children: Guidelines for Improving Communication.*[26] This small and concise book contains much information that would be helpful to guidance counselors and school psychologists working with parents of disabled children. At the end of each chapter is a useful list of additional references.

A more extensive treatment of the same topic is found in *The Disabled and Their Parents: A Counseling Challenge*, edited by Leo Buscaglia.[27] Buscaglia handles the role of the family and their special feelings and rights in addition to the feelings of parents of disabled children and the disabled themselves. Attention is paid to the person who becomes disabled later in life. Much of the book is contributed by other specialists, and problems such as the sexuality of the disabled are covered.

To assist parents in understanding their role in the educational plans that will affect their children, copies of PL 94-142 and explanatory pamphlet materials about it should be made available in the school library media center. Books and monographs that might be purchased for parents of disabled children and incorporated as part of the professional special education section of the library media center are listed in Chapter 14. Some have been written by parents of disabled children. An additional source of information for parents is *A Readers' Guide for Parents of Children with Mental, Physical or Emotional Disabilities* by Coralie B. Moore and Kathryn G. Marten (Department of HEW, publication number HSA 77-5290, 1976). Most parents of disabled children will be aware of existing parent groups and national organizations that serve children with specific handicapping conditions. It would be a good idea, however, to have such addresses available if they are needed (see Appendix I).

In Chapter 12, many sources of information for special classroom materials and programs for exceptional children are outlined. School library media specialists will need to familiarize themselves with these sources and where they can be accessed locally. They will be of inestimable assistance to classroom teachers needing such materials for the first time. There has been so much work done in this area that specific material cannot be detailed here.

Chapter 12 also contains a description of the regional resource centers concerned with implementation of PL 94-142, which calls for special materials for exceptional children to meet their educational needs. A listing of Special Education Regional Resource Centers and Direction Service Centers can be found in Appendix V. Such professional associations as the Council on Exceptional Children and the Association for Children with Learning Disabilities put out publication catalogues, which should be obtained by the school librarian for reference by the school staff.

Attitudes

The most important aspect involved in placing exceptional children in regular school programs will, of course, be attitude. Library media specialists must explore their own feelings about disability and death. Youngsters will have to be seen in terms of their abilities rather than their disabilities, and recognition will have to be given to the fact that all people have individual differences. Death must be seen as part of the life process. Whenever death occurs, it becomes easier to accept when recognition is given to the fact that the child has been helped to achieve the best possible quality of life. Simply by being accepted into a school program and being able to enjoy an educational and social experience comparable to able-bodied peers, the disabled child's quality of life will have improved a hundredfold. The library media specialist can be an important factor in that improvement.

Attitude is also of utmost importance in dealing with severely physically disabled youngsters who have communication problems. These students are usually unable to reach their full academic potential without a great deal of help and understanding. Often they are classified, mistakenly, as being less intelligent than they are. Often they are considered less mature than they are, and consequently are treated inappropriately for their age levels. It must be remembered that they have the same feelings as their able-bodied peers.

One of the obligations of the school librarian is to assist with the integration of the special child into the regular school program as far as possible. Particularly to assist with the attitudes of the other students, there is an abundance of good children's literature that offers positive portrayals of the handicapped. Although the disabled do not display an interest in reading about themselves, it is important that able-bodied people of all ages be made aware of the disabled by reading about them as they are shown in non-stereotypical ways. *Notes from a Different Drummer* by Barbara Baskin and Karen Harris is an annotated bibliography of juvenile fiction that portrays the handicapped.[28] The introductory chapters explain historical and current attitudes and trends toward the disabled as they have been and are portrayed in fiction, and it makes a worthwhile reference source for children's and young adult librarians who wish to enrich their shelves with positive portrayals of handicapped fictional characters.

As we have seen, the disabled child sometimes has a lower functioning level than able-bodied peers. In this context the librarian can play a non-threatening role by drawing on materials especially developed for lower achieving children. The library is one place where the child may perform at his or her own academic level in an accepting and uncritical environment. "Particularly in a mainstreaming situation, it may be that the greatest accomplishment of the librarian is to make the academic involvement feasible, efficient, easy and pleasurable."[29] Intellectual and cultural deprivation may have narrowed the educational background of the disabled child. The library has the potential to compensate partially for this disparity. In the library the special child can experience success on his or her own level and can share experiences with the nondisabled.

FUNDING FOR LIBRARY MEDIA RESOURCES

Some monies are available to assist in providing school library services to disabled students in public school settings. However, since legislatures and priority areas for funding change periodically, they will be mentioned here only by current titles of legislation. School librarians who wish to request funding should make their needs known to district superintendents, who will be informed by state education departments of current funding sources. The state or federal office responsible for administering each of these titles should be contacted to determine if needs could be met through funding a specific proposal.

The Education of the Handicapped Act, as amended by PL 94-142, provides some funds to local districts for programs for the handicapped child.

The Elementary and Secondary Education Act (ESEA)—as amended by Title 1, the Education of the Disadvantaged—provides some funding for handicapped children in inner-city schools or other programs in which they could be considered economically or learning disabled as well as disadvantaged. Title 4-b of the same act provides monies for library resources, a percentage of which might conceivably be tapped for programs or materials for the disabled child. However, this title is currently under revision.

Title 4-C, a competitive grant for innovative programs, provides 15 percent of its funds for programs for the disabled child. Methods of application for this grant vary from state to state.

COLLEGE AND UNIVERSITY LIBRARIES

Almost all colleges and universities receive funds from the Department of Health, Education, and Welfare and are, therefore, affected by Section 504 of the Rehabilitation Act of 1973. This is a much-needed development. Many university campuses have long been inaccessible to disabled students. Studies have shown that the higher the level of education a disabled person achieves, the better will be his or her adjustment to life.[30] Some universities —for example, the University of Illinois, University of Missouri, St. Andrews Presbyterian College in North Carolina, the University of California, and Emporia State College in Kansas—led the way some years ago in making architectural and program changes for the disabled. The number of disabled students prepared to enter college has grown in recent years because of improved high school curricula. They now outnumber the capacity of accessible institutions. In addition, students want the option of going to a school close to home.[31]

To implement Section 504, by December 1977 all colleges and universities were required to develop a transitional plan for making changes in facilities and programs over the next three years to provide accessibility to handicapped students. In the early 1970s, the Bureau of Education of the Handicapped realized that information about existing adapted college programs was sorely outdated. In July 1974 they awarded a survey contract to Abt Associates, Inc., to produce a document that would "assist in broadening the higher education options available nationally to students with all types and degrees of disability . . . by providing information about existing college-based, state, and national resources."[32] To accomplish its objective, the 3,038 two-year and four-year colleges were sent a questionnaire soliciting their cooperation. Full responses were received from 500 schools. Consequently, the resulting directory of services covered only one-sixth of the colleges and universities in the country. In addition, by the time the directory was issued in 1976, it was already outdated as many schools began to gear up for the task of developing programs and adapting facilities for disabled students. The directory requests that users inform the publisher when inaccuracies are found, since all information was provided by the schools themselves and was not validated. Users are asked not to take all information as the final word, since events are changing so rapidly in this field. It is also hoped that disabled students will use other general sources of information about colleges of their choice. The best possible action, of course, is to visit the school and inquire about special services, orientation periods, and so on. Every college that lists some services will not be appropriate for all disabled students. Specific types of support will differ according to the individual. Because not all schools answered the questionnaire and because it is now so many years later, disabled students should not assume that a school does not have the services they require simply because it is not listed in this or another directory.

Librarians in public, school, or rehabilitation libraries are sometimes approached by disabled young adults or their parents for information about colleges. The Abt directory would be a worthwhile reference source if it is used as a starting point. However, the librarian would do well to point out some of the above-mentioned points.

The August/September 1978 issue of *American Education* carried a detailed description of the program for disabled students at the University of Illinois in an article entitled "More than Ramps or Braille" by Timothy J. Nugent, an early pioneer in university service to disabled students.[33] This program, which has been in existence for over 30 years, is run by a rehabilitation-education center. Nugent has been the director since its inception. All services for disabled students are coordinated by the center.

In August 1977, a national conference entitled Disabled Students on American Campuses: Services and the State of the Art was held at Wright

State University, sponsored by the university and the Bureau of Education of the Handicapped. Proceedings of that conference, edited by Pat Marx and Perry Hall, were published and made available through Marx's office for disabled students at Wright State University, Dayton, Ohio.[34] This conference marked a milestone in the development of services to disabled college students by gathering together participants from all over the country to discuss needs of the disabled in terms of programs and facilities. Stated early in the proceedings was the very important premise that services for disabled students depend first and foremost on commitment and attitude on the part of the institution and its top administration. Implicit in this attitude must be the firm belief that "because an individual's potential will develop to the degree to which it is challenged, disabled persons should be projected into challenging situations and must be given the right to normal growth and development, including the right to fail and learn from failure."[35]

Disabled students very often come to higher education with a much lower level of academic preparation than their able-bodied peers, and they often need some remedial work and/or a great deal of support services if they are to be successful.

University Library Service for the Orthopedically Disabled

It is essential that university librarians assume their appropriate roles in services to orthopedically disabled students. What is the library's responsibility?

Use of the library is essential to all college students if they are to be able to complete assignments properly. Architectural inaccessibility is, of course, the primary cause of low library usage by the physically disabled. There is now a great deal of information available for architects who are making adaptations for libraries. Chapter 5 details this information in concise form.

In 1976 the State Library of Ohio conducted a survey of library services for handicapped students on college campuses. In it each college lists the architectural accessibility of facilities, special equipment, and special services. Such a directory would be of value if issued by every state library bureau in the country. Rehabilitation and guidance counselors would find this information helpful in counseling students as they make college choices.

The following checklist was included in the questionnaire with regard to architectural accessibility:

Is there at least one building entrance at ground level?

Are doors 32 inches wide and do they open easily (with less than 10 pounds pressure)?

Are there level thresholds to buildings and rooms?

Is there a sloping ramp to building entrance (with grade less than 8 percent)?

Is there safe and accessible parking close to the building (8-foot space with 2 feet between spaces)?

Are there level walks with no curbs at crossways from parking area to library building?

Does the student have access to an elevator?

Are rest rooms with wide stalls and grab bars provided for wheelchair users?

Are there handrails on all stairways, extending 18 inches beyond the top and bottom step?

Are there nonslip floors?

Are there lower fountains and public telephones for wheelchair users (height for accessibility 30–36 inches)?[36]

The special services reported by most of the libraries had to do primarily with providing equipment for the blind and visually handicapped and obtaining special materials from the Regional Library for the Blind and Physically Handicapped. Although this is a beginning, library service to handicapped students will have to go beyond the minimum.

In the proceedings of the Wright State University conference, additional recommendations were offered by Andrea Schein from the Handicapped Student Center, University of Massachusetts at Boston.[37] At the university, where the director of the Handicapped Student Center works closely with the library staff, disabled students are allowed to have someone else check out their books. They are encouraged to let the library staff know in advance when they wish to use the library. Disabled students who have limited hand use may be provided with a library aide, who could be either a volunteer, a work-study student, or a staff person familiar with the library.

For students in wheelchairs, library staff personnel may need to retrieve materials that are out of reach, pull drawers from the card catalogue when they are inaccessible, and design special routing when turnstiles at the main entrance prevent entrance to the library. (It would seem that with electronic surveillance available it should be possible to redesign library entrances to eliminate turnstiles.)

Disabled students could be encouraged to make greater use of the telephone by using it to renew books and ask about the availability of materials, and to arrange to have reserved items picked up or delivered by campus mail. Physically disabled students should be provided elevator keys if the library habitually cuts off service at certain times, thus making some floors inaccessible. It should be relatively easy to permit physically disabled students to take materials to restricted areas if such areas are easier to use for study. And when staff and/or catalogue is not located on each floor of the library, an accessible telephone intercom should be provided at a central location on each floor. This is also a good way to provide a system for seeking aid during emergencies. (A detailed account of the ways in which university librarians can aid blind students is found in Chapter 6 of this book, written by Hanan C. Selvin.)

Special Materials

In addition to the usual library materials that must be made available in some way, as we have seen, it would be helpful to the disabled student if the library staff could begin to acquire an understanding of the informational needs of the disabled in the area of activities of daily living. Also particularly important to the disabled college student will be information as to his or her legal rights as a disabled citizen, and information about the independent living possibilities that are developing around the country and that will make it possible for severely disabled adults to live with dignity and independence. Information about local community services, the services of the Office of Vocational Rehabilitation in particular, would also be of great importance (see Chapters 3 and 4).

Especially useful would be a file of travel guides offering information about adapted facilities, as well as Amtrak, airlines, and bus regulations (see Chapter 4). These would be of help to disabled students wishing to return home or travel independently on vacation. Recreational information about camping, skiing for the disabled, or other sports would also be welcome. Many schools now have wheelchair basketball teams and send handicapped students to participate in the national wheelchair sports events and the paralympics.

The library staff that becomes interested in the welfare of disabled students will wish to work closely with the handicapped students' service to make information available to the staff there. Utilization of the many reference sources outlined in this text will help make it possible to locate information more easily. An interesting reference is a booklet entitled *The Preparation of Orientation and Mobility Maps for the Visually and Physically Handicapped*, by F. Guthbert Salmon, Oklahoma State University, School of Architecture, Stillwater, Oklahoma, August 1977. It describes the production of a tactual map for the use of visually impaired students and an accessibility map for wheelchair students.

The library staff will find that by becoming involved it will be able to assist in myriad ways. For example, a file of maps of the campus, indicating accessible entrances to buildings, would be of great use.

The best way to become involved, of course, is to make use of the suggestions offered by the disabled-student organizations on campus. Appointing a disabled-student representative to a library staff committee charged with new programming for the disabled would bring concrete results.

CONCLUSION

The education of orthopedically disabled children has suffered from the lack of library service. The library program at Human Resources School was developed in the belief that a school library is indispensable to the total academic progress of its students and that one of the serious disadvantages of a home instructional program is the absence of professional reading guidance and the lack of diversified library materials in both print and nonprint format.

Public Law 94-142 directs that exceptional children be educated in the "least restrictive environment." For many children—severely physically disabled, profoundly deaf, deaf/blind, blind, or developmentally disabled, this will mean and should mean placement in one of the special educational facilities or special classes taught by people trained to handle youngsters with specific disabilities. It will be some time before schools of education are prepared to train all teachers adequately to understand the special problems of the severely physically disabled child.

This view is supported by Susan J. Spungin[38] in the December 1978 issue of the *Journal of Visual Impairment and Blindness*. She states that blind children have the right to remain with their families and in their communities during the course of their education and that one of the important immediate goals of special education is to give blind children adequate preparation for participation in the programs best suited to their individual needs. The phrases "least restrictive environment" and "appropriate educational program," also mentioned in PL 94-142, do not necessarily mean placement in a public school, because without adequate support services this type of program could be considered the *most* restrictive. Available services should not be considered on an either/or basis, and all programs must be viewed as feasible at various times in the child's development. It is to be hoped that the question of economics will not turn out to be the most important issue in the future placement of exceptional children. Unfortunately, early attempts at mainstreaming have shown this to be the case with some school districts.

There must be continued adequate training of teachers who specialize in teaching children with disabilities such as visual and hearing impairments and developmental problems and learning disabilities. Such specialists will be needed to help train general education teachers. Meanwhile, special school facilities continue to require more librarians, and schools that have special classes or that have mainstreamed disabled children will find the well-informed librarian a valuable member of the instructional team.

School librarians can play a constructive role in the integration of disabled children into the regular school program by influencing attitudes of staff and students, making structural changes in the library to accommodate the physically disabled, adding professional information to their collections, aiding staff and parents in obtaining specialized materials when needed, and providing a supportive library program to the disabled students themselves.

Accessible college and university libraries are of great importance to disabled students. College and university librarians can make adjustments that will make facilities, materials, and programs available to disabled students. An understanding of the special informational needs of disabled students will enable librarians to supplement their collections so as to be of help to students and the offices of handicapped students that serve them. Utilizing disabled students on library committees for program development will ensure that changes are made that will be practical and useful.

NOTES

1. National Advisory Committee on the Handicapped, *The Unfinished Revolution: Education for the Handicapped*, 1976 Annual Report, U.S. Department of Health, Education, and Welfare, Office of Education, Washington, D.C. (1976), p. 1.

2. Carrel J. Mass and Charles F. Williams, *The Assessment of College Experience of Severely Handicapped Individuals* (Gainsville, Fla.: University of Florida, 1962).

3. Ruth A. Velleman, "School Library Service for Physically Handicapped Children; An Account of the Library Program at the Human Resources School, Albertson, N.Y." (Master's thesis, Palmer Graduate Library School, C.W. Post College of Long Island University, Greenvale, N.Y., 1964), p. 46.

4. Henry Viscardi, Jr., *The School* (New York: Eriksson, 1964).

5. Ruth A. Velleman, "A Library for the Handicapped," *School Library Journal* 13, no. 1 (September 1966): 48–52.

6. _____, "Library Adaptations for the Handicapped," *School Library Journal* 21, no. 2 (October 1974): 85–88.

7. _____, "Serving Exceptional Children," *School Libraries* 20, no. 4 (Summer 1971): 27.

8. Ronald Friedman, Ph.D., "Learning Problems of Physically Disabled Children" (Speech delivered at the Human Resources School, Albertson, N.Y., and Palmer Graduate Library School, C.W. Post Center of Long Island University, Greenvale, N.Y., August 3, 1976).

9. Tomi Ungerer, *Moon Man* (New York: Harper & Row, 1967).

10. Science Research Associates, Occupational Exploration Kit and WORK (Widening Occupational Roles) Kit, Chicago, Illinois. Subscription basis, annually.

11. Judith Viorst, *The 10th Good Thing about Barney* (New York: Atheneum, 1971).

12. Carol Carrick, *The Accident* (New York: Seabury, 1976).

13. Kathryn Reggio, Ph.D., et al., *Individualized Health Incentive Program Modules for Physically Disabled Students for Grades Kindergarten through Twelve* (Albertson, N.Y.: Human Resources School, 1977). Individual titles: "Mental Health and Family Life Education," "Sociological Health Problems," "Environmental and Community Health," "Physical Health, Safety and Survival Education." (Currently under production for commercial sale; inquire Human Resources School, Albertson, N.Y.)

14. Karen H. Harris and Barbara H. Baskin, "The Exceptional Child: A Challenge for Librarians," *Louisiana Library Association Bulletin* 37, no. 1 (Spring 1974): 21.

15. Edith C. Kirk, "Designing Desirable Physical Conditions in Libraries for Visually Handicapped Children," in *The Special Child in the Library*, ed. by Barbara H. Baskin and Karen H. Harris (Chicago: American Library Association, 1976), p. 10.

16. Doris Batt, "The Hearing Impaired Child in the Library," in *The Special Child in the Library*, p. 14.

17. Harris and Baskin, "Exceptional Child," p. 22.

18. Eugene E. Bleck, M.D. and Donald A. Nagel, M.D., *Physically Handicapped Children: A Medical Atlas for Teachers* (New York: Grune & Stratton, 1975).

19. Marquis Academic Media, *Yearbook of Special Education*, 4th ed. (Chicago: Marquis Who's Who, Inc., 1979).

20. Lou Alonso, M.A., et al., *Mainstreaming Preschoolers: Children with Visual Handicaps; A Guide for Teachers, Parents, and Others Who Work with Visually Handicapped Preschoolers* (Belmont, Mass.: Contract Research Corp., 1978).

21. John F. Henne, "Serving Visually Handicapped Children," *School Library Journal* 25, no. 4 (December 1978): 36–37.

22. Jean D. Brown, "Storytelling and the Blind Child," in *The Special Child in the Library*, p. 109.

23. Mary Jane Metcalf, "Helping Hearing Impaired Students," *School Library Journal* 25, no. 5 (January 1979): 27–29.

24. Patrick Huston, "Storytelling," in *The Special Child in the Library*, p. 112.

25. Roger Kroth and Gweneth Blacklock Brown, "Welcome in the Parent," *School Media Quarterly* 6, no. 4 (Summer 1978): 248.

26. Elizabeth J. Webster, Ph.D., *Counseling with Parents of Handicapped Children: Guidelines for Improving Communication* (New York: Grune & Stratton, 1977).

27. Leo Buscaglia, Ph.D., ed., *The Disabled and Their Parents: A Counseling Challenge* (Thorofare, N.J.: Charles B. Slack, 1975).

28. Barbara H. Baskin and Karen H. Harris, *Notes from a Different Drummer: A Guide to Juvenile Fiction Portraying the Handicapped* (New York: R. R. Bowker, 1977).

29. Barbara H. Baskin and Karen H. Harris, "The Exceptional Child in the School Library: Response and Strategy" (Paper delivered at the Southwestern Library Association Biennial Conference, Galveston, Texas, October 25, 1974), p. 5.

30. Mass and Williams, *Assessment*.

31. Sharon Mistler, *Planning for Implementation of Section 504 at Colleges and Universities*, Regional Rehabilitation Research Institute on Attitudinal, Legal and Leisure Barriers, George Washington University, Washington, D.C. (March 1978), p. 2.

32. Elinor Gollay and Alwina Bennett, *The College Guide for Students with Disabilities: A Detailed Directory of Higher Education Services, Programs, and Facilities Accessible to Handicapped Students in the United States* (Cambridge, Mass.: Abt Publications; Boulder, Colo.: Westview Press, 1976), p. 1.

33. Timothy J. Nugent, "More than Ramps or Braille," *American Education* 14, no. 7 (August/September 1978): 11–18.

34. Pat Marx and Perry Hall, eds., *Proceedings of Disabled Students on American Campuses: Services and the State of the Art* (Conference held at Wright State University, Dayton, Ohio, August 21–25, 1977).

35. Ibid., p. 16.

36. *Libraries for College Students with Handicaps: A Directory of Academic Library Resources and Services in Ohio* (Columbus: The State Library of Ohio, 1976), p. iii.

37. Marx and Hall, *Proceedings*.

38. Susan J. Spungin, Ph.D., "Mainstreaming Visually Handicapped Children: Problems and Issues," *Journal of Visual Impairment and Blindness* (December 1978): 422–423.

14

A Core Special
Education Collection

A good reference collection in the field of special education would enable all school librarians to meet the information and curriculum needs of teachers and other school staff who will be dealing with disabled children in the mainstream. Parents of exceptional children will find a knowledgeable librarian to be a valuable resource person. Schools of education will be including information about the educational needs of exceptional children in their regular course work; consequently, special education collections will be needed in all colleges and universities that award a degree in education. And, finally, library schools will need to include service to the special needs child in all courses in library services to children.

The following bibliography is intended as a starter collection. Book reviews in special education journals, special bibliographies, and publishers' catalogues from those that specialize in rehabilitation and special education materials (such as Charles C Thomas in Springfield, Illinois) will help librarians to keep their collections current. Materials have been included here in the areas of the blind and visually impaired, deaf and hearing-impaired, orthopedically handicapped, and learning disabled. In addition, some of the items in Chapters 8 and 11 would be useful, depending on the special needs of the population to be served.

The areas covered in this special education collection include:

Directories, Catalogues, and Bibliographies

Special Education, General

Mainstreaming

Medical

Psychology

Parents

Death

Physical Education and Recreation

Deafness and Hearing Impairment

Blind, Deaf-Blind, and Visually Impaired

Periodicals

Newsletters

Sources and Publishers' Catalogues of Instructional Materials

Legislation and Financing

Audiovisual Materials

Starred (*) entries are suggested for building a core collection for public libraries in the field of special education (see Chapter 8 for other entries in the core public library collection).

DIRECTORIES, CATALOGUES, AND BIBLIOGRAPHIES

* Alexander Graham Bell Association for the Deaf, Inc. Books, special publications/ audiovisual materials, yearly catalogue.

American Association of Special Educators. *Directory for Special Children.* Richmond Hill, N.Y., 1975.

American Camping Association. *Directory of Camping for the Handicapped.* Martinsville, Ind.: Bradford Woods, n.d.

* American Foundation for the Blind. *Catalog of Publications.* AFB publishes the *Journal of Visual Impairment and Blindness*, as well as the *AFB Newsletter*, quarterly, free, print and braille editions. AFB Publications Series, which entitles subscriber to receive all AFB free publications and most priced publications at approximately half price. Also publishes *Washington Report*, bimonthly, free, print and braille editions.

———. *Aids and Appliances for the Blind and Visually Impaired.* Current edition. New York.

———. *Directory of Agencies Serving the Visually Handicapped in the U.S.*, 20th ed. New York, 1978. Services listed by state.

Association for Children with Learning Disabilities. *Directory of Educational Facilities for the Learning Disabled.* San Rafael, Calif.: Academic Therapy Publications, n.d.

———. *Directory of Summer Camps for Children with Learning Disabilities.* Pittsburgh, n.d.

Books for Visually Impaired Young Children: An Annotated Bibliography. Raleigh,

N.C.: North Carolina Department of Cultural Resources, Division of State Library, 1978. Compiled by Beverley Simmons, Institutional Consultant, Special Services Section, North Carolina State Library.

Council for Exceptional Children. *CEC Catalog.* Reston, Va.: Publications and nonprint media. Annual.

_____. *Directory of Federal Programs for the Handicapped.* Reston, Va.

* *Directory for Exceptional Children,* 8th ed. Boston: Porter Sargent, 1978. A listing of 3,600 special schools, private and public, day and residential. Separate sections for different disabilities, organized by state. Includes blind, deaf, retarded, emotionally disturbed, brain-damaged, and physically handicapped. Information regarding tuition, admission requirements, etc. Location maps, listings of associations, foundations, federal and state agency personnel. If only one reference book is purchased to assist library patrons seeking information about schools for children with special needs, this should be the book.

Directory of State Agencies for the Blind and *Directory of State Offices of Vocational Rehabilitation.* Washington, D.C.: Department of HEW, Rehabilitation Services Administration. Periodically updated, these directories are available free from the Administration Officer, Rehabilitation Services Administration, Room 3024, 330 C Street S.W., Washington, D.C. 20201. A valuable addition to reference rooms, they list names, addresses, and phone numbers of the personnel employed by the state offices of vocational rehabilitation and the divisions of rehabilitation for the visually impaired. Many disabled people are unaware of the law that entitles all blind and disabled persons to vocational counseling and/or financial government aid for study or work training.

Dronek, Margo. *Bibliography of Resources for Sex Education of Deaf-Blind.* Sacramento, Calif.: Southwestern Region Deaf-Blind Center, 1977.

Ellingson, Careth, and Cass, James. *Directory of Facilities for the Learning Disabled and Handicapped.* New York: Harper & Row, 1972. A directory of diagnostic facilities for children and adults, providing descriptions of remedial, therapeutic, and developmental programs. Costs (given for the 1969–1970 school year) will be higher now. Facilities are listed for the United States (by state), British Columbia, Manitoba, Ontario, and Prince Edward Island. Listings include university and hospital facilities as well as private clinics in areas such as remedial reading, speech, and hearing.

* Gallaudet College Bookstore. *A Catalog.* Washington, D.C. Annual.

Gollay, Elinor, and Bennett, Alwina. *The College Guide for Students with Disabilities.* Cambridge, Mass.: Abt Publications, 1976. Most recent survey of adapted college campuses. Architectural and special program adaptations.

Moore, Coralie, and Morton, K. *A Reader's Guide for Parents of Children with Mental, Physical or Emotional Disabilities.* Publication no. HSA 77-5290. Rockville, Md.: Department of HEW, PHS.

National Easter Seal Society for Crippled Children and Adults. *Easter Seal Directory of Resident Camps for Persons with Special Health Needs and Easter Seal Guide to Special Camping Programs.* Chicago.

Owens, Janette Alfsford, Redden, Martha Ross, and Brown, Janet Welsh. *Resource Directory of Handicapped Scientists.* Washington, D.C.: American Association for the Advancement of Science, 1978. Alphabetical listing of scientists, offering nature of disability, address, professional position, area of expertise. Includes physical and social scientists. Indexes offer listings by disability, sex, professional subject area, geographical area of the country.

Perkins School for the Blind. *Annual Accessions of Print Materials Dealing with the Blind and the Deaf/Blind.* Watertown, Mass.: Samuel P. Hayes Research Library. A complete accession list is now published twice monthly, available for a small fee.

President's Committee on Employment of the Handicapped. *Getting through College with a Disability: A Summary of Services Available on 500 Campuses for Students with Handicapping Conditions.* Washington, D.C., 1977. This information has been based on the survey done for the Abt Directory, which offers a more complete directory of all colleges surveyed. Contains listing of general handbooks on college programs that might be useful. Appendixes list, by state, organizations of handicapped students and addresses of governor's committees on the handicapped.

U.S. Office of Education, Bureau of Education for the Handicapped. *Selected Career Education Programs for the Handicapped.* Washington, D.C., n.d.

SPECIAL EDUCATION, GENERAL

* Berger, Gilda. *Physical Disabilities.* New York: Franklin Watts, 1979. Small book offering simple definitions of physical disabilities. Deals with architectural barriers, negative attitudes. Bibliography. Appropriate for upper elementary through adult.

Berko, Frances, Berko, Martin J., and Thompson, Stephanie C. *Management of Brain Damaged Children.* Springfield, Ill.: Charles C. Thomas, 1970. For parents and teachers of brain-damaged children. Descriptions of behavioral difficulties and learning disabilities, related to management and training programs and procedures both at home and at school.

Bernstein, Bebe. *Everyday Problems and the Child with Learning Difficulties.* New York: John Day, 1967. Daily living experiences in the home, school, or community; 38 different life problems delineated and a method presented for solving each one.

Best, Gary A. *Individuals with Physical Disabilities: An Introduction for Educators.* St. Louis: Mosby, 1978. Definitions of physical disabilities, suggestions for curriculum modifications, postschool and adult alternatives. Sensitive treatment of sexuality of the disabled adolescent.

Bigge, June L., and O'Donnell, Patrick A. *Teaching Individuals with Physical and Multiple Disabilities.* Columbus, Ohio: Charles E. Merrill, 1976. For teachers of children with physical and mental handicaps. Overview of handicaps plus task analyses. For the profoundly disabled, management and life experience techniques. Good chapters on communication aids, as well as aids to independent living.

Bortner, Morton. *Evaluation and Education of Children with Brain Damage.* American Lecture Series. Springfield, Ill.: Charles C. Thomas, 1968. Contributors include Herbert Birch, Marianne Frostig, Newell C. Kephart, Bluma Weiner, and other well-known experts in the field. Explains what different professions look for in evaluating brain-damaged children and brings together some representative strategies for their education.

* Cruickshank, William M. *Learning Disabilities in Home, School, and Community.* Syracuse, N.Y.: Syracuse University Press, 1977. An update of the classic *Brain Injured Child in Home, School and Community.*

* ———, and Johnson, G. O., eds. *Education of Exceptional Children and Youth,* 3rd ed. Englewood Cliffs, N.J.: Prentice-Hall, 1975. Classic text; a group of well-known educators present techniques in concepts and methods in teaching exceptional children.

Dibner, Susan S., and Dibner, Andrew S. *Integration or Segregation for the Physically Handicapped Child?* Springfield, Ill.: Charles C. Thomas, 1973. This book deals with the pros and cons of mainstreaming; however, the population studied was a camp rather than a school situation.

Dunn, Lloyd M., ed. *Exceptional Children in the Schools: Special Education in Transition.* New York: Holt, Rinehart and Winston, 1973. An updating of a classic text, which takes into account the new methods in special education, focusing upon individual needs and normalization of education for special students with the help of trained consultants available to the regular classroom teacher.

Fass, Larry A. *Learning Disabilities: A Book of Readings.* Springfield, Ill.: Charles C. Thomas, 1972. Readings selected to provide an overview of educational services for children with learning disabilities. There are specific sections on definitions, characteristics, and identifications, perceptual-motor, visual perceptional, and auditory-perceptual, and communication disorders, programming in basic skill areas, and parent counseling.

Frostig, Marianne, and Maslow, Phyllis. *Learning Problems in the Classroom: Prevention and Remediation.* New York: Grune and Stratton, 1973. Research in learning theory, behavior modification, cognitive development concept, other methods of instruction.

Gardner, William I. *Children with Learning and Behavior Problems: A Behavior Management Approach.* Boston: Allyn & Bacon, 1973. For management in the classroom of all children with emotional learning problems, brain injury, or social maladjustment.

Goodman, Libby, and Mann, Lester. *Learning Disabilities in the Secondary School, Issues and Practices.* New York: Grune and Stratton, 1976. Overview of secondary-level learning disabilities, programs, and procedures.

* Gordon, Sol. *Living Fully: A Guide for Young People with a Handicap, Their Parents, Their Teachers and Professionals.* New York: John Day, 1975. For and about young people with handicaps—blind, deaf, epileptic, or emotionally disturbed, neurologically handicapped, learning disabled. To serve as a guide toward the achievement of full adult lives.

Hallahan, Daniel P., and Cruickshank, William M. *Psycho-Educational Foundation of Learning Disabilities.* Englewood Cliffs, N.J.: Prentice-Hall, 1973. A comprehensive study of the problems that face teachers and researchers today in the field of learning disabilities.

Hammill, Donald D., and Bartal, Nettie R. *Teaching Children with Learning and Behavior Problems.* Boston: Allyn & Bacon, 1975. Diagnostic teaching techniques and remedial methods and materials for children with special learning problems.

Haring, Norris G., et al. *Teaching the Learning Disabled Child*. Englewood Cliffs, N.J.: Prentice-Hall, 1977. Prentice-Hall Series in Special Education, William M. Cruickshank, series editor. New approaches to teaching children with learning disabilities. A variety of examples of teaching methods such as DISTAR.

Harris, Mary B. *Classroom Uses of Behavior Modification*. Columbus, Ohio: Charles E. Merrill, 1972. Various methods of behavior modification. Token reinforcement programs.

Haskell, Simon H., Barrett, Elizabeth K., and Taylor, Helen. *The Education of Motor and Neurologically Handicapped Children*. New York: Wiley, 1977. Physiological, psychological, and pedagogical issues in the development of children with neurological and motor disabilities. Common handicapping conditions and recent research related to areas of learning. Education in the United States is contrasted with methods in other countries.

Johnson, Doris J., and Myklebust, Helmer R. *Learning Disabilities, Education Principles and Practices*. New York: Grune and Stratton, 1967. Classic text; point of reference for all new material in this field.

Johnson, Orville G. *Education for the Slow Learners*. Englewood Cliffs, N.J.: Prentice-Hall, 1963. Curriculum and school organization necessary to provide adequate programs for the slow learner.

Jones, Reginald L. *New Directions in Special Education*. Boston: Allyn & Bacon, 1970. Programmed instruction, diagnosis and testing, behavior modification, and innovations in curriculum and teaching methods in special education.

Karlin, Muriel Schoenbrun, and Berger, Regina. *Successful Methods for Teaching the Slow Learner*. West Nyack, N.Y.: Parker, Inc. 1969. Handbook of techniques for use with slow learners in the classroom.

Kephart, Newell C. *The Slow Learner in the Classroom*, 2nd ed. Columbus, Ohio: Charles E. Merrill, 1971. Systematic approach to the identification of slow learner behavior and learning problems. Methods of Frostig, Cruickshank, and behavior modification theories described and classroom techniques offered.

* Kirk, Samual A. *Educating Exceptional Children*, 2nd ed. Boston: Houghton Mifflin, 1972. A basic text dealing with the psychology and education of exceptional children.

Love, Harold D. *Educating Exceptional Children in Regular Classrooms*. Springfield, Ill.: Charles C. Thomas, 1972. An examination of practices in the field of special education, with a focus on those children who can be mainstreamed.

_____. *Teaching Physically Handicapped Children: Methods and Materials*. Springfield, Ill.: Charles C. Thomas, 1978. Educators who will be working with physically handicapped children in the regular classroom are addressed in this book, which may also be of interest to anyone involved with these children. A resource book on methods and materials. Background on disabilities, educational implications.

Markoff, Annabelle M. *Teaching Low-Achieving Children Reading, Spelling, and Handwriting: Developing Perceptual Skills with the Graphic Symbols of Language*. Springfield, Ill.: Charles C. Thomas, 1976. For all involved with low-achieving children. Provides a logical explanation of why the symbols of language are crucial in any program to develop perceptual skills.

Meyers, Patricia, and Hammill, Donald D. *Methods for Learning Disorders.* New York: Wiley, 1969. Descriptions of learning disorders in children, methods of teaching, glossary of terms.

* Mullins, June B. *A Teacher's Guide to Management of Physically Handicapped Students.* Springfield, Ill.: Charles C. Thomas, 1979. For teachers in both mainstream and special education situations.

Reger, Roger. *Preschool Programming of Children with Disabilities.* Springfield, Ill.: Charles C. Thomas, 1970. Concepts for programming, identification of preschool children with potential learning problems, language development of the preschool child, perceptual-motor development, children with visual disabilities, children with hearing disabilities, and a parent's view of preschool programs. Materials and their sources.

Sabatine, David A., and Miller, Ted L. *Describing Learner Characteristics of Handicapped Children and Youth.* New York: Grune and Stratton, 1978. Introductory text in assessment of preservice special education teachers and for in-service teachers seeking training in special education. Diagnostic resource book and reference guide.

Safford, Philip L., and Arbitman, Dena C. *Developmental Intervention with Young Physically Handicapped Children.* Springfield, Ill.: Charles C. Thomas, 1975. Nature of handicapping conditions in young children, interrelations of cognitive, motor, and psychosocial development in early childhood, integration of therapy and teaching goals and techniques. Development and use of curriculum guides inspired by theories of Piaget. Involvement of parents in educational process.

Schattner, Regina. *An Early Childhood Curriculum for Multiply Handicapped Children.* Foreword by Ignacy Goldberg. New York: John Day, 1971. Identification of multiply handicapped children, language development, curriculum of daily activities, two separate chapters on the blind and partially sighted child.

Smith, Sally L. *No Easy Answers: The Learning Disabled Child.* Rockville, Md.: Department of HEW, n.d. Provides answers to parents and teachers as to why children have difficulty in learning, and how parents and teachers can help the child overcome difficulties or acquire competence to manage them.

Stephens, Thomas M. *Directive Teaching of Children with Learning and Behavioral Handicaps.* Columbus, Ohio: Charles E. Merrill, 1970. For teachers and other school personnel concerned with the education and behavioral management of children with learning handicaps.

Tjossem, Theodore D., ed. *Intervention Strategies for High Risk Infants and Young Children.* NICHD Mental Retardation Research Centers Series. Baltimore: University Park Press, 1976. Collection of papers based on a conference held in 1974. Intervention programs that ensure optimum development of infants and young children with aberrant development. New developments in research, service, and training. Cognitive and language aspects of development emphasized.

Wolf, James M., and Anderson, Robert M., eds. *The Multiply Handicapped Child.* Springfield, Ill.: Charles C. Thomas, 1973. A comprehensive treatment to meet the needs of professionals working with children with more than one disabling condition.

* *Yearbook of Special Education 1978-1979*, 4th ed. Chicago: Marquis Academic Media, Marquis Who's Who. Contains an analysis of PL 94-142, a planning guide

for the development and implementation of services for handicapped children in mainstreaming context. Fuller definitions of physical disabilities than usually contained in special education texts. Much useful information.

Young, Milton A. *Teaching Children with Special Learning Needs: A Problem Solving Approach.* New York: John Day, 1967. Children with learning difficulties are not labeled in this book, which deals with using a diagnostic approach for individualized instruction according to each child's needs.

MAINSTREAMING

Alonse, Lou, et al. *Mainstreaming Preschoolers: Children with Visual Handicaps: A Guide for Teachers, Parents, and Others Who Work with Visually Handicapped Preschoolers.* Publication no. (OHDS) 78-31112. CRC Education and Human Development, Inc., a subsidiary of Contract Research Corp. for Project Head Start, Department of HEW, Office of Human Development Services, Administration for Children, Youth and Families, Head Start Bureau, 1978. Congress mandates that no less than 10 percent of funding for Project Head Start be available for Handicapped children. These booklets are valuable, however, not only for Head Start but for all people working with disabled preschoolers. Programs, activities, definitions of visual disabilities, chart of normal development, sources for additional information, valuable bibliography.

Anderson, Elizabeth M. *The Disabled Schoolchild: A Study of Integration in Primary Schools.* London: Methuen, 1973. An early study of how well disabled children perform in regular school programs. Need for special arrangements including modifications of buildings and equipment, provision of transportation, therapy, and support services.

Birch, Jack W. *Hearing Impaired Children in Mainstream.* Washington, D.C.: Gallaudet College, 1976. For teachers who have not specialized in education for the hearing-impaired.

Braun, Samuel J., and Lasher, Miriam G. *Are You Ready to Mainstream? Helping Preschoolers with Learning and Behavior Problems.* Columbus, Ohio: Charles E. Merrill, 1978. Ways in which a program can meet the needs of the young handicapped child. Attitudes, parent-teacher interaction, crises affecting children's behavior. Bibliographies, list of children's books that address crisis areas.

Brill, Richard. *Mainstreaming the Prelingually Deaf Child.* Washington, D.C.: Gallaudet College, n.d. A study of the status of prelingually deaf children in various patterns of mainstreamed education for hearing-impaired children.

Chaiken, William, and Happer, Mary Joyce. *Mainstreaming the Learning Disabled Adolescent.* Springfield, Ill.: Charles C. Thomas, 1979. A guide for staff for development of programs.

Corn, Anne Lesley, and Martinez, Iris. *When You Have a Visually Handicapped Child in Your Classroom: Suggestions for Teachers.* New York: American Foundation for the Blind, 1977. Concise but well done. Definitions, bibliography, listing of organizations.

Fairfax County Public Schools, Special Education Division, Department of Instructional Services. *Integrating the Visually Impaired Student into the Classroom.* Fairfax, Va.: Fairfax County Public Schools, n.d. Valuable information for the classroom teacher. Definitions of visual impairments, suggestions for handling, attitudes, activity suggestions, adaptations, materials, bibliographies.

Hayden, Alice H., et al. *Mainstreaming Preschoolers: Children with Learning Disabilities.* Publication no. (OHDS) 78-31117. CRC Education and Human Development, Inc., a subsidiary of Contract Research Corp. for Project Head Start, Department of HEW, Office of Human Development Services, Administration for Children, Youth and Families, Head Start Bureau, 1978. Written for teachers, parents, diagnosticians, and therapists who work directly with learning disabled preschoolers. Tries to answer questions about mainstreaming, define learning disabilities, offer programs and activities, sources for help. Chart of normal development particularly helpful.

Kieran Stokes, Shari, et al. *Mainstreaming Preschoolers: Children with Orthopedic Handicaps: A Guide for Teachers, Parents, and Others Who Work with Orthopedically Handicapped Preschoolers.* Publication no. (OHDS) 78-311114. CRC Education and Human Development, Inc., a subsidiary of Contract Research Corp. for Project Head Start, Department of HEW, Office of Human Development Services, Administration for Children, Youth and Families, Head Start Bureau, 1978. Definitions of disabilities and ways in which disabilities affect learning, chart of normal development, source directory, bibliography, glossary of terms.

Lasher, Miriam G., et al. *Mainstreaming Preschoolers: Children with Emotional Disturbance: A Guide for Teachers, Parents, and Others Who Work with Emotionally Disturbed Preschoolers.* Publication no. 78-31115. CRC Education and Human Development, Inc., a subsidiary of Contract Research Corp. for Project Head Start, Department of HEW, Office of Human Development Services, Administration for Children, Youth and Families, Head Start Bureau, 1978. How emotional disturbance affects learning in three- to five-year-olds. Mainstreaming, where to find help, chart of normal development, bibliography.

Liebergott, Jacqueline, et al. *Mainstreaming Preschoolers: Children with Speec and Language Impairments: A Guide for Teachers, Parents, and Others Who Woi with Speech and Language Impaired Preschoolers.* Publication no. (OHDS) 78-31113. CRC Education and Human Development, Inc., a subsidiary of Contract Research Corp. for Project Head Start, Department of HEW, Office of Human Development Services, Administration for Children, Youth and Families, Head Start Bureau, 1978. How communication disorders affect three- to five-year-old children. Activities, resources, bibliography, chart of normal development.

Northcott, Winifred H., ed. *The Hearing Impaired Child in a Regular Classroom: Preschool, Elementary and Secondary Years.* Washington, D.C.: Alexander Graham Bell Assn., 1973. A practical handbook for teachers, administrators, resource specialists, and parents. Bibliography, glossary of terms.

Paul, James L., Turnbull, Ann P., and Cruickshank, William. *Mainstreaming: A Practical Guide.* Syracuse, N.Y.: Syracuse University Press, 1977. The goal here is to advocate getting professionals and parents and politicians together in a "mainstreaming" effort to program for each child the best possible environment. A small book dealing with need for attitude changes through preservice and in-service courses, community cooperation, role of resource teachers, counselors, etc.

Siegel, Ernest. *Special Education in the Regular Classroom*. New York: John Day, 1969. Methods of teaching marginally disabled children with brain damage or other developmental disabilities, or emotional problems. Specific teaching techniques for solving the basic problems of the mildly handicapped child.

MEDICAL

* Apgar, Virginia, and Beck, Joan. *Is My Baby All Right? A Guide to Birth Defects*. New York: Trident, 1972. An accurate and well-written account in popular style of the birth defects that can afflict infants and how parents should cope with them. The chapter on genetic counseling will be helpful to young married couples who fear that their family history would indicate the birth of a disabled child. Apgar created the Apgar score for evaluating the health of newborn babies. Beck, a journalist with the *Chicago Tribune*, is the author of the syndicated column "You and Your Child."

Baird, Henry W. *The Child with Convulsions*. New York: Grune and Stratton, 1972. A pediatric neurologist answers questions from parents, teachers, counselors, and medical personnel.

Berkowitz, Samuel. *Cleft Palate. The Road to Normalcy for the Cleft Lip and Palate Child*. Evansville, Ind.: Mead Johnson Laboratories, 1971.

_____. *Cleft Palate. Steps in Habilitation for the Cleft Lip and Palate Child*. Evansville, Ind.: Mead Johnson Laboratories, 1971.

* Biermann, June, and Toohey, Barbara. *The Diabetes Question and Answer Book*. Los Angeles: Sherbourne Press, 1974. For the diabetic, a book of information and complete care, including menus.

* Bleck, Eugene, and Nagel, Donald A., eds. *Physically Handicapped Children: A Medical Atlas for Teachers*. New York: Grune and Stratton, 1975. A much needed handbook of medical information for teachers of physically handicapped children. Fundamental medical facts presented clearly and simply, accompanied by practical suggestions for classroom handling.

Bunch, Milton, et al. *Modern Management of Myelomeningocele*. St. Louis, Mo.: Warren H. Green, 1972. Definition of the disease of spina bifida, providing information for all who treat and work with the myelomeningocele child. Provides an understanding of the total treatment problem.

Cerami, Anthony, and Washington, Elsie. *Sickle Cell Anemia*. New York: Joseph Okpaku, 1974. Medical and legal information on this hereditary blood disease, case studies, psychosocial aspects.

Feeding Children with Cleft Lip and Palate. Olympia, Wash.: Division of Health Services, Washington State Department of Health, 1966.

Fleming, Juanita W. *Care and Management of Exceptional Children*. New York: Appleton-Century-Crofts, 1973. A guide for nurses to help them understand exceptional children in terms of their behavior and to help parents with management problems. Covers all types of disabilities. Of necessity, however, this coverage is somewhat superficial.

* Freeman, Stephen W. *The Epileptic in Home, School and Society: Coping with the Invisible Handicap*. Springfield, Ill.: Charles C. Thomas, 1979. Dealing with the educational and psychological aspects of epilepsy.

Gardner, Richard A. *MBD: The Family Book about Minimal Brain Dysfunction.* New York: Jason Aronson, 1973. In two parts, the first for parents, the second for children. The first part describes the physical and psychological aspects of the disorder. The second part is designed to be read by children, preferably along with a parent.

Goldin, George J., et al. *Rehabilitation of the Young Epileptic: Dimensions and Dynamics.* Northeastern University Studies in Rehabilitation no. 12. Lexington, Mass.: D. C. Heath, 1971. Complete study of research findings on rehabilitation of epileptic adolescents.

* Graham, Malcolm D. *Cleft Palate: Middle Ear Disease and Hearing Loss.* Springfield, Ill.: Charles C. Thomas, 1978. A full medical account of this disability. Useful to all those involved in the care of the cleft palate individual.

Jones, Peter. *Living with Haemophilia.* Philadelphia: Davis, 1974. Information for hemophiliacs and their families in understanding language (originally a British publication).

Linde, Shirley M. *Sickle Cell: A Complete Guide to Prevention and Treatment.* New York: Pavilion, 1972. Appendixes include addresses of screening clinics, international directory of genetic counseling services, voluntary health organizations, sources of information.

McKusick, Victor A., and Claiborne, Robert. *Medical Genetics.* New York: HP, 1973. Informative but highly technical, medical information on genetics. For medical departments dealing with congenitally disabled children.

Morrison, Delmont, Pothier, Patricia C., and Horr, Katy. *Sensory-Motor Dysfunction and Therapy in Infancy and Early Childhood.* Springfield, Ill.: Charles C. Thomas, 1978. Theory of and research into sensory-motor therapy. Relationship between sensory-motor and emotional development.

Nakos, Eva, and Taylor, Susan. *Early Development of the Child with Myelomeningocele: A Parents' Guide.* Cincinnati, Ohio: Children's Hospital Medical Center, 1977. Care and equipment at home for the child with spina bifida. Information as to sources of equipment and sources of information. Extremely useful.

Peterson, Raymond M., and Cleveland, James O. *Medical Problems in the Classroom: An Educator's Guide.* Springfield, Ill.: Charles C. Thomas, 1975. A book on medical problems that will be encountered in the classroom more often than previously because of PL 94-142. More medically oriented than Bleck.

* Ranch, Jean, and McWeeney, Mae. *Managing Your Diabetes.* Minneapolis: Sister Kenny Institute-Abbot-Northwestern Hospital, 1978. A patient education manual on diabetes, excellent supplement to instructions of doctor or nurse.

* Rosenstein, Solomon N. *Dentistry in Cerebral Palsy and Related Handicapping Conditions.* Springfield, Ill.: Charles C. Thomas, 1975. All aspects of dentistry for patients with cerebral palsy. The role of the dental practitioner in the team approach to total treatment for cerebral palsied individuals.

Snyder, Gilbert B., Berkowitz, Samuel, Bzoch, Kenneth R., and Stool, Sylvan. *Your Cleft Lip and Palate Child: A Basic Guide for Parents.* Evansville, Ind.: Mead Johnson Laboratories, n.d. Sponsored by the Florida Cleft Palate Association and Mead

Johnson Laboratories, and available from them. Definitions, care, dental aspects, speech, surgical procedures.

Vogel, James M. *How to Live with Hemophilia.* New York: Interbook, n.d. All about hemophilia. The appendix is a national directory of hemophilia centers.

Wender, Paul H. *Minimal Brain Dysfunction in Children.* Series on Psychological Disorders, ed. Irving B. Weiner. New York: Wiley-Interscience, 1971. Clinical and theoretical aspects. Large amount of descriptive data to make diagnosis more accurate. A good deal of management information.

* Weyman, Joan. *The Dental Care of Handicapped Children.* Baltimore: Williams & Wilkins, 1971. Information needed by dental practitioners to provide dental treatment for children with various types of handicaps.

PSYCHOLOGY

Buscaglia, Lee. *The Disabled and Their Parents: A Counseling Challenge.* Thorofare, N.J.: Charles B. Slack, 1975. A book for counselors to help them handle the special problems of families with disabled children.

* Cruickshank, William, ed. *Psychology of Exceptional Children and Youth.* Englewood Cliffs, N.J.: Prentice-Hall, 1971. Third edition of a classic dealing with the psychological problems of children with impaired vision, speech defects, crippling conditions, brain damage, auditory impairments, and other handicapping conditions.

DiLeo, Joseph H. *Young Children and Their Drawings.* New York: Brummer Mazel, 1970. Drawings of the normal child, and drawings used as diagnostic aids for the disabled child with diverse disorders.

Garrison, Karl C., and Dewey, G. Force, Jr. *The Psychology of Exceptional Children,* 4th ed. New York: Ronald Press, 1965. A classic text.

Geist, Harold. *A Child Goes to the Hospital: The Psychological Aspects of a Child Going to the Hospital.* Springfield, Ill.: Charles C. Thomas, 1965. Suggestions to parents as to what to tell or not to tell children going to the hospital, especially for surgery. Relationship of nurse to parent. Advice to physicians. How to handle terminal patient.

Hofmann, Adele D., Becker, R. D., and Gabriel, H. Paul. *The Hospitalized Adolescent: Guide to Managing the Ill and Injured Youth.* Foreword by Anna Freud. New York: Free Press, 1976. Provides insights into the special problems of the adolescent, case histories, roles of all professionals involved.

* Splaver, Sarah. *Your Handicap, Don't Let It Handicap You.* New York: Messner, 1967. A book for the young adult disabled person.

Vernon, David, Foley, Jeanne M., Sipowicz, Raymond R., and Schulman, Jerome L. *The Psychological Responses of Children to Hospitalization and Illness.* Springfield, Ill.: Charles C. Thomas, 1965. A comprehensive critical review of the literature. Includes published and unpublished studies.

Waldorn, Hilda K. *Rehabilitation of the Physically Handicapped Adolescent.* New York: John Day, 1973. Information for the professional dealing with the disabled adolescent. For all nonmedical personnel who counsel the physically handicapped adolescent. Deals with sickle cell anemia, hemophilia, epilepsy, diabetes, allergies, and brain injury.

Webster, Elizabeth J. *Professional Approaches with Parents of Handicapped Children.* Springfield, Ill.: Charles C. Thomas, 1976. For use in parent counseling. A collection of articles to help professionals improve their interaction with parents of handicapped children.

* Wright, Beatrice A. *Physical Disability—A Psychological Approach.* New York: Harper & Row, 1960. A basic text that is still in use and valid. Nothing else comparable is available.

PARENTS

The Art and Science of Parenting the Disabled Child. Symposium Proceedings, November 20–21, 1976, San Francisco. Chicago: National Easter Seal Society for Crippled Children and Adults.

* Ayrault, Evelyn West. *Helping the Handicapped Teenager Mature.* New York: Association Press, 1971. A very informative book for parents and their disabled teenagers. Deals with all of the physical, psychological, social, and sexual problems of growing up, including problems of education, recreation, and career fulfillment. Appendixes give directories of agencies providing services to the disabled, listing of special camps, and adapted college facilities.

Barsch, Ray H. *The Parent of the Handicapped Child: The Study of Childrearing Practices.* American Lecture Series, ed. Morris Val Jones. Springfield, Ill.: Charles C. Thomas, 1968. Answers to questionnaires by parents of disabled children. Much valuable information, although dated by use of such terms as "mongoloid" for "Down's syndrome children."

Educators Publishing Services, Inc. *The Rights of Parents and the Responsibilities of Schools.* Cambridge, Mass., n.d. Contains the full text of PL 94-142, with interpretive commentary.

* Finnie, Nancie R. *FCSP, Handling the Young Cerebral Palsied Child at Home.* New York: Dutton, 1975.

Gardner, Richard A. *MBD: The Family Book about Minimal Brain Dysfunction.* Part 1. For Parents; Part 2. For Boys and Girls. New York: Jason Aronson, 1973. A novel book written for both parents and children. Will serve to open much needed discussion between parents and children. There is very little written on a level for children to read about their own disabilities.

Haller, J. Alex, ed., Talbert, James L., and Dombro, Robert H., assoc. eds. *The Hospitalized Child and His Family.* Illustrated by Aaron Sopher. Baltimore: Johns Hopkins University Press, 1967. Discussions of the effects of hospitalization on the child, preparing the child for an operation, educational needs of the hospitalized child, the mother living in with the hospitalized child, the child and the family at home after the operation. For doctors, nurses, and paramedical personnel who must care for the disabled child and deal with the family.

* Heisler, Verda. *A Handicapped Child in the Family: A Guide for Parents.* New York: Grune and Stratton, 1972. The book points out ways in which parents can

discover their psychological and emotional attitudes toward their child and his disability in order to develop the inner resources necessary to meet the special demands in their lives.

Hofmann, Ruth B. *How to Build Special Furniture and Equipment for Handicapped Children.* Springfield, Ill.: Charles C. Thomas, 1970. Functional furniture for handicapped children. Includes simple blueprints for parents who might have a need to build for a handicapped child.

Hotte, Eleanor Boettke. *Self-Help Clothing for Children Who Have Physical Disabilities,* rev. ed. Chicago: National Easter Seal Society for Crippled Children and Adults, March 1979. A revised edition of the booklet produced in 1962, reflecting current clothing picture of what is available.

Katz, Alfred H. *Parents of the Handicapped.* Springfield, Ill.: Charles C. Thomas, 1961. History of the participation of parents in groups. Origin and development of four important parent organizations concerned with cerebral palsy, muscular dystrophy, and retarded and emotionally disturbed children.

Kvaraceus, William C., and Hayes, E. Nelson, eds. *If Your Child Is Handicapped.* Boston: Porter Sargent, 1969. The highly personal stories of 46 families who tell of their adjustment to the limitations of a handicapped child.

Love, Harold D. *Parental Attitudes toward Exceptional Children.* Springfield, Ill.: Charles C. Thomas, 1970. An analysis of parental attitudes. Will assist professionals who counsel parents of exceptional children as well as parents themselves to help understand and accept their exceptional children.

McCollum, Audrey T. *Coping with Prolonged Health Impairment in Your Child.* Boston: Little, Brown, 1975. Growth and changing needs of children who also have long-term disabilities, discussed by a professional counselor. Good for parents and also for professionals who come in contact with the child.

* Osman, Betty B. *Learning Disabilities: A Family Affair.* New York: Random House, 1979. For parents of children with learning disabilities. A timely book by a specialist in the field. Clearly written. Appendixes list special tests and what parents should know about them, how they should handle IEP meetings, facts about income tax deductions for handicapped children, and addresses of organizations. Bibliography.

* Spock, Benjamin, and Lerrigo, Marion O. *Caring for Your Disabled Child.* New York: Macmillan, 1965. The well-known Spock, in collaboration with Lerrigo, noted health education authority, offers a comprehensive guide on the psychological and physical impact of disability on the child and his family, medical treatment, education and vocational preparation, play and recreation. Sexual and social adjustment and equipment and appliances are also covered.

* Weiner, Florence. *Help for the Handicapped Child.* New York: McGraw-Hill, 1973. In addition to defining and describing a number of major illnesses and handicapped conditions, this practical book for parents serves as an information directory for services available from specialists; community health centers; hospitals; state, federal, and private institutions; and voluntary health agencies.

Wentworth, Elise H. *Listen to Your Heart: A Message to Parents of Handicapped Children.* Boston: Houghton Mifflin, 1974. Written by the mother of a disabled child who is also a therapist and counselor. Complete guide for parents, dealing with problems with siblings, between husbands and wives, etc. Listing of books, agencies, government publications.

DEATH

Anthony, James E., and Koupernik, Cyrille. *The Child in His Family: The Impact of Disease and Death*. New York: Wiley, 1973.

Bernstein, Joanne E. *Loss and How to Cope with It*. New York: Seabury Press, 1977.

Easson, William M. *The Dying Child: The Management of the Child or Adolescent Who Is Dying*. Springfield, Ill.: Charles C. Thomas, 1970. For anyone who must deal with the child or adolescent who is dying, problems of the family, the treatment staff, emotional involvements.

Grollman, Earl A., ed. *Explaining Death to Children*. Introduction by Louise Bates Ames. Boston: Beacon Press, 1968. Collection of articles on philosophical and religious concepts of death.

Wolf, Anna M. *Helping Your Child to Understand Death*. New York: Child Study Press, 1973.

PHYSICAL EDUCATION AND RECREATION

* Adams, Ronald C., Daniel, Alfred N., and Rullman, Lee. *Games, Sports and Exercises for the Physically Handicapped*, 2nd ed. Philadelphia: Lea & Febiger, 1975. One of the best basic texts in physical education for handicapped children. The book emphasizes the need for gross motor activities in everyday life. General characteristics and medical problems are emphasized. The authors urge absorption into regular class programs and suggest special adaptations for programs and equipment.

Alkema, Chester J. *Art for the Exceptional*. Boulder, Colo.: Pruett, 1971. A book for art teachers of exceptional children. Many special ideas and techniques offered for children with all types of disabilities.

American Alliance for Health, Physical Education, and Recreation. *Making Physical Education and Recreation Facilities Accessible to All: Planning, Designing, Adapting*. Washington, D.C.: Information and Research Utilization Center in Physical Education and Recreation for the Handicapped, 1972. Architectural adaptations for physical education facilities, as well as playgrounds, swimming pools, outdoor recreation areas, bibliography, laws pertaining to accessibility, listing of journals.

_____. *Physical Education and Recreation for Impaired, Disabled and Handicapped Individuals . . . Past, Present, and Future*. Washington, D.C., 1972. A publication based upon the final report of the Information and Research Utilization Center in Physical Education and Recreation for the Handicapped. Project was completed in 1972. Research information on physical education and recreation for all groups of disabled people. Includes creative arts, camping, and park needs.

_____. *Physical Education and Recreation for the Visually Handicapped*. Washington, D.C., 1973.

* American National Red Cross. *Adapted Aquatics: Swimming for Persons with Physical or Mental Impairments*. Garden City, N.Y.: Doubleday, 1977.

Arnheim, Daniel D., Auxter, David, and Crowe, Walter C. *Principles and Methods of Adapted Physical Education.* St. Louis: Mosby, 1969. Nature of physical and mental disability, development of programs in adapted physical education. For elementary and secondary school physical educators and for college classes offering courses in adapted and corrective physical education. Exercise-oriented.

Association for Children with Learning Disabilities. *A Directory of Summer Camps for Children with Learning Disabilities.* Pittsburgh, 1974.

Barnett, Marian Weller. *Handicapped Girls and Girl Scouting: A Guide for Leaders.* Catalog no. 19-171. New York: Girl Scouts of the U.S.A., 1968.

Bauer, Joseph J. *Riding for Rehabilitation: A Guide for Handicapped Riders and Their Instructors.* Toronto: Canadian Stage and Arts Publications, 1972.

Boy Scouts of America. *Scouting for the Deaf.* North Brunswick, N.J., 1973.

_____. *Scouting for the Physically Handicapped.* North Brunswick, N.J., 1971.

_____. *Scouting for the Visually Handicapped.* North Brunswick, N.J., 1968.

Cordellos, Harry. *Aquatic Recreation for the Blind.* Washington, D.C.: American Association for Health, Physical Education, and Recreation, 1976. Firsthand account of unique problems facing visually impaired persons in aquatic activities. Diving, survival swimming, lifesaving, small craft safety, water skiing, and scuba diving. Emphasis on safety first.

Daniels, Arthur S., and Davies, Evelyn A. *Adapted Physical Education,* 3rd ed. New York: Harper & Row, 1975.

Dibner, Susan Schmidt, and Dibner, Andrew S. *Integration or Segregation for the Physically Handicapped Child?* Springfield, Ill.: Charles C. Thomas, 1973. Integrated vs. segregated camping for disabled children. Results of both types of programs, results of interviews with campers.

Far West Laboratory for Educational Research and Development. *The Parent/Child Toy-Lending Library.* Stock no. 1780-0093. Berkeley, Calif.: Information/Utilization Division. Available from Superintendent of Documents.

Geddes, Dolores. *Physical Activities for Individuals with Handicapping Conditions.* St. Louis: Mosby, 1974. Recreational activities. Includes developmental sequences of activities.

Gordon, Ronnie. *The Design of a Pre-School Therapeutic Playground: An Outdoor "Learning Laboratory."* Rehabilitation Monograph 47. New York: Institute of Rehabilitation Medicine, New York University Medical Center, 1972.

Information and Research Utilization Center in Physical Education and Recreation for the Handicapped. *Integrating Persons with Handicapping Conditions into Regular Physical Education and Recreation Programs.* Washington, D.C.: American Alliance for Health, Physical Education and Recreation, 1974.

Lindsay, Zaidee. *Art and the Handicapped Child.* New York: Van Nostrand-Reinhold, 1972. A realistic handbook offering art activities and craft techniques adapted to different disabilities.

Marx, Orin H. *Physical Activities for Handicapped Children in the Home.* Iowa City, Iowa: University Hospital School, University of Iowa, 1972. A monograph with suggestions for parents.

Museums and Handicapped Students: Guidelines for Educators. Washington, D.C.: Smithsonian Institution, 1977. Guidelines for museum programs for the disabled. Valuable information about architectural requirements for the mobility disabled, equipment and museum programs for the deaf and the blind.

* National Easter Seal Society for Crippled Children and Adults. *Directory of Camps for the Handicapped*, 10th ed. Chicago, 1977.

Nesbitt, John A., et al. *Training Needs and Strategies in Camping for the Handicapped.* Eugene, Ore.: Center of Leisure Studies, University of Oregon, 1972. Based on the proceedings of a conference under the sponsorship of the Therapeutic Recreation Service for Handicapped Children Project, Department of Recreation and Leisure Studies, California State University, San Jose, California. Assessment of training, research and service dimensions of day and residential camp programs and outdoor recreation for handicapped children.

* Newman, Judy. *Swimming for Children with Physical and Sensory Impairments.* Springfield, Ill.: Charles C. Thomas, 1976. A book that instructs how to teach swimming to children with visual and auditory impairments, cerebral palsy, spina bifida, and other disabilities.

Reynolds, Grace Demmery, ed. *A Swimming Program for the Handicapped.* New York: Association Press, 1973. Employment of swimming skills as an aid in the improvement of the handicapped. How to set up a successful program.

Schattner, Regina. *Creative Dramatics for Handicapped Children.* New York: John Day, 1967. One title in a series of books in special education published by the John Day Company.

Sosne, Michael. *Handbook of Adapted Physical Education Equipment and Its Use.* Springfield, Ill.: Charles C. Thomas, 1973. For the assistance of teachers, parents, and nonprofessional personnel in planning for handicapped students in a program of physical education and recreation.

Stevens, Ardis. *Fun Is Therapeutic: A Recreation Book to Help Therapeutic Recreation Leaders by People Who Are Leading Recreation.* Springfield, Ill.: Charles C. Thomas, 1972.

TRIC—Therapeutic Recreation Information Center, Department of Recreation and Park Administration, California, State University, Sacramento. TRIC is a computer-based information acquisition, storage retrieval, and dissemination center specifically concerned with published and unpublished materials related to recreation services to ill, disadvantaged, disabled, and aging persons. More than 2,000 index terms have been incorporated into the 100 related abstracts or major files: those descriptor terms that have 100 or more related abstracts at a sliding scale in direct proportion to the number of abstracts produced. Information requests should be as specific as possible. Telephone requests can also be handled by calling 916-454-6182.

Vinton, Dennis A., et al. *Camping and Environmental Education for Handicapped Children and Youth. Basic Concepts and Comprehensive Bibliography.* Washington, D.C.: Hawkins and Association, Inc., 1978. Development of camping and environmental education for handicapped children and youth in the United States and educational, recreational, and therapeutic aspects of these programs. Examples of specific programs and activities and list of resources and services. Extensive bibliography.

Walter, Felix. *Sports Centers and Swimming Pools:* A study of their design with particular reference to the needs of the physically disabled. Thistle Foundation. Available from the Disabled Living Foundation, London, n.d.

Weisman, Marilee. *So Get on with It: A Celebration of Wheelchair Sports.* New York: Doubleday, 1976.

Wheeler, Ruth H., and Hooley, Agnes M. *Physical Education for the Handicapped*, 2nd ed. Philadelphia: Lea & Febiger, 1976. A new edition of a standard text by a physical therapist and a physical educator concerning physical education. Chapter on attitudes toward the disabled and mainstreaming have been eliminated. New chapters on mental retardation and learning disabled, and camping for the handicapped have been included. Emphasis is on exercises rather than on sports and movement.

DEAFNESS AND HEARING IMPAIRMENT

Many of the materials on deafness are available from the Alexander Graham Bell Association and the Gallaudet Press, both in Washington, D.C. The continued split in philosophy of the education of the deaf is represented by the publications of these two groups.

The Alexander Graham Bell Association for the Deaf believes hearing-impaired children and adults can participate independently through development of their oral and auditory capabilities. The Association bases its belief on the knowledge (quoted below from its annual catalog) that:

1. Speech is recognized by society as the universal mode of communication;
2. Deaf children who develop speech communication proficiency during early childhood ultimately have more options open to them for education and fuller participation in society than those who do not develop speech communication skills; and
3. Modern educational audiology suggests that 75 to 80 percent of hearing-impaired children have sufficient residual hearing to develop speech communication fitted with appropriate amplification and given quality educational programming.

Therefore, the Association directs its energies, resources, and services toward achieving the following objectives:

1. To gather and develop information on all ways and means to assist hearing-impaired children and adults develop and improve their language, speech, and speechreading, and to make fullest use of residual hearing.
2. To aid any school or program for hearing-impaired children in its efforts to develop or improve programs in speech communication.
3. To organize, analyze, and interpret information pertinent to the goal of the Association.
4. To disseminate information to the general public and appropriate decision-making groups throughout the world which are directly or indirectly related to the self-realization and general well-being of hearing-impaired children and adults.

Gallaudet College, the only liberal arts college for the deaf in the United States, advocates the teaching of total communication to deaf children, recognizing that profoundly deaf and many severely deaf children, for the most part, cannot develop sufficient lip reading skills or speech sufficient for total communication in a hearing world. Materials developing both of these philosophies should be available in a balanced special education collection.

American Annals of the Deaf. Gallaudet College, Washington, D.C.

American Annals of the Deaf. May issue. Available from American Annals of the Deaf Editor, Gallaudet College, Washington, D.C. The annual directory of information on personnel, facilities in education, recreational, religious, and therapeutic fields of service, teacher training, publication reviews, statistical data on American schools for the deaf, and schools and classes in Canada.

American School for the Deaf. *A Dictionary of Idioms for the Deaf.* Hartford, Conn.: American School for the Deaf, 1976. Available from Volta Bureau, Washington, D.C. Designed as a supplement to school dictionaries and for use by students in the upper grades of schools for the deaf and their teachers. The dictionary contains over 4,000 entries of idiomatic phrases, mainly those most commonly used and most likely to be difficult for the deaf. Cross-referenced; an appendix lists essential idioms.

Annual Survey of Hearing-Impaired Children and Youth. Office of Demographic Studies, Gallaudet College, Washington, D.C. Variety of data available. Write for information and to be placed on mailing list.

Bender, Ruth E. *The Conquest of Deafness: A History of the Long Struggle to Make Possible Normal Living to Those Handicapped by Lack of Normal Hearing,* rev. ed. Cleveland, Ohio: Press of Case Western Reserve University, 1970. Useful features are the bibliography of over 200 references, a chronology, and an index, mainly of persons influential in work for the deaf.

Berg, Frederick S., ed. *The Hard of Hearing Child: A Clinical and Educational Management.* New York: Grune and Stratton, 1970. Designed for those who will provide leadership in initiating, implementing, and evaluating clinical and educational programs that seek to alleviate disability from auditory disorders, this book defines the hard of hearing child, deals with basic considerations of the hearing mechanisms and communication, and suggests specific planning and programming considerations.

Birch, Jack W. *Hearing Impaired Pupils in the Mainstream.* Reston, Va.: Council for Exceptional Children, 1975. This book focuses on "translating special education now from successful programs into forms useful in the day to day work on to teachers, supervisors, administrators who want to include hearing impaired pupils in regular schools."

Blackwell, Peter M., Engen, Elizabeth, Fischgrunde, Joseph E., and Zarcadoolas, Christina. *A Language and Learning Curriculum for Hearing-Impaired Children.* Washington, D.C.: Alexander Graham Bell Association for the Deaf, 1978. Based on the Rhode Island School for the Deaf curriculum guide. An innovative approach to the development of language and reading skills. Curriculum prekindergarten through high school.

* Charlip, Remy. *Handtalk: An ABC of Finger Spelling and Sign Language.* New York: Parent's Magazine Press, 1974. By means of a striking, photographic display, *Handtalk* teaches two ways of communicating through sign language by using a sign for a word or concept and by finger spelling. Not only a pleasure to look at but also cleverly conceived to stimulate learning, this book will continue to fascinate and encourage long after a first reading.

Donnelly, Kenneth. *Interpreting Hearing Aid Technology.* Washington, D.C.: Gallaudet College, 1974. This is written for the audiologist, speech pathologist, hearing aid dealer, and others concerned with the management of hearing-impaired individuals.

* *Facts about Hearing and Hearing Aids. A Consumer's Guide from the National Bureau of Standards.* Stock no. 0303-0920. Department of Commerce Publication. November, 1971. For sale by U.S. Government Printing Office.

* Fant, Louis J., Jr. *Ameslan—An Introduction to American Sign Language.* Silver Spring, Md.: National Association of the Deaf, 1972.

Fine, Peter, ed. *Deafness in Infancy and Early Childhood.* New York: Medcom Press, 1974. Author is a doctor who became deaf at 35 and is now the medical director of Gallaudet College. Includes perspectives from a medical point of view (fairly technical, invaluable source for practicing physicians), education of deaf children (for parents and educators), and psychological aspects of deafness (also for lay and professionals).

Giangreco, C. Joseph. *The Education of the Hearing Impaired.* Springfield, Ill.: Charles C. Thomas, 1970. Following the first chapter on historical aspects, the authors provide seven chapters devoted to the deaf, their education, and social and vocational adjustment. Written for parents, nurses, teachers, and other professionals working with the hearing-impaired.

* Gregory, Susan. *The Deaf Child and His Family.* New York: Wiley, 1976. Extensive interviews carried out with 122 mothers of young deaf children provide the basis of this book, which describes the day-to-day life of the deaf child and his family. The author suggests that parents should, from their first encounter with professional workers, be treated as genuine and valued members of the therapeutic team.

Harris, Grace M. *Language for the Preschool Deaf Child,* 3rd ed. New York: Grune and Stratton, 1971. Early intervention techniques for the development of language in the young hearing-impaired child.

Hart, Beatrice Ostern. *Teaching Reading to Deaf Children.* Washington, D.C.: Alexander Graham Bell Assn., 1978. A revision of a popular classic. A practical handbook, presenting a step-by-step program to guide the deaf child's reading growth prekindergarten through high school.

Irwin, John V., ed., and Marge, Michael. *Principles of Childhood Language Disabilities.* New York: Appleton-Century-Crofts, 1972. This book is divided into four sections: Part I, Linguistic Approaches; Part II, Disabilities in Children Viewed Etiologically; Part III, Identification and Diagnosis: Part IV, Management and Corrective Education. The authors represent pediatrics, neurology, speech pathology, audiology, psychology, psycholinguistics, and special education.

Katz, Lee, Mathis, Steve L., and Merrill, Edward C. *The Deaf Child in the Public Schools.* Danville, Ill.: Interstate, 1974. By three eminently qualified and highly respected people in the field. Katz is executive director of International Association of Parents of Deaf; Steve Mathis is principal of Carver School for the Deaf; and Edward Merrill is president of Gallaudet College. Question-and-answer format, with sources for further reading.

Kretschmer, Richard, and Kretschmer, Laura. *Language Development and Intervention with the Hearing Impaired.* Washington, D.C.: Gallaudet College, 1978. An overview of the most recent thinking in the area of psycholinguistics and its application to the hearing impaired.

Lemonds, Cherry. *Choosing a Job: Information about Deaf People and Their Jobs.* Knoxville: Southern Regional Media Center for the Deaf, University of Tennessee, 1974. Introducing the deaf high school student to new and unique jobs that deaf people are entering in the hope that they will be motivated to branch out from the traditional deaf job stereotypes. A list of career programs for the deaf students is included.

* Levine, Edna S. *Lisa and Her Soundless World.* New York: Human Sciences Press, 1974. This story of Lisa is one of a series that offers innovative mental health approach to literature for the young child. Treatment techniques and lip reading are explained. The language of finger spelling is introduced.

Ling, Daniel, and Ling, Agnes H. *Aural Habilitation: The Foundations of Verbal Learning in Hearing-Impaired Children.* Washington, D.C.: Alexander Graham Bell Assn., 1978. Programs that emphasize the optimal use of residual hearing, essential to the planning of IEPs for hearing-impaired children for placement in the least restrictive educational setting. A text for students, teachers, educational administrators, speech pathologists, and parents.

Little, James A. *Answers.* Santa Fe: New Mexico School for the Deaf, 1970. If you plan to read only one book about deafness, read this one. Excellent articles are included on educating the preschool deaf child, on simple and inexpensive activities to do at home, as well as information on auditory testing and on proper selection and care of hearing aids. Also available through the International Association of Parents of the Deaf.

Mindel, E., and Vernon, M. *They Grow in Silence—The Deaf Child and His Family.* Silver Spring, Md.: National Association of the Deaf, 1971. Authors combine statements on deaf children and their families.

Moffat, Samuel. *Helping the Child Who Cannot Hear.* Public Affairs Pamphlet no. 479, New York, 1972.

* Moore, Donald D. *Educating the Deaf: Psychology, Principles, and Practices.* Washington, D.C.: Gallaudet College, 1978. Contains historical perspectives, causes of deafness, communication and teaching methods in education of the deaf.

Myklebust, Helmer R. *Auditory Disorders in Children.* Washington, D.C.: Gallaudet College, 1964. A manual for specialists suggesting clinical procedures and techniques for diagnosing hearing-impaired children.

———. *The Psychology of Deafness: Sensory Deprivation, Learning and Adjustment.* New York: Grune and Stratton, 1964. First published in 1960, this current edition contains major findings of a completed investigation of the development and disorders of written language and particularly of the acquisition of the written word by the deaf child. Intended as a text for advanced courses in audiology, language pathology, education of the deaf, and psychology. Students in other disciplines may also find it useful.

Neyhus, Arthur I., and Austrin, Gary F., eds. *Deafness and Adolescence.* Washington, D.C.: Alexander Graham Bell Assn., 1978. Monograph on all aspects of the deaf adolescent. Psychological and biological development, communication ability, educational needs, postsecondary education options.

Nix, Gary W., ed. *Mainstream Education for Hearing Impaired Children and Youth.* New York: Grune and Stratton, 1976. This collection of articles includes viewpoints on both the practice and the technology of mainstreaming hearing-impaired children. The contributing authors discuss many aspects of mainstreaming—psychological, pathological, audiological, and educational.

Northcott, Winifred H., ed. *Curriculum Guide: Hearing-Impaired Children—Birth to Three Years—And Their Parents.* Washington, D.C.: Alexander Graham Bell Association for the Deaf, 1972. This curriculum guide covers components of a comprehensive infant program, integration of a hearing-impaired preschool child into a nursery school for hearing children, stages of receptive and expressive language, developmental patterns and home-centered activities for normal children at specific ages.

Northern, J., and Downs, M. *Hearing in Children.* Washington, D.C.: Gallaudet College, 1978. A comprehensive description of the current state of knowledge of the audiological problems of children.

Oyer, Herbert J., ed. *Communication for the Hearing Handicapped: An International Perspective.* Baltimore: University Park Press, 1976.

* Pahz, James Alon, and Pahz, Cheryl Suzanne. *Total Communication: The Meaning behind the Movement to Expand Educational Opportunities for Deaf Children.* Springfield, Ill.: Charles C. Thomas, 1978. A definitive explanation of the total communication philosophy of deaf education.

Picture Books in Signed English. Washington, D.C.: Gallaudet College, series. Also available through the International Association of Parents of the Deaf.

Riekehof, Lottie. *Talk to the Deaf.* Springfield, Mo.: Gospel Publishing House, 1963.

Russell, W. Keith, et al. *Linguistics and Deaf Children: Transformational Syntax and Its Applications.* Washington, D.C.: Alexander Graham Bell Association for the Deaf, 1976. An outgrowth of an extensive study of syntax structure in the language of deaf students that was supported by the Bureau of Education for the Handicapped of the National Institute of Education, this book reports on applications of current linguistic thinking on the structure of language and language development of deaf children.

Sabatino, David A., and Miller, Ted L., eds. *Describing Learner Characteristics of Handicapped Children and Youth.* New York: Grune and Stratton, 1978. An introductory text in assessment for preservice special education teachers and for in-service training. A diagnostic resource book and reference guide.

Schlesenger, H. S., and Meadow, K. P. *Sound and Sign*. Washington, D.C.: Gallaudet College, 1972. Covers the controversy over the "either–or" question of the manual vs. the oral method of communication and proposes a combination program.

Semple, Jean E. *Hearing-Impaired Preschool Child: A Book for Parents*. Springfield, Ill.: Charles C. Thomas, 1970. Presented in simple style suited to the nonexpert, the text covers the problems faced by parents and offers helpful and practical suggestions in dealing with hearing loss.

* Spradley, Thomas S., and Spradley, James P. *Deaf Like Me*. Washington, D.C.: Gallaudet College, 1978. An account of a family that was able to communicate with a five-year-old daughter for the first time after perceiving futile hopes of oral education.

Strong, Alice, Kretschmer, Richard, and Kretschmer, Laura. *Language, Learning and Deafness: Theory, Applications, and Classroom Management*. New York: Grune and Stratton, 1978. An overview and outline of the development of language in the hearing-impaired as well as methods for incorporating language development into reading.

Vorce, Eleanor. *Teaching Speech to Deaf Children*. Lexington School for the Deaf Education Series Book IX. Washington, D.C.: Alexander Graham Bell Association for the Deaf, 1974. The book offers prospective and experienced teachers a concise and functional approach to a complex school subject. A proven and practical method of achieving slow and steady speech progress with severely deaf children is offered. The language process and the Lexington philosophy and method are discussed. Recommendations and a bibliography complete the text.

BLIND, DEAF-BLIND, AND VISUALLY IMPAIRED

Amblyopia—Lazy Eye. Washington, D.C.: American Association of Ophthalmology, 1971.

* American Foundation for the Blind. *The Preschool Deaf/Blind Child: Suggestions for Parents*. New York, 1976.

Bishop, Virginia E. *Teaching the Visually Limited Child*. Springfield, Ill.: Charles C. Thomas, 1978. Of use to teachers with visually impaired students in a mainstreaming situation.

* Bowker, R. R. Company. *Large Type Books in Print*. New York. Current edition.

Callier Center for Communicative Disorders. *Regional Planning Program for Prevocational Services to Deaf/Blind Children*. Dallas: South Central Regional Center for Services to Deaf/Blind Children through Callier Center for Communicative Disorders, 1974.

Cratty, Bryant J. *Body-Image of Blind Children*. New York: American Foundation for the Blind, 1968.

Crawford, Fred L. *Career Planning for the Blind: A Manual for Students & Teachers*. Foreword by Mary E. Switzer. New York: Farrar, Straus and Giroux, 1966. What is a career? Choosing an occupation, how blindness may affect the development of a career, community resources, laws governing employment. Sample workbook lessons.

Curtis, Scott, Donlon, Edward T., and Wagner, Elizabeth, eds. "Deaf-Blind Children: Evaluating Their Multiple Handicaps." New York: American Foundation for the Blind, 1970. Mimeographed. This book details the evaluation and examination techniques and procedures developed by members of various disciplines who participated in a special diagnostic clinic established by the Syracuse University Center for the Development of Blind Children for the purpose of providing an organized approach to the study of multiply handicapped children.

"Facts about Blindness." New York: American Foundation for the Blind, 1973. Brochure.

Freeman, Peggy. *Understanding the Deaf-Blind Child.* London: Heinemann, 1975.

Halliday, Carol. *The Visually Impaired Child: Growth, Learning, Development: Infancy to School Age.* Louisville, Ky.: American Printing House for the Blind, 1971.

_____, and Kurzhals, Ina W. *Stimulating Environments for Children Who Are Visually Impaired.* Springfield, Ill.: Charles C. Thomas, 1976. To aid visually impaired children in receiving and utilizing as fully as possible the input from their environments.

Harley, Randall K., and Lawrence, G. Allen. *Visual Impairment in the Schools.* Springfield, Ill.: Charles C. Thomas, 1977. A guide to a better understanding of the structure and function of the eye, its diseases, and the relationship of visual impairment and visual learning.

Higgins, Leslie C. *Classification in Congenitally Blind Children.* New York: American Foundation for the Blind, 1973.

Lowenfield, Berthold. *Our Blind Children.* Springfield, Ill.: Charles C. Thomas, 1971.

_____. *The Visually Handicapped Child in School.* New York: John Day, 1973.

National Braille Association. *NBA Manual for Large Type Transcribing.* Midland Park, N.J.: 1973.

* National Library Service for the Blind and Physically Handicapped, Library of Congress. *Aids for Handicapped Readers.* Washington, D.C., September 1972.

* _____. *Bibles in Special Media.* Washington, D.C., December 1973.

* _____. *Magazines: Large Type, Open Reel, Disc, Cassette, Braille, Moon Type.* Washington, D.C., June 1973.

* _____. *Reading Materials in Large Type.* Washington, D.C., August 1973.

* _____. *Sources of Braille Materials for the Visually Handicapped.* Washington, D.C., 1973.

Perkins School for the Blind. *Braille Fragrance Books.* Watertown, Mass.: Howe Press, n.d.

_____. *Braille Vision Books.* Watertown, Mass.: Howe Press, n.d.

_____. *Perkins Sign Language Dictionary: A Sign Dictionary for Use with Multi-Handicapped Deaf Children in School.* Watertown, Mass.: Howe Press, 1975.

Robbins, Nan. *The Deaf-Blind "Rubella" Child: Descriptive Characteristics of*

Children with Auditory-Visual Impairments Resulting from Maternal Rubella during Pregnancy and Discussion of Implications for Educational Planning. Watertown, Mass.: Howe Press, 1967.

———. *Educational Beginnings with Deaf-Blind Children.* Watertown, Mass.: Howe Press, 1964.

———. *Speech Beginnings for the Deaf-Blind Child: A Guide for Parents.* Watertown, Mass.: Howe Press, 1963.

* *Sex Education and Family Life for Visually Handicapped Children and Youth: A Resource Guide.* New York: Siecus, n.d. A basic guide for teachers, counselors, parents, administrators, and others that can be used for general orientation, in-service training, curriculum development, and individual counseling. Includes an introductory section on background and history, learning activities in five areas (self-identity, physical and emotional growth, human reproduction, interpersonal relations, decision making), and sources of information and materials (print, audio-visual, braille, recording, large print, models) with descriptions and addresses of suppliers.

Sherrick, Carl E., ed. *1980 Is Now: A Conference on the Future of Deaf-Blind Children.* Los Angeles: John Tracy Clinic, 1974.

Watson, Marcia J. *A Practical Guide to the Training of Low-Functioning Deaf-Blind Children.* Hartford, Conn.: Oak Hill School of the Connecticut Institute for the Blind, 1973.

PERIODICALS

American Association of Workers for the Blind. *Blindnesss,* Washington, D.C. Annual.

American Education. Office of Education, Washington, D.C. 10 issues a year.

* *American Journal of Diseases of Children.* American Medical Association, 535 North Dearborn Street, Chicago, Illinois. Monthly.

ASHA. American Speech and Hearing Association, 9030 Old Georgetown Road, Washington, D.C. Monthly.

Children Development Abstracts and Bibliography. University of Chicago Press, 5801 Ellis Avenue, Chicago, Illinois. 3 issues a year, 2 numbers per issue.

Childhood Education. Association for Childhood International, 3615 Wisconsin Avenue N.W., Washington, D.C. Monthly October through May.

Children Today. Children's Bureau, Washington, D.C. 6 issues a year.

* *The Deaf American.* National Association of the Deaf, 814 Thayer Avenue, Silver Spring, Maryland. 11 issues a year.

DSH Abstracts. Deafness, Speech and Hearing Publications, 9030 Old Georgetown Road, Washington, D.C. Quarterly.

Education of the Visually Handicapped. Association for Education of the Visually Handicapped, 1839 Frankfort Ave., Louisville, Ky. Quarterly.

Exceptional Child Education Resources. Council for Exceptional Children, 1411 S. Jefferson Davis Hwy., Arlington, Va. Quarterly.

* *Exceptional Children.* Council for Exceptional Children, 1411 S. Jefferson Hwy., Arlington, Va. 8 issues a year.

* *The Exceptional Parent.* Psy-Ed Corp., P.O. Box 101, Back Bay Annex, Boston, Mass. 6 issues a year.

Journal of Learning Disabilities. The Professional Press, 5 N. Wabash Ave., Room 1410, Chicago, Ill. 10 issues a year.

Journal of Special Education. 3515 Woodhaven Rd., Philadelphia, Pa. 19154. Quarterly.

Journal of Speech and Hearing Disorders. American Speech and Hearing Assn., 9030 Old Georgetown Rd., Washington, D.C. Quarterly.

* *Journal of Visual Impairment and Blindness* (formerly *New Outlook for the Blind*). American Foundation for the Blind, 15 W. 16 St., New York, N.Y. 10 issues a year.

New Zealand Speech Therapist's Journal. New Zealand Speech Therapist's Assn., 44 Peterborough St., Christchurch 1, New Zealand. Semiannual.

The Pointer. P.O. Box 131, Syracuse, N.Y. 13210. 3 issues a year.

* *Programs for the Handicapped.* Department of HEW, Office for Handicapped Individuals, Washington, D.C. Monthly or more often, Apply.

Special Education. Association for Special Education and the Spastics Society, 12 Park Crescent, London WIN 4EQ, England. Quarterly.

Teaching Exceptional Children. Council for Exceptional Children, 1411 Jefferson Davis Hwy., Arlington, Va. Quarterly.

* *Volta Review.* Alexander Graham Bell Association for the Deaf, 3417 Volta Place N.W., Washington, D.C. Monthly except June, July, and August.

NEWSLETTERS

Breakthrough. The National Newsletter of the Osteogenesis Imperfecta Foundation, Inc., 139 Exeter St., Hartford, Conn. 06106.

Children of the Silent Night. Perkins School for the Blind, Watertown, Mass. 02172.

Closer Look: Common Sense from Closer Look. P.O. Box 1492, Washington, D.C. A project of the Parents' Campaign for Handicapped Children and Youth. Free. May reproduce and distribute copies if credit is given to *Closer Look.*

College "Helps" Newsletter. Partners in Publishing, P.O. Box 50347, Tulsa, Oklahoma. Newsletter for school counselors describing higher education programs for disabled students, including the learning disabled; book reviews, legislative news, other valuable information.

Crusader. United Cerebral Palsy Assn., 66 E. 34 St., New York, N.Y. 10016. Bimonthly.

The Directive Teacher (replacing *Apropos*, which is no longer in print). NCEMMH, Ohio State University, Columbus, Ohio 43210. To keep the special education field up-to-date on NIMIS data base, which is continuing at Ohio State University.

Easter Seal Communicator. National Easter Seal Society for Crippled Children and Adults, 2023 W. Ogden Ave., Chicago, Ill. 60612. Bimonthly.

Education for the Handicapped Law Report. CRR Publishing Co., 1156 15 St. N.W., Washington, DC. 20002. Ring binder; extremely expensive.

Frankly Speaking. National Information Center for Special Education Materials, University of Southern California/NICSEM, Los Angeles, Calif. 90007. Quarterly. Newsletter designed to meet the information needs of persons involved in special education at the local level.

Hearing Research Developments. Official publication of CHEAR, International Foundation for Children's Hearing, Education and Research, 871 McLean Ave., Yonkers, N.Y. 19704.

Impact. Rehabilitation Specialist, Department of Human Development and the Family, University of Nebraska, Lincoln, Neb. 68583. Reports on an independent living project.

The Kurzweil Report: Technology for the Handicapped. Kurzweil Computer Products, 264 Third Ave., Cambridge, Mass. 02142.

Muscular Dystrophy News. Muscular Dystrophy Association of America, 1790 Broadway, New York, N.Y. 10019. 3 issues a year.

Nat-Cent News. Helen Keller National Center for Deaf-Blind Youths and Adults, 111 Middle Neck Rd., Sands Point, N.Y. 11050. Large type.

National CF News Bulletin. National Cystic Fibrosis Research Foundation, 3379 Peachtree Rd. N.E., Atlanta, Ga. Irregular.

National Parents' Exchange. A newsletter for parents of deaf-blind children. Southwestern Region Deaf-Blind Center, 721 Capitol Mall, Sacramento, Calif. 95814.

National Spokesman. Epilepsy Foundation of America, 1828 L St. N.W., Washington, D.C. 20036.

News. National Library Service for the Blind and Physically Handicapped, Library of Congress, Washington, D.C. 20542. Publication from Library of Congress. Also Talking Book topic. Reference, bibliographies.

The Program Tree. National Information Center for Special Education Materials, University of Southern California/NICSEM, Los Angeles, Calif. Newsletter updating the new NIMIS II data base. Also reports on other systems, workshops, programs, and publications being developed around the country, especially with regard to PL 94-142 and its implications. Single copies of materials are usually available.

Recording for the Blind News. Recording for the Blind, 215 East 58 St., New York, N.Y.

RP Foundation Newsletter. National Retinitis Pigmentosa Foundation, 8331 Mindale Circle, Baltimore, Md. 21277.

Talking Book Topics. Division for the Blind and Physically Handicapped, Library of Congress, Washington, D.C. 20542. Bimonthly.

SOURCES AND PUBLISHERS' CATALOGUES
OF INSTRUCTIONAL MATERIAL

American Printing House for the Blind, 1839 Frankfort Ave., Louisville, Ky. 40206.

Association for Childhood Education International. *Selecting Educational Equipment and Materials for School and Home.* 3615 Wisconsin Ave. N.W., Washington, D.C. 20016.

Catalog of Instructional Materials for the Handicapped Learner. Handicapped Learner Materials Distribution Center, Special Materials Project, 1979. Indiana University Audio-Visual Center, Bloomington, Ind. 47405. Curriculum materials for use with the handicapped learner.

Developmental Learning Materials, 7440 Natchez Ave., Niles, Ill. 60648.

Educational Development Laboratories. *Reading and Language Arts Catalog.* New York: McGraw-Hill. Remedial, special education.

General Learning Corporation, The Judy Company, 250 James St., Morristown, N.J.: 07960.

Ideal School Supply Company, 11000 South Laverne Ave., Oak Lawn, Ill. 60453.

Learning Concepts, 2501 N. Lamar, Austin, Tex. 78705. New Directions: New mainstreaming training series.

G. E. Miller, Inc., Special Education Materials, Inc., 484 S. Broadway, Yonkers, N.Y. 10705. Testing and evaluation, perceptual materials, gross motor activities, perceptual-motor, cognitive skills, speech and language, special physical education classroom furniture, aids for the handicapped, career education, secondary education.

Modern Education Corporation, P.O. Box 721, Tulsa, Okla. 74101. Special materials catalogue. Workbooks in speech pathology, perceptual training, and other special resource materials.

National Association for the Deaf, 814 Thayer Ave., Silver Spring, Md. 20910. Its catalogue lists publications from the Regional Research Center for the Deaf, New York University, New York City. At present, films about the deaf are also available.

NCEMMH, Publications Sales Division. *Publishers Source Directory.* Ohio State University Press, 2070 Neil Ave., Columbus, Ohio 43210. Latest edition. Producers of special education materials.

Newby Visualanguage, Inc., P.O. Box 121, Eagleville, Pa. 19408. A new way to teach language to hearing impaired, language-deprived, mentally retarded, bilingual, visually impaired, early childhood, learning disabled.

NICSEM, National Information Center for Special Education Materials, Los Angeles, Calif. 90007. Contact for special education materials information. A variety of indexes and microfiche gives access to all materials in NIMIS/NICSEM, including a special index of nonprint materials. These indexes are available through state departments of education. For on-line searching, these data files are also available through Lockheed Information Systems, 3251 Hanover Street, Palo Alto, Calif. 94302, or Bibliographical Retrieval Service, Corporation Park, Building 702, Scotia, N.Y. 12302.

NIMIS, Publications Sales Division, Ohio State University Press, Columbus, Ohio. *Instructional Materials Thesaurus for Special Education.* Latest edition. Official list of terms used to classify the more than 36,000 instructional materials listed in NIMIS. Can be used in special libraries or information centers as a cross-referenced list of keyword subject headings to facilitate cataloging or to arrange materials.

J. A. Preston, 71 Fifth Ave., New York, N.Y. 10003. Materials for exceptional children and youth: perceptual-motor equipment, adapted classroom furniture, perceptual training materials, developmental elementary physical education.

Prince, Dan, ed. *The Tool Kit.* Publication no. (OHD) 76-31093. Office of Human Development, Office of Child Development, Head Start Bureau, Department of

HEW. Washington, D.C. A catalogue of materials, methods, and media for Head Start teachers of handicapped children.

Pro-Ed, 333 Perry Brooks Building, Austin, Tex. 78701. Special education, remedial instruction, speech/language therapy.

Recording for the Blind, Inc., 215 E. 58 St., New York, N.Y. 10022. Latest catalogue of tape-recorded books. Listings by subject, general works, textbooks, college and above, and schoolbooks to grade 12.

Special Learning Corporation, 42 Boston Post Rd., Guilford, Conn. 06437.

The Stoelting Company, 1350 S. Kostner Ave., Chicago, Ill. 60623. Screening and diagnostic texts, materials in reading, math, language development, speech and hearing, motor and orthopedic materials.

Teaching Resources Corporation, New York Times, 100 Boylston St., Boston, Mass. 02116.

Texas Education Agency. *Resources on Handicapping Conditions Which Are Suggested for Use by Educators in General Education.* 1978. Resources on handicapping conditions, for the classroom teacher to assist regular students to understand and accept handicapped students in the classroom. List of vendors.

LEGISLATION AND FINANCING

Ballard, Joseph. *PL 94-142 and Section 504—Understanding What They Are and Are Not.* Reston, Va.: Government Relations Unit, Council for Exceptional Children, 1977. Questions and answers about both laws.

Bernstein, Charles D., Kirst, Michael W., Hartman, William T., and Marshall, Rudolph S. *Financing Educational Services for the Handicapped: An Analysis of Current Research and Practices.* Reston, Va.: Government Relations Unit, Council for Exceptional Children, 1976. An evaluation of current practices in financing for special education.

Biehl, G. Richard. *Guide to the Section 504 Self-Evaluation for Colleges and Universities.* Washington, D.C.: National Association of College and University Business Officers, 1978. Copies available without charge. Suggestions for how compliance may be achieved in accordance with Section 504. Suggestions for innovative services. Good listing of organizations for sources of additional information. Listing of state offices of vocational rehabilitation. Bibliography.

The Children's Defense Fund. *How to Look at Your State's Plans for Educating Handicapped Children.* Washington, D.C., Fall 1975. Description of the law, state and local responsibilities under the law, and how parents can get involved in protecting the rights of their children under the law.

————. *Your Rights under the Education for All Handicapped Children Act, PL 94-142.* Washington, D.C., March 1976.

Clelland, Richard. *Section 504: Civil Rights for the Handicapped.* Arlington, Va.: American Association of School Administrators, 1978. Title V, Section 504, employment practices, program accessibility, comparison with PL 94-142, difficulties in implementation. Appendix of checklist on building accessibility.

Coons, Maggie, and Milner, Margaret. *Creating an Accessible Campus.* Washington, D.C.: Association of Physical Plant Administrators of Universities and Colleges, with a grant from the Exxon Education Foundation, 1978. Program and building accessibility on college campuses. Special space considerations, including a short section on the library. Instructional aids, including special hardware for the blind.

Davis, Sharon, and Ward, Michael. *Vocational Education of Handicapped Students: A Guide for Policy Development.* Reston, Va.: Council for Exceptional Children, 1978. PL 94-482, the Education Amendments of 1976, calls for the expansion and strengthening of vocational education programs for handicapped students, requiring that at least 10 percent of the dollar resources provided to the states be used for this purpose. This manual is a guide to be used to establish policy in the vocational area.

Educating Children with Special Needs. Current Trends in School Policies and Programs. Arlington, Va.: National School Public Relations Association, 1974.

Education for Children with Epilepsy: The Education for All Handicapped Children Act. Washington, D.C.: Epilepsy Foundation of America, n.d. The education law with regard to children with epilepsy. Bibliography. Listing of brochures published by some individual states on legal rights for disabled children.

Hippel, Caron Von, Foster, June, and Lonberg, Jean. *Civil Rights, Handicapped Persons and Education: Section 504. Self-Evaluation Guide, Preschool, Elementary, Secondary, and Adult Education.* Belmont, Mass.: CRC Education and Human Development, Inc., August 1978. Portions of this guide are based on materials developed by G. Richard Biehl for the National Association of College and University Business Officers and printed in the *Guide to the Section 504 Self-Evaluation for Colleges and Universities.* Information on how to evaluate programs—preschool, public education, and adult education, evaluation forms, limited bibliography. Companion volume is *A Training and Resource Directory for Teachers Serving Handicapped Students, K-12.*

Kapisovsky, Peggy M., Workman, Jean, and Foster, June C. *A Training and Resource Directory for Teachers Serving Handicapped Students, K-12.* Cambridge, Mass.: Technical Education Research Center, n.d. To assist elementary and secondary level regular class teachers to find resources that will help them accommodate students with physical and mental handicaps. In-service training opportunities, network of national, state, and local agencies and organizations that are sources of materials, services and technical assistance, and literature and media on educational services for handicapped students.

Kunder, Linda H. *Barrier-Free School Facilities for Handicapped Students.* Arlington, Va.: Educational Research Service, Inc., 1977. Extensive coverage. Excellent annotated reference list and bibliography.

Mistler, Sharon. *Planning for Implementation of Section 504 at Colleges and Universities.* Washington, D.C.: George Washington University, March 1978. Accessibility on college campuses, including equipment needed for the library to accommodate disabled students.

Nix, Gary W., ed. *The Rights of Hearing-Impaired Children.* Washington, D.C.: Alexander Graham Bell Assn., 1977. PL 94-142 and its implications for the hearing-impaired, least restrictive environment, IEPs, legal and educational rights.

PL 94-142, The Education for All Handicapped Children Act. Reston, Va.: Council for Exceptional Children, 1976. The complete text of the act.

Redden, Martha Ross, Levering, Cricket, and DeQuinzio, Diane. *Recruitment, Admissions and Handicapped Students: A Guide for Compliance for Section 504 of the Rehabilitation Act of 1973.* Washington, D.C.: American Association of Collegiate Registrar and Admissions Officers and the American Council on Education. Guidelines for the admission of disabled students to universities. Covers recruitment, application forms, admission tests, financial aid, orientation, grievance procedures, etc. Appendixes include national organizations of handicapped persons, state administrators of vocational rehabilitation. Sources of additional information.

Redden, Martha Ross, Davis, Cheryl Arlene, and Brown, Janet Welsh. *Science for Handicapped Students in Higher Education.* Washington, D.C.: American Association for the Advancement of Science, n.d. Deals with barriers, solutions and recommendations for science programs wishing to accommodate handicapped students. This monograph is an outgrowth of the Office of Opportunities in Science, which seeks to open the field of science to the handicapped student.

Research for Better Schools, Inc. *Clarification of PL 94-142 for the Classroom Teacher.* Philadelphia, n.d. School responsibility under PL 94-142, preparing the IEP, meaning of "least restrictive environment," useful bibliography.

Weintraub, Frederick J., Abeson, Alan, Ballard, Joseph, and LaVor, Martin L. *Public Policy and the Education of Exceptional Children.* Reston, Va.: Council for Exceptional Children, 1976. Good overview of education rights of exceptional children, federal law, financing, administrative responsibility, etc.

AUDIOVISUAL MATERIALS

ACI Films, Inc., *Films for the Exceptional Child*, 35 W. 45 St., New York, N.Y. 10036. Captioned films, nonverbal films, motor development, fine and gross muscle control, visual discrimination, language and communication skills.

Educational Activities, Inc., P.O. Box 392, Freeport, N.Y. Records, filmstrips, cassettes, and multimedia programs for special needs students.

Film Library, Guidance Information Center, Saxtons River, Vt. Special education films, including films produced by the Perkins School for the Blind. Most films are for rental. The Perkins School films are available on free loan.

Films Incorporated, 733 Green Bay Rd., Wilmette, Ill. 60091. Films about exceptional children, including a number of the "Zoom" titles.

Media Services and Captioned Film Program. Bureau of Education for the Handicapped, Office of Education, Washington, D.C. 20202. Catalogue available from Educational Media Distribution Center.

National Audio Visual Center, National Archives and Records Service, General Services Administration, Washington, D.C. *Selected U.S. Government Audiovisuals in Special Education.* Latest edition. Hearing-impaired and deaf, learning disabilities, mental retardation, multiple handicapped, teacher training. Films, filmstrips, transparencies.

National Center on Educational Media and Materials for the Handicapped at the Ohio State University, Ohio State University Press. *National Catalog of Films in Special Education.* Latest edition. An annotated list of more than 700 films for teachers, paraprofessionals, and parents on various aspects of special education.

Parents Magazine Films, 52 Vanderbilt Ave., New York, N.Y. 10017. Special set of color filmstrips on children with handicaps.

Appendix I

Professional and Volunteer Agencies

Space limitations do not allow listing all of the organizations involved with service to disabled people. Following are the addresses of many organizations mentioned in this book. More extensive listings can be found in *The Directory of National Information Sources on Handicapping Conditions and Related Services* (Clearinghouse on the Handicapped, Office for Handicapped Individuals, Department of Health, Education, and Welfare, Washington, D.C.); the *Disability and Rehabilitation Handbook* (Robert M. Goldenson et al., eds., New York: McGraw-Hill, 1978); or the *Encyclopedia of Associations* (3 vols., Detroit: Gale Research, 1979).

This listing contains national organizations followed by agencies classified according to specific disabilities and specific areas of interest.

NATIONAL ORGANIZATIONS

American Coalition of Citizens with
Disabilities
1200 15 St. N.W.
Washington, D.C. 20005

ICD Rehabilitation and Research Center
340 E. 24 St.
New York, N.Y. 10010

Institute of Rehabilitation Medicine
400 E. 34 St.
New York, N.Y. 10016

Mainstream, Inc.
1200 15 St. N.W.
Washington, D.C. 20005

National Center for a Barrier Free
Environment
Seventh and Florida Aves. N.E.
Washington, D.C. 20002

National Center for Law and the
Handicapped
211 W. Washington St.
Suite 1900
South Bend, Ind. 46601

National Clearinghouse of Rehabilitation
Materials
Oklahoma State University
Stillwater, Okla. 74074

National Congress of Organizations of the
Physically Handicapped, Inc.
7611 Oakland Ave.
Minneapolis, Minn. 55432

National Easter Seal Society for Crippled
Children and Adults
2023 W. Ogden Ave.
Chicago, Ill. 60612

National Foundation (March of Dimes)
1275 Mamaroneck Ave.
White Plains, N.Y. 10605

National Foundation of Dentistry for the
  Handicapped
1121 Broadway
Boulder, Colo. 80302

National Institute of Rehabilitation
  Engineering
97 Decker Rd.
Butler, N.J. 07405

Rehabilitation International USA (RIUSA)
20 W. 40 St.
New York, N.Y. 10018

Sister Kenny Institute
Chicago Ave. at 27 St.
Minneapolis, Minn. 55407

TRACE Research and Development Center
  for the Severely Communicatively
  Handicapped
922 Erb
1500 Johnson Dr.
Madison, Wis. 53706

AGENCIES CLASSIFIED

Blindness and Visual Impairment

American Association of Workers for
  the Blind
1511 K St. N.W.
Washington, D.C. 20005

American Council of the Blind
818 18 St. N.W.
Suite 700
Washington, D.C. 20006

American Foundation for the Blind
15 W. 16 St.
New York, N.Y. 10011

American Printing House for the Blind
1839 Frankfort Ave.
Louisville, Ky. 40206

Association for the Education of the Visually
  Handicapped
919 Walnut St.
Philadelphia, Pa. 19107

Blinded Veterans Association
1735 DeSales St. N.W.
Washington, D.C. 20036

Braille Institute of America
741 N. Vermont Ave.
Los Angeles, Calif. 90029

Clovernook Home and School for the Blind
Cincinnati, Ohio

Guide Dog Foundation for the Blind
109-19 72 Ave.
Forest Hills, N.Y. 11375

Guide Dogs for the Blind
P.O. Box 1200
San Rafael, Calif. 94902

Hadley School for the Blind
700 Elm St.
Winnetka, Ill. 60093

G. K. Hall & Co.
(large print books)
10 Lincoln St.
Boston, Mass. 02111

Howe Press
Perkins School for the Blind
Watertown, Mass. 02172

Keith Jennison Large Type Editions
Franklin Watts, Inc.
730 Fifth Ave.
New York, N.Y. 10019

Kurzweil Computer Products
264 Third St.
Cambridge, Mass. 02142

Low-Vision Clinic
School of Optometry
University of California
Berkeley, Calif. 94720

Low Vision Clinic
Boston University School of Medicine
Boston, Mass. 02215

Low-Vision Clinic
Industrial Home for the Blind
57 Willoughby St.
Brooklyn, N.Y. 11201

National Accreditation Council for Agencies
  Servicing the Blind and Visually
  Handicapped
79 Madison Ave.
New York, N.Y. 10016

National Association for the Visually
  Handicapped
305 E. 24 St.
New York, N.Y. 10010

National Braille Association
85 Goodwin Ave.
Midland Park, N.J. 07432

National Federation of the Blind
218 Randolph Hotel Bldg.
Des Moines, Iowa 50309

National Retinitis Pigmentosa Foundation
Rolling Park Bldg.
8331 Mindale Circle
Baltimore, Md. 21207

National Society for the Prevention of
  Blindness
79 Madison Ave.
New York, N.Y. 10016

Recording for the Blind, Inc.
215 E. 58 St.
New York, N.Y. 10022

SFB Products
(special and adapted instruments and
  materials)
221 Rock Hill Rd.
Bala-Cynwyd, Pa. 19004

Southern Microfilm Corp.
(in-stock and custom large print)
900 W. 34 St., P.O. Box 1824
Houston, Tex. 77018

Telesensory Systems, Inc.
(Optacon, talking calculator, electronic
  devices)
1889 Page Mill Rd.
Palo Alto, Calif. 94304

Visualtek
(closed circuit TV and microfiche reader)
1610 26 St.
Santa Monica, Calif. 90404

Volunteer Services for the Blind, Inc.
(braille reading materials and custom
  transcriptions)
919 Walnut St.
Philadelphia, Pa. 19107

Volunteer Transcribing Services
(in-stock and custom large print books)
205 E. Third Ave., Suite 201
San Mateo, Calif. 94401

Xavier Society for the Blind
(braille, large print, and recorded textbooks
  and reading materials)
154 E. 23 St.
New York, N.Y. 10010

Deafness and Hearing Impairment

Alexander Graham Bell Association for the
  Deaf
3417 Volta Place N.W.
Washington, D.C. 20007

American Speech and Hearing Association
10801 Rockville Pike
Rockville, Md. 20852

Better Hearing Institute
1430 K St. N.W., Suite 800
Washington, D.C. 20005

Deafness Research Foundation
366 Madison Ave.
New York, N.Y. 10017

Gallaudet College Library
Edward Miner Gallaudet Memorial Library
Florida Ave. and Seventh St. N.E.
Washington, D.C. 20002

I Hear Your Hand, Inc.
6025 Springhill Dr.
Greenbelt, Md. 20770

International Association of Parents of the
Deaf
814 Thayer Ave.
Silver Spring, Md. 20910

Joyce Motion Picture Co.
18702 Bryant St.
P.O. Box 458
Northridge, Calif. 91324

Lions International, Inc.
Hearing Conservation and Work with the
Deaf
York and Cermak Rds.
Oak Brook, Ill. 60521

Media Services and Captioned Films
Educational Media Distribution Center
5034 Wisconsin Ave. N.W.
Washington, D.C. 20016

National Association of Hearing and Speech
Agencies
814 Thayer Ave.
Silver Spring, Md. 20910

National Association of the Deaf
814 Thayer Ave.
Silver Spring, Md. 20910

National Center for Law and the Deaf
Florida Ave. and Seventh St. N.E.
Washington, D.C. 20002

National Technical Institute for the Deaf
One Lomb Memorial Dr.
Rochester, N.Y. 14623

National Theatre of the Deaf
1860 Broadway
New York, N.Y. 10023

Professional Rehabilitation Workers with
the Adult Deaf, Inc.
814 Thayer Ave.
Silver Spring, Md. 20910

Quota International, Inc.
1828 L St. N.W., Suite 908
Washington, D.C. 20036

Registry of Interpreters for the Deaf
P.O. Box 1339
Washington, D.C. 20013

Teletypewriters for the Deaf, Inc.
814 Thayer Ave.
Silver Spring, Md. 20910

Western Maryland College
Total Communication Laboratory
Westminster, Md. 21157

Employment

American Organization for Rehabilitation
through Training Federation (ORT)
817 Broadway
New York, N.Y. 10003

Federation Employment and Guidance
Service
215 Park Ave. S.
New York, N.Y. 10003

Goodwill Industries of America
9200 Wisconsin Ave.
Washington, D.C. 20014

Just One Break
373 Park Ave. S.
New York, N.Y. 10016

President's Committee on Employment of
the Handicapped
Washington, D.C. 20210

Flying

Arizona Wheelchair Pilots Assn.
7008 Willetta
Scottsdale, Ariz. 85257

Bill Blackwood (flying controls)
1111 Rising Hill
Escondido, Calif. 92025

Southern California Wheelchair Aviators
671 N. Dexford
La Habra, Calif. 90631

Wheelchair Pilots Assn.
17018 102 Ave. N.
Largo, Fla. 33540

Other Disabilities

American Cleft Palate Assn.
331 Salk Hall
University of Pittsburgh
Pittsburgh, Pa. 15261

Amyotrophic Lateral Sclerosis Foundation,
Inc.
2840 Adams Ave.
San Diego, Calif. 92116

Amyotrophic Lateral Sclerosis Society of
America
12011 San Vicente Blvd.
P.O. Box 49001
Los Angeles, Calif. 90049

The Arthritis Foundation
3400 Peachtree Rd. N.E.
Atlanta, Ga. 30326

Arthrogryposis Assn. (arthropgryposis
multiplex congenita)
106 Herkimer St.
North Bellmore, N.Y. 11712
or
3204 K St.
Vancouver, Wash. 98663

Cystic Fibrosis Research Foundation
6000 Executive Bldg., Suite 309
Rockville, Md. 20852

Dysautonomia Foundation (familial
dysautonomia)
370 Lexington Ave.
New York, N.Y. 10017

Epilepsy Foundation of America
1828 L St. N.W.
Washington, D.C. 20036

Friedrich's Ataxia Group in America, Inc.
P.O. Box 11116
Oakland, Calif. 94611

Human Growth Foundation (dwarfism)
Maryland Academy of Science Bldg.
601 Light St.
Baltimore, Md. 21230

Little Peopie of America, Inc.
P.O. Box 126
Owatonna, Minn. 55060

Muscular Dystrophy Assn.
810 Seventh Ave.
New York, N.Y. 10019

National ALS Foundation, Inc.
185 Madison Ave.
New York, N.Y. 10016

National Hemophilia Foundation
25 W. 39 St.
New York, N.Y. 10018

National Multiple Sclerosis Society
257 Park Ave. S.
New York, N.Y. 10010

National Sickle Cell Disease Research
Foundation
Association for Sickle Cell Anemia
521 Fifth Ave.
New York, N.Y. 10036

National Spinal Cord Injury Foundation
369 Elliot St.
Newton Upper Falls, Mass. 02164

Osteogenesis Imperfecta Foundation, Inc.
1231 May Ct.
Berlington, N.C. 27215

Paralyzed Veterans of America, Inc.
4330 East-West Hwy.
Suite 300
Washington, D.C. 20014

Spina Bifida Association of America
343 S. Dearborn St.
Chicago, Ill. 60604

Spina Bifida Association of Greater
New York
P.O. Box 805, Radio City Station
New York, N.Y. 10019

United Cerebral Palsy Assn.
66 E. 34 St.
New York, N.Y. 10016

Rehabilitational

American Association for Rehabilitation
  Therapy
P.O. Box 93
Little Rock, Ark. 72116

American Orthotic and Prosthetic Assn.
1440 N St. N.W.
Washington, D.C. 20005

American Personnel and Guidance Assn.
1607 New Hampshire Ave. N.W.
Washington, D.C. 20009

American Psychological Assn.
Division of Rehabilitation Psychology
2658 S. Elm St.
Tempe, Ariz. 85282

American Rehabilitation Counseling Assn.
1607 New Hampshire Ave. N.W.
Washington, D.C. 20009

Association of Rehabilitation Facilities
5530 Wisconsin Ave.
Suite 955
Washington, D.C. 20015

Commission on Accreditation of
  Rehabilitation Facilities
2500 N. Pantamo Rd.
Tucson, Ariz. 85715

National Rehabilitation Assn. and National
  Rehabilitation Counseling Assn.
1522 K St. N.W.
Washington, D.C. 20005

Special Education

Association for Childhood Education
  International
3615 Wisconsin Ave. N.W.
Washington, D.C. 20016

Association for Children with Learning
  Disabilities
5225 Grace
Pittsburgh, Pa. 15236

Association for Special Education
  Technology
Exceptional Child Center
Utah State University
Logan, Utah 84322

Child Study Association of America Wel-Met,
  Inc.
50 Madison Ave.
New York, N.Y. 10010

Closer Look
P.O. Box 1492
Washington, D.C. 20013

Council for Exceptional Children
1920 Association Dr.
Reston, Va. 22091

Foundation for Child Development
345 E. 46 St.
New York, N.Y. 10010

National Association for the Education of
  Young Children
3700 Massachusetts Ave.
Washington, D.C. 20016

Sports

American Athletic Association of the Deaf
3916 Lantern Dr.
Silver Spring, Md. 20902

American Blind Bowler's Assn.
150 N. Bellaire
Louisville, Ky. 40206

American Wheelchair Bowling Assn.
2635 N.E. 79 St.
Pompano Beach, Fla. 33062

BOLD (Blind Outdoor Leisure Development,
  Inc.)
533 Main
Aspen, Colo. 81611

Braille Sports Foundation
Rm. 301
730 Hennepin Ave.
Minneapolis, Minn. 55402

Committee for the Promotion of Camping
  for the Handicapped
2056 S. Bluff Rd.
Traverse City, Mich. 49684

International Committee of the Silent Sports
Gallaudet College
Washington, D.C. 20002

International Council on Therapeutic Ice
  Skating
P.O. Box 13
State College, Pa. 16801

International Sports Organization for the
  Disabled and International Stoke-
  Mandeville Games Federation
Stoke-Mandeville Spinal Injury Center
Aylesbury, England

National Archery Assn.
Ronks, Pa. 17572

National Bleep Baseball Assn.
3212 Tomahawk
Lawrence, Kans. 66044

National Handicapped Sports and Recreation
  Assn.
10 Mutual Bldg.
4205 E. Florida
Denver, Colo. 80222

National Inconvenienced Sportsmen's Assn.
3738 Walnut Ave.
Carmichael, Calif. 95608

National Wheelchair Athletic Assn.
40-24 62 St.
Woodside, N.Y. 11377

National Wheelchair Basketball Assn.
110 Seaton Bldg.
University of Kentucky
Lexington, Ky. 40506

North American Recreation
(sporting equipment for the handicapped)
P.O. Box 758
Bridgeport, Conn. 06601

North American Riding for the Handicapped
  Assn.
P.O. Box 100
Ashburn, Va. 22011

Rehabilitation Education Center
(football)
University of Illinois
Oak St. at Stadium Dr.
Champaign, Ill. 61820

Ski for Light, Inc.
1455 W. Lake St.
Minneapolis, Minn. 55408

U.S. Association for Blind Athletes
55 W. California Ave.
Beach Haven Park, N.J. 08008

U.S. Blind Golfer's Assn.
225 Baronne St.
New Orleans, La. 70112

U.S. Deaf Skiers Assn.
2 Sunset Hill Rd.
Simsbury, Conn. 06070

Zodiac of North America, Inc.
(rubber boats)
11 Lee St.
Annapolis, Md. 21401

Appendix II

Government Offices and Agencies

CIVIL RIGHTS AND DEPARTMENT OF HEALTH, EDUCATION, AND WELFARE OFFICES

Region I (Conn., Maine, Mass., N.H., R.I., Vt.)
140 Federal St., 14th Fl.
Boston, Mass. 02110

Region II (N.J., N.Y., Puerto Rico, Virgin Isles)
26 Federal Plaza, 33rd Fl.
New York, N.Y. 10007

Region III (Del., D.C., Md., Pa., Va., W. Va.)
P.O. Box 13716
Philadelphia, Pa. 19101

Region IV (Ala., Fla., Ga., Ky., Miss., N.C., S.C., Tenn.)
101 Marietta St., 10th Fl.
Atlanta, Ga. 30323

Region V (Ill., Ind., Mich., Minn., Ohio, Wis.)
300 S. Wacker Dr.
Chicago, Ill. 60606
  For Cleveland, Ohio office, *Region V:*
  Plaza Nine Bldg.

55 Erieview Plaza, Rm. 222
Cleveland, Ohio 44114

Region VI (Ark., La., N.Mex., Okla., Tex.)
1200 Main Tower Bldg.
Dallas, Tex. 75202

Region VII (Iowa, Kans., Mo., Neb.)
Twelve Grand Bldg.
1150 Grand Ave.
Kansas City, Mo. 64106

Region VIII (Colo., Mont., N.Dak., S.Dak., Utah, Wyo.)
Federal Bldg.
1961 Stout St., Rm. 11037
Denver, Colo. 80294

Region IX (Ariz., Calif., Hawaii, Nev., Guam, Trust Terr. Pac. Isles, Amer. Samoa)
100 Van Ness Ave., 14th Fl.
San Francisco, Calif. 94102

Region X (Alaska, Idaho, Ore., Wash.)
1321 Second Ave., Rm. 5041 MS/508
Seattle, Wash. 98101

FEDERAL ORGANIZATIONS

Architectural and Transportation Barriers
  Compliance Board
Department of HEW
Washington, D.C. 20201

Bureau of Education for the Handicapped
Office of Education, Department of Health,
  Education, and Welfare
Washington, D.C. 20201

National Library for the Blind and Physically
  Handicapped
Library of Congress
1291 Taylor St. N.W.
Washington, D.C. 20542

Office for Handicapped Individuals
Department of Health, Education, and
  Welfare
Washington, D.C. 20201

Rehabilitation Services Administration
Department of Health, Education, and
  Welfare
Washington, D.C. 20201

Small Business Administration
1441 L St. N.W.
Washington, D.C. 20416

U.S. Commission on Civil Rights
1121 Vermont Ave. N.W.
Washington, D.C. 20425

Urban Mass Transportation Administration
  (UMTA)
Office of Capital Assistance
400 Seventh St. S.W.
Washington, D.C. 20590

Veterans Administration
Vermont Ave. and H St. N.W.
Washington, D.C. 20420

VOCATIONAL REHABILITATION AGENCIES

General

Vocational Rehabilitation
2129 E. South Blvd.
Montgomery, **Alabama** 36111
(205) 281-8780

Office of Vocational Rehabilitation
Pouch F, Mail Station 0581
Juneau, **Alaska** 99811
(907) 586-6500

Rehabilitation Services Bureau, Dept. of
  Economic Security
1400 W. Washington St.
Phoenix, **Arizona** 85007
(602) 271-3332

Dept. of Social and Rehabilitation Services
1801 Rebsamen Park Rd.
P.O. Box 3781
Little Rock, **Arkansas** 72203
(501) 371-2571

Dept. of Rehabilitation
830 K St. Mall
Sacramento, **California** 95814
(916) 445-3971

Division of Rehabilitation, Dept. of Social
  Services
1575 Sherman St.
Denver, **Colorado** 80203
(303) 892-2285

State Dept. of Education, Division of
  Vocational Rehabilitation
600 Asylum Ave.
Hartford, **Connecticut** 06105
(203) 566-7329

Dept. of Labor, Division of Vocational
  Rehabilitation
1500 Shallcross Ave.
P.O. Box 1190
Wilmington, **Delaware** 19899
(302) 571-2860

Social and Rehabilitation Administration,
  Dept. of Human Resources
122 C St. N.W., 8th Fl.
Washington, **D.C.** 20001
(202) 629-5896

Office of Vocational Rehabilitation, Dept.
  of Health and Rehabilitative Services
1323 Winewood Blvd.
Tallahassee, **Florida** 32301
(904) 488-6210

Dept. of Human Resources, Division of
Vocational Rehabilitation
47 Trinity Ave.
Atlanta, **Georgia** 30334
(404) 656-2621

Dept. of Vocational Rehabilitation
P.O. Box 10-C
Agana, **Guam** 96910
472-8806

Division of Vocational Rehabilitation,
Dept. of Social Services and Housing
Queen Liliuokalani Bldg., Rm. 216
P.O. Box 339
Honolulu, **Hawaii** 96809
(808) 548-6367

State of Idaho
Division of Vocational Rehabilitation
1501 McKinney
Boise, **Idaho** 83704
(208) 384-3390

Division of Vocational Rehabilitation
623 E. Adams St.
P.O. Box 1587
Springfield, **Illinois** 62706
(217) 782-2093

Indiana Rehabilitation Services
1028 Illinois Bldg.
17 W. Market St.
Indianapolis, **Indiana** 46204
(317) 633-5687

State of Iowa
Dept. of Public Instruction, Rehabilitation
Education and Services Branch
507 Tenth St., 5th Fl.
Des Moines, **Iowa** 50309
(515) 281-4311

Division of Vocational Rehabilitation, Dept.
of Social and Rehabilitative Services
State Office Bldg., 5th Fl.
Topeka, **Kansas** 66612
(913) 296-3911

Bureau of Rehabilitative Services
Capital Plaza Office Tower
Frankfort, **Kentucky** 40601
(502) 564-4440

State of Louisiana
Division of Vocational Rehabilitation, Dept.
of Health and Human Serivces, Office of
Rehabilitation Service
1755 Florida Blvd.
P.O. Box 44371
Baton Rouge, **Louisiana** 70804
(504) 389-2876

Bureau of Rehabilitation
32 Winthrop St.
Augusta, **Maine** 04330
(207) 289-2266

Division of Vocational Rehabilitation
P.O. Box 8717, Baltimore-Washington
International Airport
Baltimore, **Maryland** 21240
(301) 796-8300

Rehabilitation Commission
296 Boylston St.
Boston, **Massachusetts** 02116
(617) 727-2172

State of Michigan
Dept. of Education, Vocational
Rehabilitation Service
P.O. Box 30010
Lansing, **Michigan** 48909
(517) 373-3390

Division of Vocational Rehabilitation, Dept.
of Economic Security
Administrative Office, 8th Fl.
Capitol Square Bldg., 550 Cedar St.
St. Paul, **Minnesota** 55101
(612) 296-5619

Vocational Rehabilitation Division
550 High St.
Walter Sillers Bldg.
P.O. Box 1698
Jackson, **Mississippi** 39205
(601) 354-6825

State of Missouri
Dept. of Elementary and Secondary
Education, Division of Vocational
Rehabilitation
3523 N. Ten Mile Dr.
Jefferson City, **Missouri** 65101
(314) 751-3251

State of Montana
Social and Rehabilitation Services,
   Rehabilitative Services Division
P.O. Box 4210
Helena, **Montana** 59601
(406) 449-2590

Dept. of Education, Division of Rehabilitative
   Services
301 Centennial Mall, 6th Fl.
Lincoln, **Nebraska** 68508
(402) 471-2961

Dept. of Human Resources, Rehabilitation
   Division
Kinkead Bldg., 5th Fl.
505 E. King St.
Carson City, **Nevada** 89701
(702) 885-4440

State Department of Education, Division
   of Vocational Rehabilitation
105 Loudon Rd., Bldg. 3
Concord, **New Hampshire** 03301
(603) 271-3121

Division of Vocational Rehabilitation
   Services
Labor and Industry Bldg., Rm. 1005
John Fitch Plaza
Trenton, **New Jersey** 08625
(609) 292-5987

Vocational Rehabilitation, Department of
   Education
231 Washington Ave.
P.O. Box 1830
Santa Fe, **New Mexico** 87503
(505) 827-2266

The University of the State of New York
The State Education Department, Office of
   Vocational Rehabilitation
99 Washington Ave.
Albany, **New York** 12230
(518) 474-3941

Division of Vocational Rehabilitation
   Services, Dept. of Human Resources
State Office
620 N. West St., P.O. Box 26053
Raleigh, **North Carolina** 27611
(919) 829-3364

Division of Vocational Rehabilitation
1025 N. Third St., P.O. Box 1037
Bismarck, **North Dakota** 58501
(701) 224-2907

Rehabilitation Services Commission
4656 Heaton Rd.
Columbus, **Ohio** 43229
(614) 466-5157

Dept. of Institutions, Rehabilitation Services,
   Social and Rehabilitative Services, Division
   of Rehabilitative and Visual Services
P.O. Box 25352
Oklahoma City, **Oklahoma** 73125
(405) 521-3374

Vocational Rehabilitation Division, Dept.
   of Human Resources
2045 Silverton Rd. N.E.
Salem, **Oregon** 97310
(503) 378-3850

Bureau of Vocational Rehabilitation
Labor and Industry Bldg.
Seventh and Forster Sts.
Harrisburg, **Pennsylvania** 17120
(717) 787-5244

Dept. of Social Services
P.O. Box 1118
Hato Rey, **Puerto Rico** 00919
(809) 725-1792

Vocational Rehabilitation
40 Fountain St.
Providence, **Rhode Island** 02903
(401) 421-7005

Vocational Rehabilitation Dept.
3600 Forest Dr.
P.O. Box 4945
Columbia, **South Carolina** 29240
(803) 758-3237

Dept. of Vocational Rehabilitation, Division
   of Rehabilitative Services
State Office Bldg. Illinois St.
Pierre, **South Dakota** 57501
(605) 224-3195

Division of Vocational Rehabilitation
Suite 1400, 1808 W. End Bldg.
Nashville, **Tennessee** 37203
(615) 741-2521

Texas Rehabilitation Commission
7745 Chevy Chase Dr.
Austin, **Texas** 78752
(512) 447-0100

Division of Rehabilitation Services
250 E. Fifth S.
Salt Lake City, **Utah** 84111
(801) 533-5991

Vocational Rehabilitation Division
State Office Bldg.
Montpelier, **Vermont** 05602
(802) 244-5181

Dept. of Vocational Rehabilitation
4901 Fitzhugh Ave.
P.O. Box 11045
Richmond, **Virginia** 23230
(804) 786-2091

State Office
Division of Vocational Rehabilitation, Dept.
  of Social and Health Services
P.O. Box 1788 (Mail Stop 311)
Olympia, **Washington** 98504
(206) 753-2544

Division of Vocational Rehabilitation
P&G Bldg., Washington St.
Charleston, **West Virginia** 25305
(304) 348-2375

Administrator
1 W. Wilson St., Rm. 720
Madison, **Wisconsin** 53702
(608) 266-1683

Division of Vocational Rehabilitation
Hathaway Bldg. W.
Cheyenne, **Wyoming** 82002
(307) 777-7387

Palauni Puiasosopo
Assistant to the Governor of American Samoa
Pago Pago, **American Samoa** 96799
633-0116

Office of the High Commissioner
Trust Territory of the Pacific Islands
Saintan, **Mariana Island** 96550
9422

Dept. of Social Welfare, Division of
  Vocational Rehabilitation
P.O. Box 539
St. Thomas, **Virgin Islands** 00801

Blind

Board of Education and Services for the
  Blind
170 Ridge Rd.
Wethersfield, **Connecticut** 06109
(203) 249-8525

Delaware Bureau for the Visually Impaired,
  Dept. of Health and Social Services
305 W. Eighth St.
Wilmington, **Delaware** 19801
(302) 571-3333

Office of Blind Services, Dept. of Education
2571 Executive Center Circle E.
Howard Bldg.
Tallahassee, **Florida** 32301
(904) 488-1330

Idaho Commission for the Blind
Statehouse
Boise, **Idaho** 83720
(208) 384-3220

Commission for the Blind
Fourth and Keosauqua
Des Moines, **Iowa** 50309
(515) 283-2601

Services for the Blind and Visually
  Handicapped
State Dept. of Social and Rehabilitation
  Services
Biddle Bldg., 2700 W. Sixth St.
Topeka, **Kansas** 66606
(913) 296-4454

Bureau for the Blind
State Office Bldg. Annex
High St.
Frankfort, **Kentucky** 40601
(502) 564-4754

Dept. of Health and Human Resources,
  Office of Rehabilitation Services

Blind Services Program
1755 Florida St.
Baton Rouge, **Louisiana** 70802
(504) 389-6261

Massachusetts Commission for the Blind
110 Tremont St., 6th Fl.
Boston, **Massachusetts** 02108
(617) 727-5550

Dept. of Social Services, Office of Services
for the Blind
300 S. Capitol Ave.
Lansing, **Michigan** 48926
(517) 373-2062

State Services for the Blind and Visually
Handicapped
1745 University Ave., 1st Fl.
St. Paul, **Minnesota** 55104
(612) 296-6034

Vocational Rehabilitation for the Blind
P.O. Box 4872
Jackson, **Mississippi** 39216
(601) 354-6412

Dept. of Social Services, Division of Family
Services
Broadway State Office Bldg.
Jefferson City, **Missouri** 65101
(314) 751-4249

Visual Services Division, Dept. of Social
and Rehabilitation Services
P.O. Box 1723
Helena, **Montana** 59601
(406) 449-3434

Services for the Visually Impaired
1047 South St.
Lincoln, **Nebraska** 68502
(402) 471-2891

Commission for the Blind and Visually
Impaired
1100 Raymond Blvd.
Newark, **New Jersey** 07102
(201) 648-2324

State Dept. of Social Services
Commission for the Visually Handicapped

Ten Eyck Office Bldg.
40 N. Pearl St.
Albany, **New York** 12243
(518) 474-6739

Division of Services for the Blind, Dept.
of Human Resources
410 N. Boylan Ave.
P.O. Box 2658
Raleigh, **North Carolina** 27602
(919) 829-4231

Commission for the Blind
535 S.E. 12 Ave.
Portland, **Oregon** 97214
(503) 238-8375

Commonwealth of Pennsylvania
Dept. of Public Welfare, Bureau for the
Visually Handicapped
P.O. Box 2675
Harrisburg, **Pennsylvania** 17120
(717) 787-6176

Dept. of Social and Rehabilitation Services
Services for the Blind and Visually Impaired
46 Aborn St.
Providence, **Rhode Island** 02903
(401) 277-2300

Commission for the Blind
P.O. Box 11638, Capitol Sta.
Columbia, **South Carolina** 29211
(803) 758-2595

Services for the Blind
Dept. of Human Services
303-304 State Office Bldg.
Nashville, **Tennessee** 37219
(615) 741-3163

State Commission for the Blind
314 W. 11 St., P.O. Box 12866
Austin, **Texas** 78711
(512) 475-6810

Services for the Blind and Visually
Handicapped
309 E. First S.
Salt Lake City, **Utah** 84111
(801) 533-9393

Division for the Blind and Visually
Handicapped, Dept. of Social and
Rehabilitation Services
Vocational Rehab Division
State Office Bldg.
Montpelier, **Vermont** 05602
(802) 244-5181

Virginia Commission for the Visually
Handicapped

3003 Parkwood Ave.
Richmond, **Virginia** 23221
(804) 786-2181

Office of Services for the Blind, Dept. of
Social and Health Services
3411 S. Alaska St.
Seattle, **Washington** 98118
(206) 464-6690

Appendix III

Independent Living Centers

Letters following each entry indicate available services as explained in the codes below. States not listed contain no independent living centers. (Data listed from Office for Handicapped Individuals, 1979.)

A. Residential
B. Residential wth attendant care
C. Listing of accessible housing/placement
D. Transitional living/rehabilitation services
E. Personal care assistants (recruitment, selection, training, placement)
F. Medical services
G. Transportation
H. Independent living skills (ADL)
I. Advocacy and outreach unit
J. Information and referral/social service-state agency liaison
K. Vocational/educational liaison
L. Counseling
M. Intermediate care facility-MR
Z. Other

Our Way, Inc.
4120 W. Markham St.
Suite 314
Little Rock, **Arkansas** 72203
(501) 664-5950
(B, G, I, K, L, Z)

Center for Independent Living
2539 Telegraph Ave.
Berkeley, **California** 94704
(415) 841-4776
(C, E, G, H, I, J, K, L)

Handicapped Resource Center
114 E. Italia St.
Covina, **California** 91723
(213) 967-0635
(I, J, K, L)

California Association of the Physically
 Handicapped, Inc. (CAPH Service Center)
2031 Kern St.
Fresno, **California** 93721
(209) 237-2055
(C, E, H, J, L)

Dayle McIntosh Center for the Disabled
8100 Garden Grove Blvd.
Garden Grove, **California** 92644
(714) 898-9571; TTY (714) 892-7070
(C, E, I, J, L)

Disabled Resources Center, Inc.
330 E. Broadway St.
Long Beach, **California** 90802
(213) 437-3543
(C, E, G, J, L)

Good Shephard Center for Independent
Living, Inc.
4323 S. Leimert Blvd.
Los Angeles, **California** 90008
(213) 295-5439
(C, E, G, H, I, K)

Westside Community for Independent
Living, Inc.
11687 National Blvd.
Los Angeles, **California** 90064
(213) 473-8421; TTY (213) 477-5306
(C, E, G, J, K, L)

Center for Living Independently in Pasadena
453 E. Green St.
Pasadena, **California** 91101
(213) 440-1551
(C, G, I, J, L, Z; deaf interpreter service
available)

Mt. Diablo Rehabilitation Center
Independent Living Project
490 Golf Club Rd.
Pleasant Hill, **California** 94523
(415) 682-6330
(C, E, G, H, I, J, L)

Resources for Independent Living, Inc.
3540 42nd Ave.
Sacramento, **California** 95824
(916) 422-1733; TTY (916) 422-1805
(C, E, H, I, J, K, L)

Rolling Start, Inc.
560 W. Fourth St.
San Bernardino, **California** 92405
(714) 884-0940
(C, D, E, H, I, J, K, L)

Community Service Center for the Disabled,
Inc.
4607 Park Blvd.
San Diego, **California** 92116
(714) 293-3500
(C, G, H, I, J, K, L)

San Francisco Independent Living Project
814 Mission St.
San Francisco, **California** 94103
(415) 543-0223
(C, E, H, I, J, L)

Adult Independence Development Center
6350 Rainbow Dr.
San Jose, **California** 95129
(408) 252-8980
(D, E, G, H, I, J, L)

Community Resources for Independence
899 Second St.
Santa Rosa, **California** 95404
(707) 528-2745
(C, H, I, J, K, L)

Disability Services
2451 Country Club Blvd.
Stockton, **California** 95204
(209) 466-3684
(C, H, J, L)

Independent Living Center, Inc.
14354 Haynes St.
Van Nuys, **California** 91401
(213) 988-9525
(C, E, G, I, J, L)

Atlantis Community, Inc.
2965 W. 11 Ave.
Denver, **Colorado** 80204
(303) 893-8040
(B, E, G, I, J, K, L)

New Horizons, Inc.
c/o New Britain Memorial Hospital
2150 Corbin Ave.
New Britain, **Connecticut** 06050
(203) 223-2761
(I, J; residential facility in planning stages)

Independent Living, Inc.
4 Golden Acre
Wilmington, **Delaware** 19809
(302) 792-1547
(A, B, C, D, E, F, G, H, I, J, K, L, Z)

Independent Living for the Handicapped
3841 Calvert St. N.W.
Washington, **D.C.** 20007
(202) 338-2684
(A, B, C, D, E, F, G, H, I, J, K, L, Z)

Project Outbound
Palm Beach Habilitation Center
P.O. Box 631

Lake Worth, **Florida** 33460
(305) 967-3600
(C, D, G, H, J, K, L)

Park Villa
Association for Retarded Citizens
3100 75 St. N.
St. Petersburg, **Florida** 33710
(813) 345-9111
(A, B, C, D, E, F, G, H, I, J, K, L, Z)

Winning Wheels, Inc.
P.O. Box 121
Prophetstown, **Illinois** 61277
(815) 537-5168
(D, E, F, G, H, I, J, K, L)

The Program for Independent Living
324 E. New York St.
Indianapolis, **Indiana** 46204
(317) 635-2116
(D, E, G, H, I, J, L, Z; independent living
  for the elderly handicapped)

Cerebral Palsy Research Foundation
4320 E. Kellogg St.
Wichita, **Kansas** 67218
(316) 683-5627
(B, F, G)

The Timbers
2021 N. Old Manor
Wichita, **Kansas** 67208
(316) 688-1888
(A, B, D, E, G, H, I, J, K, L)

CONTACT (Committee on Normalization
  to Achieve Community Transition)
DHR Bldg.
275 E. Main St.
Frankfort, **Kentucky** 40601
(502) 564-2455
(A, E, G, H, I, J, K, L)

Independent Living Center
Husson College—Bell Dorm
One College Circle
Bangor, **Maine** 04401
(207) 947-7813
(D, E, F, G, K, Z; serves residents enrolled
  in education/vocational training programs)

Centers for the Handicapped
649 Lofstrand Lane
Rockville, **Maryland** 20850
(301) 340-7710
(A, F, G, I, J, L, Z)

Stavros Foundation
691 S. East St.
Amherst, **Massachusetts** 01002
(413) 253-2453
(J, L)

Boston Center for Independent Living, Inc.
50 New Edgerly Rd.
Boston, **Massachusetts** 02115
(617) 536-2187
(B, C, D, E, G, H, I, J, K, L)

Highland Heights
Fall River Housing Authority
P.O. Box 989
Fall River, **Massachusetts** 02722
(617) 678-2861
(A, E, F, G, J)

National Spinal Cord Injury Foundation
369 Elliott St.
Newton Upper Falls, **Massachusetts** 02164
(617) 964-0521
(C, D, E, G, H, J, K, L, Z)

Worcester Area Transitional Housing
507 Main St.
Worcester, **Massachusetts** 01608
(617) 757-9435
(C, D, G, H, K, Z; average stay, 8–10 months)

Ann Arbor Center for Independent Living
2462 E. Stadium Blvd.
Ann Arbor, **Michigan** 48104
(313) 971-0277
(C, E, I, J, L)

Detroit Center for Independent Living
Bicentennial Towers
4 E. Alexandrine, Suite 104
Detroit, **Michigan** 48201
(313) 494-9726
(D, H, I, J, K, L; 3–6 month transitional
  training program)

United Cerebral Palsy Association of
   Detroit, Inc.
15 E. Kirby St., Suite 210
Detroit, **Michigan** 48202
(313) 871-0177
(C, E, G, H, I, J, L)

Center of Handicapper Affairs
1026 E. Michigan St.
Lansing, **Michigan** 48912
(517) 485-5837 (TTY as well)
(H, I, J, K, L)

Comprehensive Services for Disabled
   Citizens, Inc.
4114 39 Ave. S.
Minneapolis, **Minnesota** 55406
(E, H, I, J, L)

Handicap Housing Service, Inc.
230 Metro Square Bldg.
Seventh and Robert Sts.
St. Paul, **Minnesota** 55701
(612) 222-1813
(C, Z; buys and modifies apartments for
   resale to disabled persons)

Project Independence
Independence for Impaired Individuals
1528 Iglehart St.
St. Paul, **Minnesota** 55104
(612) 489-8246
(B, G, I, J)

Community Living for Retarded Persons
5 Third St.
Bordentown, **New Jersey** 08505
(609) 298-9260
(C, G, H, I, J, K, L, Z)

Independent Living for Adults
P.O. Box 563
Hackensack, **New Jersey** 07601
(201) 488-4474
(C, D, H, I, J, K, L; serves primarily MR)

Independent Living for the Handicapped, Inc.
9 Winthrop St.
Brooklyn, **New York** 11225
(212) 462-6600
(C, E, G, H, I, J, K, L)

Center for Independence of the Disabled
   in N.Y.
432 Park Ave. S., Rm. 1202
New York, **New York** 10016
(212) 889-0381
(E, H, I, J, K, L)

United Cerebral Palsy of New York
   City
815 Second Ave.
New York, **New York** 10017
(212) 677-7400
(C, D, G, H, I, J, K, L)

Cara-More Community
625 W. Cameron Ave.
Chapel Hill, **North Carolina** 27514
(919) 967-3402
(D, H, K, L)

Bell House
Rt. 1, P.O. Box 335
Pleasant Garden, **North Carolina** 27313
(919) 674-5148
(B, Z)

New Horizons Manor
2525 N. Broadway
Fargo, **North Dakota** 58102
(701) 293-7870
(A, G)

Creative Living
472 W. Eighth Ave.
Columbus, **Ohio** 43210
(614) 422-9697
(B, D, G, K, L; serves primarily
   quadriplegics enrolled in educational/
   vocational training programs)

Vistula Manor
Toledo Metropolitan Housing Authority
615 Cherry St.
Toledo, **Ohio** 43604
(419) 243-6278
(B, G, H, K, L)

Independent Living, Inc.
P.O. Box 1004
Pendleton, **Oregon** 97801
(503) 276-8085
(C, H, I, L)

LINC Program
P. O. Box A
Pendleton, **Oregon**
(503) 276-1711
(A, D, H, I, J, K, L, Z; assistance for the
chronically mentally ill long-term patient)

Quadriplegics United against Dependency,
Inc.
3214 S.E. Holgate, Rm. 319
Portland, **Oregon** 97236
(503) 231-4976
(D, F, G, H, J, K, L, Z)

Goodwill Industries of North Central
Pennsylvania
DuBois, **Pennsylvania** 15801
(814) 371-1081
(C, G, H, I, J, K, L)

Erie Independence House
956 W. Second St.
Erie, **Pennsylvania** 16507
(814) 459-6161
(B, G, J, K)

UCP of North Central Pennsylvania, Inc.
400 Taylor Ave.
Falls Creek, **Pennsylvania** 15840
(814) 371-3571
(C, D, G, H, I, J, K, L)

Inglis House
Esther M. Klein Apts.
2600 Belmont Ave.
Philadelphia, **Pennsylvania** 19131
(215) 878-5600
(A, F, H, L)

UCP of Pittsburgh
4 Smithfield St.
Pittsburgh, **Pennsylvania** 15222
(412) 261-5831
(C, D, G, H, I, J, K, L)

Allied Services for the Handicapped, Inc.
Resident Services
475 Morgan Hwy.
Scranton, **Pennsylvania** 18508
(717) 348-1333
(C, D, G, H, I, J, K, L; serves primarily
MR and MH; average stay, 10 months)

Aberdeen Adjustment Training
612 Tenth Ave. S.E.
Aberdeen, **South Dakota** 57401
(605) 229-0263
(C, D, G, H, I, J, K, L; serves primarily
MR)

Black Hills Workshop School
3603 Range Rd.
P.O. Box 2104
Rapid City, **South Dakota** 57709
(605) 343-4550
(C, D, G, H, I, J, K, L; serves primarily MR)

Sioux Vocational School for the Handicapped
4100 S. Western Ave.
Sioux Falls, **South Dakota** 57105
(605) 336-7100
(C, D, G, H, I, J, K, L, M; serves primarily
MR)

Home II, Inc.
1514 Demonbreun St.
Nashville, **Tennessee** 37203
(615) 255-0381
(D, H, I, K, L; serves primarily MR)

Goodwill Industries of Houston
Independence Hall
6 Burress St.
Houston, **Texas** 77022
(713) 692-6237
(G, K, L)

Independent Life Styles, Inc.
1917 Augusta Dr.
Houston, **Texas** 77057
(713) 977-1545
(B, E, G, J; serves primarily quadriplegics)

Lighthouse for the Blind Residential Program
DeVille Apts.
4039 Bellefontaine
Houston, **Texas** 77025
(713) 666-4641
(A, D, G, H, J, K, L)

Willow Wood Apts.
5151 S. Willow Dr.
Houston, **Texas** 77035
(713) 729-5782
(B, E, G, H, I, J, K)

Blind Multi-Handicapped Project
1222 N. Main Ave., Suite 801
San Antonio, Texas 78212
(512) 223-3116
(D, H, K)

United Cerebral Palsy of the Alamo
    Area, Inc.
2336 Jackson Keller
San Antonio, Texas 78230
(512) 349-5267
(B, G, H, I, J, K, L)

Community Services Council
1864 S. State St.
Salt Lake City, Utah 84115
(801) 486-2136
(D, H, K, L; serves primarily quadriplegics)

Access to Independence, Inc.
3313 University Ave.
Madison, Wisconsin 53705
(608) 238-5545
(C, E, I, J, L, Z)

Karabis
Madison Housing Authority
P.O. Box 1785
Madison, Wisconsin 53701
(608) 266-4675
(A, J)

Clarendon Foundation
Cheshire Homes, Inc.
21 A Vaughn Rd.
Toronto, Ontario
M6G ZNZ, Canada

Appendix IV

National Association of Rehabilitation, Research, and Training Centers

Formerly part of the Rehabilitation Services Administration (RSA), the National Association of Rehabilitation, Research, and Training Centers is now under the National Institute of Handicapped Research. However, the Helen Keller National Center for Deaf-Blind Youths and Adults, included in this appendix, remains part of RSA.

Entries, listed by region, correspond to the following codes:

RRTC (Rehabilitation Research and Training Center): Established to conduct a continuing coordinated framework of research directed toward alleviating disability, reducing dependency, and developing more effective and efficiently integrated rehabilitation services and delivery systems. Also, to incorporate rehabilitation education into all rehabilitation-related university undergraduate and graduate curricula; conduct short- and long-term in-service and continuing education; assist in training, improving skills, and increasing the number of professional and nonprofessional rehabilitation personnel; and to widely disseminate and promote utilization of new knowledges resulting from research findings.

RRRI (Regional Rehabilitation Research Institutes): Responsible for programmed research useful to administrators, practitioners, and consumers; preparation of state-of-the-art monographs; and providing technical assistance to state rehabilitation agencies, regional offices, and the central office of RSA.

HKNC (Helen Keller National Center for Deaf-Blind Youths and Adults): Established to provide special intensive rehabilitation services for the deaf-blind, train professionals working with them, conduct research, demonstrate new methods and improved services, provide public education and understanding related to the problem of the deaf-blind, and maintain a census of deaf-blind persons.

REC (Rehabilitation Engineering Centers): Established as a national system of rehabilitation engineering centers to bring together clinicians and engineers at the patient level to utilize in rehabilitation programs the benefits of modern technology.

SCIR (Model Regional Systems of Spinal Cord Injury Rehabilitation): Established to demonstrate the benefits and cost effectiveness of a comprehensive, multidisciplinary continuum of services from emergency evacuation and transportation through acute care and to long-term community placement and follow-up.

Region I (Boston): Maine, N.H., Vt., Mass., Conn., R.I.

RRTC
  Tufts University
  Medical Rehabilitation R&T Center
  171 Harrison Ave.
  Boston, Mass. 02111
  (617) 956-5622

RRRI
  None

HKNC
  Central Office
  111 Middle Neck Rd.
  Sands Point, N.Y. 11050
  (516) 944-8900 (TTY and Voice)
  (Provides stated functions including
    residential quarters during training and
    service period)

REC
  Tufts University
  171 Harrison Ave.
  Boston, Mass. 02111
  (617) 956-5625
  (Core area: communication systems for
    individuals with nonvocal disabilities)

  Harvard–MIT
  Rm. 3-447, MIT
  Cambridge, Mass. 02139
  (Core area: sensory feedback)

  Children's Hospital Medical Center
  300 Longwood Ave.
  Boston, Mass. 02115
  (617) 734-6000 ext. 2866
  (Core area: neuromuscular control using
    sensory feedback systems)

SCIR
  Boston University Medical Center
  SCI Service
  75 E. Newton St.
  Boston, Mass. 02118

Region II (New York City): N.Y., N.J., P.R., V.I.

RRTC
  New York University
  Medical Rehabilitation R&T Center

  400 E. 34 St.
  New York, N.Y. 10016
  (212) 679-3200

  New York University
  Deafness Rehabilitation R&T Center
  80 Washington Square E.
  New York, N.Y. 10003
  (212) 598-2305

RRRI
  School of Social Work RRRI
  Columbia University
  622 W. 113 St.
  New York, N.Y. 10023
  (212) 280-5173
  (Core area: the role of the unions and
    management in improving job oppor-
    tunities for the handicapped)

HKNC
  Northeastern Regional Field Office
  111 Middle Neck Rd.
  Sands Point, N.Y. 11050
  (516) 944-8900 (TTY and Voice)
  (Service region: Conn., Maine, Mass.,
    N.H., N.J., N.Y., P.R., R.I., Vt., V.I.

REC
  New York University
  Medical Rehabilitation R&T Center
  400 E. 34 St.
  New York, N.Y. 10016
  (212) 679-3200
  (Core area: evaluation of functional
    performance of devices for severely
    disabled individuals)

SCIR
  New York University
  Institute of Rehabilitation Medicine
  400 E. 34 St.
  New York, N.Y. 10016

Region III (Philadelphia): Pa., Del., Md., Va., D.C., W. Va.

RRTC
  Temple University
  Medical Rehabilitation R&T Center,
    Suite 201
  12 and Tabor Rd.
  Philadelphia, Pa. 19141
  (215) 329-9580 ext. 61

The George Washington University
Medical Rehabilitation R&T Center
2300 Eye St. N.W., Rm. 714
Washington, D.C. 20037
(202) 676-3801

University of West Virginia
Vocational Rehabilitation R&T Center
University of West Virginia
Institute, W. Va. 25112
(304) 348-6340

RRRI
George Washington University RRRI
2201 G St. N.W.
Washington, D.C. 20052
(202) 676-6377
(Core area: attitudinal, legal, and leisure
time barriers to the disabled)

HKNC
East Central Regional Field Office
1422 Chesnut St.
Philadelphia, Pa. 19102
(215) 569-1393
(Service region: Del., D.C., Md., Ohio,
Pa., Va., W. Va.)

REC
Kruzen Research Center
Moss Rehabilitation Hospital
12 St. and Tabor Rd.
Philadelphia, Pa. 19141
(215) 329-9580
(Core area: locomotion and mobility)

University of Virginia School of Medicine
P.O. Box 3368
University Station, Va. 22903
(804) 977-6736
(Core area: spinal cord injury)

SCIR
Woodrow Wilson Rehabilitation Center
and the University of Virginia
Fisherville, Va. 22939

Region IV (Atlanta): Ky., Tenn., N.C., Ala., S.C., Ga., Miss., Fla.

RRTC
Emory University
Medical Rehabilitation R&T Center
1431 Clifton Rd.

Atlanta, Ga. 30322
(404) 329-5583

University of Alabama
1717 Sixth Ave. S.
Birmingham, Ala. 35233
(205) 934-3450

RRRI
None

HKNC
Southeastern Regional Field Office
1581 Phoenix Blvd.
Atlanta, Ga. 30349
(404) 996-2802
(Service region: Ala., Fla., Ga., Ky., N.C.,
S.C., Tenn.)

REC
The University of Tennessee
Department of Orthopaedic Surgery
1248 LaPaloma St.
Memphis, Tenn. 38114
(901) 525-2531
(Core area: mobility systems for severely
disabled)

SCIR
University of Alabama and Spain
Rehabilitation Center
1919 Seventh Ave. S.
Birmingham, Ala. 35233

Region V (Chicago): Minn., Wis., Mich., Ill., Ind., Ohio

RRTC
University of Minnesota
860 Mayo Bldg.
Minneapolis, Minn. 55455
(612) 373-8990

University of Wisconsin
Waisman Center on Mental Retardation
and Human Development
1500 Highland Ave.
Madison, Wis. 53706
(608) 263-5940

Northwestern University
Rehabilitation Institute of Chicago
345 E. Superior St.
Chicago, Ill. 60611
(312) 649-6019

University of Wisconsin-Stout
R&T Center in Vocational Rehabilitation
Menomonie, Wis. 54751
(715) 232-1389

RRRI
School of Education RRRI
University of Michigan
Ann Arbor, Mich. 58109
(313) 764-5457
(Core area: program evaluation instruments
and methodologies)

HKNC
North Central Regional Field Office
75 E. Wacker Dr.
Chicago, Ill. 60601
(312) 726-2090
(Service region: Ill., Ind., Iowa, Mich.,
Minn., Mo., Wis. Field offices are
responsible for contact with state, local,
and voluntary agencies; case findings and
referral in the geographic area serviced;
coordination of programs to assist
professionals in providing services; and
developing the coordinating community
relations activities with the director of
community education.)

REC
Northwestern University
345 E. Superior St., Rm. 1441
Chicago, Ill. 60611
(312) 649-8560
(Core area: internal total joint replacement)

Case Western Reserve University School
of Medicine
2219 Adelbert Rd.
Cleveland, Ohio 44106
(216) 791-7300
(Core area: upper extremity functional
electrical stimulation)

The University of Michigan College of
Engineering
Ann Arbor, Mich. 48109
(313) 764-8464
(Core area: automotive transportation
for the handicapped)

SCIR
University of Minnesota
860 Mayo Bldg.
Minneapolis, Minn. 55455

Wesley Memorial Hospital and
Rehabilitation Institute of Chicago
345 E. Superior St.
Chicago, Ill. 60611

Region VI (Dallas): N. Mex., Okla., Tex., Ark., La.

RRTC
University of Arkansas
Arkansas Rehabilitation R&T Center
Fayetteville, Ark. 72701
(501) 575-3656

Texas Tech University
Rehabilitation R&T Center in Mental
Retardation
P.O. Box 4510
Lubbock, Tex. 79409
(806) 742-3131

Baylor University College of Medicine
Medical Rehabilitation R&T Center
1333 Moursund Ave.
Houston, Tex. 77030
(713) 797-1440 ext. 228

RRRI
None
HKNC
South Central Regional Field Office
1111 Mockingbird Lane
Dallas, Tex. 75247
(214) 630-4936
(Service region: Ark., La., Miss., N. Mex.,
Okla., Tex.)

REC
Texas Institute for Rehabilitation and
Research
1333 Moursund Ave.
Houston, Tex. 77025
(713) 797-1440
(Core area: effects of pressure on tissue)

SCIR
Texas Institute of Rehabilitation and
Research
1333 Moursund Ave.
Houston, Tex. 77025

Region VII (Kansas City): Nebr., Iowa, Kans., Mo.

RRTC
None

RRRI
None

HKNC
None

REC
University of Iowa Orthopaedics
Department
Dill Children's Hospital
Iowa City, Iowa 52242
(319) 356-3468
(Core area: low back pain)

Cerebral Palsy Research Foundation of
Kansas, Inc.
4320 E. Kellog St.
Wichita, Kans. 67218
(316) 683-5627
(Core area: vocational aspects of
rehabilitation)

SCIR
None

Region VIII (Denver): Mont., Wyo., Utah, Colo., N. Dak., S. Dak.

RRTC
University of Colorado School of Medicine
P.O. Box C242
4200 E. Ninth Ave.
Denver, Colo. 80262
(303) 394-7267

RRRI
Colorado Seminary RRRI
University of Denver
Denver, Colo. 80631
(303) 753-2058
(Core area: Interagency linkages)

HKNC
Mountain-Plains Regional Field Office
12075 E. 45 Ave.
Denver, Colo. 80239
(303) 373-1204 (TTY and Voice)
Service region: Colo., Kans., Nebr.,
N. Dak., S. Dak., Wyo.)

REC
None

SCIR
Craig Hospital
Rocky Mountain Spinal Cord Injury
System
3425 Clarkson
Englewood, Colo. 80110

Region IX (San Francisco): Calif., Nev., Ariz., Hawaii, Guam, American Samoa

RRTC
University of California, San Francisco
Deafness and Mental Health Rehabilitation
R&T Center
1474 Fifth Ave.
San Francisco, Calif. 94143
(415) 731-9150

RRRI
None

HKNC
Southwestern Regional Field Office
120 N. Brand Blvd.
Glendale, Calif. 91203
(213) 240-2004 (TTY and Voice)
(Service region: Ariz., Calif., Nev., Utah,
Hawaii, Guam, Samoa, and the Trust
Territories)

REC
Rancho Los Amigos Hospital
7601 E. Imperial Hwy.
Downey, Calif. 90242
(213) 922-7167
(Core area: functional electrical stimulation
of paralyzed nerves and muscles)

Smith-Kettlewell Institute of Visual
  Sciences
2232 Webster St.
San Francisco, Calif. 94115
(515) 563-2323
(Core area: sensory aids—blind and deaf)

SCIR
  Good Samaritan Hospital
  1033 McDowell
  Phoenix, Ariz. 85062
  (602) 252-6611

Santa Clara Valley Medical Center
751 S. Bascom
San Jose, Calif. 95128

Region X (Seattle): Alaska, Wash., Idaho, Ore.

RRTC
  University of Washington
  Seattle, Wash. 98195
  (206) 543-3600

University of Oregon, College of Education
212 Clinical Services Bldg.

Eugene, Ore. 97403
(503) 686-3585

RRRI
  Portland State University RRRI
  P.O. Box 751
  Portland, Ore. 97207
  (503) 229-4040
  (Core area: job development/job placement
    for the severely handicapped)

HKNC
  Northwestern Regional Field Office
  649 Strander Blvd.
  Seattle, Wash. 98188
  (206) 246-2771
  (Service region: Alaska, Idaho, Mont.,
    Ore., Wash.)

REC
  None

SCIR
  University of Washington
  Department of Rehabilitation Medicine
  814 University Hospital
  Seattle, Wash. 98195

RESEARCH AND TRAINING CENTERS

The following Research and Training Centers are listed by center number (RT-).

RT-1
New York University (16-P-56801/2)
Medical Rehabilitation R&T Center
400 E. 34 St.
New York, N.Y. 10016
(212) 679-3200

RT-2
University of Minnesota (16-P-56810/5)
Medical Rehabilitation R&T Center
860 Mayo Bldg.
Minneapolis, Minn. 55455
(612) 373-8990

RT-3
University of Washington (16-P-56818/0)
Medical Rehabilitation R&T Center
cc814 RJ-30
Seattle, Wash. 98195
(206) 543-3600

RT-4
Baylor College of Medicine (16-P-56813/6)
Medical Rehabilitation R&T Center
1333 Moursund Ave.
Houston, Tex. 77030
(713) 797-1440 ext. 228

RT-6
Emory University (16-P-56808/4)
School of Medicine
Center for Rehabilitation Medicine
1431 Clifton Rd.
Atlanta, Ga. 30322
(404) 329-5583

RT-7
Tufts University (16-P-57856/1)
Medical Rehabilitation R&T Center
171 Harrison Ave.
Boston, Mass. 02111
(617) 956-5622

RT-8
Temple University (16-P-56804)
Medical Rehabilitation R&T Center,
  Suite 201
12 and Tabor Rd.
Philadelphia, Pa. 19141
(215) 329-9580 ext. 61

RT-9
George Washington University
  (16-P-56803/3)
Medical Rehabilitation R&T Center
Ross Hall, Rm. 714
2300 Eye St. N.W.
Washington, D.C. 20037
(202) 676-3801

RT-10
University of Colorado Medical Center
  (16-P-46815/8)
Medical Rehabilitation R&T Center
4200 E. Ninth Ave., P.O. Box C242
Denver, Colo. 80262
(303) 394-5144

RT-11
University of Wisconsin (16-P-56811/5)
Mental Retardation R&T Center
Waisman Center on MR and Human
  Development
1500 Highland Ave.
Madison, Wis. 53706
(608) 263-5940

RT-13
University of Arkansas (16-P-56812/6)
Vocational R&T Center
346 West Ave. Annex
Fayetteville, Ark. 72701
(501) 575-3656

RT-15
West Virginia University (16-P-56806/3)
West Virginia Vocational Rehabilitation
  R&T Center
Institute, W. Va. 25112
(304) 348-6340

RT-16
University of Oregon (16-P-56817/0)
College of Education

Mental Retardation R&T Center
212 Clinical Services Bldg.
Eugene, Ore. 94703
(503) 686-3585

RT-17
New York University (16-P-56802/2)
N.Y.U. Deafness Rehabilitation R&T Center
80 Washington Square E.
New York, N.Y. 10003
(212) 598-2305

RT-19
University of Alabama in Birmingham
  (16-P-56807/4)
Medical Rehabilitation R&T Center
1717 Sixth Ave. S.
Birmingham, Ala. 35233
(205) 934-3450

RT-20
Northwestern University (16-P-56809/5)
Medical Rehabilitation R&T Center
Rehabilitation Institute of Chicago
345 E. Superior St.
Chicago, Ill. 60611
(312) 649-6019

RT-21
Texas Tech University (16-P-56819/6)
R&T Center in Mental Retardation
P.O. Box 4510
Lubbock, Tex. 79409
(806) 742-3131

RT-22
University of Wisconsin-Stout (16-P-56821/5)
Vocational Rehabilitation R&T Center
Stout Vocational Rehabilitation Institute
Menomonie, Wis. 54751
(715) 232-1389

RT-23
University of California, San Francisco
  (16-P-59221/9)
Deafness and Mental Health Rehabilitation
  R&T Center
1474 Fifth Ave.
San Francisco, Calif. 94143
(415) 731-9150; (TTY) 731-7123

Appendix V

Special Education Regional Resource Centers and Direction Service Centers

REGIONAL RESOURCE CENTERS

California Regional Resource Center
600 S. Commonwealth Ave., Suite 1304
University of Southern California
Los Angeles, Calif. 90005
(213) 381-5231
(Area served: Calif.)

District of Columbia Regional Resource
   Center
Howard University
2935 Upton St. N.W.
Washington, D.C. 20008
(202) 686-6729
(Area served: D.C.)

Illinois Regional Resource Center
Northern Illinois University
Graham Hall 243
DeKalb, Ill. 60115
(815) 753-0534
(Area served: Ill.)

Mid-East Regional Resource Center
George Washington University
1901 Pennsylvania Ave. N.W., Suite 505
Washington, D.C. 20006
(202) 676-7200
(Areas served: Del., Md., N.C., W. Va.)

Mid-South Regional Resource Center
University of Kentucky Research Foundation

Porter Bldg., Rm. 131
Lexington, Ky. 40506
(6060) 258-4921
(Areas served: Ky., Tenn., Va.)

Midwest Regional Resource Center
Drake University
1332 26 St.
Des Moines, Iowa 50311
(515) 271-3936
(Areas served: Ark., Kans., Mo., Nebr.,
   N. Dak., Okla., S. Dak.)

New York City Regional Resource Center
City University of New York
33 W. 42 St.
New York, N.Y. 10036
(212) 790-4797; 4407; 4408
(Area served: N.Y. City)

New York State Regional Resource Center
New York State Education Department
55 Elk St.
Albany, N.Y. 12234
(518) 474-2251
(Area served: N.Y.)

Northeast Regional Resource Center
New Jersey State Department of Education
168 Bank St.

Highstown, N.J. 08520
(609) 448-4773
(Areas served: Conn., Maine, Mass., N.H.,
N.J., R.I., Vt.)

Northwest Regional Resource Center
Clinical Service Bldg., 3rd Fl.
1590 Willamette St.
University of Oregon
Eugene, Ore. 97401
(503) 686-5641; 687-6544
(Areas served: Alaska, Hawaii, Idaho, Mont.,
Ore., Wash., Wyo., Guam, Samoa)

Ohio Regional Resource Center
Ohio State Department of Education
933 High St.
Worthington, Ohio 43085
(614) 466-2650
(Area served: Ohio)

Pennsylvania Regional Resource Center
Pennsylvania State Department of Education
500 Valley Forge Plaza
1150 First Ave.
King of Prussia, Pa. 19406
(215) 265-3706
(Area served: Pa.)

Southeast Regional Resource Center
Auburn University
Montgomery, Ala. 36117
(205) 279-9110 ext. 258
(Areas served: Ala., Fla., Ga., Miss., S.C.,
P.R., V.I.)

Southwest Regional Resource Center
2363 Foothill Dr., Suite G
University of Utah
Salt Lake City, Utah 84109
(801) 581-6281
(Areas served: Ariz., Colo., Nev., N. Mex.,
Utah)

DIRECTION SERVICE CENTERS

Boston Direction Service
Federation for Children with Special Needs
120 Boylston St., Suite 338
Boston, Mass. 02116
(617) 482-2947; 2915

Community Service Society Direction Center
150 W. 105 St.
New York, N.Y. 10025
(212) 666-1300

CUNY Direction Service
144 W. 125 St.
New York, N.Y. 10027
(212) 860-6166

Delaware Direction Service
Delaware Direction Service Center
Townsend Bldg., Rm. 143
P.O. Box 1402
Dover, Del. 19901
(302) 678-5664

Fairfax County Direction Service
Fairfax County Public Schools
Staff Development Institute
6241 Meriwether Lane

Springfield, Va. 22150
(703) 971-4302

Los Angeles Direction Service
University of Southern California
600 S. Commonwealth Ave., Suite 1304
Los Angeles, Calif. 90005
(213) 645-9044

Maryland Direction Service
Maryland State Department of Education
P.O. Box 8717, BWI Airport
Baltimore, Md. 21240
(301) 796-8300 ext. 339
Also located at:
Western Maryland Direction Service
Center
Frostburg State College
Frostburg, Md. 21532
(301) 689-8879

Central Maryland Direction Service Center
County Office Bldg., Rm. 1126
Upper Marlboro, Md. 20870
(301) 952-4860

Midwest Direction Service
Midwest Regional Resource Center
1332 26 St.
Des Moines, Iowa 50311
(515) 271-3936
  Also located at:
  Jackson County Direction Service Center
  Mercantile Bank Bldg.
  3640 S. Noland Rd.
  Independence, Mo. 64055
  (816) 833-4415

Black Hills Direction Service Center
2040 W. Main No. 110
Rapid City, S. Dak. 55701
(605) 341-3944

Douglas-Lancaster Direction Service
  Center
Meyer Children's Rehabilitation Institute
444 S. 44 St.
Omaha, Nebr. 68131
(402) 541-4999

North Carolina Direction Service
North Carolina State Department of
  Public Instruction
436 Div. for Exceptional Children, Education
  Bldg.
Raleigh, N.C. 27611
(919) 733-6081

North Georgia Direction Service
5 Westside Sq.
Ellijay, Ga. 30540
(404) 635-5391

Northwest Coordination Office for
  Direction Service
1590 Willamette St.
Eugene, Ore. 97401
(503) 686-5641
  Also located at:
  E.S.D. No. 112
  Vancouver, Wash.
  (206) 694-8593

  Portland Public Schools
  King Neighborhood Facility
  4815 N.E. Seventh

Portland, Ore.
(503) 288-5167

Lane County Direction Service
1736½ Moss St.
Eugene, Ore.
(503) 686-3598

San Mateo County Direction Service
Del Green Associates, Inc.
1181 Chess Dr., Suite 200
Foster City, Calif. 94404
(415) 952-7878

Pennsylvania Direction Service
236 Union Deposit Mall
Harrisburg, Pa. 17111
(717) 783-3238

Southeast Direction Service
Auburn University at Montgomery
Montgomery, Ala. 36117
(205) 279-9110
  Also located at:
  Tri-County Direction Service
  1940A Mulberry St.
  Montgomery, Ala. 36106
  (205) 263-9700

  Tri-Cities Direction Service
  P.O. Box 1386
  Decatur, Ala.
  (205) 353-2754

Syracuse University Direction Service
Center on Human Policy
216 Ostrom Ave.
Syracuse, N.Y. 13210
(315) 423-3851

Utah Direction Service
Southeastern Education Service Center
P.O. Drawer B
Price, Utah 84501
(801) 637-5565
  Also located at:
  San Juan County Direction Service Center
  P.O. Box 807
  Blanding, Utah 84511
  (801) 678-2281

Appendix VI

Sources for Aids and Equipment

INTERNATIONAL SYMBOL OF ACCESS SOURCES

Ability Building Center, Inc.
1500 First Ave. N.E.
Rochester, Minn. 55901

C.A.P.H., Inc.
P.O. Box 22552
Sacramento, Calif. 98522

Jersey Cape Diagnostic, Training and
  Opportunity Center, Inc.
P.O. Box 31
Ocean View, N.J. 08230

Mid Michigan Stamps and Signs, Inc.
P.O. Box 2277
400 N. Larch St.
Lansing, Mich. 48912

Pict-O Signs
P.O. Box 372
Amsterdam, N.Y. 12010

President's Committee on Employment of
  the Handicapped
Washington, D.C. 20210
(indoor decals only)

Screen Art
2331 Tacoma Ave. S.
Tacoma, Wash. 98402

Seton Name Plate Corp.
592 Boulevard
New Haven, Conn. 06505

Tacoma Rubber Stamp
919 Market St.
Tacoma, Wash. 98402

Vermont Governor's Committee on
  Employment of the Handicapped
81 River St.
Montpelier, Vt. 05602

MANUFACTURERS OF AUTOMOBILE HAND CONTROLS AND ASSISTIVE DEVICES

Blatnik Precision Controls, Inc.
1523 Cota Ave.
Long Beach, Calif. 90813

Car Hand Controls (Wright Way)
266 E. Park Ave.
Elmhurst, Ill. 60126

Drive Master Corp.
61 N. Mountain Ave.
Montclair, N.J. 07042

Ferguson Auto Service
1112 N. Sheppard St.
Richmond, Va. 23230

Gresham Driving Aids
P.O. Box 405
Wixom, Mich. 48096

Handicaps, Inc.
4345 S. Santa Fe Dr.
Englewood, Colo. 80110

Hughes Hand Driving Controls
P.O. Box 275
Lexington, Mo. 64067

Kroepke Kontrols, Inc.
104 Hawkins St.
Bronx, N.Y. 10464

M.P.S. Corp.
4666 Mercury St.
San Diego, Calif. 92111

Morss Control
Star Route, P.O. Box 42
Elizabeth, Colo. 80107

Nelso Products
5960-A Sarah Ave.
Sarasota, Fla. 33577

Smith's Hand Controls
1472 Brookhaven Dr.
Southhaven, Miss. 38671

Trujillo Industries
5726 W. Washington Blvd.
Los Angeles, Calif. 90016

Wells-Engberg Co., Inc.
P.O. Box 6388
Rockford, Ill. 61125

Van Modifiers

Braun Corp. (formerly Save-A-Step Corp.)
1014 S. Monticello
Winamac, Ind. 46996

Collins Industries, Inc.
Dept. PM, P.O. Box 58
Hutchinson, Kans. 67501

Double D Industries
110 Fox Hill Rd.
St. Charles, Mo. 63301

Drive Master Corp.
61 N. Mountain Ave.
Montclair, N.J. 07042

Gresham Driving Aids, Inc.
P.O. Box 405
30800 Wixom Rd.
Wixom, Mich. 48096

Helper Industries, Inc.
832 N.W. East First St.
Fort Lauderdale, Fla. 33311

Lance Enterprises
Dave Evans
1391 Blue Hills Ave.
P.O. Box 524
Bloomfield, Conn. 06002

Medicab
Runyon Ave.
Yonkers, N.Y. 10701

Quality Motor Coach
Div. of Rec. Ve., Inc.
Route 309
Montgomeryville, Pa. 18936

Para Industries, Ltd.
6-4826 11 St. N.E.
Calgary, Alberta
T2E 2W7, Canada

Ricon Corp.
15806 Arminta St.
Van Nuys, Calif. 91406

Royce International
4345 S. Santa Fe Dr.
Englewood, Colo. 80110

Fred Scott and Sons
Dept. P, 101 Kelly St.
Elk Grove, Ill. 60007

Speedy Wagon Sales Corp.
2237 Harvester Rd.
St. Charles, Mo. 63301

Target Industries
P.O. Box 3988
8 Heywood St.
Springfield, Mass. 01101

Index